S0-AOK-600
Forsyth Library
Fort Hays State University
FOR USE IN LIBRARY ONLY
Presented by
Dr. Cecil B. Currey
to Forsyth Library

# EUROPEAN NEUTRALS AND NON-BELLIGERENTS DURING THE SECOND WORLD WAR

This collection provides the most comprehensive English-language survey of the conduct of neutral and non-belligerent states during the war for nearly fifty years.

Instead of narrowly focusing on the few neutrals that survived the war intact, the volume broadens our understanding of neutrality, by including chapters on 'non-belligerents' and those neutrals of south-east Europe, such as Romania and Yugoslavia. The chapters focus on how individual neutral governments perceived international developments and throw light on the domestic political circumstances that critically affected their response to the course of the war. They therefore provide the political context that has been overlooked in recent controversies surrounding their humanitarian and financial activities.

While based on the authors' own research, the chapters draw widely on secondary literature and provide invaluable analytical introductions to the large amount of historical writing on these countries which is unavailable in English.

NEVILLE WYLIE is Lecturer in Politics, University of Nottingham.

# EUROPEAN NEUTRALS AND NON-BELLIGERENTS DURING THE SECOND WORLD WAR

EDITED BY

NEVILLE WYLIE

CAMBRIDGE
UNIVERSITY PRESS

PUBLISHED BY THE PRESS SYNDICATE OF THE UNIVERSITY OF CAMBRIDGE
The Pitt Building, Trumpington Street, Cambridge, United Kingdom

CAMBRIDGE UNIVERSITY PRESS
The Edinburgh Building, Cambridge CB2 2RU, UK
40 West 20th Street, New York, NY 10011–4211, USA
477 Williamstown Road, Port Melbourne, VIC 3207, Australia
Ruiz de Alarcón 13, 28014 Madrid, Spain
Dock House, The Waterfront, Cape Town 8001, South Africa

http://www.cambridge.org



First published 2002

Printed in the United Kingdom at the University Press, Cambridge

*Typeface* Baskerville Monotype 11/12.5 pt.   *System* LaTeX 2ε [TB]

*A catalogue record for this book is available from the British Library*

*Library of Congress Cataloguing in Publication data*

European neutrals and non-belligerents during the Second World War/
Neville Wylie (editor).
p. cm.
Includes bibliographical references and index.
ISBN 0 521 64358 9
1. World War, 1939–1945 – Diplomatic history. 2. Neutrality – Europe – History –
20th century. I. Wylie, Neville, 1966–
D749 .E87 2001
940.53′2 – dc21   2001035694

ISBN 0 521 64358 9 hardback

# *Contents*

# *Contributors*

ALAIN COLIGNON is a research assistant specialising in the politics of neutrality at the Centre d'Etudes et de Documentation Guerre et Sociétés contemporaines, Brussels.

VESSELIN DIMITROV is lecturer in East European Politics at the London School of Economics. His most recent publications are 'The Failure of Post-war Pluralism in Eastern Europe: A Bulgarian Case Study', *Journal of Contemporary History*, 34 (1999) and 'Revolution Released: Stalin, the Bulgarian Communist Party and the Establishment of the Cominform', in F. Gori and S. Pons (eds.), *The Soviet Union and Europe in the Cold War, 1943–1953* (London, 1996).

TIBOR FRANK is director of the School of English and American Studies at Eötvös Loránd University in Budapest. He has written and edited a number of articles and books on aspects of Hungarian political and cultural history, including *Ethnicity, Propaganda, Myth-Making* (Budapest, 1999) and *A History of Hungary* (London, 1990, with Peter F. Sugar and Péter Hanák) and is currently producing an edition of the papers of a former minister in Budapest, John F. Montgomery.

ELENA HERNÁNDEZ-SANDOICA is titular professor of contemporary history at the Universidad Complutense de Madrid. Her research interests lie in the areas of intellectual history, education, and foreign policy, in particular the history of Spanish colonial policy in Cuba. Her most recent book is entitled, *Los caminos de la Historia. Cuestiones de historiografía y método* (Madrid, 1995).

HANS KIRCHHOFF is senior lecturer in the Department of History, University of Copenhagen. His published works include *Augustoprøret 1943, Samarbejdspolitikkens fald. Forundsætninger og forløb* (1979), *Kamp eller tilpasning. Politikerne og modstanden 1940–1945* (1987), 'Foreign

Policy and Rationality – The Danish Capitulation of 9 April 1940. An Outline of a Pattern of Action', *Scandinavian Journal of History*, 16 (1991), and he has recently edited a collection of papers on Denmark's national and international situation in 1940, *1940 – Da Danmark blev besat* (Copenhagen, 1990).

PAUL A. LEVINE is assistant professor at Uppsala University and works in the Centre for Multiethnic Research. He is author of *From Indifference to Activism; Swedish Diplomacy and the Holocaust, 1938–1944* (Uppsala, 2nd edition, 1998) and *'Tell ye your children' . . . A Book about the Holocaust in Europe 1933–1945* (Stockholm, 1998, with S. Bruchfeld). He has written on many aspects of anti-Semitism and the Holocaust, and was recently consulting expert to the Swedish National Commission on Jewish Assets.

BOB MOORE is reader in modern history at the University of Sheffield. His research interests include the study of prisoners of war, the Holocaust, and the history of The Netherlands. His recent publications include *Victims and Survivors: The Nazi Persecution of the Jews in the Netherlands, 1940–1945* (London, 1997) and two edited volumes, *Resistance in Western Europe* (Oxford, 2000) and *Prisoners of War and their Captors in World War II* (Oxford, 1996, with Kent Fedorowich).

ENRIQUE MORADIELLOS is lecturer in modern Spanish and European history at the Universidad de Extremadura. As well as publishing numerous articles, in Spanish and English, he is author of five books, including *La Perfida de Albión. El gobierno británico y la guerra civil española* (Madrid, 1986) and *Neutralidad Benévola. El gobierno británico y la insurrección militar española de 1936* (Oviedo, 1990).

EUNAN O'HALPIN is professor of modern Irish history at Trinity College Dublin. He is author of *Defending Ireland: The Irish State and its Enemies since 1922* (Oxford, 1999) and *Ireland and the Council of Europe: From Isolation Towards Integration* (Strasbourg, 2000). He is joint editor of the official publication series, *Documents on Irish Foreign Policy*.

MAURICE PEARTON is honorary fellow of the School of Slavonic and East European Studies, University College London, having previously been reader in political science at Richmond College, London. He has written widely on aspects of Romanian history and is the author of *Oil and the Romanian State* (Oxford, 1971) and *The Knowledgeable State – Diplomacy, War and Technology since 1830* (London, 1982).

FERNANDO ROSAS is professor of history at the Universidade Nova de Lisboa. He has written widely on many aspects of modern Portuguese history. He is author of *Portugal entre a Paz e a Guerra (1939–1945)* (Lisbon, 1990) and *O Salazarismo e a Aliança Luso-Britânica* (Lisbon, 1987). He is also editor of *Portugal e o Estado Novo (1930–1960)* (Lisbon, 1993) and *Armindo Monteiro e Oliveira Salazar – correspondência politica, 1926–1955* (Lisbon, 1996) and is director of the journal, *História.*

PATRICK SALMON is professor of history at the University of Newcastle. He is author of *Scandinavia and the Great Powers 1890–1940* (Cambridge, 1997), *The Baltic Nations and Europe: Estonia, Latvia and Lithuania in the Twentieth Century* (London, 1994, with John Hiden) and editor of *Britain and Norway in the Second World War* (London, 1995).

BRIAN R. SULLIVAN is an independent scholar and specialises on Italian military history and strategic studies. He is author of *Il Duce's Other Woman* (New York, 1993, with Philip V. Cannistraro), and numerous articles, including 'The Impatient Cat: Assessments of Military Power in Fascist Italy, 1936–1940', in Williamson Murray and Allan R. Millett (eds.), *Calculations. Net Assessment and the Coming of World War II* (New York, 1992), and 'The Italian–Ethiopian Conflict and Mussolini's Responsibility for the Second World War', in Gordon Martel (ed.), *The Origins of the Second World War Reconsidered* (London, 1998).

NEVILLE WYLIE is lecturer in politics at the University of Nottingham. He is author of *Britain and Switzerland during the Second World War* (Oxford, forthcoming) and a number of articles on Swiss history, including 'Pilet-Golaz and the Making of Swiss Foreign Policy: Some Remarks', *Schweizerische Zeitschrift für Geschichte*, 47/4 (1997), 'Le rôle des transports ferroviares en Suisse, 1939–1945: les aspects militaire, économique et politique', *Relations Internationales*, 95 (1998), and 'La Suisse et la liste noire britannique: le cas du Credit Suisse en 1940', in Michel Porret, Jean-François Favet and Corine Fluckiger (eds.), *Guerre et Paix. Mélanges offerts à Jean-Claude Favez* (Geneva, 2000).

DRAGOLJUB R. ŽIVOJINOVIĆ is professor of modern history at the University of Belgrade. He received his doctorate from the University of Pennsylvania and has been visiting professor at various European and US universities, including Cornell and the University of California, Santa Barbara. His publications include *America, Italy and the Birth of Yugoslavia 1917–1919* (New York, 1972), *The Vatican and the First World*

*War 1914–1918* (Belgrade, 1978), *The Vatican, Serbia and the Inception of Yugoslavia 1914–1918* (Belgrade, 1980), *The Vatican, the Catholic Church and the New Regime in Yugoslavia 1941–1958* (Belgrade, 1994), and a three-volume biography of *King Peter I. Karadjordjevic* (Belgrade 1988–94).

# *Acknowledgements*

This book has taken considerably longer to bring to fruition than was initially anticipated! The time taken to find appropriate contributors, assemble their chapters to a timetable that met their own busy schedules, take account of readers comments and allow for revisions to be made, far exceeded my original, wildly optimistic, calculations. I would like to express my gratitude to the fourteen contributors, for their commitment to the project, their willingness to respond to my various letters and emails, and for their patience in seeing the project through to an end. I am likewise enormously grateful for the support, encouragement, and assistance of William Davies at Cambridge University Press and of Jean Field, who meticulously copy-edited the book. My thanks also go to Jean Lundskær-Nielsen, Philip Wylie, and Heloisa Stroppa for their translations of chapters 1, 4, 10, and 11, and to the Syndics of Cambridge University Press and the Managers of the Prince Consort and Thirlwall Fund, University of Cambridge, for help in covering the costs entailed. Richard Aldrich and Mauro Mantovani generously gave their time to comment on various parts of the manuscript. Finally, I greatly benefited from being able to test out some of the ideas and concepts addressed in the collection on some excellent students who attended my courses at the Graduate Institute of International Affairs in Geneva and University College Dublin over the academic year 1999/2000. Their incisive comments and criticisms have, I hope, made for a better book.

# *Introduction: Victims or actors? European neutrals and non-belligerents, 1939–1945*

*Neville Wylie*

Neutrality has been one of the most enduring features in the history of international relations. The desire of individuals, groups or states to stand aside from the conflicts that convulse their neighbours is a natural one. Self-preservation and the wish to avoid the deprivation and hardship that so often accompany wars generally prevail over the temptation to enter the fray. Although various attempts have been made to outlaw war from international relations, war has remained an accepted, common, and perhaps even natural way for states to pursue their interests on the international stage. In these circumstances, the recourse to neutrality has generally been considered an entirely legitimate and appropriate form of behaviour. Neutrality's impact on modern history has thus been a profound one. It has helped shape the conduct of international affairs from the 1790s to the Cold War: from Jefferson's declaration of US neutrality, to the 'spectre of neutralism' in Europe in the early 1950s, and the emergence of Third World non-alignment in the 1960s and 1970s.

The pervasiveness of neutrality in international relations has not, however, encouraged people to look upon it with affection. Machiavelli, the fifteenth-century Italian philosopher, strenuously counselled against it, warning that 'the conqueror does not want doubtful friends [while]... the loser repudiates you because you were unwilling to go, arms in hand, and throw in your lot with him'.[1] Six hundred years later, John Foster Dulles, United States secretary of state, substantiated Machiavelli's claims: neutrality was, he warned on 9 June 1956, 'except under very exceptional circumstances ... an immoral and shortsighted conception'.[2] Historical writing on the Second World War has tended to

[1] N. Machiavelli, *The Prince*, cited in Efraim Karsh, *Neutrality and Small States* (London, 1988), 1.

[2] Cited in Jürg Martin Gabriel, *The American Conception of Neutrality since 1941* (Basingstoke, 1988), 185–6.

reflect this mood. The neutrals have been painted as immoral free-riders, ready to benefit from the successes of one side or another but unwilling to contribute actively themselves. At their worst they amply confirmed Chateaubriand's caustic description of the Swiss: 'neutral in the grand revolutions of the states that surround them, they enrich themselves by the misfortunes of others and found a bank on human calamities'. At the other end of the spectrum, neutrals have been depicted as naïve simpletons, who mistakenly assumed that by reiterating the mantra of neutrality they might lull the warring factions into respecting their wishes. Only rarely are they seen in a positive light, like 'gallant little Belgium' in 1914, standing Canute-like before the consuming evils of barbarism and symbolising the last vestiges of international decency.

The caricaturing and general neglect of neutrality in histories of the Second World War stem in part from the influence exerted by the writings of the principal protagonists. To these men, writing shortly after the war, the great issues had all been decided on the battlefield or in the allied conference halls. Victory had not turned on their success in playing to the neutral gallery in Europe. Historians have tended to remain wedded to the issues that impressed contemporary observers. Neutrality's abysmal record in the war – only five states avoided being sucked into the conflict – appeared to confirm neutrality as an anachronism to the modern world, or at least to modern warfare. As a consequence, few historians saw the neutrals as subjects worthy of serious attention.

With the benefit of hindsight it is clear that many of the assumptions that governed attitudes towards the neutrals were misplaced. Victory in 1945 may indeed have been one the Allies had to fight hard for, but the need to resort to total war in the first place in part arose from their failure to win the diplomatic contest while the war remained a purely European affair. It was during this period that the British, their French allies, and their supporters across the Atlantic may have squandered the chance to tackle the German menace by capitalising on their moral superiority and the sympathies of the neutral gallery. Even after the fighting intensified and expanded over the second half of 1941, diplomatic manoeuvring in Europe did not cease. International relations continued, and the neutrals, courted and cajoled by the belligerents, were clearly central to this process. However much events between 1939 and 1945 might then, at one level, revolve around belligerent concerns, we would be wrong to confine our study of the period to an examination of only those powers actively engaged in the fighting. Moreover in scripting the neutrals into the story, we would be mistaken to view them as simply appendages to the military struggle. Clearly account must be taken of their substantial economic, political, and military contribution to the fighting, but this was by no means the sum total of their activity during the five and a half years of war. The war was one of many factors which demanded the attention of neutral statesmen after 1939, and its importance was by no means foreordained. With this in mind, it is worth recalling that the neutrals were not always mere victims, powerless to resist belligerent demands. The neutrals not only *chose* to stay out of the war, they also *chose* how to define and conduct their neutrality thereafter.

The current book places fourteen neutral and non-belligerent states under the spotlight.[3] Its aim is not so much to uncover the neutrals' place in the actual fighting, but to explain what the war looked like for those states standing on the 'touchlines of war'. Why, did these states believe that a policy of neutrality provided the best means of securing their national interests? How did their domestic circumstances affect their estimation of events on the international stage? Why, ultimately, did some neutrals end up being put to the sword, while others appeared consciously to fall on it, and others still passed through the tumult with their territorial and political integrity preserved?[4]

By 1939 the neutrals could point to a rich and sophisticated corpus of international public law to define their position. They had the right to defend their borders by force, the right to trade with both camps in goods of a non-military character, and the right to maintain communications with all sides. Above all, however, they were obliged to treat the belligerents with strict impartiality, not only in their commercial dealings but also in preventing their territory from being used for military purposes or acting in such a way as to favour one side over the other. These principles had been enshrined in the 5th Hague Rules of War in

3 For a brief discussion of the principal countries not covered in the book, see Appendix.

4 The number of books dealing with a broad range of neutrals is small. Arnold and Veronica Toynbee (eds.), *The War and the Neutrals* (Oxford, 1956), is a good 'first cut'. The conference papers collected by L.-E. Roulet, *Les Etats Neutres Européens et la Seconde Guerre Mondiale* (Neuchatel, 1985) are excellent, as are some of the short essays published by the University of Caen: *L'année 40 en Europe* (Caen, 1990), and the conference papers collected under the editorship of Jukka Nevakivi, *The History of Neutrality / L'Histoire de la neutralité* (Helsinki, 1993). Jerold M. Packard's synthesis, *Neither Friend Nor Foe. The European Neutrals in World War II* (New York, 1992) is rather impressionistic. Christian Leitz's, *Nazi Germany and Neutral Europe during the Second World War* (Manchester, 2001) appeared as this book went to press, but his ideas are summarised in 'Les aspects économiques des relations entre l'allemagne nazie et les pays neutres européens pendant la seconde guerre mondiale', *Guerres mondiales et conflits contemporains*, 194 (1999), 7–28. For general studies on neutrality, see Karsh, *Neutrality and Small States*; A. B. Fox, *The Power of Small States* (Chicago, 1959); Alan T. Leonhard, *Neutrality: Changing Concepts and Practices* (Lanham, 1988), and Roderick Ogley, *The Theory and Practice of Neutrality in the Twentieth Century* (London, 1970).

1907 and represented the cumulative experience of nearly a century of learned discussion and state practice.[5]

If the basic rules governing the application of 'neutrality' were relatively straightforward the same could hardly be said for non-belligerency, a concept that Mussolini mischievously conjured up to explain Italy's ambiguous position in September 1939. In its essentials, the concept harked back to the form of neutrality common in the eighteenth century in which neutrals were effectively allowed to do as they pleased and discriminate against those belligerents they thought were in the wrong. It drew its rationale not from abstract legal principles, but from the state's capacity to convince the principally aggrieved party that its interests were best served with the *status quo*. In the last resort, a non-belligerent's strength rested on the functioning of the balance of power. Non-belligerency was, then, what states made of it, and its implications had to be worked out as the war progressed. For Mussolini, it allowed Italy to retain her ideological and political alignment with the Axis, while stopping short of either full belligerency, a situation for which Italy was ill prepared, or strict neutrality, a position which Mussolini found repugnant. Vichy France, Spain, Turkey, Egypt, and the Argentine can all be considered 'non-belligerent' at various times in the war. The term could equally be applied to the United States, after the passing of the Lend Lease legislation in March 1941, and the Soviet Union, before Germany's invasion in June 1941. In all these cases, the states' individual strategic, political, and economic resources allowed them to establish their own position, unimpeded by the constraints of strict neutrality. Yet, despite the clear differences between the two concepts, non-belligerency and small-state neutrality nevertheless occupy the same position in international relations. In both cases, the defining issue is the relationship between the state and the belligerents. There was therefore considerable overlap between the two concepts, and in practice 'aggrieved' belligerents frequently chose to afford non-belligerent states the same legal entitlements as they gave to neutrals. Indeed, in some cases non-belligerents were treated significantly better than their neutral counterparts.[6]

One of the points borne out in the chapters which follow is the sheer variety of neutral 'cloaks' donned by European states between 1939 and

[5] For a survey of the law of neutrality see Stephen C. Neff, *The Rights and Duties of Neutrals. A General History* (Manchester, 2000).

[6] After the summer of 1940, for example, Britain allowed Spain to accumulate stocks of blockaded goods equal to two and a half months' domestic requirements; the neutral Swiss and Swedes on the other hand had to make do with rations based on two months' supplies.

1945. Whatever its different cut and colour, it is clear that the institution of 'neutrality' was largely inadequate in providing for the basic needs of these states in an era of ideological and total war. The reason for this apparent failure can be traced to three developments. The first concerns the changing nature of modern warfare. It is one of the bitter ironies of history that progress towards the codification of neutral rights by the turn of the twentieth century coincided with technological and military developments which would ultimately overwhelm the fragile legal edifices within less than a decade. The First World War began with the violation of two 'permanent neutrals,' Belgian and Luxembourg, and by the time it ended fighting had spilled over to affect nearly every aspect of neutrality. Neutral ships were requisitioned, torpedoed, and forced to follow routes prescribed by the belligerents, their cargoes were seized as contraband, and their firms subjected to enforced rationing and trade discrimination. It was not just the expansion of warfare that precipitated the sudden collapse of neutrality but, as Geoffrey Best has shown, the general withering of self-restraint on behalf of the belligerents over all aspects of their military conduct. Once one belligerent crossed the Rubicon, others soon followed, and even those who mourned the passing of a golden age quickly found that the advent of total war left precious little opportunity to put the clock back. All too often the pursuit of military advantage was used to justify the abuse of neutral rights. War fighting after 1914 showed little regard for the rights of those wishing to stand aside, irrespective of the clarity with which these rights had been enunciated less than a decade before.[7]

Disquieting though the First World War had been for the neutrals, it proved merely a foretaste of the misery that was to befall them after 1939. Further military and technological developments between the wars ensured that when war returned to the continent the neutrals found it almost impossible to insulate themselves from the corrosive effects of the fighting. Maintaining control of their economic destiny was perhaps the highest hurdle. The problem partly lay in their heightened importance to the warring factions. Germany's close economic ties with south-east Europe, coupled with the enormous pressures exerted by total war after 1941, meant that the neutrals' manufactures, raw materials, financial resources and facilities were substantially more valuable to Germany than they had been quarter of a century before. Their ability to resist German

[7] Geoffrey Best, *Humanity in Warfare. The Modern History of the International Law of Armed Conflicts* (Oxford, 1980).

demands was likewise reduced by the scale of Germany's victories in the first years of the war. Economic relations with the Allies were little better. The blockade was a cherished weapon in Britain's depleted armoury, but in fact all sides quickly developed a level of sophistication in their economic warfare which far outstripped anything the neutrals had been forced to endure before. By the middle of 1943 Portugal, Spain, and Switzerland each had well over one thousand companies 'black-listed' by the Allies for collaborating with the Axis. The Swedes, though more fortunate, still had over five hundred names listed by the second half of 1944. To make matters worse, the neutrals' willingness to meet Allied demands, forgo economic advantages, and introduce restrictions on their trade with the Axis was diminished by the enduring effects of the Depression. The social and political unrest of the 1930s, added to memories of the dislocation that occasioned the return to peace in 1918, persuaded most neutral officials, businessmen, and financiers to err on the side of caution.[8] Some neutrals may well have lived up to Chateaubriand's caustic judgement, but for many exploitation of the war's business opportunities was neither a question of ethics nor of commerce, but simply a way of maintaining political order at home and the socio-economic structures upon which that order relied.

The emergence of air power in the inter-war period further undermined the utility of neutrality after 1939. Air power made neutrals part of the strategic landscape. Britain's ability to strike the Ploesti oilfields in Romania from bases in Greece worked against Athens' attempt to keep Germany at arm's length in the spring of 1941. Likewise, the Turkish government never really overcame Moscow's suspicions that it had connived in the Anglo-French plans to bomb Russian oil installations at Baku during the Phoney War. At the other end of Europe, the mere existence of the airfield at Ålborg in northern Jutland was used to justify Germany's pre-emptive occupation of Denmark on 9 April 1940. Even when neutrals avoided being drawn into the belligerents' strategic plans, air warfare aggravated their political relations and exacerbated the already huge disparities between their military forces and those of any potential aggressor. Three days after the war began, Berlin ominously announced that neutrality would only be respected if governments provided for the adequate defence of their airspace.[9] None of the neutrals

8 See Nils Ørvik, *The Decline of Neutrality, 1914–1941* (London, 1971, 2nd edition) and Hans A. Schmitt (ed.), *Neutral Europe between War and Revolution, 1917–1923* (Charlottesville, 1988).

9 Some neutrals blatantly departed from their obligations in relation to aerial overflights. Madrid turned a blind eye to Italian use of its airspace in bombing Gibraltar and happily repatriated Axis

possessed the necessary equipment to mount a credible air-defence system and over subsequent years most suffered the indignity of having their neutrality repeatedly violated by belligerent aircraft traversing their territory. Germany's threat could not be ignored, nor the possibility of Hitler using the Luftwaffe to punish any neutral that stepped out of line. For all neutral governments, the fate of Rotterdam and Belgrade was a sobering reminder of the cost of failure.[10]

The last military development to erode neutral sovereignty after 1939 was the emergence of 'irregular warfare'. Neutral states had traditionally provided fruitful environments for intelligence gathering. While this could occasionally lead to embarrassment, on the whole so long as the belligerents' activities were not directed against the host state, neutral governments were usually prepared to turn a blind eye.[11] 'Irregular warfare', including subversion, 'psychological warfare', and sabotage, was, however, a different proposition, not just because it represented another stage in the escalation of total war but because it further eroded that vital, but increasingly fragile, distinction between belligerent and neutral. The 'fifth column' was used to devastating effect by Germany in the Low Countries in May 1940; both sides subjected the neutrals to a barrage of propaganda, through newspapers, newsreels, and radio broadcasts, with the aim of influencing public opinion and bending neutral governments to their will.[12] As the war progressed, the neutrals were used as sanctuaries for mounting covert military operations into enemy territory and on occasion became operational theatres in their own right. Britain's hand in the *coup* that ousted Prince Paul in March 1941 is the most outstanding example, but Salazar's discovery in early 1942 of secret British networks in Portugal showed how even those neutrals enjoying good relations with the belligerents were not immune from the threat of subversion.[13]

It was not, however, merely the expansion, radicalisation, and intensification of warfare that undermined neutrality before the Second World

crews who were forced down on Spanish soil. The Irish afforded the same facilities to the British, while denying them – like the Spanish – to the opposing side.

[10] These fears played a part in Portuguese anxieties over allowing the British onto the Azores islands in August 1943, and Turkish reluctance to enter the war in 1943 and early 1944.

[11] Dutch claims to neutrality were damaged by the Abwehr's seizure of two British agents who were lured to the Dutch–German border, together with Dutch security officials, in November 1939.

[12] See Robert Cole, *The War of Words in Neutral Europe* (London, 1989).

[13] David Stafford, 'SOE and British Involvement in the Belgrade Coup d'Etat of March 1941', *Slavic Review*, 36/3 (1977), 399–419; Antonio Telo, *Propaganda e guerra secreta em Portugal 1939–1945* (Lisbon, 1990), 104–7, and Neville Wylie, 'An Amateur Learns his Job'? Special Operations Executive in Portugal, 1940–1942', *Journal of Contemporary History*, 36/3 (2001), 455–71.

War. Two events in the inter-war period eroded the basic assumptions that sustained neutrality's status as an acknowledged and respected institution in international relations. The first was the emergence of 'internationalism', symbolised by the creation of the League of Nations in 1919, which saw a reversion to the medieval ideas of a 'just war' and at a stroke cast neutrality in a war against aggression as not merely inappropriate but positively immoral. Neutrality was clearly out of place in an age when peace was considered indivisible and security deemed the responsibility of the entire international community. The collapse of collective security in the mid-1930s triggered a general drift towards neutrality, but the fifteen-year experiment in liberal internationalism which preceded this did nothing to improve neutrality's standing after its debacle in the First World War, and eroded the confidence of those small western European states who had most to gain from the reinforcement of neutral rights in time of war.

The corrosive effects of the League's internationalism on neutrality paled into insignificance in comparison with the assault inflicted by the new authoritarian ideologies. It was the appearance of aggressive political extremism, with its attendant ideas of perpetual conflict, survival of the fittest and elevation of the *Volk* or class above all else, which ultimately made neutrality the threadbare garment that it was for most of the Second World War. Fascism, National Socialism, and Communism all explicitly challenged the 'accepted norms' of international relations and rejected the principles of restraint and 'balance' that were essential for the survival of small-state neutrality. All three, in their own fashions, embraced ideological warfare during the Second World War – a concept that not only entailed the jettisoning of humanitarian standards on the battlefield, but also involved harnessing the airwaves, newspapers, and movies to propagate their ideological beliefs abroad. While all the neutrals tried, with varying degrees of success, to accommodate Italian, German, and Soviet wishes, it was Hitler's National Socialism that posed the greatest threat and confronted them with a challenge that few could meet. Hitler's racial ambitions entailed merging the Nordic races and Swiss-Germans with the Aryans of the Reich, and subordinating all other peoples, especially those in the Balkans, to their will. Politically, National Socialism was more exclusive than Soviet Communism or Italian Fascism. The march to create a thousand-year Reich had little time for such arcane ideas as neutrality. 'It was not the neutrals or luke-warms,' Hitler insisted, 'who make history.' Those whom destiny had summoned had to answer the call: he who was not for Nazi Germany was against her.

In such a world, it was not sufficient for the neutrals simply to adhere to The Hague's – increasingly incongruous – 'rules': they had instead to be unfailingly impartial in their statements, sentiments and press reporting. This was clearly an impossible task, even for those neutral governments prepared to go to the limits in controlling public expression. Endeavouring to live up to these intolerably high standards after June 1940 became a consuming concern for all neutrals.

One of the striking features of European neutrality after 1939 was the neutrals' failure to capitalise on their numerical strength. In the eighteenth century, when the modern laws of neutrality were first crystallised, neutrals had habitually formed 'leagues of armed neutrality', often under the patronage of a benevolent Great Power. Though by no means an unqualified success, there is little doubt that the practice served these states well. From the 1950s, neutral and non-aligned states likewise benefited from joint action, with both groups successfully developing common sets of ideas and practices that helped insulate them from the pervasive influence of the two Superpowers. Collective neutrality was, however, largely absent during the Second World War. The benefits of forging regional neutral blocs had long been recognised. The Oslo pact (1930), Balkan entente (1934), and Luso-Spanish treaty (1939) all in their way looked towards the emergence of neutral zones and sought to gain international endorsement for their efforts.[14] Part of their difficulty lay in the absence of Great Power sponsorship. The one practice of his Tsarist predecessors Stalin chose not to emulate was their promotion of 'neutral leagues' or advancement of international law, and while most neutrals, at one time or another, appealed to Washington for assistance, the Roosevelt administration ultimately showed little interest in anyone's neutrality other than its own. The various Balkan projects ultimately fell victim to Bulgaria's refusal to renounce its revisionist ambitions and the anxiety most felt towards encouraging a resurgence of Turkish influence in the region.[15] Though more internally cohesive, the Oslo pact suffered from a lack of agreement over which of their overbearing neighbours posed the greatest danger. Russia's attack on Finland momentarily cemented public opinion behind the concept of 'Nordic solidarity' but none of the governments was willing to promote the idea, least of all Stockholm,

[14] The Oslo group emerged in late 1930 and eventually consisted of Sweden, Norway, Denmark, The Netherlands, Belgium, Luxembourg, and Finland. Although primarily concerned with economic matters, the group became a forum for political action by the mid-1930s, actively promoting neutral rights and making some efforts towards coordinating defence planning. See Ger van Roon, *Small States in Years of Depression: The Oslo Alliance 1930–1940* (Assen, 1989).

[15] The Balkan entente, formed in 1934, comprised Romania, Yugoslavia, Turkey, and Greece.

whose geographical position and resources ultimately gave it the decisive voice. The neutrals remaining after June 1941 sought to expand their trade with each other but no concerted efforts were made to coordinate their activities, except on a humanitarian level, although even here the initiatives were often marked by a sense of competition as much as cooperation. The opening of the Allied propaganda offensive against them in April 1944 encouraged all the neutrals to pay more attention to each other's activities, but apart from wolfram exports from Iberia, despite Allied suspicions to the contrary there was little overt coordination of policies between the different neutrals.[16]

The institution of neutrality, in which so many European states had sought sanctuary by 1939, was thus a much less robust institution than that which had entered the First World War a quarter of a century before. The practicalities of modern warfare, with its increasing confusion of combatant and non-combatant status; belligerent and non-belligerent distinctions; the experiment in liberal internationalism, with its implicit assault on the validity of neutrality; and finally the emergence of aggressive authoritarian ideologies in Russia, Italy, and above all Germany resulted in the erosion of those diplomatic norms, values, and beliefs which had underpinned the classical neutrality of the nineteenth century. Few states could claim that their neutrality was guided by anything other than political pragmatism. In the majority of cases, the neutral proclamations in September 1939 sounded hollow when voiced by statesmen who had either made Geneva their second home for nearly two decades or whose societies found Bolshevism and Hitler's pact with Stalin so demonstrably repulsive.[17] Moreover, the role that neutrals had traditionally made their own, of interceding between the belligerents and facilitating their mutual humanitarian concerns, became increasingly difficult to sustain in a war which, after 1941, descended into such barbarity and excess, and whose belligerents rejected the moral assumptions upon which neutral interventions had been based. Yet, for all its patent shortcomings, neutrality was the obvious, preferred, and indeed only option for some twenty-two European states when faced with the prospect of war in the late summer of 1939. Despite the enormous changes that took place in Europe in the months and years that followed, neutrality remained the

[16] For Allied suspicions see Selim Deringil, *Turkish Foreign Policy During the Second World War* (Cambridge, 1989), 168, and the relationship between Spanish and Portuguese policy over wolfram: W. N. Medlicott, *The Economic Blockade*, 2 vols. (London, 1959), vol. II, 598–607.

[17] See Neville Wylie, 'The Neutrals', in Robert Boyce and Joe Maiolo (eds.), *The Origins of the Second World War: The Debate Continues* (London, forthcoming).

desired status for many of these states. The neutrals continued to be an influential group within the European state system, and 'neutrality' a key element in wartime international relations.

The chapters presented in this book address the phenomena of neutrality and non-belligerency from the perspective of fourteen different European states. The particular approach taken in each case has been left to the individual authors, all of whom are experts in their fields and eminently qualified to provide an overview of the particular problems that beset their countries before and during the war. Their chapters are based on their own research, but also draw widely on the secondary literature so as to give not just a balanced appraisal of the issues involved, but also an insight into the ways in which successive generations of historians have understood and explained their country's wartime experience. In so doing the chapters provide invaluable analytical introductions to a vast corpus of historical literature, the great majority of which is unavailable in the English language.

The collection is split into three sections in order to emphasise certain broader themes about the nature of neutrality and European international politics during the war. Part I examines the policies of those neutrals who succumbed to German aggression in the spring and summer of 1940: Denmark, Norway, The Netherlands, and Belgium. This was a period when European politics were still absorbing the implications of Hitler's startling pact with Stalin, and shaped by the impact of the five-month long Soviet–Finnish 'winter war'. It was also a time when the war appeared capable of leading in almost any direction. For most people, the war's most likely outcome appeared to be a compromise peace between Germany and the Anglo-French alliance. At the same time, however, the possibility of the British and French deliberately broadening the war, by striking at Hitler's Soviet ally via Finland or the Caucasus, could never be discounted. Nor could the prospect be overlooked of Hitler being ousted by 'the generals' or his underlings. Each of these scenarios promised to transform the political environment and dramatically affect the future viability of neutrality on the continent.

The Phoney War was a time for preparing for the worst and hoping for the best. It was also a period of intense diplomatic activity that centred largely on the fate of neutral Scandinavia and the Low Countries. For the neutrals and non-belligerents of western Europe the Phoney War was, then, anything but phoney. The Allies' blockade made deep inroads into their economic sovereignty: all were subjected to a relentless barrage of propaganda and criticised for remaining impassive at a time when Europe's fate was being decided. 'Each one,' Winston Churchill, Britain's First Lord of the Admiralty, warned in a famous radio broadcast on 20 January 1940, 'hopes that if he feeds the crocodile enough, the crocodile will eat him last.' Such attitudes might have been dismissed as quaint relics of some bygone age were it not for the fact that the neutrals were critical to the strategic interests of both sides. Swedish iron ore fed Germany's blast furnaces and helped to prevent Hitler's war economy from grinding to a halt; Dutch airfields were needed for the Luftwaffe's future battles over southern England, and, in the words of one recent survey, Belgium's retention of neutrality in 1939 'signified nothing less than the collapse of French hopes for a secure defence of the Allied north-western flank'.[18]

A mere handful of Danish soldiers died resisting the German occupation of 9 April 1940, and in his chapter Hans Kirchhoff explains the reasons why Copenhagen was prepared to surrender its neutrality at apparently such little cost. Denmark's political position was perhaps the least contested of all the Phoney War neutrals. Its economy was critically reliant on foreign markets, particularly in Britain and Germany, but it was widely recognised that politically Denmark lay squarely within Germany's sphere of interest. For the Danes, therefore, it was 'not so much a question of whether to adapt to the powerful southern neighbour as of how best to do it'. In retrospect, Copenhagen proved remarkably adept in meeting German demands without losing British and French goodwill. Instead of competing over Denmark's agricultural output, Copenhagen convinced the two belligerents of their mutual advantage in keeping Danish farmers in business.[19] So long as all sides refrained from contesting Berlin's *de facto* political suzerainty, Denmark's political future looked secure. Few complaints were voiced at Denmark's non-aggression pact with Germany in May 1939, nor its mining of the Belts, the waters leading into the Baltic Sea, at Berlin's behest once war began. Danish neutrality, especially in the eyes of Foreign Minister Peter Munch, aimed not at securing Denmark's full independence – an impossible task – but at providing the country with sufficient freedom to permit Denmark's survival as a social, political, and cultural unit. The logical development of this view led to Munch's concept of neo-neutrality, a form of neutrality capable of existing even in the event of a foreign

[18] Martin S. Alexander, *The Republic in Danger. General Maurice Gamelin and the Politics of French Defence, 1933–1940* (Cambridge, 1992), 208.

[19] For a recent English survey: Philip Giltner, 'Trade in 'Phoney' Wartime: The Danish–German 'Maltese' Agreement of 9 October 1939', *International History Review*, 19, 2 (1997), 333–46.

occupation. It is in this sense that Kirchhoff sees Denmark's capitulation as the rational outcome of Danish foreign policy, and a logical consequence of Denmark's historical experience and traditions.

If Denmark was a prisoner of its past, the same could equally be said of Norway. Like Denmark, Norwegian neutrality had passed the test of the First World War. Like Denmark, Norway's geography bequeathed her a political alignment, this time with Britain, which was beyond discussion. Britain had guided Norway in its path to statehood in 1907, and thereafter acted as the ultimate guarantor of Norwegian sovereignty and independence. After 1939, however, more than any other neutral, Oslo was caught in the conundrum of relying on the one power that was both capable of and, if the right circumstances prevailed, willing to violate its neutrality. As Patrick Salmon's essay shows, Oslo had traditionally resolved this dilemma by playing on Britain's moral scruples and economic self-interest. The competitive relationship that developed between the Norwegians and their British patrons after 1939 was therefore nothing new: 'ever since Amundsen beat Scott to the South Pole, Norway had been defying the British and getting away with it.' What was new was Norway's elevation in British and, subsequently, German strategic considerations. Though British thinking was muddled and confused, by early March 1940 the cabinet had effectively resolved to act irrespective of Norwegian wishes. The prize of severing Germany's iron-ore traffic through Narvik, luring the Scandinavians into the war, and finally alleviating political pressures in France, all led to London abandoning its former self-restraint. The increasingly desperate efforts of Norway's foreign minister, Halvdan Koht, to respond to belligerent actions were to no avail. Oslo lacked the means to prevent belligerent encroachments, and its fixation with the British threat ultimately blinded it to the German danger. Norwegian historians have variously explained Norway's misfortune in 1940 with reference to the country's military weaknesses, the government's prioritising, or the rigid attitudes of its leading statesmen. Salmon, however, sees Oslo's difficulties as part of a broader problem. Norwegian neutrality was bound up with a sense of a national identity that prevented, or at the very least hampered, successive governments from appreciating the changes that were under way in international affairs. Long accustomed to life at the margins of European politics, Norway's leadership failed to recognise that their isolation, and consequently their neutrality, had been progressively eroded by economic, cultural and technological developments over the inter-war years.

If the Danish and Norwegian assessments of the political situation in Europe were ultimately flawed, it nevertheless remains true that there were good historical reasons why both countries approached the outbreak of war in 1939 with a sense of guarded optimism. The same could not be said of the Dutch and the Belgians, who were the first and most celebrated victims of German aggression twenty-five years before. Neither belligerent made much distinction between Belgian and Dutch neutrality. Yet, as the chapters by Bob Moore and Alain Colignon demonstrate, the two countries' neutrality sprang from very different roots. The Dutch case rested on a pragmatic assessment of The Netherlands' place in international affairs. Domestic considerations were not entirely absent: Dutch 'pacifism' and the debilitating effect of the Depression clearly encouraged the adoption of neutrality. But for most Dutch historians the principal rationale lay in The Hague's evaluation of European international relations in the late 1930s. Neutrality was not only attuned to The Hague's imperial aspirations – the possession of the empire was The Netherlands' only claim to middle-power status – but also reflected a belief that Dutch neutrality was in the interests of the international community as a whole. The Hague was after all the home of the international law of war and Dutch statesmen had been particularly vocal in espousing the virtues of 'new diplomacy' since its inception in 1919. At the same time, however, no alternative policy seemed better able to provide for The Netherlands' needs. The Allies could scarcely offer any tangible military assistance, the Dutch were unable to mount a credible deterrent from their own resources, and the option of appeasement, reaching an accommodated settlement with the Reich, was barred by the latent anti-German sentiment of the vast bulk of the population. This is not to deny that there was more than a touch of wishful thinking in Dutch attitudes towards the war, especially after the war scares over the winter of 1939, but Dutch policy-makers were neither blind to the German danger, nor dazzled by the self-evident merits of their own neutrality.

By contrast, Belgium's return to neutrality, or 'independence', on 6 March 1936, a day before Hitler's occupation of the Rhineland, was critically affected by domestic political considerations. In his chapter on Belgium's 'fragile neutrality, solid neutralism', Alain Colignon investigates the kaleidoscopic changes in Belgian domestic politics and society which did so much to shape the course of Brussels' foreign policy over the 1930s and 1940s. Colignon emphasises how domestic political cleavages in Belgium, especially the rise of Flemish nationalism, placed severe constraints on Belgian policy-makers by the middle of the 1930s. The adoption of an 'independent' foreign policy averted a domestic political crisis and pacified Flemish Francophobia, but also reflected Brussels' growing disenchantment with the leftward shift in French politics from the early 1930s, and accorded with the express wishes of the country's young king from 1934, Leopold III.[20] Paris' subsequent conciliation of Berlin merely seemed to confirm the prudence of Brussels' actions. Colignon notes the efforts made to equip the country for war in the last years of peace, and the hesitant, belated, feelers put out to the Allies by the king and his military adviser, General van Overstraeten, once the war began. But whether the court was correct in overriding the appeals of the cabinet and keeping the country's erstwhile allies at arm's length, particularly after Germany's aggressive intentions were laid bare in January 1940, remains a matter of debate. Colignon's conclusion, that Belgium ultimately practised the policy of an ostrich, echoes the sentiments of numerous French and British officials at the time, who spared little breath in castigating Belgian for its 'blind' adherence to neutrality in the face of the German menace.[21]

Part II concentrates on the 'wait-and-see neutrals', those states which had abandoned, willingly or otherwise, their neutrality by April 1941.[22] France's defeat in June 1940 left Germany as the undisputed power in central and western Europe. Hitler's stunning successes appeared to wipe the slate clean. The historical Franco-German struggle for mastery of Europe was at an end, and Britain's position as an extra-European power had, despite Churchill's defiant rhetoric, been confirmed: if Britain landed an army on the continent, Hitler would have it arrested. A new chapter seemed to open, which, depending on one's historical perspective, led either inexorably to an ideological war of annihilation in the East or to a period of inconclusive sparring between Britain and Germany. In both cases, the states of east-central and south-eastern Europe have

20 For studies in English of these problems see D. O. Kieft, *Belgium's Return to Neutrality* (Oxford, 1972) and the rather partial account of Roger Keyes, *Outrageous Fortune: Leopold III of the Belgians* (London, 1990).

21 See Martin S. Alexander, 'In Lieu of Alliance: The French General Staff's Secret Co-operation with Neutral Belgium, 1936–1940', *Journal of Strategic Studies*, 14/4 (1991), 413–27 and *The Republic in Danger*, 172–209. Brain Bond is more sympathetic to Leopold: *Britain, France and Belgium, 1939–1940* (London, 1990, 2nd edition), 96–8. See also the 1990 conference papers collected under the title *1940 Belgique, une société en crise, un pays en guerre*, published by the Centre de recherches et d'études historique de la Deuxième Guerre Mondiale (Brussels, 1991).

22 As with Part I, the periodisation is not a strict one; Sweden and Italy were key members of the 'neutral' gallery before June 1940, just as the question of Spanish 'non-belligerency' dominated much of Britain's attention during the autumn and winter of 1940/1. Likewise, although Italy jettisoned its non-belligerency in June 1940 it is included in Part II since its involvement in the Balkans is central to any understanding of the actions of the states in this region.

traditionally been seen as victims rather than actors in their own right. There is little doubt that these states were unwittingly drawn into Great Power calculations, as Soviet and German interests first diverged and then came into direct conflict.[23] Italy signalled its intention to expand into the Balkans with its occupation of Albania in April 1939 and its incessant political intrigues against the Yugoslavs and Greeks. The prospect of German involvement encouraged Rome and Moscow to bury their differences, forge ties with actors in the region and finally take matters into their own hands. Their actions ultimately brought about the result they had both sought to avoid. Over the autumn of 1940, Germany's extensive economic interests in south-east Europe became progressively interwoven with its political objectives. Soviet ambitions over the Straits, territorial demands on Romania, and diplomatic moves in Hungary and Yugoslavia were increasingly seen in Berlin as symptomatic of Moscow's desire to contest German hegemony on the continent. Mussolini's bid for independence through a 'parallel war' meanwhile spectacularly misfired. Within days of his abortive attack on Greece on 28 October 1940, he was reluctantly forced to appeal to Hitler for assistance, and thereby precipitate the very intervention that he had hoped to avert. Britain, for its part, looked at the region as a trouble spot, which, if given the right encouragement, might turn into the ulcer for Hitler that Spain had been for Napoleon a century and a half before.

Given the extent of external intervention in the region, it may seem perverse to argue that the states of east-central and south-eastern Europe were 'independent' in any meaningful way. This is no less true when one considers that all of these states were either occupied or became embroiled in a war that brought them only further misery and foreign occupation. Yet it is equally true that focusing exclusively on the belligerents obscures the existence of other processes at work in the region at the time. While Hitler's successes in June 1940 affected the political landscape, the agendas pursued by the states in this region were anything but a passing phenomenon. The politics of peace merged seamlessly into the politics of war; the opportunities created were new, but the basic ideas governing state behaviour can be traced back into the region's complex historical past. What this suggests is that Germany, Italy, Russia, and Britain were to some extent prisoners of the local political geography. They may have warily circled each other, teasing out their weaknesses and testing their

[23] Gabriel Gorodetsky, *Grand Delusion. Stalin and the German Invasion of Russia* (New Haven, 1999), 316.

intentions, but all were ultimately forced to tailor their activities to take account of the particular political dynamics of the region.

The 'neutral' most closely associated with the revisionist label was Italy. Indeed so abhorrent was the idea of Italian neutrality in a general European war that Mussolini could barely bring himself to admit that he was anything less than a full belligerent. As Brian Sullivan shows, though Italy edged from non-alignment to non-belligerency and finally war, throughout Mussolini behaved as a man already at war. His appetite for territorial expansion was insatiable and fundamentally unappeasable. His ambitions, from avenging the mutilated peace of 1919 to founding an empire stretching from the Horn of Africa to the Balkans, were almost unlimited. For Sullivan, Mussolini was a restless warmonger, who ceaselessly tested and provoked his victims and worked to create the international conditions necessary for the fulfilment of his aspirations. Italy's actual position in European politics, both before and after the onset of war, was, however, by no means as transparent as Mussolini's aggressive pronouncements and Fascist dogmas might suggest. In the same way as Russia, Italy was to many observers 'a riddle wrapped in a mystery inside an enigma'. Its antagonism towards France and ideological affinity with Germany might be beyond doubt, but whether its national interests were always or best served by the expansion of German power was a matter upon which opinion was sharply divided. Hitler's pact with Stalin, conflict with France, and growing economic and political interest in the Balkans all diminished Italian standing and threatened to thwart Mussolini's imperial designs. For many Italians, including the king, senior army officers, and Mussolini's mercurial son-in-law and foreign minister, Count Ciano, neutrality in a German–French war was neither shameful nor necessarily ill advised. Their hesitation, coupled with the deplorable state of Italian armed forces and the constantly changing international situation, repeatedly denied Mussolini the war he so passionately desired. And while the Duce was as conscious as anyone of the limits of Italy's alliance with Germany, it was ultimately only through Germany that Mussolini could hope to realise his ambitions or overcome the chronic disparity between Italy's goals and its resources.

Mussolini harboured territorial ambitions at almost every point of the compass. When Ciano talked of Italy's national aspirations in late 1938 he was greeted with shouts of 'Tunis, Jibuti, Corsica, and Nice'. By the spring of 1939, however, the principal thrust of Italian foreign policy lay in the Balkans. It was in Albania, Yugoslavia, and Greece that Mussolini envisaged founding his new Roman empire and one of the points emphasised in Sullivan's chapter is the extent to which the Italians cooperated with other revisionist powers, notably Hungary. Hungarian aspirations were as extravagant as Italy's. The treaty of Trianon of June 1920 had shown no respect for Hungarian 'national self determination' and left successive Hungarian governments with only one *raison d'être*, to restore Hungary to a position commensurate to its population size and historical status. In retrospect, it is easy to see why Hungarian neutrality was so short lived. Berlin was ultimately able to satisfy the bulk of Budapest's claims. Nevertheless the interests of the two countries were not identical. German arms sales to Romania, its alliance with Russia, and demand for assistance against Poland all contradicted Hungarian wishes. Instead of relying on others, therefore, Budapest had to make its own opportunities, through its secret links with Rome or by threatening unilateral action against the Romanians. Hungary's final subordination to German wishes arose not simply out of Hitler's decision to intervene more actively in the region than he had felt inclined to do before, but fundamentally because Hungary found that its territorial ambitions could neither be ignored, nor satisfied through its own resources. Tibor Frank's chapter further elucidates the complexity of Hungary's position in the war. For Frank, Hungarian foreign policy was in many respects Janus faced. The logic of treaty revisionism may indeed have tied Hungary to Germany's coat tails by 1941 but this was by no means an inevitable or even desirable outcome for Hungary's foreign policy élite. Under Count Teleki, Hungary developed a policy of 'double-speak': affirming its solidarity with the Axis powers whilst simultaneously endeavouring to maintain control of its own interests and sustain amicable relations with the western powers. Such a policy can be found in its treaty with Yugoslavia in December 1940 and is also evidenced, as Frank demonstrates, in the work of Hungarian academics and essayists. One might suggest that, while neutrality may indeed have deprived Hungary of its ancient lands, in demonstrating Hungary's independence from its powerful German neighbour, it did, at some subliminal level, allow Hungarians to conceive of their country as a major power, and the rightful heir to the legacy of the Dual Monarchy.

Romania had the most to lose from border changes in the Balkans. The post-war peace settlements had given her the whole of Transylvania, plus the provinces of southern Dobrudja, Bukovina, and Bessarabia. These arrangements had assured Bucharest of the perpetual hostility of Hungary, Bulgaria, and Russia, and forced her in response to cultivate the support of France and the cooperation of the other satiated powers in the region, Yugoslavia and Greece. Given the inherent fragility of its position, Bucharest had good reason to be pleased with its choices by 1939. Its initiatives in Paris had been rewarded by a treaty in 1926 and an Anglo-French guarantee in April 1939, and its efforts to promote regional cooperation had borne fruit with the establishment of the Balkan Entente in 1934. It even, for a while, attracted Italian interest in the idea of a neutral Balkan bloc. The limits of Romania's policy were, however, cruelly exposed in the summer of 1940. As Ciano gleefully commented a day after the French sued for peace, the Allied guarantees in the Balkans had turned out to be like 'a bottle of wine which has been preserved for many years with the hope of producing strong and good wine, but when the bottle is finally opened, it [was] found to contain vinegar instead of wine'.[24] Within five months, Romania had been shorn of its disputed territories, and compelled to sign over its independence and accept German 'protection'. In his chapter on Romania, Maurice Pearton examines how King Carol's policy of neutrality gradually collapsed under the pressure of these events. Of the many points to emerge in his chapter, two warrant special mention. The first is the complex and flexible operation of Romania's economic neutrality. Oil was the one card Bucharest could play in its external relations and, given the circumstances, it played its hand remarkably well. 'As long as the Romanian Government considered it had any room for manoeuvre at all, it was an active, not passive participant in a *triangle* of relations in which it could lay down the rules.' The second point to note is Bucharest's fixation with the Russian menace. Bessarabia was not only important in itself, commanding the mouth of the river Danube, but Moscow's claim to the province was taken in Bucharest as merely the first step in a plan to subjugate the entire country to Soviet control. Accepting German arbitration over Transylvania and Dobrudja and finally adhering to the Tripartite pact were thus justified by reference to the continued Russian threat. It was Romania's misfortune that throughout the autumn of 1940, when its fate was being decided, Hitler was still inclined to abide by his pact with Stalin.

Bulgaria's relations with Russia were, on the face of it, very different from Romania's. Russia was Bulgaria's historic patron and had actively promoted pan-Slavism. Popular sympathies towards Russia were so strong that King Boris once quipped that he was the only genuine Bulgarian patriot in the entire country. Yet, as Vesselin Dimitrov notes, it

24 Ciano's remarks as recorded by Soviet ambassador in Rome, 22 June 1940, cited in Gorodetsky, *Grand Delusion*, 28.

was again the looming threat of Russian influence that finally propelled Bulgaria into German arms. Historical studies of Bulgarian neutrality, especially the attitude of King Boris, have tended to fall into one of two camps. Boris can be depicted as essentially pro-German: letting his revisionist ambitions, like the Hungarians, dictate the direction of his foreign policy. Alternatively, he can be seen as an unwilling warrior, reluctantly prised out of a neutrality which he sincerely believed was in Bulgaria's best interests. Dimitrov by contrast offers a more nuanced appraisal of Boris' conduct. Memories of Bulgaria's mistakes in the First World War reinforced Boris' desire to keep his country free from foreign entanglements. Nevertheless, as early as April 1939 the logic of Bulgaria's territorial 'entitlements' in Romania, Greece, and Yugoslavia, made Boris rule out any overt alignment with the Western Powers. By early 1940, while still temperamentally inclined towards neutrality, he had decided that Dobrudja could only be secured through closer orientation with Berlin. What put paid to Boris' hopes of achieving his goals without sacrificing Bulgarian autonomy was not so much Germany's entry into Balkan affairs, but rather Moscow's sudden determination to reactivate its old historical ties and make Bulgaria its springboard into Balkan politics. Like Romania, the chances of successfully playing Berlin off against Moscow were slim and always threatened to compromise Bulgaria's standing. Boris' pained reaction at the price demanded for German protection was, in Dimitrov's view, merely theatrical. By the time his premier, Bogdan Filov, left for Berlin, Boris' mind had already been made up; indeed, he deliberately chose the pro-German premier to lead the delegation in order to put the result beyond doubt. Neutrality was not ripped from Boris' hands. Rather it was relinquished in the hope of forestalling further Russian demands.

If the end of Bulgaria's neutrality was signalled by Filov's signature on the Tripartite pact, Yugoslavia's was ultimately brought to an end by the arrival of German bombers over Belgrade in the early hours of Palm Sunday, 1941. Over the preceding months, Yugoslavia had come under intense pressure to leave the path of neutrality, not only because of its geographical position, but also because it had emerged by the spring of 1941 as the lynch-pin of Balkan politics. As Dragoljub Zivojinović notes in his chapter, Yugoslavia had lived under the threat of an Italian invasion for the previous five years, and had during this time been forced repeatedly to shift its position and its neutrality to contain this latent threat. Italian aggression was the 'given' in Yugoslavian diplomatic calculations and all the other numerous claims on Yugoslav territory, arising from its foundation in 1919, were essentially secondary to and contingent on the problem posed by Italy's imperial pretensions in the Adriatic. Zivojinović charts the course of Yugoslavian diplomacy, and illuminates the basic attitudes that shaped Yugoslav policy, especially the views of the Regent, Prince Paul. His chapter shows how Yugoslavia's options gradually evaporated over the course of the war, leaving Paul with no option other than to submit to German wishes. Zivojinović's conclusion – that Paul's decision, painful though it was, was ultimately a correct one – may not find agreement in all quarters; less contentious is the point that until the spring of 1941 Paul played a poor hand, rather well. So long as Germany remained outside Balkan politics, Belgrade could check Italian ambitions by playing up the prospect of Anglo-French intervention. The problem was that both Paul and his Allied interlocutors wildly exaggerated the extent of western capabilities. Paul's assumption that British forces could conduct operations in Yugoslavia from their base in Salonika was considered unfeasible by Britain's military planners (although they were careful not to publicise these views in Belgrade!). Paul's decision to extract the maximum concessions out of Berlin before finally acceding to its wishes reflected a prudent and perhaps accurate reading of the situation. What it failed to do, however, was take sufficient account of the likely domestic ramifications. Paul's 'neutrality' was analogous to Leopold's 'independence': its logic rested on Yugoslavia's own political complexion as much as the balance of international forces. The domestic peace ushered in by constitutional reforms before the war began proved short lived, and evaporated altogether under the strain of Belgrade's entry into the Tripartite pact. Paul's misery then was twofold. His alignment with Germany ran counter to his deepest political convictions, but also resulted in his denunciation not only by his British friends, but also by his Yugoslav 'subjects', by the very people whose interests he had sought to serve.

Zivojinović, Dimitrov, Pearton, and – to a lesser extent – Frank, comment on how the political make-up of the states critically shaped their approach towards neutrality. In all states of this turbulent region, a sense of history and acute awareness of the recent past coloured popular attitudes and ultimately affected foreign policy decisions. For some, it was the necessity of avenging the injustices of 1919/1920; for others, it was the choice of allies and choice of enemies. The 'wait-and-see neutrals' of east-central and south-east Europe were, then, neutral by design rather than by inclination. Though all expressed their desire to remain at peace, their devotion to neutrality reflected their own long-term interests and their relations with the warring factions. The decisive events which shaped European history over these years did not so much wipe the slate clean as merely create the opportunity for the politics of this region to resume in a different form. In these conditions, neutrality was always likely to be a matter of tactical convenience. As Romania showed in the handling of its oil exports, the 'rules' of neutrality could be used to good effect. But while they might take a detached view of the Franco-German struggle, in the last resort no-one could afford the luxury of neutrality towards the historical conflicts within their own region, nor towards the intrusion into their affairs of the wider European war.

It has been revelations about the conduct of those neutrals that survived the war that have recently brought the issue of neutrality to the forefront of public and scholarly attention. Beginning in early 1997 the World Jewish Congress began publishing US official documents from the war that cast doubt on the 'neutrality' of these states, and questioned the extent to which they had been made to account for their misdemeanours by the Allies immediately after the war. The neutrals, it was found, had played a pivotal role in Germany's war effort. Switzerland was the worst culprit – purchasing nearly half of Berlin's entire gold stocks, three-quarters of which had been acquired through illegitimate means – but other neutrals and their banks were also found to have used a short spoon when supping with the devil. Not only, was it argued, had the neutrals been let off the hook after the war, but many of their banks and insurance companies had held on to the accounts of those who had perished in Hitler's death camps. At a practical level, the unprecedented campaign yielded impressive results; those 'named and shamed' made *ex gratia* payments to Holocaust survivors and their families, and the process of tracing heirless assets and returning them to their rightful owners has been accelerated. At an historical level, the event has been highly instructive. One of the first points to emerge was just how little the historical community knew about the issues being discussed. The neutrals had been a *terra incognita* for so long that much of the early discussions were marred by an ignorance of the basic facts, and an over-reliance on preconceptions and assumptions that were later found to be faulty. Three years on, the findings of the various historical commissions created to 'set the record straight' have illuminated numerous aspects of the neutrals' role during the war.[25] Nevertheless, there is still a need to contextualise

[25] See Department of State, *U.S. and Allied Wartime and Postwar Relations and Negotiations with Argentina, Portugal, Spain, Sweden, and Turkey on Looted Gold and German External Assets and U.S. Concerns about*

these findings, to understand how neutrality functioned during the war, and how it was perceived by the neutral governments themselves. It is this broader context that Enrique Moradiellos, Elena Hernández-Sandoica, Fernando Rosas, Eunan O'Halpin, Paul Levine, and Neville Wylie provide in the five chapters on the 'long-haul neutrals' in Part III.

The one country that could not be accused of duplicity in its attitude towards the democracies was Spain. As Moradiellos and Hernández-Sandoica make clear, although some historians have depicted Franco as the guardian of Iberian tranquillity, his actions, utterances, and attitudes tell a different story. In ostentatiously following Mussolini's footsteps and shifting from neutrality to non-belligerency in June 1940, Franco was not simply playing with words, but was consciously embarking on a road that would lead his country into war. This bellicosity could not be put down to mere political opportunism. His visceral hatred of Communism and disdain for parliamentary democracy was genuine, and his desire to expand Spain's imperial frontiers in North Africa was entirely sincere. Above all, Spain's position in the war was affected by Franco's romantic image of Spain, as an historic nation and bastion of Catholicism. It was not the exorbitant price tag Franco attached to Spain's entry into the war that kept Spain from crossing the threshold, but rather Hitler's mistaken belief that Spain's interests coincided with Germany's and that Franco would calmly consent to submitting some of Spain's sacred soil to alien rule. Franco may have appreciated Spain's strategic value after June 1940, but his outlook was ultimately governed by his own sense of Spain's place in the world and dependent on his ability to control the shifting balance of political forces at home.

It is significant that when the time came for Franco to start reviving his neutralist credentials, he did so explicitly within a regional context. His meeting with Salazar in February 1942 and their subsequent ratification of the Luso-Spanish treaty of March 1939 and its additional protocol of July 1940 symbolised not just Spain's retreat from non-belligerency but also its tacit recognition of and support for the neutralisation of the entire peninsula. This rare success of 'collective neutralism' was by no means foreordained. Nonetheless, Portuguese support for the idea, in particular

*the Fate of the Wartime Ustacha Treasury* (Washington, 1998); Independent Commission of Experts, *Switzerland and Gold Transactions in the Second World War. Interim Report* (Berne 1998), *Switzerland and Refugees in the Nazi Era* (Berne, 1999); Foreign and Commonwealth Office, *Nazi Gold. Information from the British Archives*, Parts I and II (London, 1997); António Telo, *A neutralidad portuguese e o ouro nazi* (Lisbon, 2000). I am grateful to the late Albert Lovet for bringing this book to my attention.

the efforts of Salazar and his ambassador in Madrid, Pedro Teotónio Pereira, ensured that when Franco decided to return to neutrality in early 1942, his wishes could be accommodated within a coherent regional framework.[26]

Portugal's commitment to neutrality was, as Fernando Rosas shows, far from straightforward. Initially biased in Britain's favour, it became increasingly 'equidistant' after the arrival of German troops at the Pyrenees, and only returned to its pro-Allied stance hesitantly in the last years of the war. This flexibility was, Rosas emphasises, largely a function of Salazar's attitude towards the Luso-British alliance and the growing room for manoeuvre that opened up in Lisbon's relations with its historic ally. Rosas traces this change to the Spanish Civil War, when developments within the region first challenged the assumptions that had underpinned Portugal's traditional Atlanticist orientation. But even though the alliance might remain the touchstone of Portuguese foreign policy, Salazar's particular, not to say peculiar, reading of his own and his country's interests inevitably affected the form of Portuguese neutrality. Portugal's profitable trade in wolfram was viewed by Salazar as a 'moral' (or rather 'immoral') issue, as much as a matter of politics and economics. He loathed and feared American capitalism almost as much as he despised Soviet Communism, and his resentment over any action that tainted Portuguese honour – such as Britain's presumptuous occupation of Portuguese Timor in December 1941 – was allowed to sour relations with foreign governments for extended periods.

Although the Allies railed at Salazar's seemingly incomprehensible obduracy, in the end the Portuguese dictator bowed to their wishes and furnished the concessions they desired. A useful comparison might be made with Ireland, another country on Europe's periphery whose long-term political interests lay with an Allied victory. Like Portugal, although the opposition never seriously advocated any alternative policy the actual form of Irish neutrality bore the hallmark of its maker, Eamon de Valera. De Valera did not quibble with the basic premise of Irish foreign policy after 1921, that Britain's defence, especially the security of the western approaches, should not be endangered by Irish independence or neutrality. This assumption was, however, tested in the second half of 1940, when de Valera's refusal to bring Ireland into the war or allow Britain access to its former 'treaty ports' undeniably complicated British

[26] For a discussion of this issue in English, see Charles R. Halstead, 'Consistent and Total Peril from Every Side. Portugal and its 1940 Protocol with Spain', *Iberian Studies*, 3 (1974), 15–29.

defence planning and, potentially at least, provided Berlin with a springboard for an invasion of the British Isles. As Eunan O'Halpin points out, de Valera worked hard to placate both sides; keeping Germany at arm's length and assuaging, if not entirely dissipating, British anxieties by authorising close contacts with London and Belfast on intelligence and military matters. Yet despite the apparent flexibility, it could be argued that the most remarkable feature of Irish neutrality was its rigidity. It was first and foremost a policy based on a principled rather than a pragmatic answer to Ireland's political and security needs. Beyond the areas where surreptitious cooperation with Ireland's neighbour complemented his own sectional interests, such as using Britain's labour shortage to offset the declining employment opportunities at home, de Valera did little to soften Irish neutrality, even after the war turned in the Allies' favour. In contrast to Salazar's attitude towards the Azores bases, the status of the 'treaty ports' remained beyond discussion. Unlike the Turks, Axis diplomats were not expelled and diplomatic protocol was observed until Hitler's last gasp, and whether de Valera's strict adherence to neutrality accorded with the wishes of the population after America's entry into the war or indeed lay in the country's long-term interests remains a vexed historical question.[27]

Sweden and Switzerland, like Ireland, entered the post-war world with their faith in neutrality confirmed. Both countries were traditional neutrals, vibrant democracies, and possessed important industrial sectors that depended on export markets for the bulk of their business.[28] Both lay sufficiently close to the centre of events to ensure that their actions inevitably impacted on some aspect or other of the war. The question of whether, in these circumstances, Swedish neutrality was a 'tactical success' or a 'moral compromise', as posed in Paul Levine's chapter, could equally be asked about Switzerland. Against the odds, both countries survived the war, and in remaining neutral after 1945 it could be argued that both governments regarded their policy as much a 'strategic' as a 'tactical' success. Recent research has, in both countries, called into question the 'heroic simplicities' that dominated earlier, especially

[27] See Brian Girvin and Geoffrey Roberts, *Ireland and the Second World War. Politics, Society and Remembrance* (Dublin, 1999) and Michael Kennedy and Joseph Morrison Skelly, *Irish Foreign Policy, 1919–1966. From Independence to Internationalism* (Dublin, 2000).

[28] For a comparison of the two see R. L. Bindschedler, H. R. Kurz, W. Carlgren, and S. Carlsson (eds.), *Schwedisch und schweizerische Neutralität im Zweiten Weltkrieg* (Basle, 1985) and John F. L. Ross, *Neutrality and International Sanctions. Sweden, Switzerland and Collective Security* (Westport, 1989).

public, perceptions of the war years. The compromises, moral or otherwise, that both made during the war are now being integrated into public discussion of the period. Fundamental to this re-evaluation is the two countries' response to the humanitarian catastrophe that overwhelmed Europe after 1941. While both can be charged with 'doing too little too late', it would appear that it was Swedish officials who, notwithstanding the efforts of individual Swiss diplomats, moved most quickly from 'indifference' to 'activism' and adopted bureaucratic procedures that promoted humanitarian aims, rather than obstructed them. In both however, the claim to 'self preservation' or neutrality were frequently used to justify initiatives that had, at their time of conception, little to do with any coherent, or even conscious, national strategy of deterrence or dissuasion. The intelligence services of both countries knew only too well that, even if it could never be entirely discounted, the German 'threat', especially after 1943, was ultimately more apparent than real. Neither government could claim that it did the utmost to confound Hitler's ambitions, even though these ambitions contradicted everything that the two democratic and pluralistic societies held dear. 'Neutrality' in both cases was a multifaceted and highly complex phenomenon that continues to defy simplistic categorisation.

The fourteen chapters collected in this book attest to the size, scope, and significance of the neutral (and non-belligerent) gallery for the international history of the Second World War, and offer insight into possible directions that future research might take.[29] They underscore the fact that when in late 1939 the 'war' began, the vast majority of European states was still at 'peace' and wished to remain so. Even after German forces had triumphed in western Europe, there were still almost as many states standing aside from the war as those who had been consumed by it. Moreover, whether the neutrals' attitudes towards the course of the war, as illuminated in these chapters, were malevolent or simply misplaced, the point that comes across is that the neutrals ultimately had greater control over their destinies than it has been fashionable to assume. Though unique and, in retrospect, ludicrously optimistic, Sidney 'George' Strube's cartoon of 22 April 1940, featured on the jacket of this book, reminds us that the neutrals were more than capable of taking

[29] Research on some of the neutrals suffers from a dearth of archival material; however the former Soviet and eastern bloc archives and the recently released Allied diplomatic decrypts might help compensate for these gaps. *Vostočnaja Evropa meždu Gitlerem i Stalinem, 1939–1941*, ed. V. K. Volkov and L. J. Gibjanskii (Moscow, 1999), and Gabriel Gorodetsky's *Grand Delusion* draw on material from Soviet, Polish, and Romanian archives.

decisions for themselves: whether, as in this case, to root out Nazi Quislings, two weeks after the German invasion of Norway, or later in the war when it was up to the neutrals to decide whether to offer 'safe-havens' to war refugees or to war criminals and their fortunes.

# PART I

## *The 'Phoney War' neutrals*

CHAPTER I

# *Denmark, September 1939–April 1940*

*Hans Kirchhoff*

Denmark's policy of neutrality from September 1939 to April 1940 was rooted in a centuries-old tradition of alliance-free neutrality, which was conditioned by the country's geo-strategic position, its role as a small country and historical experience. The Danish government tried to maintain its position of neutrality even during the German occupation, and continued this policy after 1945, until the Cold War compelled Denmark to join NATO in 1949.

## HISTORICAL EXPERIENCE

In 1864, Denmark tried to resolve the Schleswig-Holstein question by means of a war against Austria and Prussia. This decision was the result of a foolhardy, unrealistic foreign policy that counted on help from outside, but which led to defeat and the loss of North Schleswig. The loss of two-fifths of its territory and of a million inhabitants led to a profound national crisis and intense heart-searching. It placed a question mark against whether Denmark could maintain its existence as an independent state and created a small-country neurosis that affected several generations of foreign policy makers. The 1870–1 Franco-German War briefly rekindled the hope that North Schleswig could be regained via an alliance with France, but Prussia's victory crushed any hopes in this direction and made a policy of neutrality a *sine qua non*. Fear of the increasing military might of Germany became the dominant element of Danish defence policy and acknowledgement of Denmark's extremely limited freedom to manoeuvre became a maxim in defence policy circles. It was not so much a question of whether to adapt to the powerful southern neighbour as of how best to do it. Successive governments, both conservative and liberal, attempted to adjust the defence policy in order to make it acceptable to Berlin, in other words to convince Germany that under no circumstances would Denmark become an opponent in any future war.

During the First World War, the small social–liberal party, the Radical Liberals, had been the governing party and consequently responsible for safeguarding neutrality and preventing Denmark from being dragged into a conflict between the Great Powers. They did succeed in keeping the country out of the war, in spite of its vulnerable position between Germany and Great Britain. This was primarily because neither London nor Berlin had any wish to occupy Denmark, as long as the other side kept out as well; a precondition that was not present in the next war in 1940. This successful policy was assisted by a cleverly executed balancing act that did not observe the classical requirement in international law for impartiality, but which made adroit adjustments to changing situations and changing pressures from the Great Powers. Thus the foreign trade that was so vital to the foodstuff and manufacturing sectors was successfully maintained, not only with Germany and Britain but also with overseas territories. This created an economic boom in the shelter of neutrality. Foreign policy was skilfully conducted by the diplomat Erik Scavenius, in times of crisis often via secret talks with the German ambassador in Copenhagen. The neutrality, therefore, had an obvious bias towards Germany, but this was accepted by London, which had written off the Baltic as an operational field and regarded Denmark as within the German sphere of influence. Several of the leading politicians held government posts again during the Second World War and were profoundly influenced by their experiences from the previous war. This was the case with the Radical politician, Peter Munch, the undisputed leader of foreign policy in the 1930s, and with the Social Democrat, Thorvald Stauning, who became prime minister when the Radical Liberals and Social Democrats formed a coalition government in 1929.

Hopes that pro-Danish North Schleswig might one day return to the kingdom had never died out, and they were realised after the defeat of Germany and the Versailles Treaty of 1920. In a referendum, the North Schleswigers voted to come home and a new border was drawn which was as ethnically fair as possible. But it brought Denmark a German minority of about ten thousand people who demanded to come *heim ins Reich* after the Nazi take-over in 1933. The German government had never recognised the 1920 border and in the 1930s fear that Hitler might insist on its being moved further north became a permanent source of anxiety to the Danish government and was a factor in the policy of appeasement towards Germany.

In 1920, however, the border problem seemed to have been resolved and the great bone of contention that for decades had divided Denmark and Germany had thus been removed. With Germany's fall as a Great Power and the Soviet Union in splendid isolation with its own internal problems, the Baltic was an area of low tension and Denmark faced no threats to its national security. It joined the League of Nations and its system of sanctions, albeit with some reservations concerning military and economic sanctions. Denmark had no wish to be forced to take action against a future Greater Germany, for example. The decision to join provoked an internal debate about whether membership was compatible with the classical definition of neutrality (which it was not) and whether the duty to undertake sanctions committed Denmark to a higher level of defence (which the Right and the Liberal Party insisted it did, but which the Social Democrats and the Radical Liberals denied). This conflict reveals the strong desire to continue a balanced policy of neutrality regardless of the security system and it shows the intimate relationship between domestic and foreign policy.

## THE CONCEPT OF DEFENCE

During the First World War, Denmark had possessed a relatively strong defence force, with a conscripted army of about 50,000 men. The aim was to reassure Germany that Denmark could and would defend its neutrality (against Britain) and might have been a factor in keeping the German Supreme Command quiet. But with the disappearance of the military threat after the German defeat in 1918, the defence force was drastically reduced, reaching its nadir with the defence agreement of 1932 during the world Depression. This led to a reduction of the army and the navy to what from a military point of view was a weakly underpinned defence force for a neutral state. Its primary duty was to prevent accidental breaches of neutrality, such as overflying, enemy action in Danish territorial waters, or accidental crossings of the border by, for example, SA (Sturm Abteilung) bands, but not to engage in a battle for the country's existence. In the event of an attack by a Great Power – that is, Germany – the defence force would merely record, not oppose, the breach of neutrality. The two governing parties, the Radical Liberals and the Social Democrats, had strong pacifist traditions and saw no ideological, economic or strategic grounds for believing that the use of military power would be a solution to Denmark's security problem. They did not believe that it would ever be possible to build a defence force strong enough to prevent a German attack. On the contrary, a strong army in weak hands would act as a magnet to the Great Powers. They believed that the Danish nation would endure, independently of state and territory, as long as the people could survive as a social, political, and cultural unit. Instead of wasting money on a military force that would not be of much use anyway, they aimed at building a welfare, consensus state, with enough cohesion to withstand a foreign occupation – if it should come to that. So the overriding aim was to keep Denmark out of the war, a war in which the small state had no vested interest, since it would be the egoistic work of the Great Powers. The Foreign Secretary Peter Munch even developed a theory, called neo-neutrality, whereby a small country preserves the right of non-involvement in a war, even if it is physically occupied; a scenario that arose in April 1940.[1]

Nor did the Opposition, the Liberals and the Conservatives, operate with the idea of an army capable of withstanding an attack from Germany. But they wanted a military force which was sufficiently strong to prevent Denmark from forming a vacuum that the Great Powers could occupy at no cost and which, in case of an attack, could demonstrate through its fighting power the nation's will to preserve its independence. Again, there was a split between the army and the navy, both in the competition for the meagre funds available and on the question of the right strategy to adopt. The army operated with the concept of a marginal force, on the assumption that Germany would never be able to use its full power against Denmark in a war because it would be engaged elsewhere – a prediction that came true in 1940. Plans were therefore made for a bridgehead defence, in direct contradiction of the government's ideas. Unlike the army, the navy thought that Germany could force her will upon Denmark at any time, for example via a blockade, and that the primary aim, as in the First World War, must be to convince Germany of the country's ability to protect its neutrality (against Britain). They therefore planned a peripheral defence that came close to the government's guarding and marking strategy. The bad atmosphere between the government and the generals, in particular, created problems of coordination and weakened the management of the crisis when war actually came. It is symptomatic that the operational orders from the First World War, in which troops were instructed to fight to the last man, were not updated until after the Munich crisis of 1938.

In 1937 the defence regulations were revised. This involved some modernisation of the forces but no expansion. On the contrary: the

[1] P. Munch and his neo-neutrality are analysed from a political science point of view in Ole Karup Pedersen, *Udenrigsminister P. Munchs opfattelse af Danmarks stilling i international politik* (Copenhagen, 1970).

army was reduced from eight to seven regiments and the yearly number of recruits from 8,900 to 7,840. During the parliamentary debate the government agreed that breaches of neutrality other than accidental ones should be repulsed, to the extent that it was considered feasible. This did not change the underlying idea that the forces should not be used against a major attack, but it strengthened public expectation of an actual fight for existence. Because of the need to maintain the credibility of the military with the Great Powers and to avoid internal unrest, the government had no wish to clarify the situation. The great majority of the electorate supported the government's defence policy without realising what the consequences would be in a war. This created a backlash of public opinion when the uncontested occupation took place on 9 April 1940.

## APPEASEMENT TOWARDS GERMANY IN THE 1930S

The international crisis in the 1930s resulting from the aggressive foreign policies of dictatorships pushed Denmark into an increasingly isolated position. Foreign Secretary Munch was a strong supporter of the League of Nations. He hoped that it could promote disarmament and international law – one of the strongest cards for a small country at a time of international anarchy – and he was not prepared to rule out the possibility of the League coming to the aid of Denmark in a border dispute with Germany. Munch's efforts were often dismissed as naive, but he had no illusions about the role of the League of Nations in a conflict involving the Great Powers. Denmark still supported sanctions against Italy in 1935, because of the war in Abyssinia, but with the breakdown of this policy and heightened international tension Denmark gradually distanced itself from its League of Nations commitment to sanctions, notably in 1936 and 1938, and returned to isolated neutrality.[2]

[2] The study of the period of neutrality from September 1939 until April 1940 has been hampered by the highly political nature of the subject. The debate about blame for the war started immediately in 1940 and really took off after the occupation, when it was bound up with the political struggle and the action against collaboration. The parliamentary Commission of Inquiry set up in 1945 investigated complaints against the government of incompetence and collusion, but found them to be groundless (*Bilag til Beretning til Folketinget afgivet af den af Tinget under 15. juni 1945 nedsatte Kommission*, I–III (1945–51)). The Commission performed a thorough clearing-up operation and obtained important source materials. However, for many years the strong focus of the report and the public on the events immediately before the German invasion helped deflect attention away from the determining influences behind the security and defence policy decisions in the 1930s. A comprehensive scholarly study that sees the subject in its widest context is still to be written. We have to make do with partial studies. The standard work on Danish foreign policy in the

The break with the international security system took place together with the other six ex-neutral, so-called 'Oslo States', which also included Norway and Sweden. It has often been debated whether a Nordic defence league might have been able to keep Denmark and Norway out of the Second World War in 1940. Feelers had been put out by the Danish Prime Minister in 1933, but the response from Oslo and Stockholm had been negative and later on Stauning firmly rejected the idea. The Nordic foreign ministers met at regular intervals to coordinate their policies, but the geo-strategic interests were too divergent for real cooperation on defence: Sweden's defence policy was focused on the east, Norway's on the west and Denmark's on the south. This can also be seen in Denmark's acceptance of a non-aggression pact with Germany in 1939, which the other Nordic countries declined, and in the failed Nordic defence negotiations after the war, in 1948–9. On the whole, Nordic cooperation was kept on a back burner during these years. In spite of the many points of similarity in their political and democratic cultures, their respective economic interests, including policies on trade, were too dissimilar. Thus the three countries never succeeded in building up a joint economic state of preparedness for the war.

In his search for an alternative to isolated neutrality, Stauning contacted the British government during a visit to London in 1937. This took place without the knowledge of Munch, who represented a more passive line and preferred not to make any moves that might disturb the Great Powers. It is difficult to gauge how serious his approach was, but there was nothing ambiguous about Foreign Secretary Anthony Eden's response: Britain would be unable to give military aid to Denmark in the event of an armed conflict with Germany. The reply was confirmed as late as February 1940 to a group of Scandinavian journalists when Winston Churchill, First Lord of the Admiralty, expressed understanding for Denmark's total dependence on Germany. There has been some discussion as to whether with a stronger defence force Denmark could have been brought under the umbrella of a British guarantee in 1939. There is evidence of reflections of this kind in British archive materials, but a guarantee would hardly have prevented the occupation, in view of what happened in Poland and later in Greece. The Danish prime minister

1930s is still, despite criticism for its traditionalism and lack of a theoretical framework, Viggo Sjøqvist, *Danmarks udenrigspolitik 1939–1940* (Copenhagen, 1966). This investigation is based on comprehensive unpublished source materials from the Danish Ministry for Foreign Affairs and from the Auswärtiges Amt, and was the first work to raise the discussion of foreign policy in the 1930s above the polemical level.

was no doubt told what he wanted to hear in London, but this does not alter the fact that the British neither could nor would give any military guarantees to Denmark. As Chamberlain said in the Cabinet Committee on Foreign Policy in June 1939, 'German domination of Denmark would increase Germany's military strength and this therefore was not a case in which we should be bound to intervene forcibly to restore the *status quo*.' In fact, British diplomats could see some benefits in a German occupation, partly because of the strains in supply it would cause the Germans if Denmark was cut off from its trade connections to the West. This assessment proved to be wrong, but was shared by Berlin in 1940.

With its extensive foreign trade, Denmark was very dependent on international trade conditions for its prosperity and social stability. This was especially true of agriculture, which accounted for 73% of all exports in 1939 and which obtained 40% of its foodstuffs from abroad. Industry's share of exports was only 22%, but it was expanding rapidly and 30% of all imported raw materials were for industrial purposes. It added to Denmark's vulnerability that trade was mainly centred on two countries, Britain and Germany. Thus 90% of exports went to these two countries in 1939 and 60% of all imports came from them. In the 1930s Britain and Germany were engaged in a trade war for the Scandinavian market. This also influenced relations with Denmark and resulted in a minor victory for Britain. In 1929, 57% of exports went to Britain and 20% to Germany, but by 1939 the figures had changed to 51% to Britain and 23% to Germany. As for imports, in 1929 15% came from Britain and 33% from Germany, in 1939 33% from Britain and 27% from Germany. At the outbreak of war, therefore, Britain was easily the dominant trading partner, but Germany was no less indispensable, not least as a counterbalance to Britain. In a world that hid itself behind protectionism and bilateral agreements, most of the efforts of Munch and the Danish Ministry for Foreign Affairs went into securing the interests of foreign trade. This happened in negotiations that were often very difficult, and for which the Danish diplomats have since been highly praised by historians. In order to avoid dependency on one market, a balance had to be maintained between the two Great Powers and the policy of neutrality was an essential precondition for the achievement of this. The extent to which trade policy thereby also became an instrument for defence policy is less clear, for Denmark increased its trade with Britain at the same time as it stepped up its appeasement of Germany. It must be said, however, that when the war at sea broke out in September 1939 the economic threat to Denmark's existence seemed to be just as great as a possible military threat.

Viewed from a Danish perspective, there appeared to be two kinds of threat after Hitler came to power, one applicable in peacetime, the other in a time of war. The first, as mentioned above, related to the 'open wound' of the southern border. This threat was particularly evident during the so-called 'Eastern storm' of the Schleswig-Holstein Nazis in March and April 1933. But fears were assuaged when it looked as though Berlin did not support the irredentist demands of the German minority. It was Danish policy to avoid all disturbances in or near the border area. In 1938, the *Anschluß* and the Sudeten crisis brought the danger of a revision of the border, in which Hitler could use the now completely Nazified German minority as a battering ram, back into focus. But once the war broke out in 1939, this threat slid once more into the background. It never disappeared completely, however, and during the occupation, one of the most important arguments of those supporting the policy of collaboration against a break with Germany was that it could lead to a border revision that might force Danes into active service for Germany.

The second perceived threat involved an attack on – or some other form of aggression against – Danish territory during an Anglo-German war. Scenarios sprang to mind in different combinations and with varying degrees of probability. There might be accidental hostilities in or over some area of Denmark, there could be a war at sea or a blockade; or there might be demands for air bases in Jutland or naval bases in the Kattegat. The army command, extrapolating from its own concept of defence, focused especially on Jutland. The naval command shared the government view that the Germans would have no wish to occupy Denmark, which already lay within their sphere of interest. The government was aware of the German navy's plans for an offensive in the Atlantic and its demand for free passage through the Belts, which it was ready to grant. But it calculated, erroneously as it turned out, that this strategy would not become a reality until the rearmament of the German navy (the so-called Z-plan) had been completed.[3]

Whatever scenario the government chose, Denmark's isolated position meant that the primary aim must be to inspire German confidence in Danish neutrality. Government and Opposition were in agreement about

3 National and international developments leading up to the occupation were presented in a series of lectures at the University of Copenhagen in 1990; see Hans Kirchhoff (ed.), *1940 – Da Danmark blev besat* (Copenhagen, 1990), which includes a contribution by Carsten Due-Nielsen, who argues that Denmark's isolation was not quite the foregone conclusion that it has been claimed to be.

this pro-German line. Its most prominent spokesman and executor was Foreign Secretary Munch. His policy was to avoid all questions that might offend or provoke Germany and to take as few initiatives as possible that could embroil Denmark in the rivalries between the Great Powers, but if a choice between the parties became unavoidable to support the German side and, finally, to curb and moderate anti-German sentiments in the population at large. It was a foreign policy characterised by passivity and defeatism.

Accommodation to Germany occurred across a broad front. In 1935, Denmark failed to condemn German rearmament at the League of Nations. As we have seen, once the policy of sanctions broke down, Denmark withdrew from the League of Nation's system of sanctions, which Berlin had always regarded as being aimed at Germany. In 1938, the regulations governing neutrality were modified to comply with German requests for free passage through Denmark for its planes and warships, a move that prompted criticism from an otherwise generally understanding Britain. German warships were permitted to hold manoeuvres in Danish territorial waters; German emigrants were subjected to a restrictive, discriminatory refugee policy, and the Danish police cooperated with the Gestapo in the fight against international Communism.

At the same time, the ministry for foreign affairs attempted to muzzle the press. 'Having tea with Dr Munch' became a euphemism for the meetings at which the foreign secretary asked the editors to curb their criticism of Nazi atrocities and Nazi leaders. The German ambassador constantly registered disapproval of anti-Nazi articles, and in some cases succeeded in getting particularly exposed journalists removed. Indirect censorship acted as a restraint on theatre and publishing ventures. By and large, the media and institutions loyally complied with the government's requests, but a left-wing minority protested against the appeasement, embraced the causes of republican Spain and the fugitives from Hitler, and demanded a popular alliance against the forces of Fascism, which was unrealistic in the late 1930s. Foreign critics depicted Denmark as an economic and political vassal state of Hitler, which, though not correct in every sense, was not without an element of truth.

The high-water mark of the policy of appeasement came in May 1939, when Denmark alone of the Nordic countries accepted the offer of a pact of non-aggression with Germany. In 1937, behind the back of his foreign secretary, Prime Minister Stauning had sounded out the possibility of a non-aggression pact to prevent a German attack on Denmark, but had been rebuffed by the Auswärtiges Amt. Now the situation had changed because the offer was part of Hitler's propaganda offensive to mollify American criticism of his policy of aggression in Europe. However, the government did not think it could refuse, hoping that the pact would constitute some kind of guarantee of protection for the border, and negotiated an agreement that Denmark would be able to continue trading with Britain in the event of an Anglo-German conflict. The pact was signed on 31 May. But nobody in Copenhagen really believed that the agreement would be observed in a war involving the Great Powers.[4]

## THE OUTBREAK OF WAR AND THE THREAT TO THE DANISH ECONOMY

When war broke out in Europe, Denmark proclaimed its neutrality on 3 September 1939. Despite the catastrophe, the government viewed the situation with a certain amount of optimism. The German–Soviet pact of non-aggression seemed to guarantee peace in the Baltic area and the swift defeat of Poland turned the German thrust westwards, towards France. The ministry for foreign affairs regarded the war as a purely imperialist struggle between the Great Powers; the ideological overtones came much later, and they hoped for a peace compromise that would safeguard the balance of power in Europe and prevent a weakened Germany drawing in the Soviet Union. By contrast, public opinion was strongly pro-British. When British planes accidentally bombed Esbjerg, the largest town on the North Sea coast, most of the population, to the great dismay of the government, were firmly convinced that they were German bombs! The overflights led to the government setting up anti-aircraft guns in North Schleswig to quash German suspicions that the country might not defend itself against British breaches of its neutrality. For the same reason, a battalion of soldiers was stationed in North Jutland.

The extent to which the defence strategy was geared to complying with German security interests was also demonstrated by an incident in November. The German navy asked for the Belts to be mined on

[4] For Denmark's position between the Great Powers see Susan Seymour, *Anglo-Danish Relations and Germany 1933–1945* (Odense, 1982), which is based on documents from the Foreign Office and articles by Patrick Salmon, the latest in *Scandinavia and the Great Powers* (Cambridge, 1997). To these should be added Harm Schröter, *Aussenpolitik und Wirtschaftsinteresse – Skandinavien im aussenwirtschaftlichen Kalkül Deutschlands und Grossbritanniens 1918–1939* (Frankfurt am Main, 1983). Scandinavia in the struggle between the Great Powers in 1939–40 was the subject of a seminar in Oslo in 1976, but with Denmark naturally allocated only a minor role. See 'The Great Powers and the Nordic Countries 1939–1940', *Scandinavian Journal of History*, 2 (1977).

the grounds that enemy submarines had been detected in the Baltic. The government did not believe the reason but fears that the Germans would lay the mines themselves, thereby committing a breach of neutrality, made Copenhagen comply with the request. The situation closely resembled that of a similar German offensive in 1914. Munch was then minister of defence and was strongly in favour of complying with German demands even though the mining was aimed against Britain. In response to the political opposition, he had declared that the alternative would involve not only allowing the Germans to lay the mines themselves, but allowing them to establish bases on Danish territory without this being regarded by Denmark as a cause of war. As in 1914, the laying of mines in November 1939 was merely noted in London and Paris. The handling of the situation in 1914 was a historic lesson that proved a heavy burden to bear in April 1940.

In general, Munch regarded the military threat against Denmark as negligible because, in accordance with the strategic concept outlined above, he assumed that none of the belligerent parties had any interest in occupying Danish territory. By far the most important issue in the first and longest period of neutrality, therefore, was foreign trade and the problem of supplies that was bound up with it. But even here it was possible to find bright spots, since large stockpiles of goods had been accumulated so that right from the start it was possible to refer back to experiences from the First World War and put the necessary control and regulatory mechanisms in place. In this connection, it seemed crucial that the belligerent parties had reaffirmed their consent to Denmark maintaining its full level of trade with the other side. Nevertheless, this was to prove the source of major foreign policy problems and a threat to the welfare of the people and the nation's existence.

In the inter-war years, Scandinavia had been a secondary arena for the rivalry between Britain and Germany. But on the outbreak of war the Nordic scene moved more into focus. This was due to Britain's economic warfare, which was aimed at forcing the neutral countries to join the blockade against German rearmament and the German economy. The Western Powers thus emerged as the most aggressive side who ultimately wanted to bring the Nordic countries into the war, while Germany, partly because of its dependence on important strategic raw materials from Norway, Sweden, and Finland and foodstuffs from Denmark, wished Scandinavia to remain neutral, and therefore behaved reactively.

The British started their economic warfare where it had successfully left off, at Germany's defeat in 1918. They drew up lists of contraband, demanded control of exports and a ban on the re-export of certain goods to Germany, and imposed a comprehensive system of supervision on all neutral shipping. The Germans retaliated by drawing up their own lists of contraband, the primary aim of which was presumably to spread propaganda, but which in the case of Denmark involved broken promises and threatened all trade with Britain. At the beginning of September, the German warships, on the order of the Seekriegsleitung, began to torpedo and seize Nordic ships on their way to and from Britain. The Danes had argued, in defence of their continuing to export to England, that a German attack would make the British stop their import of foodstuffs, which would cause such a drastic drop in Danish agricultural production that it would harm exports to Germany. This argument proved to be wrong after 9 April, but it was accepted by Auswärtiges Amt, and the diplomats succeeded in stopping the warships. This resulted in the so-called 'Maltese Cross Arrangement', which allowed the export of Danish food products to England in special ships and under strict supervision, and only on condition that trade with Germany was maintained. It was a secret agreement and it is a good illustration of the difficult balancing act between the belligerent parties. It continued right up to the German invasion, but did not prevent further torpedoing when the war at sea was renewed in the winter of 1940.

The bilateral trade agreements were another instrument in the economic warfare. These, too, reflect the conflicting aims of Britain and Germany. The Germans were interested in importing as much as possible from Denmark, but had to accept that the Danish government, in order to maintain a balance with Britain, could not exceed the 1939 level, and an agreement was hammered out within a month, without any major problems. In contrast, trade negotiations with the British were exceptionally long and difficult, and were not completed until just before 9 April 1940. Partly as a result of its policy of self-sufficiency, Britain was less dependent on Danish food imports than earlier and was thus able to push a hard line, the primary aim of which was to reduce Danish agricultural exports to Germany. One method would be to limit the import of foodstuffs to a quantity sufficient only to produce goods for Britain. Another would be to lower prices to avoid a large balance of payments surplus being imparted to Germany in its trade with Denmark as payment for the Danish import surplus there. Both methods were adopted and promised very bad consequences for Denmark. The invasion prevented the agreement from being implemented, but it is doubtful whether exports to England could have been maintained at the low prices dictated by the British. The agreement caused great bitterness in the agricultural sector and made the farmers more favourably disposed towards the occupation, when it turned out that the occupying power could buy up everything that was produced, and at high prices.

## IN THE SHADOW OF THE WINTER WAR

On 30 November 1939, peace in Scandinavia was shattered by the Soviet Union's attack on Finland. The Winter War created a huge wave of sympathy for little Finland in its fight against the Great Power. In Norway and Sweden, there was widespread support for military intervention on behalf of Finland and the governments refrained from issuing any declarations of neutrality. The Danish government also held back, but consideration for Germany as the ally of the Soviet Union weighed more heavily in the end than Nordic solidarity.

Although the Winter War was primarily a problem for the other Scandinavian countries, it caused concern in Copenhagen. There were fears that Norway and Sweden might be drawn in if, as was rumoured, the real target of the Red Army was ice-free harbours on the west coast of Norway. There were also reports that the Non-Aggression pact had divided Scandinavia into spheres of interest, with Denmark and southern Sweden in the German one, and that Germany would strike if the war spread westwards. On 14 December, the League of Nations, at the instigation of the Western Powers, expelled the Soviet Union and asked the member states to send material and humanitarian aid to Finland. Munch objected to the League of Nation's setting itself up as a court of law and all three Nordic countries abstained from voting. But fears that Britain and France would send weapons and soldiers to Finland via the Northern Cap, under cover of the League's action, and that Germany would retaliate, placed increasing pressure on Copenhagen.

This pessimistic mood was highlighted when Prime Minister Stauning, in his New Year speech to the nation, denied that Denmark was capable of conducting a war. This merely spelt out what was inherent in the defence strategy, but it triggered a storm of protest from the Conservative Party and the officers who formed part of its hinterland. It resulted in a parliamentary declaration supported by the Social Democrat Party and the Radical Party, which could be interpreted as acquiescence to a strategy that committed the country to fight for its existence. The declaration of 19 January 1940 was later to play an important part in the debate about culpability for the war at the time of the capitulation on 9 April, because the Opposition maintained that the government had deliberately misled the public. It does look as though the government's desire to put a damper on the defence question had led it further than was justified. At any rate, the declaration had no effect on the state of preparedness.

Throughout the winter, the Western Powers increased pressure on Scandinavia, and thereby also indirectly on Copenhagen. This occurred in connection with both the 'minor' plan, aimed at halting German ore traffic by the mining of Norwegian territorial waters, and the 'major' plan, which involved preparations to send an expeditionary force of 100,000 men to the Finnish front via Narvik, but whose main purpose was to occupy the ore beds of Swedish Lapland. As part of their overall strategy, Britain and France cynically calculated on a military retaliation from Germany, which would drag Scandinavia into the war, create a second front, and thus ease the pressure on France. For the same reason, Oslo and Stockholm opposed the allied initiatives with every possible diplomatic means. The aid to Finland was common enough knowledge to be written about openly in the Western press. On the BBC, the First Lord of the Admiralty, Winston Churchill, pugnaciously called on the neutral countries to make common cause with the Allies. At the same time the war at sea escalated. In January and February twelve Danish ships, including two 'Maltese ships', were torpedoed and 143 sailors lost their lives. Other ships carrying agricultural products to Britain were attacked from the air. Nordic shipping magnates asked for the ships to sail in British convoys, but the Danes rejected this idea for fear of provoking Germany. The situation became so tense that Munch, in defiance of his own character and his lie-low policy, took several initiatives to promote peace and negotiations, which did not come to anything. The so-called '*Altmark*-affair' took place on 16 February 1940 when a British ship cornered a German prison ship in Norwegian territorial waters and set the British sailors free, without the Norwegian navy taking any action. We know that this incident was a turning-point for German planning because it convinced Hitler that the British had no scruples about breaching Norwegian neutrality and that the Norwegians had neither the will nor the ability to defend it. The '*Altmark* affair' sent shivers down spines in Copenhagen, because Denmark might well be next on the list. Characteristically, Munch showed complete understanding of the Norwegian passivity, whereas his strategic sparring partner, the Commander-in-Chief of the Navy, from his own military standpoint thought that the Norwegian navy should have offered some resistance.

It is easy to understand why the peace treaty between Finland and the Soviet Union, in the night between 12 and 13 March, was greeted with the utmost relief in the Nordic capitals. It removed the pretext for intervention from both the Allies and Germany.

## THE MILITARY THREAT AGAINST DENMARK, APRIL 1940

It turned out that the peace in Moscow only marked a slowing down in the race between the Great Powers for the ore and Norway. On 28 March, the Supreme War Council decided to implement the 'minor plan' (Operation Wilfred), and in the early hours of 8 April Norwegian territorial waters outside Narvik were mined, without the British being aware that a German attack was imminent. On 2 April, nervous about his 'soft' Northern flank and calculating that Britain would retaliate against an attack on France with a counterattack against Norway, Hitler decided to initiate Operation Weserübung at 4.15 a.m. on 9 April, and the next day the first transport ships set off on the long voyage to northern Norway. With the main force tied down on the western front, the Wehrmacht could spare few resources for the Scandinavian campaign. This meant that risks had to be reduced to a minimum which, in turn, required minimal opposition and maximum exploitation of the surprise element. It proved 100 per cent effective, for both the Scandinavian governments and the Western Powers were taken completely by surprise. Nobody had believed the Germans would dare to attempt such an ambitious naval operation while the Royal Navy had command of the seas.[5]

It is important to remember that Denmark was only a minor player in the wider plan. Denmark did not enter into German calculations until a relatively late stage, and even then only via the use of Jutland as a

[5] There is a comprehensive literature on government policy in 1940, but it is often of a rather polemical nature. The best overview is Hans Branner, *9. april – et politisk lærestykke? En udenrigspolitisk krises baggrund, indhold og perspektiver* (Copenhagen, 1987). The book is written from a political science viewpoint and does not pretend to include unpublished materials. For a penetrating analysis of, among other things, the warnings from Berlin see Bjørn Svensson, *Derfor gik det sådan den 9. april* (Copenhagen, 1965). For the decision-making process during April see also Viggo Sjøqvist, *Besættelsen 1940. De danske forudsætninger for den 9. april* (Copenhagen, 1978) and Hans Kirchhoff, 'Foreign Policy and Rationality – The Danish Capitulation of 9 April 1940. An Outline of a Pattern of Action', *Scandinavian Journal of History*, 16 (1991), which, using partially new diplomatic materials, views the capitulation as the rational response to the German invasion, from the standpoint of the defence and security strategy. The periodical *Vandkunsten*, vol. 3 (Copenhagen, 1990), contains a number of articles about the experience of 9 April in the post-war period and the way it has influenced the debate on defence policy.

transit area and of North Jutland as a port of embarkation for Norway, the whole venture being conducted as a purely political arrangement. It was not until the Luftwaffe demanded permission to touch down in Ålborg that the whole country became involved, the idea being, perhaps, that Germany would have a bigger hold on the government if Copenhagen was occupied as well. However, we can see that when the Danish government thought that a German action could be confined to demands for bases and transit rights, they were reflecting the actual role allocated to Denmark in the preliminary plans.

When the war broke out in September, five year-groups of the army were called up, bringing its strength up to 36,000 men. Three year-groups were sent home after a brief inspection, the remaining two after government decisions in December 1939 and January 1940. In other words, in April 1940 the army consisted of about 15,000 men, compared with the approximately 58,000 men in the period of minimal defence during the First World War. Half the force was stationed in Jutland, the other half on the islands. Without mobilisation it would not be an effective fighting force, nor was it intended to be, according to the accepted defence plan. Most of the navy was deployed in northern waters, to afford protection against British breaches of neutrality. This meant that Copenhagen was virtually devoid of military personnel, in keeping with the government view that the capital was of no strategic importance to the belligerent parties.

With our present knowledge that it was Germany which invaded and occupied Denmark for five years, it may be difficult to understand that Munch and the government envisaged a threat coming from the north and the west, that is, from Britain. This perception and the defence strategies that evolved from it were mainly due to the general belief that Germany would not use resources to occupy Denmark, as long as the Danes showed themselves willing to uphold the neutrality against Britain. In Munch's view, it was London, with its aggressive line towards Norway (and Sweden), that held the key to whether Germany would retaliate or not. This explains why the usually so dispassionate foreign secretary blamed Britain on 9 April, the day Denmark was invaded, for the occupation of Denmark!

This perception of the potential threat also coloured the Danish attitude towards the defence problem that seemed to overshadow all others in 1940: the war at sea. It cast doubts on whether Danish foreign trade could be maintained at all, between the Scylla of increasingly rigorous controls on contraband by the British and the Charybdis of German torpedoes and mines. For if Britain attacked Norway, Germany might be expected to halt all Danish agricultural exports to Britain and this would put a bomb under the country's economy and welfare that seemed to pose no less of a threat than an actual occupation. So it was with some trepidation that the Ministry for Foreign Affairs processed information from the Embassy in London about Allied war policy in Northern Scandinavia and similar briefings from Oslo (and Stockholm) about concrete allied initiatives, culminating in the laying of mines on the morning of 8 April.

In contrast, information from the Embassy in Berlin painted a much calmer picture in the winter and spring of 1940. The reports focused exclusively on the Western Offensive which, after several cancellations throughout the winter, now seemed imminent. Reports of German troop movements south of the border had provoked the Army Supreme Command on their own initiative to alert the garrisons in North Schleswig in January. The panic annoyed the government and the Commander-in-Chief of the Navy, who feared any provocation of Germany, but it fitted in perfectly with the generals' overall strategy, which regarded a German advance into Jutland to acquire aircraft and naval bases for use against Britain as the main danger to Denmark. As we have seen, this view was not shared by the government or the Commander-in-Chief of the Navy. On the contrary, the narrow focus of information from the Berlin Embassy on the Western Offensive seemed to confirm their view that Germany's military attention was fully concentrated on the land war against France.

The first dispatch of direct relevance to Denmark came from Berlin on 4 April. It referred to an 'aggression' in the coming week and linked it to an invasion of Holland and Belgium. After that it mentioned the probability of operations continuing towards southern Norway. The dispatch originated in disaffected officers of the Oberkommando der Wehrmacht – we know now that it came from Colonel Oster in Abwehr – so it was from an incredibly reliable source, but as it stands it is by no means as clear and unambiguous as it was made out to be during the debate about who was to blame for the war. A joint campaign against Denmark and Holland/Belgium seemed to have no military coherence, and would also be quite irrelevant to Operation Weserübung, whose strategic centre of gravity lay in northern Norway. Moreover, the term 'aggression' could mean various things, not necessarily a military action. The same distorted picture reached the Norwegian and Swedish ambassadors, the Norwegian ambassador not even being aware of the fact that Norway was also included! So when a worried Danish government asked Oslo and Stockholm the following day whether there was any danger, it received a categorical denial. The Embassy staff too played safe in the days that followed by warning that it might be a German bluff and went completely along with the government line that Germany had nothing to gain from obtaining air bases in Denmark. Simultaneous reports of concentrations of troops and ships in the German Baltic were dismissed with the explanation that these were aimed at Norway rather than Denmark, and would only be used in the event of a British attack. The warning on 4 April caused a great deal of alarm in Copenhagen and precipitated a frenzy of government activity. But the obscure picture of the enemy and counter-reports in the next few days strengthened the belief, or at any rate the hope, that any escalation of the war would take place outside Denmark. The Army Supreme Command wanted to mobilise, but this was refused on the grounds that it might send out the wrong signals to Germany and lead to countermeasures. The watchword was to avoid any move that could cause provocation.

It was not until 8 April, the day before the invasion, that further news brought things seriously to a head. During the morning, it became known that the British had mined Norwegian territorial waters and throughout the day reports were received of German fleet movements through the Belts. At the same time, the Germans moved a division up south of the border. In the eyes of a critical later age, the government must have known on 8 April that an attack, in the form of an invasion, would materialise the following day. Charges against Munch for having overlooked or deliberately disregarded the many warning signs came to play an important part in the debate over culpability for the capitulation and war. But too much weight is being given to hindsight here. The signals were not as clear as they appear to us today, and a number of scenarios would have been possible. For example, the German fleet movements could have indicated an outbreak of hostilities in the North Atlantic. This was certainly the view in Oslo and London; an intelligence lapse which sent the Royal Navy on the wrong tack and gave the German navy a free run to the fjords of western Norway. The ships could also be seen as a response to the British mining operation of that morning, directed at Norway or specific parts of Norway. There had been open speculation in the last few days in the Danish and international press about a possible counterattack of this kind and the idea was supported by reports that the German fleet was heading for Norway. In either eventuality, there were good reasons for Copenhagen to hope that the operation would bypass Denmark. In this context, the German division south of the border could be seen as a military back-up for a diplomatic request for transit for German troops through Jutland on the way to Norway. An invasion into Jutland of this nature could occur without any warning, but it was commonly believed that Berlin would first issue an ultimatum, which would give time to negotiate. In the government's view, this was the most likely scenario the night before 9 April. Neither the politicians nor the army envisaged the situation that actually resulted, namely a total invasion of the country, without any warning. Here, the strategic plan combined with historical experience and general wishful thinking acted as a bar to the correct perception of what was happening. When judging the government's behaviour, however, it is important to remember that no matter what scenario was adopted, it would still have to exercise the utmost care to avoid provoking Germany. The German ambassador, who knew as little about Operation Weserübung as the Danish government (he was only informed of it by courier late on the evening of 8 April) and who shared the Danish assessment of the situation, warned Munch repeatedly throughout the day against any actions that could sow doubts about the sustainability of Danish neutrality and force the Wehrmacht to intervene.

Therefore, the government again rejected the Army Supreme Command's request for mobilisation, which would actually, at the eleventh hour, have created chaos. Furthermore, the troops were kept away from the border to avoid accidental shooting incidents that might lead to a warlike situation that would be out of the government's control. It was also in accordance with this line that, on the morning of 9 April, the Commander-in-Chief of the Fleet circumvented operational instructions and ordered ships in Copenhagen not to fire without further orders. At a meeting with party leaders on the evening of 8 April, which had been called in order to pacify the Opposition, Munch stated unequivocally that Denmark could not wage war against Germany or Britain and that Denmark must thus, according to Munch's neo-neutral line, remain neutral, even if there were German troops inside the country. This meant yet again that the important thing was to avoid violence likely to jeopardise the search for a non-violent solution. It was obvious that any armed resistance would be merely symbolic. As a result, every effort would be made to maintain neutrality in the form of non-participation in the war within the tight limits that would be imposed by the acceptance of a foreign occupation.

### CAPITULATION

On 9 April, at 4.15 a.m., German troops advanced across the border and there were minor skirmishes with Danish units. In all, sixteen Danish soldiers were killed. Parachute troops landed in Ålborg, and the most important ports were occupied. The small Danish air force was destroyed on the ground. A warship conquered the capital without a shot being fired. At the same time, the German ambassador went to the foreign secretary with an ultimatum demanding an immediate laying down of arms. In return, Germany promised to 'preserve Denmark's territorial integrity and political independence'. This promise should be seen in relation to the necessity of acquiring as speedy and painless a control of Denmark as possible. The chief government ministers met the king and the military commanders and after a brief consultation decided to accept the ultimatum under protest. The king asked whether, considering the reaction in other countries, there had been enough resistance. Munch thought that armed conflict would make no difference at all. The Army Supreme Commander wanted the fight to be continued from North Zealand, but this was rejected. At around 6 p.m., the order went out for a ceasefire.

In this way the so-called peaceful occupation, *occupatio pacifica*, came into being, which by and large lasted until the end of the Second World War. It would be wrong to say that it had been a foregone conclusion. Alternative situations and different German plans could have changed the course of events, as was the case in Norway, where the Nazi Quisling suddenly appeared on the scene and destroyed their 'Danish' solution. But there it is clear that the German offer of non-interference and continued non-participation in the war went hand in hand with Munch's concept. In that respect, capitulation was a logical consequence of historical experience and a historical tradition. Seen in this light, the government's strategy throughout April 1940 showed a marked continuity and a clear, rational coherence between ends and means, in the handling of the threat, in the anticipation of the attack, and in the response to the invasion.

### CONTINUITY AND BREACHES IN THE DANISH POLICY OF NEUTRALITY

The government and official Denmark, supported by the population in general, responded to the peaceful occupation of 1940 by following a line of collaboration and appeasement, the greatest virtue of which was that it allowed Denmark to emerge from the war as the occupied country in Hitler's Europe which had suffered least harm and destruction. On the basis of the fiction that it retained its neutrality and sovereignty, Denmark succeeded in holding on to its democratic institutions and in containing German repression for the longest period of time. At the material level, too, it succeeded in maintaining a higher level of welfare than that in Germany. The price was a pro-German line which, despite its involuntary nature, harnessed Denmark to the German war machine, morally, politically and, not least, economically. The opponents of collaboration from 1942 consisted of extreme nationalists and Communists and other left-wingers, who from the 1930s had opposed the policy towards Germany and who became the nucleus of an organised resistance. In August 1943, the pro-Allies mood in the population exploded in a revolt that forced the government and parliament to step back and allow the resistance movement to take charge. The movement's main organ, the Danish Freedom Council, declared war on Germany and embraced the Western Allies' invasion strategy. For both foreign policy and domestic reasons, the politicians had to adjust to the new centre of power, but from the wings they tried to contain the Freedom Council's war programme as far as they could.

After the German capitulation, the old political system was quickly restored to power. Denmark was recognised as an Allied Power and joined the UN with the flag flying high. Under the slogan 'Never again a 9 April', the resistance movement had demanded a break with the isolationist neutrality policy from before the war, but it is difficult to distinguish between the so-called 'bridge-building policy' between East and West from 1945 to 1948 and the earlier, alliance-free defence policy. When the Cold War forced Denmark to choose sides, the first response was to try and form a Nordic defence pact with Norway and Sweden. The great advantage of this was that Scandinavia would be able to remain a neutral bloc at a time of increased international tension. It was therefore not so much as an act of positive enthusiasm as a choice of the lesser of two evils that the government committed Denmark to membership of NATO after the breakdown of negotiations between the Nordic countries.

Political and historical literature has viewed the membership of NATO in April 1949 as a decisive break with a foreign policy that had prevailed for two hundred years, but the latest studies of Denmark's role in NATO draw particular attention to the elements of continuity. This may be seen, for example, in the attempts of successive governments to preserve Scandinavia as an area of low tension and their efforts to tone down a more aggressive American policy that might provoke the Soviet Union and threaten Denmark's vulnerable position on the north-eastern flank of NATO. These elements of lie-low policy and non-provocative behaviour show fidelity to the policy of neutrality and thereby the importance of historical experience and geographical factors in the shaping of Denmark's defence policy.[6]

[6] For a discussion of Denmark's policy of non-provocation in NATO see Poul Villaume, *Allieret med forbehold. Danmark, NATO og den kolde krig. En studie i dansk sikkerhedspolitik 1949–1961* (Copenhagen, 1994).

CHAPTER 2

# *Norway*

*Patrick Salmon*

On Monday 8 April 1940 the Oslo newspaper *Dagbladet* carried a leading article protesting against the Allied decision, announced early that morning, to lay mines in Norwegian territorial waters. It was, the paper declared, one of the most serious blows inflicted on Norwegian interests since the beginning of the war: Norway must protest in the strongest possible terms against this violation of the country's neutrality. The late-afternoon edition of the paper carried new headlines: '100 armed German ships in Kattegat today, heading northward'; 'Two mysterious sinkings off Lillesand'; 'Koht to speak in Storting open session this evening.'[1] The Storting, the Norwegian parliament, met shortly after 5 o'clock and, after an opening statement by the foreign minister, Halvdan Koht, went into closed session to discuss the events of the last few days: the diplomatic notes of 5 April in which Britain and France reserved to themselves the right to take action – as yet unspecified – to prevent Germany from obtaining resources and facilities from Norway and Sweden; and the proclamation, issued early on the 8th, that mines were to be laid in three specified areas in order to force German shipping out of Norwegian waters and expose it to interception by the Royal Navy.[2]

Norway's parliamentarians had already had ample opportunity to explore the implications of the Allied declaration. While Koht had urged the prime minister, Johan Nygaardsvold, to hold a cabinet meeting first thing that morning, the latter had insisted that ministers must consult the Storting's influential foreign affairs committee.[3] The meeting, chaired by Storting President Carl Hambro, lasted for two and a half hours as one member after another insisted on having his say. Only at 1.30 in the afternoon, after a brief cabinet meeting, was Koht able to announce

[1] *Dagbladet i krig og fred 1930–1954* (Oslo, 1968), 261–2.
[2] *Møter før lukkede dører. Stortinget 1939–1945* (Oslo, 1995), 322–41.
[3] Halvdan Koht, *For fred og fridom i krigstid 1939–1940* (Oslo, 1957), 213.

to the press the government's protest against the Allied minelaying; and only then could he sit down in the foreign ministry to prepare his speech to the Storting. Engaged in that task, he thus missed the dramatic headlines in the afternoon newspapers. At one point Koht was interrupted by a telephone call from London reporting 'alleged German naval movements towards Narvik,' beyond the Arctic Circle; but he was reassured by the thought that the British must already be taking steps to intercept any German fleet which had the temerity to penetrate so far north.[4]

The Storting debate that evening provided further evidence of the extent to which the flagrant Allied violation of Norwegian neutrality dominated the attention of Norwegian politicians to the exclusion of all other considerations. When the minister of war, Col. Birger Ljungberg, reported that the survivors of one of the ships torpedoed earlier that day, the *Rio de Janeiro*, were wearing military uniforms and claimed to have been heading for Bergen to defend Norway against the British and French, 'the ominous portent of this story did not seem to strike the members of the Storting'.[5] They continued to lecture the government on how it should respond to Britain and France and refused requests from the prime minister and foreign minister to curtail their debate. When the session ended at 9 o'clock the cabinet was finally able to discuss the day's events. By now the danger from Germany was uppermost in their minds; but during their thirty-minute meeting ministers decided against the advice of the chief of the general staff that they should order a full mobilisation. They resolved instead to summon the two battalions in the Østfold district which were ready for immediate mobilisation, and to lay mines in the Oslo fjord. 'The day was at an end,' wrote Koht.[6] Shortly after midnight, however, with air-raid sirens sounding and German warships reported in the Oslo fjord, it was evident that the German invasion of Norway had begun.

The events of 8 April epitomise all the elements which made neutral Norway so peculiarly ill prepared to meet the ultimate challenge to its national existence. Inexperience, confusion, uncertainty, lack of preparation, lack of realism all played their part. So too did the deference of ministers towards parliament in a state whose key formative experiences – and, indeed, the essence of its modern national identity – were bound up with the assertion of democratic parliamentarism against an alien

[4] Ibid., 216–17.
[5] *Stortinget 1939–1945*, 326; Carl J. Hambro, *I Saw it Happen in Norway* (London, 1940), 9–10.
[6] Koht, *For fred og fridom*, 219.

(i.e. Swedish) monarchical authoritarianism: the constitution of 1814, the establishment of parliamentary sovereignty in 1884, and finally the achievement of independence in 1905. Most of all, however, it was the British minelaying that diverted attention from the impending German menace. For Britain's action fulfilled the most deep-seated fears of ministers and parliamentarians – of the foreign minister most of all. Only Great Britain, it was believed, had both the capacity to violate Norwegian neutrality and a vested interest in doing so. Only British action would rouse Germany to retaliate against a country which it would otherwise prefer to leave in peace. On 8 April 1940 the most plausible threat to Norwegian neutrality had finally been realised. And yet this mistrust of British intentions had gone hand in hand with an equally powerful faith that in the last resort Britain would always be willing and able to defend Norway. Should the unthinkable happen – should either Germany or the Soviet Union wish to launch an attack on Norwegian territory – the Royal Navy would always be able to stop them. This duality characterised – and fatally weakened – the entire conduct of Norwegian neutrality policy between 1905 and 1940.

## NEUTRALITY IN THE SHADOW OF GREAT BRITAIN, 1905–39

Norwegian neutrality, as it emerged as a self-conscious political programme in the last two decades of the nineteenth century, displayed many contradictory features.[7] It was isolationist in the sense that it rejected foreign entanglements but also in the sense that Norway was literally isolated: on the northern periphery of Europe and relatively free from the danger of attack. Secure as they felt themselves to be, Norwegians nevertheless took an active interest in promoting peace. Emerging in the 1880s, the Norwegian peace movement demanded international arbitration as a means of settling disputes among states and – somewhat paradoxically – that the neutrality of the united kingdoms of Sweden–Norway should be guaranteed by the Great Powers. It may have been the Storting's resolution in favour of arbitration treaties in 1890 which led Alfred Nobel to entrust the Norwegian parliament with the award of his peace prize.[8] But Norwegian neutrality was also an

[7] Trygve Mathisen, 'Nøytralitetstanken i norsk politikk fra 1890-årene og til Norge gikk med i Folkeforbundet', *Historisk tidsskrift*, 36 (1952), 29–60; Narve Bjørgo, Øystein Rian, and Alf Kaartvedt, *Norsk utenrikspolitikks historie*, vol. 1, *Selvstendighet og union. Fra middelalderen til 1905* (Oslo, 1995), 328–43.

[8] Oscar J. Falnes, *Norway and the Nobel Peace Prize* (New York, 1938), 13.

assertion of national identity. It was a response to Swedish threats to Norway's constitutional position and democratic institutions – especially acute in the mid-1890s – and the fear that Sweden's close relations with Germany might involve both kingdoms in war with Russia.[9] Nationalism and neutrality, a commitment both to international peace and a strong defence force for Norway, were therefore closely linked, for example in the early writings and activities of the future foreign minister, Halvdan Koht.[10]

After 1905 Norwegian neutrality lost much of its anti-Swedish tinge. Indeed as early as 1906, in its negotiations for a neutrality guarantee by the Great Powers, the Norwegian government wished to include a reservation clause allowing Norway to go to the assistance of Sweden or Denmark if either should be attacked. But after 1905, when the Norwegian government took charge of the country's foreign policy for the first time, a division opened up between those who held political responsibility and those who did not. Official neutrality policy was both ideological and deeply pragmatic. Formally, the government sought security through a Great-Power guarantee: a goal realised, albeit only in part, with the conclusion of the 'integrity treaty' of 1907.[11] Informally, however, it sought an 'implicit guarantee' from Great Britain, based on the assumption that British self-interest could not permit a hostile power to establish itself on Norwegian territory, and reinforced by ties of sentiment.[12] Prince Carl of Denmark, elected King Haakon VII of Norway in 1905, was married to the daughter of Edward VII. The calculation behind his election was exposed somewhat incautiously by prime minister Gunnar Knudsen a few years later, when he told a visiting British naval squadron that in times of trouble 'we place our trust in the British nation, mindful of the new link forged by our Queen'.[13]

Both formal and informal dependence on the Great Powers were resented by the rising generation of Norwegian politicians, irrespective of party. The intellectual Halvdan Koht, the Bergen shipowner Johan Ludwig Mowinckel, and the journalist and politician Carl J. Hambro held that the integrity treaty of 1907 and the North Sea *status quo* agreement of 1908 (to which Denmark was a party but Norway was not,

[9] Mathisen, 'Nøytralitetstanken', 36.
[10] Sigmund Skard, *Mennesket Halvdan Koht* (Oslo, 1982), chs. 4–6.
[11] Patrick Salmon, *Foreign Policy and National Identity: The Norwegian Integrity Treaty, 1907–24* (Oslo, 1993).
[12] For further discussion of the 'implicit guarantee', see, 73–4.
[13] Quoted in Roald Berg '"Det land vi venter hjælp af." England som Norges beskytter 1905–1908', in Rolf Tamnes (ed.), *Forsvarsstudier vol.* IV (Oslo, 1985), 168.

owing to its status under the 1907 treaty) placed Norway in a position of 'tutelage' which allowed the Great Powers too much influence over the country's affairs.[14] Among such men feelings towards Great Britain in particular were frequently ambivalent. Koht had received part of his training as a historian in Leipzig and Paris; Mowinckel, though always conscious of Norway's dependence on Britain as protector, ran foul of British blockade measures during the First World War; Hambro, editor between 1913 and 1920 of the Oslo daily *Morgenbladet*, was a vociferous critic of British imperialism: 'a fanatic, pro-German, pro-Irish, and, in practice, everything that is anti-British', as the British legation later complained.[15] It was these men who came to dominate Norwegian politics between the wars: Hambro as Conservative leader, chairman of the Storting's foreign affairs committee and Storting President; Mowinckel as Liberal prime minister and foreign minister three times between 1924 and 1935; Koht as foreign minister in the Labour government from 1935 onwards. The generation of 1905 still held key positions of power in 1940.

Between 1905 and 1940 patterns of learnt behaviour were built up in the British–Norwegian relationship. Norwegians came to know Britain as their ultimate protector (albeit against threats which they perhaps never really expected to materialise) but also as a power which must not be antagonised where important Norwegian interests were at stake, for example in the Antarctic whaling industry. They learned that there could be conflicts of vital interest between the two countries. Norway's attempt to protect its fishing industry by extending the limit of its territorial waters from three to four miles was stubbornly resisted by the British before the First World War and again in the inter-war period.[16] Norwegians learned that Great Britain had the power of life or death over all aspects of their economic life. In the exceptionally cold winter of 1916–17 the British brought economic activity to a standstill – and inflicted much hardship – by imposing a coal embargo in order to enforce Norwegian compliance with their blockade of Germany.[17]

And yet the Norwegians also learned that there were circumstances in which they could defy Great Britain. In 1911 the British foreign secretary,

[14] Skard, *Koht*, 59; Roald Berg, *Norsk utenrikspolitikks historie*, vol. II, *Norge på egen hånd 1905–1920* (Oslo, 1995), 85; Salmon, *Foreign Policy*, 12–13.

[15] Quoted in ibid., 21.

[16] Berg, *Norge på egen hånd*, part III, chs. 2, 4; Odd-Bjørn Fure, *Norsk utenrikspolitikks historie*, vol. III, *Mellomkrigstid 1920–1940* (Oslo, 1996), part II, chs. 1–2.

[17] Patrick Salmon, *Scandinavia and the Great Powers, 1890–1940* (Cambridge, 1997), 138–9.

Sir Edward Grey, told the Norwegian minister that the territorial waters question was so important that Britain was prepared if necessary to go to war, 'even with a great power', to enforce acceptance of the three-mile limit. Privately, however, Britain's minister in Norway was advising his government that it was 'morally impossible ... to coerce Norway by force'.[18] Towards the end of the First World War, when Admiral Beatty was ordered to lay mines in Norwegian waters even in the face of Norwegian resistance, he declared that 'it would be most repugnant to the officers and men of the Grand Fleet to steam in overwhelming strength into the waters of a small but high-spirited people and coerce them'. If blood were shed, it would 'constitute a crime as bad as any the Germans had committed elsewhere'.[19] These scruples, published in an official war history, were read and digested by Norwegians. The lesson seemed to be that Britain might wish to violate Norwegian neutrality, but in the last resort would always draw back from doing so.

Ever since Amundsen beat Scott to the South Pole, Norwegians had been defying the British and getting away with it. They could rely on British self-restraint and sense of honour even when issues of real importance to both countries were at stake. They could not be so sure about their other formidable neighbours, Russia and Germany, but until 1939 neither power seemed to pose a serious threat to Norwegian security. After 1917 the close links between the Norwegian labour movement and the Soviet Communist Party were a source of anxiety for bourgeois Norwegian society, but there was little to disturb the correct and, indeed, largely amicable relations between the two countries. In 1936, when the Soviet Union exerted pressure to secure Trotsky's expulsion from Norway – ending in 'a total Norwegian capitulation' – a more menacing attitude was revealed; but it was only after the Soviet invasion of Finland on 30 November 1939 that Norwegian politicians began to worry seriously about Soviet intentions towards Norway.[20]

There seemed equally little reason to fear Germany. Despite the ruthlessness of the U-boat campaign against Norwegian shipping during the First World War and the revulsion for the Nazi regime felt by most Norwegians, few believed Germany capable of launching an attack. Nor would there be any reason to do so since Germany would gain more from Norwegian neutrality, in terms of access to Norwegian resources and the

[18] Quoted in Berg, *Norge på egen hånd*, 121.
[19] Quoted in Sir Henry Newbolt, *History of the Great War: Naval Operations*, vol. v (London, 1931), 349.
[20] Fure, *Mellomkrigstid*, pp. 269–73, 322–34 (quotation from p. 272 – my translation).

world's oceans via Norwegian territorial waters – not to mention the Swedish iron ore exported from Narvik – than from involving Norway in war. The view of Admiral Wegener that in a future war the German navy would need to redress the strategic imbalance with Great Britain by seizing bases in Norway, though little noticed outside Germany, was known to the Norwegian defence authorities as early as 1936.[21] Government ministers and their military advisers – especially the naval staff – nevertheless assumed that Germany would attempt an attack on Norwegian territory only if provoked into doing so by British action, and that Britain's naval supremacy would make a German landing impossible. Koht drew further comfort from what he saw as the lesson of recent advances in military technology: that the long range of modern aircraft had reduced the need for advanced bases and made control of Norwegian territory *less* important to the Great Powers than it had been in the last war.[22] A rare expression of dissent came in 1937 from Colonel Otto Ruge, chief of the general staff, in an appreciation which anticipated almost exactly the events of April 1940.[23] Ruge believed that Germany might have an independent interest in seizing bases in south-west Norway, and would not necessarily act only in response to a British move. He regarded the Royal Navy as an uncertain barrier against a German landing; he understood the importance of air supremacy; and he believed the attack would come as a surprise. But Ruge's insight that Norwegian territory was of heightened strategic importance was not shared by his political superiors or military colleagues.

It would nevertheless be unrealistic to criticise the Norwegian authorities for failing to base their security policy on this isolated insight. Norway's defences had, admittedly, been run down to dangerously low levels throughout virtually the whole of the inter-war period. Only after 1937 were significant sums devoted to military spending – far too late to have much impact after two decades of cuts – for which the responsibility lay with politicians of all major parties, backed by the overwhelming support of public opinion.[24] The 'anti-military prejudice' of ministers such as Koht and Nygaardsvold precluded effective coordination between the government and the chiefs of the armed forces, or any realistic discussion of the country's security position.[25] But the task of any country's security policy is to guard against all conceivable threats: to demand

[21] Salmon, *Scandinavia and the Great Powers*, 185. [22] Fure, *Mellomkrigstid*, 307.
[23] Ibid., 305–7. [24] Salmon, *Scandinavia and the Great Powers*, 184–5.
[25] Olav Riste, 'The Foreign Policy-Making Process in Norway: An Historical Perspective' in *Forsvarsstudier. Årbok for Forsvarshistorisk forskningssenter, Forsvarets høgskole 1982* (Oslo, 1983), 239.

more is unreasonable. The only conceivable threat to Norwegian security came from Great Britain, which was also the country's only conceivable defender. It would therefore have been not only ruinously expensive but also illogical to have constructed a defence force to meet all eventualities unaided. What Norway needed, so it was believed, was not a 'neutrality defence' but a 'neutrality guard': a defence force which would register violations of neutrality and lodge protests, but would not actually shoot.[26] If the unthinkable happened, and Norway was attacked, then its armed forces might just be strong enough to hold out until external (i.e. British) support arrived. Norway's leaders cannot be blamed for failing to anticipate the unique conditions of the Phoney War, in which the belligerents were not bogged down in costly, largely static continental warfare as in 1914 to 1918 but, on the contrary, had both the resources and the leisure to contemplate adventures against small states on the strategic periphery.[27]

## NEUTRALITY UNDER THREAT, 1939–40

If the function of Norwegian neutrality policy was to deter Britain from taking action that might provoke a violent German response, Koht's policy in 1939–40, as Magne Skodvin has pointed out, must be judged a success.[28] Koht was in no doubt that in the last resort Norway's values and interests lay with the Allies and that the country must never enter the war 'on the wrong side'. But 'this must never be said aloud. Any hint in that direction would endanger neutrality and be tantamount to betrayal.'[29] His task was therefore to repel any suggestion of cooperation between Norway and the Allies and protest vigorously against British breaches of Norwegian neutrality.[30] If Norway could not demonstrate its will and capacity to protect its own territory, Germany might be provoked into taking counter-measures which would bring Norway into the war. There was also a domestic political dimension to Koht's policy. He had to guard against the risk that pro-Allied sympathies or simple fear of Germany or the Soviet Union might lead his colleagues,

[26] A Labour politician quoted in Halvdan Koht (ed. Steinar Kjærheim), *Rikspolitisk dagbok 1933–1940* (Oslo, 1985), 200.
[27] Magne Skodvin, 'Norwegian Neutrality and the Question of Credibility', *Scandinavian Journal of History*, 2 (1977), 127.
[28] Magne Skodvin, 'Aspects of Neutrality: The Norwegian Experience', in Karl Rommetveit (ed.), *Narvik 1940: Five-Nation War in the High North* (Oslo, 1991), 22.
[29] Skodvin, 'Norwegian Neutrality', 143.
[30] See the penetrating analysis in Skard, *Koht*, 129–31.

or other politicians, or Norwegian public opinion, to demand prior consultation with Great Britain on ways of meeting a future attack. This might conceivably enhance Norwegian security, but it would also spell the end of Norwegian neutrality. Koht had no intention of seeking British assistance until Norway was actually at war, an eventuality which did not arise until the morning of 9 April 1940.

Until a very late stage, Koht's strategy worked. From the earliest days of the war the British government took initiatives that were designed, at the very least, to bring about a more accommodating Norwegian attitude towards the blockade of Germany, and ultimately to force Norway into the war on the Allied side. As early as 5 September 1939 the British chiefs of staff approved a proposal to give Norway a limited guarantee of military support against German attack. The offer, conveyed to Koht on 16 September, met with no response. There is no evidence that Koht informed his cabinet colleagues of this approach; and he certainly broke with his almost invariable practice by failing to put it before the Storting's foreign affairs committee.[31] There followed months of difficult negotiations for war trade and shipping agreements with Great Britain. They followed the pattern of the negotiations over fisheries limits in the 1930s: tough Norwegian resistance followed by British threats – which the British government in the last resort refrained from putting into effect, even though it had not achieved all it wanted. The Norwegians successfully exploited Britain's pressing need for their large merchant fleet, especially oil tankers, to extract concessions. They may also have benefited from the growing Allied preoccupation with military intervention in Scandinavia and the consequent need to avoid jeopardising Norwegian goodwill.[32]

The corollary of Norway's tough stance towards Great Britain was a much more accommodating attitude towards Germany. During the autumn of 1939 a series of cases arose which revealed the extent to which Norwegian territorial waters were being utilised by German ships for military purposes. In the cases of the German auxiliary ship *Westerwald* and of the captured American cargo ship *City of Flint* the Norwegian government found legal reasons to pretend that there was no conflict with neutrality regulations.[33] A far more blatant case arose when, between 7 and 13 December, three ore ships bound for Britain were knowingly torpedoed inside Norwegian waters by the German submarine U-38.

[31] Fure, *Mellomkrigstid*, 340. [32] Ibid., 322.

[33] For a discussion of these cases see Skodvin, 'Norwegian Neutrality,' 136–7.

Again, the Norwegian government sought to make as little as possible of the incidents, arguing that the sinkings might have been caused by mines.

The outbreak of the Soviet–Finnish Winter War at the end of November 1939 greatly increased both the complexity and the risks of neutrality policy.[34] Hitherto, Norway had been obliged to navigate between Britain and Germany, as in 1914 to 1918, and the Soviet Union had not been a significant power factor. It now had to manoeuvre between three Great Powers. In early December the Soviets seemed poised to conquer Finland and perhaps to press on into the far north of Sweden and Norway: it was only towards the end of the month that the Finnish defensive victory at Suomussalmi opened up the prospect of a longer and more inconclusive conflict. The Norwegian government strengthened its northern defences, but also distanced itself from Russia's expulsion from the League of Nations and – in contrast to Sweden – took a strictly neutral line towards the Soviet–Finnish conflict, for example by making it as difficult as possible for Norwegians to volunteer to fight for Finland. Good relations with Moscow had always been an axiom of Koht's foreign policy. Appeasement of Russia thus came naturally, but Koht also feared that helping Finland would associate Norway too closely with the Western Powers, and allow Germany to claim it was acting unneutrally.[35]

But as the stalemate in the larger European war continued, British intentions became less predictable. The Soviet attack on Finland provided the Allies with an opportunity to exploit what they regarded as one of Germany's most vulnerable points: its dependence on imports of iron ore from Sweden.[36] Military assistance to Finland would offer a pretext for depriving Germany of Swedish iron ore, either by cutting its winter supply from the Norwegian ice-free port of Narvik or – more ambitiously – by sending an expeditionary force to occupy the northern Swedish iron ore fields.

In both cases, but especially in that of military intervention, Norwegian and Swedish cooperation would be indispensable. The Allies had neither the resources nor the political will to attempt a landing in the face of even token military resistance, and passive resistance would cripple their

[34] Ibid., 326.

[35] Arne Bergsgård, 'Utrikspolitikk', in *Instilling fra Undersøkelsekommissjonen av 1945. Bilag*, vol. 1 (Oslo, 1947), 213, 217.

[36] From the extensive literature on this subject see Thomas Munch-Petersen, *The Strategy of Phoney War: Britain, Sweden and the Iron Ore Question 1939–1940* (Stockholm, 1981); Jukka Nevakivi, *The Appeal that was Never Made: The Allies, Scandinavia and the Finnish Winter War 1939–1940* (London, 1976).

operations (for example, if the Swedes switched off the electricity which powered the railway between Narvik and Kiruna – the only route by which the Allies could reach northern Sweden). In the minds of some Allied leaders – notably Winston Churchill, Britain's First Lord of the Admiralty – Scandinavian cooperation would serve another and more important function: that of bringing Norway and Sweden into the war on the Allied side. For the French, military operations in Scandinavia would have the additional benefit of diverting the war well away from France. But there was also a division between Churchill and his cabinet colleagues in that, while he favoured immediate action against German ore ships in Norwegian waters, either by sending in naval patrols or by laying mines, other ministers favoured the so-called 'larger scheme' of full-scale military intervention. This promised to deal with Germany's entire supply of Swedish iron ore, not merely the Narvik traffic. An additional attraction, one suspects, was that it was so large and required so much preparation that there was a good chance it would never materialise.

This disagreement remained unresolved as Allied military plans began to take shape at the end of December 1939. The British and French governments nevertheless started to lay the diplomatic groundwork for military intervention. Diplomatic notes to the Norwegian and Swedish governments on 27 December sought to play on Scandinavian sympathies for Finland, informing Norway and Sweden that the Allies intended to give the Finns 'unofficially . . . all the indirect assistance in their power' and promising Allied support if the two governments did the same.[37] A second pair of notes, on 6 January 1940, was intended to prepare the way for naval action against the Narvik traffic by arguing that the German sinkings in December had turned Norwegian waters into a theatre of war.

Knowing nothing of the background, Koht's first instinct was to characterise the December note as an attempt to re-establish Great-Power 'tutelage'. For an analogy he reached back not merely to the integrity treaty of 1907, but much further: to the 'November treaty' of 1855 in which Britain and France had guaranteed Sweden–Norway against Russia in the aftermath of the Crimean War.[38] The note of 6 January he rightly regarded as far more alarming, with its threat of immediate naval action in Norwegian waters, and coinciding as it did with a menacing Soviet note of the same date accusing Norway and Sweden of permitting blatantly pro-Finnish activities on their soil.[39] Faced with

[37] Quoted in Sir Llewellyn Woodward, *British Foreign Policy in the Second World War* (London, 1962), 22.

[38] Fure, *Mellomkrigstid*, 346. [39] Ibid., 334.

these threats, Koht reacted in characteristic fashion, returning a conciliatory reply to the Soviets and using delaying tactics and legalistic arguments to challenge the Allied claims regarding Norwegian territorial waters. As the weaker power, these were the only tactics the Norwegians had available. The British were not persuaded by the objections (they found Swedish arguments more impressive), but together the two Scandinavian governments succeeded in exploiting the hesitations and divisions within the British war cabinet. On 12 January Churchill's Narvik scheme was shelved indefinitely.

The Norwegians and Swedes did not know this; and planning for the 'larger plan' – still predicated on Scandinavian cooperation – went ahead, receiving the endorsement of the Allied Supreme War Council on 5 February 1940. However, British (though not French) doubts about the Scandinavian response were heightened by the continuing diplomatic fall-out from their earlier approaches. On 19 January Koht went so far as to insinuate in a speech to the Storting that the British might have torpedoed the three ships themselves. Churchill's frustration was expressed in the notorious wireless broadcast of 20 January in which he accused the neutrals of each feeding the crocodile in the hope that they would be eaten last. But, again, Norwegian tactics worked to the extent that they reinforced British moral scruples and left an element of doubt as to how Norway might respond to a British landing. In fact it could be argued that the height of Norwegian persuasiveness was reached in the aftermath of the most spectacular violation of Norwegian neutrality of the entire Phoney War. On 16 February 1940 the German auxiliary ship *Altmark* was boarded in Norwegian territorial waters by the British destroyer *Cossack*, resulting in the release of the 299 British prisoners of war who had been concealed in the ship's hold.

In terms of international law the *Altmark* case was complex, though with clear evidence of mistakes on the part of the Norwegian authorities and deliberate violation of neutrality by both the Germans and the British.[40] The consequences of the incident were profound, especially, as we shall see, for their influence on Hitler's attitude to the Norwegian question. Yet the *Altmark* incident is also remarkable for what it did *not* lead to. Churchill seized the opportunity to revive his plan for laying mines in Norwegian waters – this time with the clear intention of provoking a German reaction – but once again the proposal was turned

[40] Documents printed in Reidar Omang (ed.), *Altmark-saken 1940* (Oslo, 1953).

down.[41] The war cabinet was swayed by political objections from the Dominion prime ministers and the leaders of the Opposition, as well as fears about the reactions of the United States and Italy. Ministers were also warned by the Ministry of Economic Warfare (MEW) that Oslo was likely to react by denouncing the recently negotiated shipping agreement, thus depriving Britain of oil at a time when stocks were dangerously low. Once again, a combination of moral scruple and economic self-interest deterred Britain from taking action against Norway.

From this point onwards, however, British inhibitions diminished. By early April 1940 they had reached vanishing point. The first stage was marked by the grotesque exchanges between cabinet ministers and the commanders of the Allied expeditionary force, Operation Avonmouth, on the eve of its scheduled departure for Narvik on 11 March 1940.[42] The instructions to the two commanders, Major-General Macksey and Admiral Evans, were unsatisfactory to say the least. It was clear that ministers had failed to confront in their own minds the implications of the decision to send an expedition to Finland. It appeared that force was not to be used except as a last resort, and that if passage was barred it should merely be demanded 'with the utmost energy'. General Macksey understood his instructions to mean that, if passage was nevertheless refused, he should not attempt to get through by fighting, an impression reinforced by Halifax's observation that 'if we can't get in except at the cost of a lot of Norwegian lives, I am not for it – ore or no ore'.[43]

Nevertheless, the meeting concluded with a decision, forced by Chamberlain, that the commanders had to be allowed to use force if they judged it necessary. It is true, of course, that the entire meeting took place on the eve of Finland's capitulation to Russia. Finnish negotiators were already in Moscow, and the British knew it. Probably no-one present at the meeting expected the expedition to set sail. It is also true that the Norwegian government had decided on 2 March not to offer resistance to the Allies, should they demand passage to Finland. Koht had advised his colleagues that Norway must satisfy itself with a protest since it could not under any circumstance allow itself to be drawn into the war 'on the

[41] Patrick Salmon, 'British Strategy and Norway 1939–40', in P. Salmon (ed.), *Britain and Norway in the Second World War* (London, 1995), 9–10.

[42] Revealing accounts of these meetings are contained in R. Macleod and D. Kelly (eds.), *The Ironside Diaries 1937–1940* (London, 1962), 226–8, and Sir John Kennedy, *The Business of War* (London, 1957), 46–51.

[43] Quoted in ibid., 50.

wrong side'.[44] But in March Norway's territorial integrity was preserved not by Norwegian protests or British scruples but by a peace treaty in Moscow.[45] In principle, the war cabinet had resolved to land British forces in Norway regardless of Norwegian objections.

The second stage in the hardening of British attitudes occurred in the period between the peace of Moscow on 12 March and the meeting of the Supreme War Council in London on 28 March. The Finnish debacle damaged Allied prestige and led to the fall of the Daladier government in France. In both countries there was a search for ways to regain the initiative and demonstrate Allied resolve. Apart from operations against the Soviet Union, which were now being contemplated seriously by a number of senior military commanders and politicians in both France and Britain,[46] the main proposals were to drop 'fluvial mines' in the Rhine (Operation Royal Marine) and, once again, to lay mines in Norwegian territorial waters (Operation Wilfred). The Supreme War Council decided that the two operations should be carried out simultaneously. In the end, Royal Marine was abandoned and Wilfred was postponed from 5 to 8 April, thus ensuring that it would be the Allies, not Hitler, who 'missed the bus'.

For the Norwegians, the most tangible evidence of a tougher British stance was the increasing readiness of British warships to pursue German ships into Norwegian waters. None were actually sunk, but the obvious British presence was 'a cautious demonstration of power towards both Norway and Germany'.[47] Violations of Norwegian air space by British aircraft also increased. The new pattern of British behaviour activated a key element in Koht's thinking: British breaches of Norwegian neutrality would provoke German counter-measures which might bring Norway into the war. Koht tried to avert German action by means of strong diplomatic protests against British violations and by ordering greater activity on the part of Norwegian patrol ships: escorting German ships and warning the British. Finally, on 23 March, he threatened that all foreign warships entering Norwegian waters would be fired on.[48] His actions were not directed solely against the Allies: German vessels and aircraft were also operating in Norwegian waters and air space with

[44] Minutes of the cabinet meeting captured by the Germans and published in White Book No. 4, *Britain's Designs on Norway: Documents Concerning the Anglo-French Policy of Extending the War* (New York, 1940), 61–4.
[45] Fure, *Mellomkrigstid*, 357.
[46] Hans-Joachim Lorbeer, *Westmächte gegen die Sowjetunion 1939–41* (Freiburg im Breisgau, 1975).
[47] Fure, *Mellomkrigstid*, 358. [48] Bergsgård, 'Utrikspolitikk', 254.

increasing impunity. On 28 March Koht ordered the internment of a German submarine, with its crew, which had run aground near Mandal. But it was now far too late to influence either the Allies or Germany.

It had taken a long time for Hitler to be finally convinced that it was in Germany's interest to destroy rather than preserve Norwegian neutrality. Until December 1939 he had proved unresponsive to suggestions from Admiral Raeder, the head of the German navy, that it might be advantageous to occupy bases on the coast of Norway.[49] The visit of the Norwegian national socialist leader Vidkun Quisling to Berlin in mid-December opened Hitler's eyes to the danger posed by Great Britain to Norway's neutral status.[50] Quisling's apparently authoritative (but entirely spurious) information on the close links between Jewish politicians in Norway and Britain – Carl Hambro and the British minister of war Leslie Hore-Belisha – and the two countries' armed forces and intelligence services were used by Raeder and the Nazi ideologue Alfred Rosenberg to promote their respective naval and racial visions. Hitler's response was to order planning for two scenarios: a political coup through Quisling and his party, and a military occupation by the German armed forces. As German planning developed between December 1939 and February 1940, the political option receded into the background; but the notion planted by Quisling of Norwegian–British collusion survived. Koht's candid conversations with the German minister in Oslo, Curt Bräuer, which revealed the depth of his mistrust of British intentions, were simply ignored or disbelieved.

The *Altmark* incident prompted Hitler to accelerate preparations for a military solution. The official directive for Weserübung, the German occupation of Denmark and Norway, was issued on 1 March 1940. Germany's plans, like those of the Allies, were temporarily stalled by the end of the Soviet–Finnish war; but by late March Raeder was employing new arguments to persuade Hitler to take action: the threat posed to Germany's ore supplies by the increasing activity of British warships in and around Norwegian waters, and the need to prevent the German fleet from being tied up inactive any longer. On 2 April Hitler finally agreed, designating 9 April as the date for the invasion. Over the next few days, there was mounting evidence that a large-scale German action was impending, and that its probable destination was Norway. But intelligence reaching London was discounted as 'another move in the

49 Salmon, *Scandinavia and the Great Powers*, 332–3.
50 Hans Fredrik Dahl, *Quisling: A Study in Treachery* (Cambridge, 1999), 148–59.

war of nerves' or misinterpreted as the long-anticipated break-out of the German navy into the North Atlantic. Preoccupied with its own plans for laying mines in Norwegian waters and landing token forces in Norway's west coast ports to meet an expected German response, the British Admiralty never imagined Germany taking action against Norway in its own right. Very little intelligence appears to have penetrated as far as Oslo; but here, as we have seen, attention was wholly occupied by the diplomatic preliminaries to the British minelaying operation planned for 8 April.

## THE END OF NORWEGIAN NEUTRALITY, 1940–9

From the morning of 9 April 1940 Norway was at war, but the Norwegian government in exile did not sign a military agreement with the United Kingdom until May 1941; and it was only with the signature of the North Atlantic Treaty on 4 April 1949 that neutrality was finally abandoned. Before April 1940, alliance with Great Britain was a position of last resort for Koht, to be contemplated, if at all, only when Norway was actually at war. One of the very few occasions when the question was openly discussed came during a meeting of the Storting's foreign affairs committee after the Allied notes of 27 December 1939.[51] One member of the committee regretted that the government had not pursued the Allied offer of a military guarantee; another, Mowinckel, suggested that the Norwegian reply ought not to be too negative, since Norway might need full British cooperation some time in the future. The only member of the government who actively sought cooperation with the British at this time was Trygve Lie, the minister of supply, who hinted to MEW in February 1940 that the signature of an Anglo-Norwegian war trade agreement might be followed by secret military and naval conversations between the two countries – a prospect that helped to persuade ministers against Churchill's Narvik scheme after the *Altmark* incident.[52]

After April 1940 Norway was *de facto* an ally of Great Britain. It was, however, difficult for many of the country's political leaders to adjust to the new situation. Pursued by the Germans through Norway and then dispersed to London, Stockholm, or the United States, Norway's political elite found itself challenged to acknowledge the bankruptcy of the foreign and security policies which had guided the country since 1905. Koht, most of all, was the victim of this mood of recrimination

[51] Fure, *Mellomkrigstid*, 347. [52] Salmon, 'British Strategy and Norway', 10.

and redefinition. This was partly a product of resentment against Koht's dominance of Norwegian foreign policy since 1935, and his intellectual contempt for most of his colleagues. He was also, naturally, made the scapegoat for the catastrophe of April 1940; although in fact, as we have seen, his basic assumptions about Norway's position were shared by almost all Norwegians in positions of authority, and his culpability for the country's military unpreparedness was almost certainly less than that of, for example, the minister of defence. As the Norwegian government in exile established itself in London and the home counties during the summer of 1940, Koht was also accused of holding himself aloof from the British and of being too concerned to remain on good terms with the Soviet Union. In both accusations there was more than an element of truth.[53]

The summer and autumn of 1940 marked a sea change in Norway's relations with Great Britain. In July a group of intellectuals in London associated with the most ambitious and dynamic member of the government-in-exile, Trygve Lie, argued in a letter to the government that Norway must associate itself wholeheartedly with the Allied cause: 'If the British government sees the Norwegian government as a co-belligerent that is half-hearted, unreliable, or which goes its separate way, then this will sooner or later lead to the British authorities pushing aside our own military and administrative authorities.'[54] The change was symbolised by Koht's resignation as foreign minister in November 1940 and his replacement by Trygve Lie. Advised by the chief author of the July letter, Arne Ording, Lie announced Norway's new alliance policy in a wireless broadcast on 15 December. He went on to articulate his vision of a wartime alliance developing into peacetime cooperation between Norway and the West, embracing not only Britain but also the United States. The vision may have been idealistic, but it also reflected vital national interests. The policy of isolated neutrality, of keeping Britain at arm's length while relying on British naval power as a last resort, had failed. Only coordination of defence in peacetime could prevent a repetition of the disaster of April 1940.

By the end of 1940 the generation of 1905 had been sidelined and a new generation had taken over in London, even though Nygaardsvold remained at the head of the government. It was augmented in the course

[53] Olav Riste, *'London-regjeringa.' Norge i krigsalliansen 1940–1945*, vol. I, *1940–1942: prøvetid* (Oslo, 1973), 61–6.

[54] Quoted in Olav Riste, 'Relations between the Norwegian Government in Exile and the British Government', in Salmon (ed.), *Britain and Norway in the Second World War*, 42.

of the war by the emerging leaders of the home front resistance to German rule in Norway: men like Einar Gerhardsen and Halvard Lange who were to emerge from German concentration camps to become, respectively, prime minister and foreign minister in the first post-war government; or Jens Christian Hauge, the leader of Milorg, the underground army, who became minister of defence. Norway, meanwhile, had moved from isolationist neutrality to being the most articulate advocate of post-war Atlantic cooperation – in advance of Britain itself, and long before the entry of the United States into war. In the process it became one of the most loyal and respected of Britain's wartime allies.

There was, however, no smooth transition from wartime to Cold War alliance. In the immediate post-war years Anglo-Norwegian military ties remained strong, but the Norwegian government, still mindful of the power of the Soviet Union which had liberated northern Norway, attempted a policy of 'bridge-building' between east and west. It was only following the dramatic deterioration of east–west relations in 1948 and, even then, in the face of strong Swedish pressure to form a neutral Scandinavian defence alliance, that Norway resolved to make a firm commitment to an American-led security system.

## THE HISTORIOGRAPHY OF NORWEGIAN NEUTRALITY

The historiographical debate on Norwegian neutrality was long dominated by an attempt to find explanations – and scapegoats – for the events of 1940. The earliest such attempt was made less than three weeks after the German invasion, by the German foreign minister Joachim von Ribbentrop. At a press conference on 27 April 1940 he presented 'White Book No. 4', a volume of captured British and Norwegian documents which purported to show that an Allied occupation of Norway had only narrowly been prevented and – using the record of the cabinet meeting of 2 March discussed earlier – that the Norwegian government had contemplated coming into the war on the side of Britain and France.[55] The Norwegian government responded with its own White Book in July 1940, and in 1941 a large collection of documents on the period from September 1939 to December 1940 was published under the auspices of the Royal Institute for

[55] *Britain's Designs on Norway.*

International Affairs.[56] In 1941 Koht published his *Norway Neutral and Invaded*, which dealt with the German allegations but also outlined a defence of his foreign policy on which he was to elaborate after the end of the war.[57]

After the liberation of Norway, the debate began in earnest. Unpopular before the war, Koht quickly became the most convenient hate-figure, thanks not least to the long vendetta waged by Johan Scharffenberg, a courageous and outspoken opponent of Nazi rule in Norway, but also a man of eccentric judgement. Scharffenberg's early attacks castigated Koht's 'incomprehensible blindness' and defeatism before the German invasion. Later, in criticising Norway's membership of the UN and NATO, he alleged that the German invasion had been a justified response to Koht's pro-British conduct.[58] A more judicious, though still critical, assessment was delivered by the parliamentary commission of inquiry into the events of 1940 when it reported in December 1946. Much of the blame for Norway's lack of preparedness was allotted to the defence minister and prime minister, while Koht was praised for his patriotic reply to the German minister on the morning of 9 April. The commission nonetheless criticised the general thrust of Koht's policy: 'The foreign policy leadership cannot be blamed for not foreseeing the German invasion in February–March 1940, but they can be blamed for being so one-sidedly fixed on the danger from the west that they closed their eyes to other dangers.'[59]

Among the reports prepared for the parliamentary commission, one, Arne Bergsgård's study of the government's foreign policy, stands in a class of its own.[60] It was the judgement of one eminent historian on another and also, until very recently, the only scholarly account of Norwegian foreign policy between 1933 and 1940 based on primary sources.[61] But his account also represents a sustained critique of Koht's beliefs and actions, made all the more effective by drawing extensively

[56] *Ny norsk kvitbok* (London, 1940); Monica Curtis (ed.), *Norway and the War, September 1939 – December 1940* (Oxford, 1941).

[57] London, 1941. Carl J. Hambro's *I Saw it Happen in Norway*, published in 1940, had little to say about the neutrality period, focusing almost entirely on the German invasion and afterwards.

[58] Skard, *Koht*, 219, 225; Johan Scharffenberg, *Norske akstykker til okkupasjonens forhistorie* (Oslo, 1951).

[59] Quoted in Skard, *Koht*, 221 (my translation).

[60] Bergsgård, 'Utrikspolitikk'. For a detailed understanding of the 1939–40 period in particular, Bergsgård remains indispensable.

[61] For recent assessments of Bergsgård and Koht, see William H. Hubbard, Jan Eivind Myhre, Trond Nordby, and Sølvi Sogner, *Making a Historical Culture: Historiography in Norway* (Oslo, 1995), 45, 187–90.

on the foreign minister's own words. Admitting his mistakes, but unrepentant about his core assumptions, Koht wrote prolifically in response to his critics.[62] In his first riposte, *Norsk utanrikspolitikk fram til 9. April 1940* ('Norwegian foreign policy up to 9 April 1940'), he repeated many of the arguments of his wartime book, but also expressed his scepticism towards the claims of the Western Powers in a way that he had been unable to do in 1941: '"Ideologically," Great Britain under Chamberlain was closer to Germany than Russia . . . For me the great danger was not bolshevism but nazism', and so on.[63] Ten years later the 84-year-old historian produced *For fred og fridom i krigstid 1939–1940* ('For Peace and Freedom in Wartime 1939–1940'), a much more substantial work, in response to the memoirs of his old adversary, Trygve Lie.[64]

The scholarly reappraisal of the events of 9 April began in the 1950s with the work of Nils Ørvik and Magne Skodvin. Ørvik first approached the problem of Norwegian neutrality in 1939–40 as part of his wider study of the American and Nordic experience, *The Decline of Neutrality 1914–1941*.[65] He argued that the legal norms on which neutrality had been based since the nineteenth century had become irrelevant in an era of ideological warfare. In 1939–40 Norway had been squeezed between German ruthlessness and the moral imperatives of the Allies, expressed most famously in Churchill's demand that 'The letter of the law must not in supreme emergency obstruct those who are charged with its protection and enforcement . . . Humanity, rather than legality, must be our guide.'[66] Norwegian neutrality was untenable 'because it rested on an artificial basis': it was an attempt to stick to the letter of international law which 'was not backed up by a strong and undiscriminating military force'.[67] This first study was to be reinforced by substantial works on Norwegian–British economic negotiations in 1939–40 and Norwegian security policy between the wars.[68]

[62] Apart from the works discussed here, see *Frå skanse til skanse* (Oslo, 1947), an autobiographical account of the weeks following the German invasion, and 'Mr. Winston Churchill and the Norwegian question', *The Norseman*, 8 (1950), 73–84, which contains much intriguing detail and plays up Churchill's interest (shared by Koht) in good relations with the Soviet Union.

[63] Koht, *Norsk utanrikspolitikk*, 12–14 (my translation).

[64] Oslo 1957. Trygve Lie, *Leve eller dø*, vol. I, *Norge i krig* (Oslo, 1955).

[65] Oslo, 1953, 2nd edn, London, 1971.

[66] Memorandum of 16 December 1939, printed in Winston S. Churchill, *The Second World War*, vol. I, *The Gathering Storm* (2nd edn, London, 1949), 490–2.

[67] Ørvik, *Decline of Neutrality*, 244.

[68] Nils Ørvik, *Norge i brennpunktet: Fra forhistorien til 9. April 1940*, vol. I, *Handelskrigen 1939–40* (Oslo, 1953); Ørvik, *Sikkerhetspolitikken 1920–39* (2 vols., Oslo, 1960–1).

If Ørvik, with his acceptance that neutrality was no longer viable, represented the post-1949 view of Norwegian neutrality, Magne Skodvin's work showed more sympathy with the neutralist tradition. Skodvin never wrote the one great work on the period 1939–40 of which he, more than anyone, would have been capable. Instead, his profound insights appeared piecemeal over a forty-year period.[69] Apart from inspiring the work of younger historians, especially through the 'contemporary history research group' (Samtidshistorisk Forskningsgruppe) founded in 1968, Skodvin's great service was to rehabilitate Halvdan Koht from the caricature and vilification of his critics.[70] In the early 1970s Skodvin moved on to examine Norway's decision to join NATO.[71] He was to be followed by a new generation of Norwegian historians, including Geir Lundestad, Helge Pharo, and Knut Einar Eriksen, who were to win an international reputation as Cold War scholars.[72] From this point onwards, Norwegian scholarship – benefiting from an exceptionally open policy on access to official documents – followed the moving frontier of the archives into more and more recent times, and the pre-1940 period suffered from neglect.

As it happened, however, one of the first of the new Cold War studies was to prompt the most fundamental post-war reappraisal of Norwegian neutrality. Nils Morten Udgaard's *Great Power Politics and Norwegian Foreign Policy* described Norwegian policy as travelling full circle between 1940 and 1948, from wartime solidarity with the Atlantic powers, to non-alignment and accommodation of Soviet interests at the end of the war, and back to a strong commitment to the West in 1948–9.[73] In a review published in 1973 Olav Riste praised the book but challenged the thesis. By focusing on the public swings of Norwegian foreign policy between neutrality, collective security, isolationism, and alliance, Udgaard – and others – had failed to notice the fundamental continuity of Norwegian foreign policy since 1905. Throughout the period from 1905 to 1949, Norway had relied on an 'implicit guarantee' that in the last resort the

[69] Some have been collected in Magne Skodvin, *Samtid og historie. Utvalde artiklar og avhandlingar* (Oslo, 1975).

[70] See also e.g. the essays collected in *Mellom nøytrale og allierte* (Oslo, 1968). See the appreciative comments in Skard, *Koht*, 243.

[71] Magne Skodvin, *Norden eller NATO?* (Oslo, 1971).

[72] For discussions of these developments see John Sanness, 'Norske historikere og den kalde krig', in Tamnes (ed.), *Forsvarsstudier*, vol. IV 169–85; Tor Egil Førland, 'International History', in Hubbard, Myhre, Nordby, and Sogner, *Making a Historical Culture*, 360–76.

[73] *Great Power Politics and Norwegian Foreign Policy. A study of Norway's foreign relations November 1940–February 1948* (Oslo, 1973). The term 'implicit guarantee' was actually first used by John Sanness in 1978 (see Førland, 'International History', 364).

Anglo-Saxon Great Powers – Great Britain in the first instance – would be willing and able to defend Norway against external aggression. All that changed in 1949 was that the implicit guarantee became explicit with Norway's accession to the North Atlantic treaty.

Riste's argument, of which the outlines were already visible in his 1965 study of Norway during the First World War, *The Neutral Ally*, was developed in his two-volume history of the government-in-exile, *London-regjeringa*, as well as in a number of shorter pieces, of which the best known was probably his 1985 article 'Was 1949 a turning point?'.[74] The notion of the implicit guarantee remains the most powerful interpretative tool for the understanding of Norwegian foreign policy between 1905 and 1949. It also provides an explanation for the strong neutralist and isolationist tendencies still evident in Norway between 1949 and the present day.[75] Intellectually, the Riste thesis has proved hard to challenge.[76] It has also become entrenched through Riste's energy, organisational ability, and strong institutional base at the Norwegian Institute for Defence Studies. Roald Berg's 1983 thesis on 'England as Norway's protector 1905–1908', was supervised by Riste and filled an important gap.[77] However, much detail remained to be established, especially for the inter-war period.

The deficiency was remedied in the 1990s with the appearance of another Riste-inspired project, the six-volume history of Norwegian foreign policy, *Norsk utenrikspolitikks historie*.[78] Perhaps the most interesting of the earlier volumes was the one by Odd-Bjørn Fure, dealing with the period from 1920 to 1940.[79] Fure did not belong to the relatively closed circle of Norwegian international historians, with their predominantly Anglo-Saxon orientation. Instead, he drew on the work of the French Annales school and the Norbert Elias' concept of 'habitus' to link the domestic tensions of inter-war Norway to the wider ideological and political conflicts in the world outside. Fure explicitly avoided conducting

74 *The Neutral Ally: Norway's Relations with Belligerent Powers in the First World War* (Oslo, 1965); *'London-regjeringa.' Norge i krigsalliansen 1940–1945* (2 vols., Oslo, 1973–9); 'Was 1949 a Turning Point? Norway and the Western Powers 1947–1950', in Olav Riste (ed.), *Western Security: The Formative Years* (Oslo, 1985), 128–49.

75 See e.g. Olav Riste, *Isolasjonisme og stormaktsgarantier* (Oslo, 1991).

76 See Tor Egil Førland, '1949 som "vendepunkt": Er NATO-medlemskapet bare kulisse?', *Internasjonal politikk* (1988), 69–85; and Riste's reply, 'Merkeår i norsk utanrikspolitikk: Vendepunkt eller ledd i ein gradvis prosess?', ibid., 187–91.

77 Summarised in Berg "Det land vi venter hjælp af." See also Berg, *Norge på egen hånd.*

78 For a discussion of the first four volumes and their context, see Patrick Salmon, 'How to Write International History: Reflections on *Norsk utenrikspolitikks historie*', *Diplomacy and Statecraft*, 9 (1998), 208–23.

79 Fure, *Mellomkrigstid.*

yet another autopsy on the traumatic events of 9 April 1940 (though his chapters on 1939–40 contain profound reflections on the subject), and rejected the emphasis placed on security policy by most previous studies. Until 1937, he declared, security policy had been 'a marginal and sometimes wholly absent element of Norwegian foreign policy'; moreover, there were many aspects of foreign policy in the inter-war period which had no connection with the catastrophe of 1940.[80] By examining the full range of Norway's international preoccupations, Fure showed how far Norway's marginal, peripheral position was becoming undermined in the inter-war period by its increasing integration with the wider world in terms of communications, foreign trade, and cultural interaction. By the 1930s this integration had clear security implications which the country's leaders were unwilling or unable to acknowledge.[81]

Within the pages of *Norsk utenrikspolitikks historie* and in the recent controversy between international historians of the 'Skodvin' and 'Riste' schools on the one hand, and the Norwegian political scientist Iver Neumann on the other, are the outlines of a new, 'post-modern' debate on Norwegian foreign policy which addresses such issues as national identity, and the dichotomies between nation and state, and state and citizen.[82] In this context the debate on Norwegian neutrality during the Second World War may appear *passé*. In fact, as we have seen, neutrality was bound up with Norwegian national identity: the identity of a country proud to be isolated from an imperfect and menacing world and reluctant to acknowledge that its security was inseparable from that of others. During and after the Second World War this image was succeeded by another: that of a country more than willing to involve itself in the collective endeavour to win the war and preserve peace through involvement in an ultimately victorious Western alliance. However, Norway remains the home of the Nobel Peace Prize, the place where the Oslo Accords were negotiated, and the country which has twice rejected membership of the EEC and the European Union. It has therefore not abandoned the idealism and practical commitment to peacemaking – or the isolationism – which formed part of the Norwegian neutrality tradition.

[80] Ibid., 11–12 (my translation). [81] Ibid., 15.
[82] For a brief outline of this controversy, with references, see Salmon, 'How to Write International History'.

CHAPTER 3

# *The Netherlands*

*Bob Moore*

Early in the morning of 10 May 1940 the might of the German armed forces rolled into The Netherlands bringing to an end more than a century of jealously guarded and carefully maintained neutrality. To explain the nature of this central tenet of Dutch foreign policy, it is necessary to look at its origins and development in the inter-war period, before examining the ways in which Dutch and other historians have interpreted it and passed judgement.[1]

## I

Neutrality, as practised in the 1930s, owed its form primarily to the experiences of The Netherlands as a neutral state during and immediately after the First World War. In 1914, the Dutch had proclaimed their neutrality in line with the second Hague Peace Conference (1907). Unable to defend all their frontiers, they trod a fine line between the belligerent states on military, political, and economic matters, protesting violations where they thought it possible or necessary to impress others and reaching tacit agreements where positions could not be maintained. Apart from the military issues raised by the belligerents in relation to Dutch territory, the most vexed questions on The Netherlands' neutrality related to her economic role. Germany was anxious to exploit all the possibilities which the neutrality of its neighbour provided to break the British blockade, while Britain, France, and later America sought to limit these same opportunities.[2] Although some accommodations were reached with the

[1] Parts of this chapter are adapted from an article that appeared in *Diplomacy and Statecraft*, 3/3 (1992), 468–93 and I wish to thank the journal's editors for permission to reproduce them here. I also wish to express my thanks to the British Academy and the Research Committee of the former Bristol Polytechnic Humanities Department, whose grants made possible the research for this article.

[2] C. B. Wels, *Aloofness and Neutrality: Studies on Dutch Foreign Relations and Policy-Making Institutions* (Utrecht, 1982), 68–75.

belligerent powers and the creation of the Nederlandsche Overzee Trustmaatschappij (NOT) helped in the practical operation of Dutch external trade, at the war's end all sides remained unsatisfied with the outcome.[3] The Dutch had particularly resented the restrictions placed on their abilities to trade and also the Anglo-American seizure of Dutch shipping in March 1918 which led to food shortages in The Netherlands in the last months of the war.[4] Conversely, the belligerents had all resented Dutch policies which failed to meet their demands and there was widespread anger at the profits made by Dutch merchants during the conflict. Moreover, after the armistice, the dominant Allied powers tended to focus on aspects of Dutch behaviour which were perceived as having been pro-German, a spotlight which was made all the more uncomfortable by the appointment of the (supposedly) pro-German H. A. van Karnebeek as Foreign Minister in the new government of September 1918, the asylum given to Kaiser Wilhelm II on 9 November, and the permission granted for the evacuation of unarmed German soldiers across Dutch territory after the armistice was signed.

There is no doubt that although The Netherlands' neutrality had been preserved, the war had demonstrated some serious weaknesses in the formulation and execution of Dutch foreign policy. This was in no small part due to the low status of the foreign affairs portfolio within pre-1914 Dutch governments. The ministerial office was often regarded as a make-weight in coalition cabinets and this was reflected by the rather anonymous men appointed in the years before 1918. Domestic and colonial affairs had a far higher priority and there had been an almost consistent neglect of the ministry and its organisation since the 1840s and a tendency to regard diplomatic representation as a prime target when it came to cost-cutting.[5] On taking office, van Karnebeek embarked on a programme of reorganisation and modernisation which helped to raise the prestige of the ministry *vis-à-vis* other departments and also prepared it for the difficult negotiations which peace would bring.

In many respects, the end of hostilities brought more dangerous problems for the Dutch than the war itself. The worldwide esteem gained before 1914 as the host of international conferences had been entirely dissipated and The Netherlands' neutrality had served to distance and

[3] For further details of the creation and workings of the NOT, see C. Smit, *Nederland in de Eerste Wereldoorlog 1899–1919* (Groningen, 1972), vol. II (1914–17), 76–97. Charlotte A. van Manen, *De Nederlandsche Overzee Trustmaatschappij*, 8 vols. (The Hague, 1935).

[4] Wels, *Aloofness and Neutrality*, 70–4. [5] Ibid., 206.

alienate all her nearest neighbours. Moreover, in an attempt to reinforce her security and revise the treaties of 1839, the Belgians raised a series of territorial questions at the Paris Peace Conference. In particular they pointed to the deficiencies of the treaties of 1839 which had been exposed by the recent conflict. The strategically important crossing points of the River Meuse (Maas) in Limburg were in Dutch hands as was *Zeeuws Vlaanderen,* which gave them control of the Scheldt estuary and had served to block British access to the port of Antwerp. The Belgians hoped to use their influence with the major powers to force the issue but received little encouragement except from the French. In the meantime, the Dutch continued to adopt an intransigent stance against Belgian annexationism and demands against Dutch sovereignty based on their knowledge of the Powers' views and the need to placate domestic public opinion which would not countenance concessions. Offers were made to improve some of the waterways and joint control of the Scheldt in peacetime, even though these might be detrimental to the economy, but the package failed to impress the Belgians. The negotiations dragged on unresolved until September 1920 when the Belgians withdrew, having signed a secret military alliance with the French.[6] While the issues remained unresolved, there is no doubt that van Karnebeek's personal standing at home was markedly improved by his 'success' in fending off the Belgians.

Although The Netherlands had escaped from this potentially very damaging diplomatic threat unscathed, van Karnebeek was clearly conscious that the pre-war policy of passive neutrality would no longer be sufficient to maintain the country's interests in the post-war world. To that end, he encouraged Dutch membership of the League of Nations (1920) and its various institutions in spite of substantial domestic scepticism and hostility.[7] Many in The Netherlands regarded the League as the forum of the victorious powers and thought that enforcing League sanctions might compromise Dutch neutrality. Others harked back to the Congress system of the post-1815 period which was also perceived as having been detrimental to Dutch interests.[8]

[6] E. H. Kossmann, *The Low Countries 1780–1940* (Oxford, 1978), 576–7, 580; E. H. Kossmann, *De Lage Landen 1780–1980: Twee Eeuwen Nederland en België*, 2 vols. (Amsterdam/Brussels, 1986), vol. II, 60–1; Wels, *Aloofness and Neutrality*, 76–7; Sally Marks, *Innocent Abroad: Belgium at the Paris Peace Conference of 1919* (Chapel Hill, 1981), 280–6, 292–3.

[7] Kossmann, *The Low Countries*, 579.

[8] Wels, *Aloofness and Neutrality*, 77–8. He was also partly instrumental in the creation of the Permanent Court of International Justice in The Hague, for which he was rewarded with chairmanship of the second session of the League Assembly (1921–2).

Nonetheless, this more active approach to the defence of Dutch neutrality gained some favour. Even those Dutch men and women who continued to think that passive neutrality as practised between 1914 and 1918 had preserved their security and served their country extremely well were prepared to concede that there had been a change in European attitudes – away from war and towards collective security and multilateral agreements. In particular, the four-power agreement at the Washington Conference on security in the Far East (1921), British, French, American, and Japanese guarantees to the Dutch East Indies (1922), and the Locarno Pact (1925), seemed to provide concrete evidence of the success of van Karnebeek's approach to international relations.[9]

The apparent guarantee of imperial security in the Far East, together with the European treaties and the growth of social democracy as a force at home, all conspired to increase pacifist tendencies which governments could not ignore. In general, it led to a questioning of the amounts spent on defence if there was no real chance of a small power defending itself against aggression from a larger neighbour and, specifically, to parliamentary rejection of a proposed naval programme in 1923. While van Karnebeek's attempts to adopt a more active foreign policy were assisted by the international situation in the first half of the 1920s, his attempts to resolve the outstanding differences between the Dutch and Belgians after Locarno met with disaster. His search for a compromise produced an almost immediate agreement on economic differences and the question of access to rivers and waterways, but when the terms of this treaty became known they caused a storm of protest in The Netherlands. The opening of the Scheldt and the construction of a canal giving Antwerp direct access to the Rhine were considered to be highly detrimental to Dutch mercantile interests in general and potentially fatal for the port of Rotterdam. Consequently, businessmen and their employees were united in opposition to the agreement.[10] Although passed by the lower house of the Dutch parliament with a small majority, the bill was decisively defeated in the upper house on 24 March 1927. As a result, van Karnebeek resigned and no further negotiations were attempted.[11] Having attempted to 'break with tradition' in order to bring about a closer relationship with Belgium, he had clearly overstepped the boundaries of what the Dutch public and politicians were prepared to accept in the interests of

[9] Wels, *Aloofness and Neutrality*, 78. [10] Kossmann, *The Low Countries*, 581.
[11] Ibid.; Wels, *Aloofness and Neutrality*, 79.

regional stability and the resolution of outstanding disputes with their neighbours.[12]

In the following two years, relations with Belgium reached an all-time low but were resurrected as the economic depression hit all the smaller states of Europe and they combined to try to resist the rising tide of international protectionism through dialogue and cooperation at Oslo (1930) and with more concrete proposals for tariff reduction at Ouchy (1932). While nothing practical came of these ideas due to British and American opposition, the continued involvement of The Netherlands in multilateral talks on matters of common interest indicated that even as the power of the League was seen to be waning, the country would still try to safeguard its economic interests and free trade through bilateral treaties with neighbours. With the failure of the League to help Abyssinia against Italian aggression, the Dutch along with the other Oslo States decided that membership of the League afforded little protection and might conversely involve them in the imposition of sanctions at the behest of the major powers which would be in conflict with their own national interests. Thus, in 1936 The Netherlands declared itself no longer bound by article 16 of the League Covenant.

When war broke out in September 1939, The Netherlands reacted in much the same way as it had in 1914 with Minister-President de Geer making a public announcement that the policy of independence would be maintained 'fully and undiminished'.[13] In practice, this meant trying to defend Dutch national security and economic interests. Belligerent powers entered into negotiations with the Dutch to safeguard their economic interests and to hamstring those of their enemies. As in the First World War, the Dutch prevaricated on the question of a war trade agreement with the British and the document was still unsigned in May 1940.[14] In addition, British sources reported that the Dutch had also been secretly moving some of their gold reserves overseas to New York and South Africa.[15] A prudent course perhaps, but one

[12] For a more detailed explanation of van Karnebeek's position and the collapse of his policy on Belgium see Wels, *Aloofness and Neutrality*, 216–24.

[13] Amry J. Vandenbosch, *Dutch Foreign Policy since 1815: A Study in Small Power Politics* (The Hague, 1959), 280.

[14] W. N. Medlicott, *The Economic Blockade*, 2 vols. 2nd edn (London, 1978). Bob Moore, 'British Economic Warfare and Relations with the Neutral Netherlands during the "Phoney War," September 1939 – May 1940', *War and Society*, 13/2 (1995), 65–89.

[15] Moore, 'British Economic Warfare', 77–8. Nevile Bland to Cadogan, 29 October 1939, reported a conversation with H. M. Hirschfeld of the Dutch Foreign Office, P(ublic) R(ecord) O(ffice) CAB63/129.

which the government was anxious should not become public knowledge. In the military sphere, while consistently upholding the principles of neutrality and eschewing any open contacts with Belgium, France, or Britain there were some unofficial military and intelligence contacts, including the ill-fated Venlo Affair in November 1939 which gave the Germans at least the pretence of a *casus belli*.[16] Even if there was a degree of hypocrisy in the Dutch government's public pronouncements, both to the people and to the outside world, it remains the case that nothing the last peacetime Dutch cabinet could have done would have materially changed the events of May 1940 and saved the kingdom from invasion.

## II

To provide a complete picture, it is necessary to examine the ways in which Dutch historiography on The Netherlands' foreign policy has developed since the beginning of the Second World War. Certainly, the invasion brought an abrupt end to any illusions that neutrality could be maintained in the face of a malevolent European neighbour. In the occupation period, the policy was widely derided as bankrupt and those who had carried it out as consigned to the dustbin of history. In the years following liberation, a number of elements militated against a deeper analysis of the motives behind Dutch foreign policy in the 1930s: the relative unimportance of The Netherlands to European diplomacy in the pre-war era, the destruction of documents during the war, the limited nature of the sources, and the attitudes of post-war Dutch historians to the inter-war period. For the most part, judgements about the country's foreign policy have taken second place to debates on domestic affairs or the economy. Until the 1970s, analyses of successive Dutch governments' domestic and international policies pursued in the 1930s were almost uniformly critical. The cabinets led by Hendrik Colijn between 1933 and 1939 were usually portrayed as conservative, colourless, and lacking in originality. The reason for this is not hard to fathom. After the war, a reconstructing Netherlands had no need to rehabilitate discredited pre-war politicians. As a result, the view that inter-war Dutch governments had failed to deal adequately not only with the economic crisis, but also with the approaching international storm of the late 1930s became an orthodox standpoint in popular, if not in academic circles.

[16] S. Payne Best, *The Venlo Incident* (London, 1950); C. A. MacDonald, 'The Venlo Affair', *European Studies Review*, 8 (1978), 443–64; C. M. Andrew, *Secret Service: The Making of the British Intelligence Community* (London, 1989), 609–16.

Kossmann has argued that in 1936 The Netherlands 'reverted completely to the position it had been in before the First World War',[17] and there is strong evidence for this. However, the period between 1918 and 1936 did see a change in the theoretical formulation of neutrality. While public opinion had seen no reason to abandon the winning formula of the First World War, van Karnebeek in particular had seen the threat posed by continued isolation and had used his position to create a new variant, namely *zelfstandigheidspolitiek*, best defined as a policy of independence or active neutrality,[18] and this was precisely the formulation used by Minister-President de Geer in September 1939. Moreover, this stance was no longer justified purely in terms of Dutch interests but was expressed as an international duty. A. A. H. Struycken, an influential figure in Dutch foreign policy-making in the 1920s went so far as to say that 'the inviolate character and independence of our territory is an indispensable condition of the political balance of power in Europe.'[19]

The 'shock of 1940' inevitably produced a reappraisal of neutrality and *zelfstandigheidspolitiek* in the post-war era, a reappraisal given added import by the loss of most of the East Indian colonies and the realisation that The Netherlands could no longer regard itself even as a 'middle power'.[20] For this reason alone, the neutralism and neutrality of the pre-war era were widely condemned for having failed to prevent the disaster of 1940. Yet even as the war in Europe began, there were already academics prepared to explain and justify their country's position. A notable contemporary commentator, B. M. Telders of Leiden, was quick to highlight the differences between The Netherlands and the Western allies.[21] In 1939, his strident defence of neutrality included extensive use of concepts like trust, duty, and fulfilling a function within the European political structure. In other words, he reiterated the traditional justification for the policy – that a neutral Netherlands not only took a rightful stance but also fulfilled a moral duty to the security of Europe. This was nothing new, but the professor went much further by taking issue with the motives of London and Paris. Had not the Hitler menace come about largely through the 'peace policy' of Britain and France in

[17] Kossmann, *The Low Countries*, 584.

[18] Wels, *Aloofness and Neutrality*, 20, cites B. W. Kranenburg, *De hartslag van ons buitenlandse beleid* (Assen, 1949), 221.

[19] A. A. H. Struycken, *De Hoofdtrekken van Nederlandsch Buitenlands Beleid* (Arnhem, 1923), 18, cited in Wels, *Aloofness and Neutrality*, 81.

[20] A. E. Kersten, 'In de ban van de Bondgenoot', in D. Barnouw, M. de Keizer, and G. van der Stroom (eds.), *1940–1945: Onverwerkt Verleden* (Utrecht, 1985), 102–3.

[21] B. M. Telders, *Nederlands Onzijdigheid: Grondslagen en Gevolgen* (The Hague, October 1939).

1919? How could they claim to be protecting the peace of Europe when their policies (on reparations and the Ruhr) had created the danger in the first place? Moreover, Britain and France had portrayed themselves as the protectors of small powers, yet they had watched while Austria, Czechoslovakia, and Albania had fallen, and only intervened when their own interests were threatened.[22]

Vandenbosch, writing from the United States during the war, provided a more sober analysis of Dutch neutrality but was still somewhat critical of Anglo-French policies.[23] He took the line that if Britain and France had given decisive leadership to the international community in the 1930s, the Dutch might have followed a different policy, but even he still thought this unlikely. Moreover, after the Germans reoccupied the Rhineland in March 1936 there was 'little else the Dutch could do. It was too late to adopt another policy.'[24] In any case, an alliance was unlikely to increase their security. After January 1939, The Netherlands was assured of British aid, 'which in all probability would not have been adequate'.[25] In making these points, Vandenbosch identified two major constraints on Dutch action. Firstly, that it was impossible to reverse a policy which had been in place for so long – especially at short notice. Neither the will nor the resources to change course existed. Secondly, even if the will had been there, it seemed unlikely that acceptance of an Anglo-French security alliance could have benefited The Netherlands. Certainly the views of the British Chiefs of Staff bear out Vandenbosch's contention. While advising that the territorial integrity of The Netherlands was of vital strategic interest to Britain and that there should be intervention if the country were to be attacked, they did have reservations:

> The only doubt in our mind arises from the present strength of our defensive preparations. Our examination ... of the military action which could be taken shows that there is no hope of preventing Holland from being overrun, and that the restoration of her territory would depend upon the later course of the war.[26]

These ideas were further developed in Vandenbosch's major study of Dutch foreign policy in the nineteenth and twentieth centuries. Here he highlighted other important considerations for the Dutch. Although

[22] Telders, *Nederlands Onzijdigheid*, 7, 10.
[23] Amry J. Vandenbosch, 'Netherlands Foreign Policy', in B. Landheer, (ed.), *The Netherlands* (Berkeley/Los Angeles, 1944).
[24] Vandenbosch, 'Netherlands Foreign Policy', 147.
[25] Ibid.
[26] PRO CAB16 D(efence) P(lans) P(olicy) 43 and Annexes, cited in N. H. Gibbs, *Grand Strategy:* vol. 1: *Rearmament Policy* (London, 1976), 500.

their neutrality was seen as a hindrance by the Allies, London and Paris still preferred this to any Dutch–German accommodation. The foreign minister of the 1939–40 de Geer cabinet, Eelco van Kleffens, had outlined the rationale for continued neutrality in January 1940 by referring to a series of principles.

Firstly, Dutch neutrality was the means of safeguarding a sensitive strategic and economic area.[27] By staying out of the conflict, the Dutch denied all belligerent states the advantage of using Dutch territory for military purposes while at the same time protecting for everyone the trade routes along the major rivers. While the strategic argument was certainly valid, the economic one carried less weight. Germany had already achieved a high degree of autarky by 1939 and had planned her rearmament and war economy on the assumption that European trade and waterways would be disrupted in wartime. The major economic beneficiaries of Dutch neutrality would therefore be the Dutch themselves, since they could thereby preserve their existing and vitally important ties with all the belligerent powers without having to make uncomfortable choices between them.

Van Kleffens' second point was that, by remaining neutral, the Oslo States provided the obvious mediators in the conflict; the peacemakers who could step in as and when required. This can be seen as a *post facto* rationale for the events of November 1939 when Queen Wilhelmina together with King Leopold of the Belgians made an abortive attempt to offer themselves as mediators between the belligerents. Moreover, he argued, the Dutch were under no obligation to go to war, and there was no obvious cause for them to support. Finally, there was the question of morality. The Dutch perceived the war as a private affair between the belligerent states. The British and French had asserted that they had gone to war for the protection of civilisation, but how could they claim this when they had asked for Soviet help? In Dutch policy-making, the antipathy and animosity towards the Soviet Union (which The Netherlands refused to recognise) or anything which smacked of bolshevism could not be underestimated. The confessional base for much of Dutch politics made it impossible to associate The Netherlands with the Soviet Union. Indeed, the Dutch deliberately raised the question of the Soviet attack on Finland at the League of Nations in December 1939, and also raised money for the Finnish Red Cross.[28] Even though Stalin had reached an agreement

[27] Vandenbosch, *Dutch Foreign Policy*, 281–2, cites *Handelingen Tweede Kamer 1939–1940*, 25 October 1939, 312–17.
[28] Vandenbosch, *Dutch Foreign Policy*, 286.

with Hitler in August 1939, thus removing the immediate prospect of an Anglo-French–Soviet pact, the Dutch still questioned whether London and Paris could be trusted not to involve the godless bolsheviks in future alliances.

In effect, van Kleffens had outlined the moral and economic rationale for The Netherlands staying neutral, stung by Churchill's BBC broadcast of 20 January 1940 which had urged the neutral states to join the Anglo-French alliance. While he struck a high moral tone in relation to bolshevism, this merely reflected the views of many Dutch men and women who regarded Communism as a scourge worse even than Nazism. By stressing the need to keep The Netherlands free to trade, he was also fulfilling the wishes of the majority who realised that the well-being of the Dutch economy required stability and independence – freedoms which had been traditional aims stretching back for centuries. Whatever van Kleffens might have said for public consumption at home, this could not hide some inherent hypocrisy in the Dutch position. The British Foreign Office was certainly unimpressed by the Dutch attitude, especially after the invasion scare of November 1939, and the complaints made about Churchill's comments. Reporting the Dutch reaction to the latter, Minister Plenipotentiary Nevile Bland noted:

> Strict neutrality remains as strongly as ever the keystone, although it may one day become a millstone, for Dutch foreign policy. It seems to be regarded as a panacea for all ills, and as the best weapon for sterilising the German invasion bogey. Although the great majority of Dutchmen realise in their heart of hearts where their true interests are placed in an emergency and on which side their sympathies lie, years of uninterrupted peace and the intense desire for personal gain have had the effect of making many people in this country close their eyes instinctively to the realities of an unpleasant prospect. And whenever the spectre of war appears to get nearer it is always the neutrality drug which is taken out of the cupboard to give confidence and lull the nation into a sense of security.[29]

Whatever Whitehall may have thought, continued Dutch adherence to strict neutrality was not designed primarily to annoy Britain, nor was it based on traditional, and perhaps outmoded, objectives, but rather on a pragmatic assessment of The Netherlands' contemporary international position and an accurate reflection of the opinion, not only of the ruling élite, but also of large sections of the population. Such a groundswell of opinion, whether based on economic self-interest, visions of international

[29] Nevile Bland to Lord Halifax, 29 January 1940, PRO FO837/541 (C2007/1046/29).

morality, or just an inability to envisage alternatives, was ignored by Dutch foreign ministers and cabinets at their peril.

In the post-war Netherlands, the history of the 1930s, both diplomatic and domestic, became bound up with the history of the occupation period. Many general works and monographs saw the 1930s merely as an introductory phase to the war, the most notable being Louis de Jong's fourteen-volume history of The Netherlands in the Second World War, which attempted to cover every aspect of the war as it affected the country and its colonial empire. Consequently, there are detailed examinations of the policy of neutrality and its execution before May 1940 as well as an in-depth study of Dutch defence and security policy. Like many other authors on the pre-war Netherlands, De Jong implicitly criticises the conservative character of the Dutch political system and condemns neutrality as 'a policy of make believe',[30] concluding that The Netherlands effectively lost the war in the 1920s and 1930s, having neither the capacity nor the structures, nor the manpower, nor the resources, nor the mentality necessary for stubborn defence.[31] At the same time, his writing does reinforce two existing trends in Dutch historiography of the Second World War. The first of these trends is to see the occupation as a separate period, largely unconnected with what went before, or with what came after. Thus, his introductory sections tend to concentrate on issues of importance to a study of the war period, rather than dealing with the pre-war era in its own right. Although the advantage of hindsight is not used excessively, this separation remains implicit in the structuring of the first two volumes of his work. The second trend is of much greater importance, namely to see behaviour patterns in the immediate pre-war and wartime periods in terms of *goed en fout*.[32] In essence, this involves an interpretation of the occupation in terms of what was either beneficial or detrimental for The Netherlands as a whole. For the study of topics such as resistance or collaboration, this might be regarded as appropriate (albeit not uncontentious), but becomes more problematic when applied to 'grey areas'. Moreover, it leads to the danger of trying

[30] Madelon de Keizer, 'Dutch Neutrality in the Thirties: Voluntary or Imposed?', in L. E. Roulet (ed.), *Les Etats Neutres Européens et la Seconde Guerre Mondiale* (Neuchatel, 1985) 178–9.

[31] Louis de Jong, *Het Koninkrijk der Nederland in de Tweede Wereldoorlog.*, vol. III, May 1940 ('s-Gravenhogg 1970), 509.

[32] For a detailed commentary on this tendency in Dutch historiography, see J. C. H. Blom, 'In de ban van goed en fout', in G. Abma, Y. Kuiper, and J. Rypkema (eds.), *Tussen Goed en Fout. Nieuwe Gezichtspunten in de Geschiedschrijving, 1940–45* (Franeker, 1986). A review of some of the relevant literature also appears in B. Moore, 'Occupation, Collaboration and Resistance: Some Recent Publications on the Netherlands during the Second World War', *European History Quarterly*, 21 (1991), 109–18.

to judge all behaviour, both before and during the war, on the basis of these two categorisations.

De Jong's work undoubtedly reinforced the picture of the pre-war Dutch administration as less than capable of dealing with the crisis of the later 1930s. Moreover, the 'official' nature of this history, its sheer size and its widespread popularity with the public made it *the* authority on every aspect of the occupation and therefore difficult to challenge. In effect, interpretations of Dutch pre-war policy, at least for a time, dragged along in the wake of *goed en fout*, before being liberated by the reaction to De Jong's work in the later 1970s. This took two forms. One was a rejection of his methodology by historians anxious to analyse the continuities in Dutch society between the pre-war and post-war periods, rather than the uniqueness of the occupation.[33] The other was a reappraisal by Dutch diplomatic historians of their country's policy in the inter-war years.

A critique of de Jong came from von der Dunk, who argued that the question of preparedness for a future war was only of secondary importance. While the conservatism and naïvety of Dutch governments undoubtedly played a role, they genuinely believed that there was no real alternative available to them. Thus, however imperfect it may have been, continued adherence to neutrality remained the best possible option in the 1930s. Moreover, the belief in neutrality was so deeply rooted in the Dutch mentality that it prevented any government from changing its line. Von der Dunk argues that the long-standing commitment to a neutral stance meant that The Netherlands had to show its faith in the credibility of such a policy, as any preparations for war would have been seen as signalling a lack of real commitment.[34] This critique from the domestic perspective provided a necessary counterweight to de Jong, but in the field of diplomatic history there were also new initiatives.

While the study of Dutch foreign policy in its own right did not cease altogether after 1945, scholars and contemporary commentators tended to be more preoccupied with the loss of empire. In the 1970s, attention was refocused on Dutch foreign affairs in the post-war world, with four discrete lines of enquiry. These were a reappraisal of the continuities in Dutch foreign policy from the nineteenth century to the present, most

[33] For an analysis of this, see J. C. H. Blom, *Crisis Bezetting en Herstel: Tien Studies over Nederland, 1930–1950* (The Hague, 1989), 102–20.

[34] H. W. von der Dunk, 'Negentienveertig. Van Neutralism naar Nazi-heerschappij', in C. B. Wels, G. A. M. Beekelaar and J. C. H. Blom (eds.), *Vaderlands Verleden in Veelvoud* (The Hague, 1980), 311–36; De Keizer, 'Dutch Neutrality', 179–80.

notably by Wels;[35] a detailed examination of the restructuring of the machinery of foreign policy during the Second World War by Kersten;[36] the study of post-war policy formation synthesised by Voorhoeve;[37] and increasing attention to the role of The Netherlands in post-war European integration.[38]

These new approaches to the subject allowed a further reappraisal of pre-war Dutch policy. Voorhoeve argued that the reasons for the Dutch clinging to the policy of neutrality in the 1930s rested on six contentions. The first was that the Dutch were unaware of the German intention to break up the European equilibrium, and thus destroy the international balance which allowed The Netherlands to stay neutral.[39] This is undoubtedly the least convincing of the contentions. If Dutch decision-makers had been inclined to assume that no state would risk leading the continent into another conflict after 1918, the war scare of January 1939 and the German march into Prague some two months later should have been enough to enlighten them.[40] Where this idea may have more validity is in explaining the mentality of the Dutch public at large. Many did not want to believe in the aggressive intent of their German neighbour *towards them*. Even if Hitler had designs on eastern Europe, or even Belgium and France, was it not possible that The Netherlands might be able to stay out of the fray, as it had done in the First World War? The outbreak of war in September 1939, far from shaking this confidence, if anything, seemed to reinforce it.[41]

This links in with the second contention, namely that the policy of neutrality conformed to the 'spirit of the age' in The Netherlands. The climate was one of pacifism, idealism, and a belief in international goodwill and the traditions of diplomacy. Pacifism was certainly as popular in The Netherlands as it had been in Britain and France, and the same might have been said about support for the League of Nations. Even if the Dutch government had believed wholeheartedly in the aggressive intent

35 Wels, *Aloofness and Neutrality*, 29–96.

36 A. E. Kersten, *Buitenlandse Zaken in ballingschap: Groei en verandering van een ministerie, 1940–45* (Alphen a/d Rijn, 1981).

37 J. J. C. Voorhoeve, *Peace, Profits and Principles. A Study of Dutch Foreign Policy* (The Hague, 1979).

38 While there are many works which examine the post-war development of Benelux and the European Economic Community, Ger van Roon, *Small States in Years of Depression. The Oslo Alliance 1930–1940* (Assen, 1989, translated from Dutch, 1985), looks explicitly at the pre-war antecedents of European unity.

39 Voorhoeve, *Peace*, 37.

40 Wels, *Aloofness and Neutrality*, 80.

41 Wels, *Aloofness and Neutrality*, 82, cites H. Daalder, 'Nederland en de Wereld, 1935–1945', *Tijdschrift voor Geschiedenis*, 66 (1953), 170–200.

of its German neighbour, the problem would have been to convince the population that a change was both desirable and necessary. Indeed, the few changes which were made took the opposite direction and involved further retreats into total neutrality, such as abrogating article 16 of the League covenant after the Abyssinian crisis.

To some extent, the Dutch were trapped by their own justification for continued neutrality. Until the First World War, neutrality had been a pragmatic response to the geographical and economic position of the country. During and after the war, the policy was elevated to the status of a God-given mission, becoming almost a part of the *raison d'être* of the Dutch state.[42] Even allowing for the fact that upgrading of neutrality to some sort of holy grail was partly just an extenuation for the practical advantages which neutrality gave to The Netherlands, it nevertheless made it almost impossible for any later Dutch government to try to alter this perception in the public mind. A vivid illustration of this came in 1940, with the adverse reaction to Churchill's radio broadcast.[43]

In these first three contentions, Voorhoeve rightly concentrated on the limitations which public opinion placed on the ability of the Dutch government to react to the changing European diplomatic scene in the later 1930s. Yet even if we ignore both the effect which public opinion had on Dutch policy, and the presumed lack of realism on the part of Dutch politicians and their inability to see the coming storm, we are still left with the question, what else could the government have done?[44]

Undoubtedly the options were very limited, as Voorhoeve's remaining three contentions demonstrate. First of all, it could be argued that there really was no other policy available. There had been some limited government discussion about The Netherlands involving itself in a system of guarantees in the later 1930s, but this had effectively been ruled out.[45] Any approach to Britain and France was likely to be seized upon by the Germans as an aggressive and unfriendly act, and this would add to friction over border incidents and refugees which the Nazis had already provoked.[46] Moreover, it was apparent that in the event of German

[42] Wels, *Aloofness and Neutrality*, 81–2.

[43] M. Gilbert, *Winston S. Churchill*, vol. VI (London, 1983), 136. Nevile Bland to Lord Halifax no. 154, 6 March 1940, PRO FO432/6 (C3725/1046/27).

[44] A. F. Manning, 'Nederland en het buitenland 1918–1940', in D. P. Blok, W. Prevenier, and D. J. Roorden, *et al.* (eds.), *Algemene Geschiedenis der Nederlanden*, vol. XIV: *Nederland en België, 1914–1940* (Haarlem: Fibula-van Dishoeck, 1979), 364, 'Dutch foreign policy was far from grandiose, but was there really an alternative?.'

[45] Wels, *Aloofness and Neutrality*, 82.

[46] A. F. Manning, 'Nederland en het buitenland 1918–1940', 361–2. Wels, *Aloofness and Neutrality*, 82.

aggression, the Western Powers could provide little immediate material help to counteract a direct German assault on Dutch territory. The alternative, some form of understanding with Germany, would have run counter to the trend of worsening Dutch–German relations, and also counter to majority public opinion, which had little sympathy for Nazism or the Hitler regime.

A change in The Netherlands' diplomatic and alliance policy would also have entailed a change in military policy. Yet as Voorhoeve and others have pointed out, no realistic amount of military spending could have enabled the country to withstand the Germans for long. At a time of economic depression and innumerable calls on the Dutch exchequer, there were bound to be objections to increased defence spending, based partly on moral grounds, and partly on the view that there were other priorities to be considered first. Even those politicians who had no objections to increases in the defence budget often regarded these as necessary in terms of colonial defence and security rather than in European terms.

Defence planning for the kingdom in Europe was predicated on the eventual arrival of outside help. The inevitable lack of manpower and resources in a small country necessitated a defensive strategy which minimised these disadvantages and maximised the natural advantages of the Dutch terrain. The plans of the Dutch general staff involved flooding certain areas to form a barrier against advancing armies and then retiring behind this 'Fortress Holland' and holding out for as long as possible. The fact that the Dutch general staff accepted that they would be fighting alongside the French, Belgians, and British at some point made it seem more logical to outside observers for them to open contacts with their counterparts, but official attempts by the British and French to foster such collaboration came to nothing and were shunned by the Dutch cabinet in 1939 and again in 1940.[47] At a military level some contacts were maintained, but without the knowledge of cabinet ministers, and planning inevitably remained *ad hoc*. In the end, the Dutch armed forces were tied to the secret plans lodged in Brussels, Paris, and London which were to be opened only if Dutch territory was violated. It is intriguing to note that the post-war investigation into the conduct of Dutch ministers and civil servants contented itself with ensuring that the policy of neutrality had been scrupulously carried out before the German

[47] Donald Cameron Watt, *How War Came 1938–39: The Immediate Origins of the Second World War* (London, 1989), 563. De Jong, *Het Koninkrijk*, II, 27–30.

invasion rather than enquiring whether the policy itself had been appropriate.[48]

The greater depth of analysis by Dutch international historians of their country's foreign policy prior to May 1940, while not producing uniform conclusions, has nevertheless shown a tendency to reflect the traditional views of Dutch policy-making as a whole. While Vandenbosch shows a degree of sympathy for the policy-makers of the 1930s, Wels makes the point that there really had not been a policy before May 1940, more a faith or a hope.[49] Voorhoeve goes even further. Commenting on the loss of the East Indies in 1941–2, he says, 'again, a lack of foresight into world politics, wishful thinking and the absence of a strong will to defend one's position led to disaster'.[50] The 'again' provides an implicit reference to the events of 1939 and 1940 in Europe, and acts as a condemnation of the policies adopted not just by the de Geer cabinet after August 1939, but by successive Dutch governments in the inter-war period.

These judgements, based as they are on detailed analysis of Dutch foreign policy, are in many cases harsher that those passed by the British and other outside contemporary observers. Nevertheless, they do highlight many of the problems for the Dutch in the later 1930s. In the short term, there was very little room for manoeuvre. Policies were too firmly entrenched and alterations would have required not only an act of will but also a massive reorientation of priorities and totally unreasonable financial commitments. Thus it could be argued that in the crises of 1939 and 1940 there was little more the Dutch government in The Hague could have done besides what it actually did. This, however, prompts the question of why they found themselves in this position in the first place. Could there have been a different long-term strategy which would have increased the options available when the crisis arose?

In the first instance, such a hypothesis requires a belief that the existing policy was in some way faulty or restrictive, yet successive governments had looked on neutrality as the best way of maintaining The Netherlands' international security. The country's inability to compete either militarily or economically with the major powers of the twentieth century was offset by the assumption of a mediating and balancing role in Europe and a colonial role in the East and West Indies. This relative isolation did not require formal treaties with neighbouring states beyond the regulation of

[48] Enquêtecommissie Regeringsbeleid 1940–1945 *Verslag houdende de uitkomsten van het onderzoek*, 8 vols. (The Hague, 1949–56), especially vol. IIa, 14–33.

[49] Wels, 'Foreign Relations', 98. [50] Voorhoeve, *Peace*, 38.

normal frontier relations, or indeed anything other than a general affiliation to the international security system of the League of Nations. Close military cooperation in the 1920s with neighbouring states would have involved a relationship with Belgium, a tall order in itself given the animosity between the two states. Moreover, against whom was this cooperation to be directed? While the future could not be guaranteed, post-Versailles Germany presented very little in the way of a threat and the belligerence of the Belgians and French over the Ruhr made it doubly important that the Dutch did not choose sides. Even if one takes the long-term view, there seem to have been few reasons for the Dutch to change their policy direction, and it is difficult to see where they might have been negligent.

More recent research has concentrated not so much on the details of foreign policy, which have been well documented, but on some important long-term domestic factors which had a bearing on Dutch foreign relations in the inter-war period, namely public opinion, defence, and colonial policy. In some respects, the debate has shifted away from external to internal factors in an attempt to understand the fundamental determinants of neutrality prior to 1940. Prime examples can be found in more recent work by von der Dunk and Blom. Von der Dunk takes the traditional view of Dutch foreign policy as his starting point, in other words that the 1930s were the decade of shortsightedness, bad decisions, lost chances, illusions, and defeatism. He notes that the traditions of neutrality have received a great deal of attention, but not how these were interrelated with public opinion. Specifically, he links the popular support for neutrality to the traditionally un-military character of The Netherlands. While the antimilitarism of pacifists and the Left did play its part in the 1930s, it was seen as dangerous utopianism by those in power. More nebulous, but perhaps far more prevalent, was the ambiguous attitude which the Dutch population had towards its armed forces. Part of this might be traced to a general dislike of spending money on defence, but the roots of the problem are seen to go much deeper. While the army was regarded as a necessary evil, each of the major political groupings had a different view of what its structure and organisation ought to be. Part of this stemmed from the traditions of the Dutch republic against centralism and monarchy, but even after 1918 Conservatives and Liberals continued to disagree about the army's organisation and the Liberals were also keen to make economies in the defence budget. Anti-revolutionary Protestants saw the army as a force of law and order and as a symbol of defence against evil and Papism, whereas Catholics found it hard to come to terms with a body which had traditionally been used against their religion and its supporters.

Only the Social Democrats and Communists had a clear line against the military in the 1930s, and even this was watered down as Dutch social democracy moved more into the mainstream of 'respectable' politics.

If the army could not compete with those of neighbouring countries, then questions arose as to how strong or how symbolic the armed forces should be, and how much attention should be paid to their views on national security. Von der Dunk comes to the conclusion that even better intelligence on German intentions and closer alliances with their Western neighbours were unlikely to have made much difference in May 1940. Nevertheless, there was an aversion to allowing the armed forces to dictate policy, combined with a tendency to give priority to domestic questions. While there was undoubtedly a sense of weakness, the politicians felt that they could delegate or defer important decisions about national security because the geographical position of the country might afford a degree of protection.[51] While acknowledging that much research still needs to be done in this field, von der Dunk has at least opened up a new area of enquiry into the relationship between politicians, defence, and foreign policy.

Blom takes a different approach, concentrating on the defence policy of The Netherlands, but looking at the influence of foreign policy, economic factors and the 'spirit of the nation' upon that policy in the inter-war years. His conclusion mirrors those of Manning:[52] 'there was no alternative, no-one sought an alternative and there were perfectly reasonable (and some less reasonable) arguments for this standpoint'.[53] The military and the politicians realised only too well that the army and navy could not defend the country for long, and even in the nineteenth century policy had been based around the idea of help from allies. Thus in the 1930s, strategy was based on defending 'Fortress Holland' and other fortified lines for as long as it took for help to arrive. While this was a rational plan to adopt, it did have drawbacks. Neutrality meant not having any formal contacts with potential allies. Clandestine discussions between the Dutch general staff and their neighbours had to take place without the knowledge of the cabinet, and also held many risks for the Dutch in their relationship with Germany.[54]

[51] H. W. von der Dunk, 'Neutralisme en Defensie: het dilemma in de jaren dertig', in G. Teitler (ed.), *Tussen Crisis en Oorlog: Maatschappij en Krijgsmacht in de jaren dertig* (Dieren, 1984), 21.

[52] A. F. Manning, 'Nederland en het Buitenland', 364.

[53] J. C. H. Blom, '"Durch kamen sie doch." Het Nederlands defensiebeleid in de jaren dertig opnieuw beschouwd', in G. Teitler (ed.), *Tussen Crisis en Oorlog*, 118–19.

[54] Ibid., 119–20.

Blom's research also suggests that, in spite of incomplete and in some cases unreliable data, the general view that inter-war governments neglected defence spending needs some revision. International comparison shows that The Netherlands spent as much per head as many other countries in the period from 1928 to 1930, and increased its expenditure from the mid-1930s in response to the worsening international situation. This is perhaps even more remarkable when the depth of the economic crisis in The Netherlands and its persistence into the later years of the decade are taken into account.[55] Finally, there is the question of the 'spirit of the nation'. Blom takes issue with the assumption that anti-militarism, if not the sole cause of Dutch defeat in 1940, was the main reason for the rapidity of the defeat.[56] Instead Blom points to organisations in the 1930s which supported the armed forces and claims that these were equally influential, if not more so, than those of the anti-militarists. Although this remains a difficult area for concrete conclusions, it seems that the 'spirit of the nation' in The Netherlands was little different from that of countries elsewhere in Europe.[57] In emphasising these factors, Blom reinforces the picture of powerlessness of inter-war Dutch governments, both in the short and in the long term. If there was no neglect of defence spending, nor any particular Dutch phenomenon of anti-militarism or unmilitarism, were the pursuit of neutrality and the defeat in 1940 merely the results of a country being too small to defend itself in the modern era?

Before leaving this topic, it is worth stressing two further considerations which are almost unspoken realities in foreign policy-making, namely economic relations and the question of imperial defence. The first of these factors centred on the vexed question of how to deal with a powerful and increasingly unreliable neighbour whose trading accounted for a substantial proportion of Dutch imports and exports.[58] As de Keizer

[55] Ibid., 122–3. It is also pointed out that there is a good deal of defence spending 'hidden' in the budget of the Netherlands Indies which remains outside the quoted figures.

[56] J. J. Bout, 'The Nature and Extent of Anti-Militarism in the Netherlands from 1918–1940 and the Degree to Which They Contributed to the Quick Defeat in May 1940' (PhD, University of British Columbia, 1975), cited in Blom, 'Het Nederlands defensiebeleid,' 125.

[57] Ibid., 125–7.

[58] See, for example, H. M. Hirschfeld, *Herinneringen uit de jaren 1933–39* (Amsterdam/Brussels, 1959), 196, who cites his report to the Minister of Economic Affairs and M. P. L. Steenberghe, 9 April 1935, which quotes Dutch exports to Germany at 21.5 per cent and imports from Germany at 31.3 per cent. It is also worth noting that more than half of Dutch exports to Germany between 1923 and 1938 were of agricultural produce. De Keizer, 'Dutch Neutrality', 186. For even more recent analyses, see Johannes Houwink ten Cate, *'De mannen van de daad' en Duitsland, 1919–1939. Het Hollandse zakenleven en de vooroorlogse buitenlandse politiek* (The Hague, 1995) and Madelon de Keizer, *Appeasement en aanpassing. Het Nederlandse bedrijfsleven en de Deutsch-Niederländische Gesellschaft 1936–1942* (The Hague, 1984).

points out, all Dutch governments were aware of the need to maintain cooperation and acceptable working relations with Germany.[59] Any attempt by the League of Nations to apply sanctions would have had severe ramifications for the Dutch, and this goes a long way towards explaining their abrogation of article 16 of the League Covenant in 1936. In spite of Germany's increasing espousal of economic autarky, its 'stranglehold'[60] over The Netherlands did not really diminish in the later 1930s, and continued to exert an enormous influence on all Dutch cabinets. Dutch neutrality was not a blind adherence to a policy rooted in tradition, but a pragmatic response to the realities of The Netherlands' international economic position.

The second consideration, imperial defence, has received less attention but was a crucial element in the formulation of a global foreign policy. By the 1930s, the Japanese threat to the East Indies was becoming increasingly apparent, as was the ideological and economic penetration of the United States into both the East and West Indies. In trying to deal with the former, the Dutch had to consider what if any alliances were necessary to assist in imperial defence. In other words, the construction of Dutch foreign policy went way beyond the consideration of protecting the kingdom in Europe.

One explanation for the apparently different justifications for pursuing a policy of neutrality put forward by the Dutch in the 1930s has been suggested by Porter. He argues that the policy itself was never a coherent one, but was driven by two separate elements within government circles. Firstly, there were the 'idealists' who felt that international survival was best guaranteed by a strict adherence to the principles of neutrality. Secondly, there were the 'pragmatists' who saw neutrality as the best compromise, especially to protect the country's economic interests.[61] Indeed, his characterisation of this neutrality as a bifurcated policy, with no single government department in charge of all its ramifications, may

[59] The whole question of Dutch economic dependence on Germany and its effects on foreign policy was first explored in H. Lademacher, 'Niederlande Zwischen wirschaftlichem Zwang und politischer Entscheidungsfreiheit', in E. Fondran (ed.), *Innen- und Aussenpolitik unter nationalsozialistischer Bedrohung. Determinanten internationaler Beziehungen in historischen Fallstudien* (Opladen, 1977), cited in de Keizer, 'Dutch Neutrality', 177–8. More recently, Dutch commercial relations with western Europe in the inter-war period have been examined in H. Klemann, *Tussen Reich en Empire: De Economische Betrekkingen van Nederland met zijn Belangrijkste Handelspartners: Duitsland, Groot-Brittanniëen België en de Nederlandse Handelspolitiek, 1929–36* (Amsterdam, 1990).

[60] De Keizer, 'Dutch Neutrality', 189.

[61] J. J. Porter, *Dutch Neutrality in Two World Wars* (Ann Arbor, 1983), vi, cited in De Keizer, 'Dutch Neutrality', 191–2.

well help to explain the mixed messages which were sometimes picked up by other governments in western Europe.

A different interpretation questions whether The Netherlands was truly neutral in the inter-war period at all.[62] It has been argued that there was a good deal of Dutch support for a revision of the international order and the Treaty of Versailles on which it was based. This emanated partly from sympathy for Germany, and partly from the view that the existing system itself was a threat to long-term international security. Moreover, even Colijn accepted that if a European war led to a German occupation of The Netherlands on strategic grounds, the Dutch would be able to call on British help in spite of London's refusal to make any formal arrangements. What von der Dunk has called 'pseudo-neutralism' could also be seen in Colijn's attempts to engineer some Anglo-Dutch co-operation on defence in the Far East.[63]

In conclusion, it should be stressed that this cannot claim to be a comprehensive survey of the available literature. Attention has been focused on a few of the more important interpretative books and articles on the subject. Although Dutch historians have themselves been very critical of the course pursued in the 1930s, revisions and reinterpretations have occurred in the last twenty years which cast some doubt on this orthodoxy. Recent research makes it clear that Dutch neutrality in the inter-war years was not based on the 'posture of an ostrich', deaf and blind to the threat from a resurgent Nazi Germany, but on a rational appraisal of The Netherlands' position in the world. Moreover, it was not entirely a static and traditionally based policy, but was also adapted, within defined limits, to meet the changing needs of Dutch security in the inter-war years.

[62] R. van Diepen, '"Schuldige mannen?" Neville Chamberlain, Hendrikus Colijn en de Duitse dreiging, 1933–1938', *Tijdschrift voor Geschiedenis*, III/1 (1998), 3–17.

[63] Van Diepen, 'Schuldige mannen?', 14–15, cites von der Dunk, 'Neutralisme', 21 and Bob de Graaff, 'Colijn: premier in de buitenlandse politiek', in D. A. Hellema, C. Wiebes, and B. Zeeman (eds.), *Jaarboek buitenlandse zaken 1994* (The Hague, 1994), 31–55 esp. 35.

CHAPTER 4

# *Belgium: fragile neutrality, solid neutralism*

*Alain Colignon*

In the course of 1936, the apparent return of Belgium to a policy of so-called 'independence' (in fact, neutrality) was the reason for much comment in chancelleries and stimulated considerable controversy in the press. This policy appeared to have major implications for the balance of power in Europe, a fragile equilibrium liable to be shattered by the diplomatic game to which the great western European states had entrusted their fate.

The German invasion on 10 May 1940, followed by the rapid military collapse and dissolution of the institutions, should have put an end to the public careers of those who had conceived and then assumed responsibility for this policy. Nevertheless, its main protagonists, although (or perhaps because) they were divided concerning both their ends and their means, managed to re-emerge – some in the very short term – in occupied Belgium. And others, in the relatively long-term and after many ups and downs, surfaced again in a country which had been liberated by the Allied armies.

Needless to say, the propagandists and historians continued to write long after the events, either to attack or defend this policy, or to try to understand and explain it. The time for anathemas now seems to be past. In this chapter I will not attempt to describe for the umpteenth time the course of events in these brief pages: other historians have taken care of that well before me.[1] What I will merely try to do is to

[1] The first 'historical' approach to the policy of neutrality seems to be that of J. Wullus-Rudiger, *La défense de la Belgique en 1940* (Villeneuve-sur-Lot, 1940). Destined for 'chancelleries, universities, military colleges, and national libraries', this work was written in the summer of 1940. The author, a French-speaker from Flanders, returned to the subject in 1945 with a more thorough study, *La Belgique et la crise européenne. 1914–1945* (2 vols Brussels, 1945). These publications, like those that followed, resort to history with a decidedly apologetic goal; they look to justify the validity of Belgian policy and are the accounts of personalities attached to the French-speaking establishment (Pierre Van Zuylen, the Ambassador Davignon, Count Capelle, General Van Overstraeten). The Flemish version of these facts was for a long time expressed *mezzo voce*. The most detailed

show that neutrality resulted to a differing degree from a combination of external factors and internal factors, the latter being partly linked to the former.

Belgian neutrality, as it existed from autumn 1936 to the month of May 1940, is a historical fact. It is men who, having designed it, endowed it with a particular content, with the result known by all. 'Fatality' has probably less to do with it than the tactical stance of individuals or collective groups linked to a certain vision of the world, or a certain understanding of interests they judged to be vital.

## DEEP-ROOTED NEUTRALISM

Both jurists and historians fix the starting point of Belgium's status of neutrality to 20 January 1831, that is, during the first months of 'national' independence.[2] Did not the Protocol of separation from the Kingdom of The Netherlands concocted at the time under the auspices of the great European Powers stipulate in article 5: 'Belgium ... will constitute a

work for many years was that of Omer De Raeymaeker, *België's International Beleid, 1919–1939* (Brussel/Antwerpen/Leuven/Gent, 1945). An historical account apparently more detached from the political context probably started with the article by Jacques Willequet entitled 'Regards sur la politique belge d'indépendance 1936–1940', published in the *Revue d'Histoire de la Deuxième Guerre Mondiale.* It was followed in 1960 by other different contributions in the May issue of *Revue générale belge.* It was still a very factual approach to the controversy, however, with an argument based on political or military considerations in the straight sense. With the extensive research that prolonged the finalising of his doctorate, 'Les avertissements qui venaient de Berlin *(9 octobre 1939–10 mai 1940)*' (Brussels, 1977), Jean Vanwelkenhuyzen seemed to situate himself in this historiographic strain, with a decidedly pro-Belgian and Francophone bias. The same opinion had another opportunity to be heard at an international symposium held in Neuchatel and Berne in 1985: 'La neutralité du Pays-Bas, du Luxembourg et de la Belgique pendant la "drôle de guerre"', in L. E. Roulet (ed.), *Les Etats Neutres Européens et la Seconde Guerre Mondiale* (Neuchatel, 1985), 195–206. But it was perhaps its last moment. On the other hand, *L'an 40. La Belgique occupée* by José Gotovitch and Jules Gérard-Libois marked a complete change in the study of the question. Published in Brussels in 1971, the book tried to describe the successive postures adopted by the different ideological families of the country during the period 1936–40. It cast a more forthright light on the game played by the different pressure groups and does not worry about defending any given policy, or individual. This founding work remains a standard reference. From the Dutch-speaking side, we have witnessed an increase in scientific production as from the seventies, after Jan Dhondt expressed his scouring analyses in a synthesised form in *Bulletin critique d'histoire de Belgique 1968–1969* (1970). For the latest bibliographical works see C. Koninckx, *Léopold III. Roi et Diplomate. La politique étrangère belge et les initiatives de paix pendant l'entre-deux-guerres 1934–1940* (Anvers, 1997), 255–70. See also the conference proceedings published under the auspices of the Centre de Recherches et d'études historiques de la Deuxième Guerre Mondiale, *1940. Belgique, une société en crise, un pays en guerre* (Brussels, 1991).

[2] Article 9 of the Treaty of the XVIII Articles thus specified the international status of the young state: 'The Five Powers, without wishing to interfere with the internal regime of Belgium [*sic*], guarantee her this perpetual neutrality, as well as the integrity and inviolability of her territory in the limits mentioned in the present article.'

perpetually neutral state. The five Powers guarantee her this perpetual neutrality, as well as the integrity and inviolability of her territory'? The article had been 'suggested' by Lord Palmerston, the British foreign secretary, who would not stand for the new state, barely born, falling one way or another into the French sphere of influence. In Brussels, the deputies of the National Congress, hastily assembled to bestow the country with a constitution, vigorously protested against this statute imposed from abroad, 'without the consent of the national representation', though to no avail. Neutrality survived the upheaval of the period, through a military defeat, from the treaty of the XVIII Articles (26 June 1831) to that of the XXIV Articles (19 April 1839).[3] It had nevertheless given rise to discussions, as bitter as they were futile, among the deputies, newcomers to the rostrum who were ready to invoke the sovereign right of peoples to determine their own future. The arguments developed on this occasion by the supporters and opponents of neutrality had, with the help of circumstances, conserved a slight air of topicality a century later, when neutral Belgium worriedly observed developments in the Phoney War. In fact, even by 1831 a certain Mr Lecocq congratulated himself on putting neutrality into practice, explaining crudely:

> What a rich and seductive perspective . . . with Belgium neutral and respected, between the belligerent armies of England, Germany and France. Belgium, so productive, due to circumstances was turning into the general store of provisions; supplying everyone, receiving from all quarters and, despite the storm raging on its borders, enjoying the bliss of a period of tranquillity and peace.[4]

Others rejected the principle no less vehemently. Thus, Eugène Defacqz:

> Besides, what is this neutrality? A brake, yes, but for you who are weak . . . But for your powerful neighbours, it is a vain word, a useless convention in peace, derisory in war; for, when war comes, each will violate your neutral territory as often as their military manoeuvres deem it necessary.

It was quite well considered. In any case, neutrality was grudgingly accepted, together with the rest of the international conventions. Belgium's political decision-makers had no choice, however, as geopolitical necessities linked to the European order demanded such a position. As often happens, the Belgian leaders did not take long to make a virtue out

[3] The latter reaffirmed in Article 7: 'Belgium . . . will form an independent and perpetually neutral state. She will be obliged to observe this neutrality towards all states.' On this matter see: A. De Ridder, *Histoire diplomatique du traité de 1839* (Brussels/Paris, 1920) and F. De Lannoy, *Histoire diplomatique de l'indépendance belge* (Brussels, 1930).

[4] Quotes extracted from E. Banning, *Les origines et les phases de la neutralité belge* (Brussels, 1927), 47.

of necessity when they realised that it would grant them vast room for manoeuvre if they used it at the right time. The consequent reductions in the military budget, justified by the adoption of neutrality, were welcomed by all, for from now on Europe became the guarantor for the young kingdom. As from 1840, King Leopold I could state that 'to maintain a sincere, loyal and strong neutrality should be our constant goal.' His minister to Paris, Count Charles Le Hon, declared at the same time: 'Perpetual neutrality was not at first to our taste, but Europe imposed it on us in absolute terms as a condition for our independence, and since then we have openly accepted it, unreservedly.'[5]

The Belgians had the chance to appreciate the convenience of their international position during the Franco-Prussian war of 1870–1. They attributed to it the merit of not being pulled into the conflict, without wondering too much as to whether they had not benefited from an exceptional balance of power in the 1830s and which, as a result, was unlikely to happen again. From then on, the parties in power – and above all the Christian family, which was continually involved in state affairs from 1884 to 1914 – raised neutrality to the status of an article of faith. Charles Woeste, the all-powerful spokesman of the Catholic Right, considered that neutrality was 'the national solution to the Belgian question ... A restricted country surrounded by powerful rivals, devoid of frontiers, forming a barrier, neutrality (was) ... the best patriotic formula.'[6]

The eruption of the Kaiser's regiments in August 1914 was going to give this keystone of European international law a testing time. Its violation turned out to be an excellent propaganda weapon in the hands of the Entente. For the rest, embarked on a conflict that it had not wished to see approaching and for which it was badly prepared, official Belgium clung for a long time, too long, to what was no longer anything more than juridical fiction. Rejecting the hard-line policy, King Albert I still confided in a letter to his Bavarian brother-in-law, Count Toerring, on 30 October 1915, that neutrality remained in his opinion 'the principle inscribed by the Powers at the very base of our national structure ... It was not only the origin but also the very condition of our existence as a nation.' The prolonging of the war and its increasing violence made the leaders realise the futility of their efforts. In July 1916 the Belgian government decided to send a memorandum to the Western Powers in which it was stated that 'the Belgians were unanimous in no longer desiring a conventional neutrality' which henceforth was considered as a

[5] Quoted by R. Devleeshouwer, *Les Belges et le danger de guerre 1910–1914* (Paris/Louvain, 1958), 19.
[6] C. Woeste, *La neutralité de la Belgique doit-elle être maintenue?* (Brussels, 1919), 23.

'weakening of their sovereignty'. Subsequently, a statute was demanded in its place establishing 'absolute independence', 'with no obligation on our part towards anyone' (11 October 1917). Coming from a third-class military power, these demands were laughable. As the Under-Secretary of State to the British Foreign Office pointed out, with a touch of irritation, this demand, if fulfilled, would have eventually 'exempted Belgium from any obligations towards powers from whom they were requesting intervention for their defence'.[7]

After the signing of the Armistice on 11 November 1918, as Belgium found herself on the right side – that of the victors – hesitations and doubts were no longer the order of the day. The tone of the official speeches was considerably more categorical. Albert I had solemnly pronounced in his King's Speech on 22 November 1918: 'Victorious Belgium, emancipated from the neutrality imposed on her by treaties, the foundations of which were shattered by war, will now enjoy complete independence.' Paul Hymans, the liberal minister of foreign affairs, for his part affirmed that neutrality 'eliminated from the diplomatic civil-state', was dead and 'would not come back to life'. However, there were many ulterior motives both among the Catholic Right and the top diplomatic staff, where traditions and nostalgia were nurtured. No sooner had the desire for 'independence' been exhibited than Belgian diplomacy started the search for guarantors. They first consulted their old allies. The United Kingdom turned a deaf ear, much to its regret: in 1919 they feared complications concerning Belgium's designs in the Dutch Limburg. With no guarantees forthcoming from the Foreign Office, Belgium turned to France.

After long hard bargaining, the two parties eventually signed, on 7 September 1920, a 'Franco-Belgian defensive Military Agreement, in case of unprovoked German aggression'. This convention, insistently sought after by the French high command, had an undeniably defensive character. Directed against Germany, it responded to the wishes of the French-speaking establishment in general, and the enthusiastically pro-French liberals in particular. However, as far as its terms had not been made public (the arrangements agreed between military staffs remained secret), it contained a degree of ambiguity. Besides, the French tended to consider it as a real treaty of alliance, whereas their partners saw it as 'a purely technical arrangement, with no binding force'.[8]

[7] Quoted by F. Van Langenhove, *La Belgique en quête de sécurité 1920–1940* (Brussels, 1969), 10.

[8] For an analysis of its content see F. Van Langenhove, *L'élaboration de la politique étrangère de la Belgique entre les deux guerres mondiales* (Brussels, Académie royale de Belgique. Mémoires de la classe des Lettres, vol. LXV, 1980), 96 ff.

Then time passed. With the Treaty of Locarno, the new Belgian borders were guaranteed. In the late 1920s, European appeasement seemed to be on the right track. It is at about this time that Flemish circles began to express with some intensity their hostility towards this 'Military Agreement'. They willingly presented it as 'a kind of subterfuge disguising a secret alliance' (as Paul Hymans put it) which would transform the country into a satellite of the Third Republic. The vehemence of their accusations can perhaps be attributed to the fact that Flemish-speaking Flanders, at the time immersed in an economic, cultural, and demographic boom, had forged an identity by standing up against the Gallicised élite. Since the middle of the nineteenth century, Flanders, with its strong Catholic and rural roots,[9] had adopted the custom of opposing the French language, and showed little sympathy for the 'great principles' of 1789. They likened them to a deadly evil for traditional community solidarity, for a society where Authority lived happily alongside the Holy. Stemming from both the anti-modernist Right and the first Christian democracy, Flanders at that time combined romantic populism with acute anti-militarism. The latter allowed them periodically to join forces with the professed pacifism in the ranks of the socialist left. These internal political factors, combined with the loss of influence of the great democracies and their inability to maintain the European order as established in the treaties of 1919–20, would pull Belgium back into neutrality as surely as a river flows into the sea.

## POLICY OF INDEPENDENCE?

As from the autumn of 1930, faced with the rivalries and the impotence of the former Franco-British guarantors, King Albert had come to lament to his close friends the relinquishing of the statute of neutrality:

> If it [neutrality] had not existed we would have had to invent it. It has been of incalculable value to us. Without the cover of neutrality, the Great Powers would never have accepted our presence in the Congo . . .[10]

[9] Intellectually speaking, the weight of rural society had a more lasting influence over the Flemish population than their French-speaking Walloon counterparts, dispersed, from the second half of the nineteenth century, around the powerful industrial axis of Haine-Sambre-Meuse-Vesdre, from the French border to the German border. Moreover, for cultural reasons, the Walloon élite adhered mainly to the ideas of a laic society, in contrast to what happened in Flanders.

[10] General Van Overstraeten, *Albert Ier – Léopold III. Vingt ans de politique militaire belge 1920–1940* (Brussels, n.d.), 60.

In March 1931, after the withdrawal of the occupation forces from the Rhineland, the minister of foreign affairs re-evaluated and downgraded the obligations of the Franco-Belgian Military Agreement. Finally, in October 1934, a few months after the death of King Albert, his successor, Leopold III praised, in front of former combatants, the international situation of the country as it had been before 1914. At the time, the kingdom wanted to 'be free of all tutelage, and follow the tradition which granted us, during the eighty-four years of our independence, uninterrupted peace'.[11] Basically, King Leopold applied himself to following in the footsteps of Albert I.

This attitude on the part of the authorities was perhaps inspired by what was going on in the north of the country. A latent conflict of nationalities had been brewing for many years. It set the French-speaking minority – 2 or 3 per cent of the Flemish population, but situated in the upper echelons of society – against the Flemish-speaking elements of the middle classes and the petite bourgeoisie. The demise of suffrage based on property in 1893–4, and its replacement by a form of universal suffrage, had already struck a serious blow to Belgium's traditional establishment, dominated by influential French-speaking figures 'from Ostende to Arlon'. The coming into force of genuine universal suffrage (though limited even for males), the economic development of Flanders, and the implementation of legislation in favour of regional mono-lingualism would progressively sideline those who, in Flanders, shared the language of Voltaire. The beneficiaries of the operation belonged mainly to the Christian sphere of influence. Their spokesman, following the spirit of the system, opposed everything that came from France. Liberal democracy, stemming from the 'ideas of 1789', was no longer fashionable in these circles. A minority of this obscure group, which appeared after the tensions and splits of the First World War, could be qualified as Flemish Nationalists. It professed a profound hatred for the Belgian nation state, which it considered an instrument of oppression against the 'Flemish People'; during the 1930s, under the ensigns of the Vlaamsch Nationaal Verbond (VNV – Flemish National Federation), it slowly joined the family of European Fascist parties.

This multiform, diffuse, powerful anti-French opinion encouraged in the Flemish masses a strong antimilitarist sentiment, of both peasant and Christian origins. This anti-militarism was able to associate itself with

[11] C. Koninckx, *Léopold III roi et diplomate. La politique belge et les initiatives de paix pendant l'entre-deux-guerres 1934–1940* (Anvers, 1997).

the professed pacifism in the ranks of the laic Left. The militant wing of the Belgian workers' party was not up to the same standard.

As from the end of the 1920s, a first wave of recriminations against the Military Agreement with France made itself heard. In 1928, for example, the Catholic deputy De Bruyne had demanded 'protection against the south'. His socialist colleague Eeckelers for his part refused to recognise Germany as a danger (though the Weimar regime was still in existence) and went so far as to pronounce the following rash words: 'We will walk in front of the German with the bread and salt of fraternity.'

The initiatives undertaken by the Quai d'Orsay with a view to countering the desire for vengeance of the Reich by creating new adversaries on her eastern frontiers kindled fear among a good number of Belgian politicians, and not only in Flanders. The French minister Barthou, a staunch Liberal, had negotiated in May–June 1934 with the USSR an 'Eastern Pact', which was later to become the 'Franco-Soviet Pact' under the government of Laval (2 May 1935). In the Belgian kingdom, this defensive treaty, a pure product of *Realpolitik*, had disturbed a large number of conservatives. They were not far from thinking that this pact would possibly allow the propagation of Communism throughout the old continent and that their country, 'ally of an ally', would have been tarnished as an accomplice. As for some Flemish Catholics, they had seen in the pact a forewarning of a new European war, which they blamed on French 'imperialism'.

After June 1935 the federation of the Vlaamse Oud Strijders (former Flemish combatants), pacifist and autonomist, embarked upon a new campaign against the 'bloody agreement' *(sic)* of September 1920. In the course of the summer they published a leaflet in which it was stated:

> All Flanders, and especially the Flanders that is loyal to the Belgian State, demands with one united voice, from the lips of its former combatants, the cancellation of the Franco-Belgian Military Agreement and the return to a policy of voluntary neutrality.[12]

On 18 August 1935, the traditional Flemish pilgrimage to the Tower of Yser concluded with the cry: 'Los van Frankrijk!' ('Let's separate from France!'). Pronounced at Dixmuide, this slogan was repeated during numerous meetings. Before the year was out, Catholic opinion proved to be increasingly sensitive to this controversy. The

[12] Cited by G. Provoost, *Vlaanderen en het militair-politiek beleid in België tussen de twee wereldoorlogen*, vol. II (Leuven, 1977), 203 ff.

Algemeen Christelijk Werkersverbond (Christian Workers' Association), the Davidsfonds (Flemish cultural association) and the parliamentary faction of the Flemish Right joined the position of the VNV.[13] In February 1936, following the proposal of a law by a VNV deputy, this same parliamentary Right wing insisted that 'in the interests of the country, the Franco-Belgian Military Agreement should be deemed null and void'.

At that time Belgium possessed a government of national unity, a tripartite coalition presided by the French-speaking Catholic Paul Van Zeeland. Anxious to ease the pressure that threatened the unity of his cabinet, the prime minister won the consent of the minister of foreign affairs and the French to reduce the contents of the famous Agreement to a simple exchange of information between military staffs according to the circumstances. That was on 6 March. The following day, Hitler occupied the demilitarised Rhineland without shedding a drop of blood. The French and British went no further than uttering verbal protests. Then, in April–May, legislative elections were held in France, resulting in a majority for the Popular Front and a series of strikes which reached the Walloon industrial basin. A part of the French-speaking Catholic bourgeoisie joined the Flemish Catholic Right in denouncing their southern neighbours; as 'pledged to the Soviets,' 'sliding into demagogy and anarchy'. The politico-literary weekly *Cassandre* served as a platform for these recriminations. The relative upsurge of the extreme right – Rexist among the French-speakers, VNV in Flanders – which had made its presence felt in the ballot on 24 May 1936 revealed discontent amongst the middle classes. As from this moment Belgian official circles emphasised their diplomatic disengagement.

On 20 July 1936, the minister of foreign affairs, Paul-Henri Spaak, recently converted to the virtues of very moderate socialism, in a speech given at the banquet of the union of foreign press lauded 'an exclusively and fundamentally Belgian foreign policy'. In Walloon circles and in traditionally pro-French socialist and liberal newspapers the speech provoked great indignation, but the protests proved to be futile, as these groups lacked contacts in the corridors of power. In high places the new orientation of Belgian diplomacy appeared indispensable for the vote of military credits in parliament, as well as for the survival of the ministerial triumpherate. On 9 September, Prime Minister Van Zeeland made this policy publicly his own in the course of a radio broadcast. The sovereign

[13] R. Coolsaet, *Buitenlandse zaken* (Leuven, 1987), 47.

personally used his weight to tip the scales. On 14 October 1936, while presiding over a session of the council of ministers, the king insisted on clearly specifying the objectives of the 'policy of independence,'[14] the only one capable of ensuring national consensus and of securing the agreement of the majority of Flemish deputies – necessary for a major military effort. The old leader of the Socialist Party (Parti Ouvrier Belge), Emile Vandervelde, succeeded in making the text of the royal intervention known to the public. It immediately brought about an intense reaction, and a no less intense displeasure in the chancelleries of France and Great Britain, who interpreted it as a rupture in the alliance against Germany.

In Belgium, the policy of independence, qualified by some as the 'policy of the King' after his speech of 14 October, only really aroused opposition among the communists and groups and individuals of Walloon sensibility. The capacity of opposition of the latter proved to be perfectly malleable. Indeed, several interpolations had been presented in the Chamber on 28–29 October concerning the 'royal speech'. They demanded the continuing of contacts with the military staff of France. The skill of Spaak was added to the necessity to maintain the triumpherate, exposed to the vigorous opposition of the extreme Rexist right. This allowed the government to win a comfortable majority, as a total of 126 deputies approved the 'royal speech'; 42 voted against while 10 abstained.[15] Among the favourable votes appeared the names of several leading figures of the Walloon movement who had until then been opposed to it. The various leaders had hastened to point out that it was not a question of returning to the pre-1914 situation, and that they reserved the right to renew contacts with France whenever necessary. This was little more than a white lie. In fact, the last real contact with Paris had taken place from 16 to 18 July 1936. After that date, the meetings became more *ad hoc*, less and less formal, and with an ever greater gap between one and the next. They were finally interrupted for good in the course of the months that led up to the war.

France and Great Britain tried to make the most of a bad situation. On 24 April 1937, their representatives had submitted to Spaak an official note freeing Belgium from its previous obligations. At the same time they renewed their promises of assistance. Earlier, on 30 January, Hitler

[14] He had only taken up again the main ideas laid out for him in a memorandum by his military adviser, Colonel (later General) Van Overstraeten.

[15] Ph. Destatte, *L'identité wallonne. Essai sur l'affirmation politique de la Wallonie (XIXe–XXe siècle)* (Charleroi, 1997), 165.

had declared in the Reichstag that he was willing to recognise the Low Countries as 'neutral territories'. On 13 October 1937, his minister of Foreign Affairs transmitted a note to the Belgian ambassador in Berlin in which the Reich guaranteed Belgian territorial integrity 'unless ... Belgium, in an armed conflict in which Germany was engaged, collaborated towards a military action against her'. From that point on, Brussels' leaders were able to believe that the 'policy of independence', which was none other than a return to neutrality, although everyone refused to call it by that name, had achieved its primary objective. The repeated lack of resolve shown by the western democracies throughout 1938, first during Germany's *Anschluß* with Austria in March and then during the Munich conference in September, confirmed this attitude. Shortly before, they had scarcely appreciated the fact that Great Britain had attempted to carry out its appeasement of the Third Reich by offering Hitler part of the Belgian Congo and Portuguese colonies.[16] In short, they clung to this diplomatic position all the more energetically as they were only too well aware how fragile it really was. And then, apparently, it began to bear fruit. Belgium's military forces seemed to reinforce themselves little by little. Within the space of six years, from 1934 to 1939, the part of the budget reserved for the armed forces had risen from 11.4 per cent to 24 per cent. The approach of the conflict was not accompanied by a diplomatic rebalance, indeed quite the opposite.

## POLICY OF NEUTRALITY = POLICY OF THE OSTRICH?

On 1 September 1939, Germany invaded Poland. On the 3rd, France and Great Britain decided to declare war against her. On the same day, Belgium proclaimed herself officially neutral.[17] The next day, speaking on the radio, King Leopold asked 'each person to observe the rigorous discipline, obliged by neutrality, when giving voice to his feelings'. The concept of neutrality had finally been baptised. The sovereign and his ministers were in full agreement as to the general principles of its application. The government of national union (a reconstruction of the tripartite in times of crisis), presided over by the Catholic Hubert Pierlot, professed its faith in neutrality, which kept the country out of the war. But for most of its members it was merely a means to avoid the loss of life and material

[16] C. S. Pansaerts, 'Anglo-German Conversations on Colonial Appeasement and the Involvement of the Belgian Congo (October 1937–March 1938)', *Cahiers-Brijdragen*, 16 (1994), 41–80.

[17] The declaration of independence appears in the official journal, *Le Moniteur belge*, 3 September 1939, 6045–48.

destruction for as long as possible. For the king and his close advisers, on the other hand, it had become an end in itself. From 16 September, the king advised the prime minister: 'We must create a neutralist mentality in Belgium', and he would repeat this axiom until May 1940.[18] In October, in a message broadcast to the American nation, he showed how much interest he attached to it when he affirmed that it corresponded to 'the traditions and aspirations of the Belgian People'.[19] Subsequently, he was heard to rise repeatedly against the newspapers that he considered to be insufficiently neutral: *Le Soir, La Gazette* (of Brussels) and *La Flandre libérale* (of Ghent), 'detestable but [who] at least do not hide their hand'.[20]

This kind of thought reflected the general frame of mind of the monarch. Leopold III belonged to a generation which had witnessed the decline of the liberal democracies. Mistrustful of Nazi totalitarianism, of which the plebeian vulgarity and brutality repulsed him, he had observed that authoritarian regimes were a welcome change to the sluggishness of parliament, characterised by multiple ministerial crises. Above all, he was appalled by the rise of organised political parties which, following the example of what was happening in other European monarchies, tended to gnaw away at what he considered to be his prerogatives. Too aware of his duties towards the state to aspire to a dictatorship, he would have favoured without a shadow of doubt a return to the constitutional monarchy enjoyed by his ancestors, Leopold I and Leopold II. His immediate entourage, who moved in general in markedly right-wing spheres, encouraged him in this direction.[21] The only socialist of any calibre who had managed to penetrate his intimate circle and influence him intellectually, Hendrik De Man, had since 1937–8 ceased to believe in a parliamentary regime, and had told him so. Having evolved 'beyond Marxism', De Man hoped for no more than a 'government of public health'.[22] Leopold III, having few ideas, valued all the more those he did have. The 'obstinacy' and 'pigheadedness' that many politicians

18 According to Hubert Pierlot in *Le Soir* 6 July 1947 (*Pages d'Histoire*, vol. II).

19 *Contribution à l'étude de la question royale. Evénements-documents* (Brussels, 1945), vol. I, 101.

20 Koninckx, *Léopold III roi et diplomate*, 178 ff.

21 Among the advisers to the sovereign were Baron (after February 1940, Count) Robert Capelle, the king's private secretary; Baron Pierre Van Zuylen; Count Jacques Davignon, ambassador to Berlin; General Raoul Van Overstraeten, his military adviser, a vehement Anglophobe; Count Cornet de Ways-Ruart, Grand Marshall to the Court. The jurist Louis Wodon, former head of the cabinet of King Albert and a great believer in the 'pre-eminence of the royal function', also gave King Leopold his advice. A personality who stood out from this group, which was decidedly to the right of the political spectrum: the liberal Louis Frederiq, head of the cabinet of the sovereign.

22 M. Brelaz, *Léopold III et Henri De Man* (Genéve, 1988), 58.

subsequently discovered in him (but which they had tolerated for a long time) made him assume afterwards a larger part of the responsibility in the eventual failure of neutrality.

Public opinion, on the whole unaware of these states of mind, was generally speaking satisfied with the situation. Tormented by material concerns, the public generally confided in those who had taken the reins of the state in order to avoid the worst. This did not save them from unease. Though the real opponents of the system, whether from the right or the left, remained out on a limb, this system was saturated with antagonistic currents, a reflection of the tensions that war exerted on the traditional pillars of society.[23] To simplify matters, we could say that these currents consisted of the hard neutralists, pure neutralists, mute neutralists, and anti-neutralists, the latter a tiny minority, in reality no more than camouflaged interventionists. Overlaps and links could exist between tendencies close to one another.[24]

In the first category the main Fascist or neo-Fascist elements could be found, whether pro-Belgian like Rex, or Flemish nationalist like the VNV. Having rejected parliamentary democracy long before, they feared, without daring to say so openly, a victory of the Western Powers. Such a victory would have brought about the disappearance of a regime which was at least, for them, a reference model, and which to their mind served as an efficient rampart against Communism. For that reason, they could rely on the benevolent support of the ultra conservatives, hard-line anti-Communists. This group was led by some authentic agents of Reich influence, such as Staf De Clercq, *leider* of the VNV, or Léon Degrelle, the head of the Rexist movement. For the theorists, neutrality dominated not only the expression of their thoughts but the very thoughts themselves.

The family of pure neutralists proved to be more widespread, less monolithic. Within it could be found the whole of the Catholic party, confused Flemish and Francophones, but with some nuances. The Right was especially particular in this matter and transmitted their opinion in their publications, either in the *Revue catholique des Idées et des Faits*, or in

[23] In the last legislative elections before the conflict (April 1939), 82.26 per cent of the electorate remained faithful to the three traditional parties (Socialists, Liberals and Catholics). The support for the extreme right Rex and the VNV accounted for some 12.37 per cent of the electorate.

[24] For an overview of the politico-social structures during the Phoney War, refer to J. Gotovitch and J. Gerard-Libois, *L'an 40. La Belgique occupée* (Brussels, 1971), 23–67. For a survey of the economic situation, D. Martin, 'De onafhankelijkheidspolitiek: enkele aspekten van de Duits-Belgische ekonomische betrekkingen 1936–1940', in *Vlaams Marxistische Tijdschrift*, 12 (1980), 47–75 and P. Klefisch, *Das Dritte Reich und Belgien* (Frankfurt, 1988).

the *XXe Siècle*, or in the very Flemish *Standaard*. Had not this last publication called for prison sentences for the authors of articles hostile to a belligerent neighbour? The conservative and French-speaking wing of this tendency had, at the end of 1939, set up a League for Independence, endowed with the weekly publication, *L'Ouest*. Here staunchly patriotic Belgians rubbed shoulders with crypto-Rexists. Therefore, other pages expressed more conditioned sentiments towards neutrality. This list included *La Libre Belgique, La Cité chrétienne, La Gazette de Liège* and even the Maurrasian *Nation Belge*. As for *La Cité nouvelle*, the voice of the Christian Democracy, its neutralism was decidedly questionable.

Next to these neutrals, as particular as they were right-thinking, appeared a certain number of Flemish socialists marked by demanism (that is to say, by a socialism with strong authoritarian and technocratic leanings). It was thanks to them that the inspirer of the 'Plan of Work' had been able to succeed Vandervelde in the presidency of the Belgian Workers' Party in May 1939. Re-appointed as minister on 3 September, he began to fight for neutrality in the doctrinal review *Leiding*. At the end of October, he published an article entitled: 'Stop the sabotage of neutrality' (*Genoeg sabotage van de onzijdigheid*). It earned him the wrath of the anti-neutralists in his party, who were numerous on the Walloon side and who had gathered together around the *Revue socialiste*. Strangely, after a few soundings, the communists had ended up rejoining the pure neutralist camp.[25] The signing of the German–Soviet non-aggression pact and the geopolitical convulsion it had provoked had given them no choice. The Third International had given out new directives by means of Andor Berei, the instructor of the Comintern in Brussels.

Like a good soldier, the Belgian Communist party had obeyed. By the end of September, their press had begun to spread the slogan: 'Neither London, nor Berlin', and to propagate the theory that what was being witnessed was a conflict of rival imperialists and that the proletariat had nothing to gain by adhering to one side or the other. Prosaically, they launched a campaign – qualified as demagogic by their adversaries – to raise the pay of the mobilised conscripts. To confront this campaign the government resorted to an old decree to pursue publications that were liable to affect troop morale. Le Parquet banned *La Voix du Peuple*, the party's daily newspaper, in November. Nevertheless, they managed to distribute thirty-nine numbers under a series of twenty-two successive titles until 1 May 1940. Moreover, the structure of the Belgian

[25] J. Gotovitch, *Du rouge au tricolore. Résistance et parti communiste* (Brussels, 1992), 65–82.

Communist party was used as a haven for the French Communist party, pursued in France because of their defeatism. With body and soul in alignment with the Soviet Union, the Belgian Communist party maintained most of its members, but evolved in an atmosphere that had become very hostile since the outbreak of war between the Soviet Union and Finland.

Then there was the bulk of the mute neutralists. These nurtured few illusions. They were more numerous mainly in the French-speaking area and Brussels and in laic circles. The majority socialists or liberals, supported by a well distributed press (*Le Soir, La Meuse, La Gazette de Charleroi, Le Peuple, La Province de Namur*, etc.), expected a German attack, rendered inevitable, in their opinion, by the very nature of the Nazi Reich. According to them, neutrality should be no more than a way of winning time in order to prepare for war in optimum conditions. They willingly subscribed to the reasoning of Henri Rolin, an eminent jurist who likened neutrality to 'the natural reaction to flee before the dangers from the outside world' which had merely served to convert 'selfishness into a virtue.' These people multiplied their distress signals to their leaders in government to convince the latter to renew contacts with France and Great Britain. Their demands, which became more and more urgent as the danger increased, partially overlapped with those of the interventionists, who were to be found in French-speaking circles or among personalities of Radical–Socialist tendencies. They only disposed of newspapers of limited readership (*L'Action wallonne, La Wallonie nouvelle*) or leaflets controlled from the Quai d'Orsay (*Vérité, Alerte*). Thus their warnings went unheeded. A prisoner of its policy of neutrality, the Pierlot government seemed unshakeable, even when most of its members had lost faith in their beliefs. The king, who refused to change course, tired himself out trying to prop up their resolve. He had personally permitted General Van Overstraeten to maintain, with absolute discretion, verbal exchanges with the British and French military attachés (Col. Blake and Col. Laurent, later Col. Hautecoeur). These conversations took place on the quiet from the end of September to 17 November 1939. They never went very far, as Belgium feared giving Germany the ideal pretext for attacking her while she struggled to maintain the supposed 'moral capital' of neutrality. The conversations were abruptly broken off as the Wehrmacht assembled its units on Belgium's borders.[26]

[26] J. Vanwelkenhuyzen, *Neutralité armée. La politique militaire de la Belgique pendant la 'Drôle de guerre'* (Brussels, 1979).

A first alert had in fact occurred in November 1939. From 6 to 12 November, an invasion was believed to be imminent. Already at this stage, Prime Minister Pierlot had had a confrontation with the king, disagreeing with him over the necessity to renew contacts with the Allied Powers. Things had finally calmed down, thanks to the mediation of Spaak and the 'serious misunderstanding' had been smoothed out. A second alert, more serious this time, occurred on 10 January 1940. The affair is now well known. A German liaison aircraft, lost in the fog, landed by chance at Mechelen in the Belgian Limburg area. The two German officers it was carrying were in possession of documents which contained the plans for the attack on the west. After consultations, General Van Overstraeten submitted a synthesis to General Gamelin. Meanwhile King Leopold endeavoured to obtain guarantees from Britain in the event of Belgium being plunged into the war. However, he carried out this manoeuvre without informing his ministers, resorting to the services of a friend of the royal family, Admiral Keyes. Due to circumstances beyond his control, the operation was a complete failure. It reached the ears of Spaak on 15 January, at the end of the morning, but he agreed to support the sovereign. Later, he was to regret not having reacted more vigorously to what was in effect a demonstration of personal – and therefore anti-constitutional – politics on the part of Leopold III. Those who heard about the problem attributed the action to his acute sense of duty, but they could no longer have much faith in their chances to remain out of the fight.

On 10 April 1940, the alarm bells rang once again. Norway and Denmark, two neutral states, had just suffered a surprise attack. The Allies exerted particularly intense diplomatic pressure to secure the entry of their armies into Belgium as a preventive measure. Leopold opposed this yet again. What is more, he extracted a communiqué from his ministers in which they reaffirmed 'the desire of the government to persevere in the policy of independence and neutrality adopted since the beginning of the European conflict'. If Pierlot increasingly annoyed the sovereign with his veiled threats to do away with neutrality, the former shortly afterwards had the satisfaction of seeing his line of policy approved by a huge majority in the Senate: the budget for foreign affairs was accepted by 133 votes out of 138.[27] This satisfaction, however, was short lived. As from 20 April 1940, the signs indicating an invasion grew in number.

[27] Only two abstentions and three negative votes, those of the communist senators, were recorded.

But had the lapse of time that was believed to have been won permitted the state to reinforce its structures, given the modest dimensions and capacity of the country? Economically speaking, Belgium had absorbed the shock of the declaration of war by her neighbours quite well. The Allied Powers had, after some hesitation, allowed Brussels to maintain its exports to Germany at the same level as 1938, with the natural exception of typically military products and those of strategic interest. Nonetheless, they established a maritime blockade which impeded transatlantic imports and upset provisions. The Department of Economic Affairs took a series of steps to prevent a denuding of the country. For example, a list of consumer goods whose export was prohibited was drawn up, and regularly updated. The results: though one could have feared the worst in September 1939 with the spectacular fall of imports from 1,835 to 905 million Francs and a 400-million Franc decrease in exports, the situation stabilised as from October. In November, imports rose to 1,540; thereafter, as from January, they constantly remained above the 1,500 million mark. As for exports, they had increased sharply in December 1939 to reach the record figures of 2,450 and 2,310 million in March and April 1940. During the month of April, the Belgian balance of payments presented a profit of 800 million.

The state of war favoured the rush of orders in the textile and metallurgic industries, which enabled the Belgian franc to remain steady during this period. The gold reserves in the National Bank even rose from 22,700 million Belgian francs (August 1939) to 23,250 million (beginning of May 1940). This euphoric commercial situation did not save the population from experiencing hard times due to the slump in other economic sectors (construction, ports, consumer goods and luxury industries). Thus in January–February of 1940 there were 190,000 unemployed, 20,000 more than a year before.

From a military point of view, a considerable effort had been made.[28] It did not fail to impress, at least on paper. By the beginning of the month of May 1940 the army had been able to assemble twenty-two divisions (though experts considered that six of these were not up to much). Altogether the army had a theoretical strength of 4,800 officers, 19,000 NCOs and professional soldiers, and 47,000 conscripts. The mobilisation would add to this number about 20,000 reserve officers and 550,000 recalled soldiers (out of a population of about 8 million inhabitants) but these figures varied constantly because of special leave, release for

[28] De Fabribeckers, *La campagne de l'armée belge en 1940* (Bruxelles/Paris, n.d.).

economic reasons, etc. Therefore, at the beginning of March, the army had demobilised nearly 100,000 men, of whom 30,000 were unsuitable, 10,000 fathers of large families, and 15,000 miners. The 'agricultural leave', every month, reduced the strength of the infantry by 28 per cent. Above all, this force had been conceived with one great defect. Following the example of France, Belgium, marked by the experience of the First World War, had created an army designed purely for defence, or for delaying rearguard actions. A lot of effort and money had therefore been invested in fortifications, including the fortified towns of Liège, Antwerp, and Namur, the 'bridgehead of Flanders' (around Gent), the 'K–W line' between Antwerp and Namur, alignments of fortresses in the Ardennes and – obliged by neutrality – facing the southern border. The modernisation of the fortified position of Liège had itself alone consumed 833 million francs, that is 20,000 million francs at today's prices.

Because of this strategic decision, the army suffered from a serious lack of modern tanks (8 heavy 16-ton tanks, 200 light armoured vehicles – but all obsolete) and of aircraft (Belgium possessed exactly 184 airworthy aircraft, but two-thirds of these could be considered museum pieces) and the motorisation of the infantry was still superficial. Finally, anti-aircraft artillery was minimal, while field artillery was still horse drawn, except for the Cavalry Corps and the Ardennes Chasseurs. The excellence of the anti-tank piece – a 47 mm cannon – did not compensate for these weaknesses. Belgium had preferred concrete to mobility. Neutrality had obliged her to defend herself in all directions. Both were to cost her dearly.

To crown it all, these sluggish units did not have a high morale. The neutralist spirit inspired by the hierarchy, refraining to identify the potential enemy, had lowered the army's guard. The long months of inactivity in the cold of winter, broken by manoeuvres and counter-manoeuvres, now against France, now against Germany, had not solved anything. Boredom, stemming from indecision, had no doubt inflicted more damage than the defeatist campaign carried out by the Flemish, Neo-fascist and crypto-separatist VNV.

On 10 May 1940, the Wehrmacht made a surprise attack – a very relative surprise – on Belgium, The Netherlands, and the Grand Duchy of Luxembourg. In this way it put an end to the calculations and other hesitations of the leaders who, whether they liked it or not, had practised a policy of the ostrich throughout the Phoney War. The behaviour under fire of the Belgian army was not precisely glorious. After eighteen days of combat, it was beginning to collapse. Only the act of capitulation signed by King Leopold, who no longer had any faith in an Allied victory, prevented it from complete destruction. In the meantime, the monarch had broken with his ministers following a dramatic interview in the castle of Wynendaele, as the latter had advocated continuing the struggle alongside the French and British. After much hesitation and not a few tribulations, Pierlot and Spaak eventually found a haven in the capital of the British Empire at the beginning of autumn 1940.[29]

A strange kind of prisoner in his castle at Laeken, during the course of this 'ambiguous summer'[30] of 1940 the sovereign hinted at forming another government which would then function under the control of the occupying power. The German authorities refrained from following up these covert advances, which saved him from a tremendous *faux-pas*. Leopold III from then on sank back into a prudent silence, which was perhaps another kind of neutrality. In September 1944, with the Allies' blessing, the Pierlot government was restored to power, and public opinion, which had in the past reviled them so much, agreed to forget their weaknesses, and their lack of foresight.

As for King Leopold, he was obliged to renounce the throne at the end of a 'royal debate' that had gone on for five years: less for having assumed the 'policy of independence' than for letting his contempt for parliament and its members show through. The royal function in Belgium lost at this moment any possibility of maintaining its preeminence in the heart of executive power. Following the example of other European monarchies, it shrank from then on to a simply symbolic function.

Neutrality had long since belonged to bygone days, rejected by everyone, including those who had most vociferously supported it but who, prudent or opportunist, had survived its demise. Spawn of the political moment, a good many Belgians for a long time found neutrality attractive – for various reasons, sometimes contradictory. And it was disowned by all when the political circumstances let it blow away in the winds of history.

[29] J. Stengers, *Léopold III et le gouvernement: les deux politiques belges de 1940* (Gembloux, 1980).

[30] According to the title of a work by Désiré Denuit, *L'été ambigu de 1940. Carnets d'un journaliste* (Brussels, 1978).

# PART II

## *The 'wait-and-see' neutrals*

South-East Europe and the Balkans, 1939–1941.

CHAPTER 5

# 'Where one man, and only one man, led.' Italy's path from non-alignment to non-belligerency to war, 1937–1940

*Brian R. Sullivan*

Few times have I seen Mussolini so happy. He has fulfilled his real dream: that of becoming the military *condottiero* of the Country in war.
Entry in Ciano's diary, 29 May 1940[1]

Mussolini was never neutral after August 1939. He had long schemed to subjugate Europe in alliance with Germany. If the Duce embodied the state, neither was Italy neutral. But his 'l'état c'est moi' – like conceit and his posture of representing all Italians – reflected wishful thinking and propaganda. Italian society encompassed many political segments: Fascist hierarchs; Party and militia members; the monarchy; military leaders; diplomats; industrialists; large landowners; professionals and smaller landowners; workers, shopkeepers, petty bureaucrats, and white-collar employees; and peasants and farm workers, the largest group. From August 1939 to April 1940, they favoured peace.[2]

Catholic leaders and the Vatican formed a special group. Church authorities were simultaneously Italian subjects, Fascist-ruled citizens, and papal appointees. Thirty-five Italian cardinals out of a total of sixty-two dominated the Roman Church in 1939–40. Pius XII was latest in a continuous succession of Italian pontiffs since 1523. While Italian-born priests in Vatican posts became papal subjects, they retained their national identity. The 1929 Lateran Accords required Italian priests' loyalty to Italy. But Italian clergy could not ignore papal pronouncements. War and peace have moral and political aspects. Nazi aggression against Catholic Poland troubled even pro-Fascist Italian prelates.[3]

[1] Galeazzo Ciano, *Diario 1937–1943* (Milan, 1980), 435.

[2] *Documents on British Foreign Policy, 1919–1939*, third series (hereafter *DBFP*), vol. VII, nos. 86, 96; *Foreign Relations of the United States* (hereafter *FRUS*), *1939*, vol. I, 363, 416; ibid., *1940*, 114–15; Gianluca André, 'La non belligeranza e l'intervento dell'Italia', in R. H. Rainero and A. Biagini (eds.), *L'Italia in guerra. Il primo anno – 1940* (Rome, 1991), 151–2.

[3] '5 Cardinals Lead in Vatican Contest', *The New York Times*, 13 February 1939, 1; Arturo Carlo Jemolo, *Chiesa e Stato in Italia negli ultimi cento anni* (Turin, 1948), 637–59; John Cornwell, *Hitler's*

In August 1939, Mussolini realised most Italians did not want to – possibly *would not* – follow him into battle. Yet he longed to join Hitler. When the Duce announced Italian 'non-belligerency' – an unrecognised international status – he made a crucial distinction. Could Europe's first radical-right dictator balance between Nazism and Democracy?[4]

Historians have questioned the similarity of Fascism and Nazism.[5] Neither Mussolini nor Hitler doubted that they shared an ideology. Both reviled Liberalism and Democracy, despised Marxism and Bolshevism. They condemned capitalism and class warfare, praised social cooperation and economic justice. They denounced parliaments for causing internal chaos and external weakness, proletarian dictatorships for rule by terror and international subversion. Fascists and Nazis advocated nation-states based on meritocracy and disciplined mass devotion, and demanded a similar international 'New Order': stronger states dominating weaker, under Italian–German supremacy. This required war. Neither Democrats nor Communists could peacefully accept a civilisation antithetical to their ideologies and interests.[6]

Mussolini proclaimed the twentieth century as the Fascist era. Before 1933, however, he felt isolated and threatened. After Hitler came to power, the Duce considered Nazism and Fascism fraternal movements facing common enemies. Hitler encouraged Mussolini. However, Mussolini's megalomania, and Hitler's temporary vulnerability and repeated declarations of discipleship, led the Duce to assume the senior role. Mussolini welcomed Hitler's assurances that the Balkan–Mediterranean

*Pope. The Secret History of Pius XII* (New York, 1999), 228–34; Pierre Blet, Angelo Martini, and Burkhart Schneider (eds.), *Records and Documents of the Holy See Relating to the Second World War*, vol. 1, (London, 1968) (hereafter *Holy See*), no. 182.

4 Ciano, *Diario*, 326–43; Giuseppe Bottai, *Diario 1935–1944*, (Milan, 1982), 153–60; André, 'La non belligeranza', 153.

5 Enzo Collotti, *Fascismo, fascismi* (Florence, 1989), 3–90, 163–91; R. J. B. Bosworth, *The Italian Dictatorship. Problems and Perspectives in the Interpretation of Mussolini and Fascism* (London, 1998), 53–7, 205–38; Roger Griffin (ed.), *International Fascism. Theories, Causes and the New Consensus* (London, 1998); Renzo De Felice (ed.), *Il fascismo. Le interpretazioni dei contemporanei e degli storici*, 2nd edn (Bari, 1998).

6 *Opera Omnia di Benito Mussolini*, Edoardo and Duilio Susmel (eds.), 44 vols. (Florence/Rome, 1951–80) (hereafter *OO*), vol. XXIV, 283; vol. XXIV, 86–96, 133–6; vol. XXVIII, 67–71; vol. XXIX, 1–2; *The Speeches of Adolf Hitler, April 1922–August 1939*, 2 vols., ed. Norman H. Baynes (London, 1942), vol. II, 1000–4, 1086, 1167, 1341, 1352–3, 1360–4, 1399–1400, 1461–4, 1471–2, 1515, 1599–1600; *Hitler's Secret Conversations, 1941–1944* (New York, 1972), 8–9, 217, 480–1, 498; Renzo De Felice (ed.), *Autobiografia del fascismo. Antologia di testi fascisti 1919–1945* (Bergamo, 1978), 352–61, 365–83, 389–409, 451–4, 459–78; Adrian Lyttelton (ed.), *Italian Fascisms: From Pareto to Gentile* (New York, 1975), 39–58, 225–41, 285–97, 301–15; P.J. Morgan, 'The Italian Fascist New Order in Europe', in M.L. Smith and Peter M. R. Stark, (eds.), *Making the New Europe. European Unity and the Second World War* (London, 1990), 27–30.

region formed future provinces of Italy's new Roman Empire. Yet Hitler contradicted his words by preparations to seize Austria and dominate south-east Europe.[7]

The Fascist–Nazi concept of a healthy – therefore Social Darwinian – European order created the paradox of Italy and Germany as philosophical twins yet national rivals. In 1932, Mussolini's 'Doctrine of Fascism' proclaimed his ideology meant expansion, imperialism, and conflict. Three months after that tract appeared, the Nazis took over Germany. They accepted Fascist concepts while threatening Italian interests. Both soon sought a *modus vivendi.* But the bad impression Hitler made in his June 1934 talks near Venice damaged Mussolini's wary trust of his German admirer. Hitler demolished it with the Nazi *putsch* in Vienna in July. Rushed to the Brenner Pass, Italian divisions forced a Nazi retreat; eighteen months of tension followed.[8]

Competition between regimes fostered internal pressures in Italy. Despite Fascist and Nazi horrors, many young Italians and Germans applauded their national revolutions. Nazi economic successes sustained exhilarating hopes in young Germans. Mussolini's older dictatorship had disappointed younger Fascists by 1933–4. Employment and wages rose spectacularly in Germany. In Italy, unemployment remained high; income declined. Contrasts between national mortality rates, consumption, radio and automobile ownership, and production grew. When Mussolini learned that Hitler planned to offer every German family an affordable car, he theatrically sneered that this would stimulate hedonism and sap German aggressiveness.[9]

Fascist social programmes inspired Nazi projects. But Italian economic weakness, inefficient arms spending, and pervasive corruption diminished resources for such programmes. The powerful German economy,

[7] *The Memoirs of Field-Marshal Keitel*, ed. Walter Gorlitz (New York, 1969), 83–4; *OO*, vol. XXVIII, 251; *I documenti diplomatici italiani* (hereafter *DDI*), 7, vol. XII, 364; vol. XIII, 61, 69, 595; *Documents on German Foreign Policy* (hereafter *DGFP*) C, vol. I, 12, 14, 27, 35, 51, 83, 365, 388, 397, 485; vol. II, 28, 67, 104, 126, 145, 282, 332, 354, 368, 420, 472; D, vol. V, 272, 365; *The Speeches of Adolf Hitler*, vol. II, 1018, 1086, 1120, 1167, 1421, 1462; Jens Petersen, *Hitler e Mussolini. La difficile alleanza* (Bari, 1975) 165–8, 426–44; Renzo De Felice, *Mussolini il duce. I. Gli anni del consenso 1929–1934* (Turin, 1974), 433–98; Brian R. Sullivan, 'From Little Brother to Senior Partner: Fascist Italian Perceptions of the Nazis and of Hitler's Regime, 1930–1936', *Intelligence and National Security* (1998), 95–6; Donald W. Treadgold, *Twentieth Century Russia*, 8th edn (Boulder, CO, 1995), 243–6; Jean Lacouture, *Leon Blum* (New York, 1982), 214–24.

[8] Benito Mussolini with Giovanni Gentile, 'The Doctrine of Fascism', in Lyttelton, *Italian Fascisms*, 47, 56; Sullivan, 'From Little Brother to Senior Partner', 96–102.

[9] Vera Zamagni, *The Economic History of Italy, 1860–1990* (Oxford, 1993), 259–89, 303–17; B. R. Mitchell, *International Historical Statistics: Europe 1750–1988*, 3rd edn. (London, 1992), 119–20, 163, 183–4, 715–16, 755, 848–9; Ciano, *Diario*, 143.

stimulated by rearmament, permitted realisation of its Fascist-inspired welfare laws. For Italians, armaments programmes led only to higher taxes and consumer goods shortages. This created discontent not just among workers but in the Party, foreign service, officer corps, and industrial circles. Fascist propaganda inculcated Corporativist ideals within many educated Italians. Fascist economics made their realisation impossible. The Depression worsened matters. American investment, which had put hundreds of millions of dollars into Italian industry, ceased. Fascists presented the Italian model as the solution to the world crisis. Conditions in Italy belied such boasts. After 1933, German penetration of Balkan markets crushed Italian competition, damaging Fascist attempts at economic recovery. Mussolini's need for economic revival partially inspired his decision to conquer Ethiopia.[10] However, the League of Nations punished Mussolini's African aggression with economic sanctions and threatened an oil embargo. Mussolini sought Hitler's assistance. Impressed by Fascist defiance and eager for Italian support, Hitler reciprocated with economic aid and political encouragement. Fascist–Nazi cooperation revived.[11]

Victory enhanced Fascism's prestige. Anticipated material benefits of empire proved illusory, however, while Fascist brutality ignited a massive revolt in late 1937. This prevented Italian exploitation of the rich Ethiopian soil. The *Impero* consumed billions of lire in construction projects and counterinsurgency operations but yielded little return. Yet the enthusiasm the conquest aroused provoked Fascist overconfidence and demands for additional success. Mussolini himself proved a victim of such aspirations. His yearning for new triumphs explains the assistance he gave to the Nationalists in the Spanish Civil War.[12]

[10] Filippo Anfuso, *Roma Berlino Salò (1936–1945)* (Milan, 1950), 89; Zamagni, *The Economic History of Italy*, 253–5, 268–71, 309; Lucio Ceva and Andrea Curami, *Industria bellica anni trenta. Commesse militari, l'Ansaldo ed altri* (Milan, 1992) passim; Maria Sophia Quine, *Population Politics in Twentieth-Century Europe. Fascist Dictatorships and Liberal Democracies* (London, 1996), 43–51; Luciano Zani, *Fascism, autarchy, commercia estero. Felice Guarneri un technocrate al servizio dello 'Stato nuovo'* (Bologna, 1988), 55–166; Piero Bairati, *Sul filo di lana. Cinque generazioni di imprenditori: i Marzotto* (Bologna, 1986), 202–27; Valerio Castronovo, *Storia di una banca. La Banca Nazionale del lavoro e lo sviluppo economico italiano 1913–1983* (Turin, 1983), 124–89; Mariuccia Salvati, *Il regime e gli impiegati. La nazionalizzazione piccolo-borghese nel ventennio fascista* (Bari, 1992), 170–204; Brian R. Sullivan, 'More than Meets the Eye: The Ethiopian War and the Origins of the Second World War', in Gordon Martel (ed.), *The Origins of the Second World War Reconsidered*, 2nd edn (London, 1999), 184–5.

[11] For an overview of the role of Mussolini's foreign policy, 1922–36, see MacGregor Knox, ' "The Fascist Regime, its Foreign Policy and its Wars." An "Anti-Anti-Fascist" Orthodoxy?', *Contemporary European History*, (July 1995), 349–54, 358–62.

[12] Brian R. Sullivan, 'The Italian–Ethiopian War, October 1935–November 1941: Causes, Conduct, and Consequences', in A. Hamish Ion and E. J. Errington, (eds.), *Great Powers and Little Wars.*

Italian–German cooperation in Spain renewed trust between the regimes. Meanwhile, Italian military strength declined. The conquest and pacification of Ethiopia, followed by intervention in Spain, left the Italian forces gravely weakened by mid-1937. In three years, Italy declined from being able to deter Germany to needing the Nazi regime for support and security. Visiting Berlin in September 1937, the Duce proclaimed: 'When you have friends, you march together all the way to the end.' Mussolini implicitly declared if Italy allied with Germany again, 1914–15 events would not reoccur. Comradeship, faith, and loyalty underpinned Fascist morality. But Mussolini also had practical needs for Nazi help.[13]

Experience left Mussolini uneasy about Hitler's reliability but his carefully choreographed 1937 tour of the Third Reich deeply impressed him. Advisers tried to temper the Duce's enthusiasm. But after his return, Mussolini called Germany Europe's dominant state. Fascist ideology and Mussolini's imperial dreams made an Italian–German alliance irresistible.[14]

The Duce still attempted to balance German power. In mid-1937, Mussolini and Prime Minister Neville Chamberlain began contacts leading to the April 1938 Easter Accords. Mussolini pretended Italian–British differences could be settled. But in early 1937 he had defined Britain as 'the principal enemy'. More significant, in the middle of March 1938, Hitler extracted the Duce's reluctant acquiescence to the *Anschluß*. Military weakness forced Mussolini to surrender Austria sooner than anticipated. Next day, he decided to increase the army by ten divisions. That summer, he ordered vast fortifications to be constructed along the new Italian–German border. This would strain Italian resources but strengthen Mussolini's diplomacy.[15]

*The Limits of Power* (Westport, 1993), 185–94; Enrico Caviglia, *Diario (aprile 1925–marzo 1945)* (Rome, 1952), 145; Bottai, *Diario*, 109–16; John F. Coverdale, *Italian Intervention in the Spanish Civil War* (Princeton, 1975), 12, 19; Antonello Biagini and Alessandro Gionfrida, (eds.), *Lo Stato Maggiore Generale tra le due guerre. (Verbali delle riunioni presiedute da Badoglio dal 1925 al 1937)* (Rome, 1997), 373–82.

[13] Sullivan, 'More than Meets the Eye', 187–91; *The Speeches of Adolf Hitler*, 1672; *OO*, vol. XXVIII, 253 (Mussolini quotation); *Keitel Memoirs*, 38; Ciano, *Diario*, 40; *DGFP*, D, vol. I, 3–4; Renzo De Felice, *Mussolini il duce. II. Lo Stato Totalitario 1936–1940* (Turin, 1981), 414.

[14] Ciano, *Diario*, 40–1; Anfuso, *Roma Berlino Salò*, 51–63; Bottai, *Diario*, 120; Massimo Magustrati, *L'Italia a Berlin* (Milan, 1956), 65–71; Rachele Mussolini, *Mussolini: An Intimate Biography* (New York, 1974), 141–2; Edda Ciano, *La mia testimonianza* (Milan, 1975), 142; Vittorio Mussolini, *Vita con mio padre* (Milan, 1957), 85.

[15] Donatella Bolech, *L'accordo di due imperi. L'accordo italo-inglese del 16 aprile 1938* (Milan, 1977) *passim*; *Lo Stato Maggiore Generale tra le due guerre*, 420 ('principal enemy' quotation); William I. Shorrock, *From Ally to Enemy. The Enigma of Fascist Italy in French Diplomacy, 1920–1940* (Kent, 1988),

The *Anschluß* connected Italian and German security geopolitically and ideologically. If the Nazi regime collapsed, Mussolini would face an anti-Fascist neighbour across the Brenner, as well as the Maritime Alps. Thus, he could no longer be neutral if Hitler's destruction threatened. If the Nazis fell, the Fascists would follow. From March 1938, Mussolini's policies combined self-preservation, Fascist–Nazi solidarity, and imperial expansion.

Simultaneously, relations between the Duce and Vittorio Emanuele III deteriorated. In March 1938, the Chamber of Deputies 'spontaneously' acclaimed Mussolini and the king as First Marshals of the Empire. Mussolini's self-promotion corresponded to Hitler's February assumption of Wehrmacht command and granted Mussolini dignity when the Führer visited Italy that May. Mussolini's elevation also reinforced his prestige, damaged by the *Anschluß*. But this placed him and Vittorio Emanuele III on the same level. The king had long feared that the Duce would eventually seek to abolish the monarchy. Now Mussolini's goal seemed obvious.[16]

While visiting Italy, Hitler suggested forming an alliance. Mussolini replied positively but vaguely. German Foreign Minister Joachim von Ribbentrop acted more insistently with Galeazzo Ciano, the Duce's son-in-law and foreign minister, presenting him with a draft treaty. The Nazi foreign minister insisted Italy and Germany could destroy France and Britain. Next, the Axis could conquer the Soviets and defeat the Americans. Despite Mussolini's imperial appetite, he found Ribbentrop's assertions excessive. However, the Germans denied that they sought immediate expansion. They explained pressure on Czechoslovakia as simply to form a Swiss-type federation with Sudeten cantons.[17]

206–29; Lacouture, *Leon Blum*, 344–9; Philip V. Cannistraro and Brian R. Sullivan, *Il Duce's Other Woman* (New York, 1993), 450–7, 480–4, 495–9, 505–7; Sullivan, 'The Italian–Ethiopian War', 185–92 and 'From Little Brother to Senior Partner', 101–6; *DGFP*, D, vol. I, 94, 399; Alberto Pirelli, *Taccuini 1922/1943*, ed. Donato Barbone (Bologna, 1984), 207; *L'esercito italiano tra la la e la 2a guerra mondiale . Novembre 1918 – giugno 1940* (Rome, 1954), 114–15, 180, 187, 260; Alberto Rovighi and Filippo Stefani, *La partecipazione italiana alla guerra civile spagnola (1936–1939)*, 4 vols. (Rome, 1992–3), vol. III, 72–3, 98; Archivio Centrale dello Stato (hereafter ACS), Carte Graziani, folder 38, report of 4 Jan. 1938; Public Record Office, FO 371 22012/J29, J 284, J372, J468; National Archives (hereafter NA) T-973, reel 15, frames 352–70; *Documents diplomatiques français, 1932-1939*, 2nd series (hereafter *DDF*), vol. X, no. 240; J. E. Kaufmann and Robert M. Jurga, *Fortress Europe. European Fortifications of World War II* (Conshohocken, PA, 1999), 191–9.

[16] *DDF*, vol. VII, no. 424; De Felice, *Mussolini il duce. II*, 22–44; Fortunato Minniti, 'Profilo dell'iniziativa strategica italiana dalla "non belligeranza" alla "guerra parallela"', *'Storia contemporanea*, Dec. 1987, 1123–5. The king's fears were well-founded. See Ciano, *Diario*, 306; Anfuso, *Roma Berlino Salò*, 123.

[17] Ciano, *Diario*, 133–6; *DGFP*, D, vol. I, 759; Paul Schmidt, *Hitler's Interpreter*, ed. R. H. C. Steed (London, 1951), 83–4; *DGFP*, vol. II, nos. 220, 223; Pirelli, *Taccuini*, 208.

In May 1938, Mussolini considered an alliance with Hitler inevitable but premature. War in Spain provided one reason. An Italian-led offensive had severed Catalonia from the remainder of Republican Spain in mid-April 1938, and Mussolini expected victory by the summer. Thereafter, he could better negotiate with Hitler. By deterring the French and British, an Italian–German alliance would facilitate the Duce's plans to invade Albania, gaining Adriatic dominion. Mussolini could then reduce Yugoslavia to an Italian satellite.[18]

As the Duce insisted in his May speech at Genoa, he welcomed the *Anschluß*:

> The German world and the Roman world are in direct contact. Their friendship is lasting ... the so-called Great Democracies [may not be] preparing a war based on ideologies. Nonetheless, it's just as well for them to know that, in such a case, the Totalitarian States will immediately ally and march together all the way to the end.[19]

Acquiring more territory, wealth, and power also inspired Mussolini to ally with Germany. Paradoxically, he delayed, simultaneously threatening France and Britain. The Duce sought concessions by encouraging false hopes of Italian neutrality. His actual goal was to form a Fascist–Nazi alliance from a stronger position. Recognising Mussolini's duplicity, French Foreign Minister Yvon Delbos called this the policy of 'kicks in the rear end'.[20]

Ciano and other Fascist leaders had lost much pro-Axis enthusiasm after Hitler seized Austria with one day's warning. Many Italian diplomats shared this increasingly anti-Nazi attitude. They doubted the wisdom of aligning closely with Germany. But as Ciano realised when Hitler suggested an alliance in May 1938: 'The Duce intends to do it, and he will do it because he has a thousand and one reasons to distrust the Western Democracies.' Ciano reluctantly followed his father-in-law's lead, seeking concessions from the West, especially the British. He recognised the logic of Mussolini's approach towards Berlins, although he did not agree.

[18] Ciano, *Diario*, 66–7, 112, 125–8, 131, 136, 141, 147–9, 159; Mario Toscano, *Le origini del Patto d'Acciaio* (Florence, 1948), 4–18; Jens Petersen, 'Bernardo Attolico a Berlino', in Leonardo A. Losito (ed.), *Bernardo Attolico. Atti e Documenti dal convegno internazionale di studi nel primo cinquantenario di morte* (Brindisi, 1994); Rovighi and Stefani, *La partecipazione*, vol. III, 126–51.

[19] *OO*, vol. XXXIX, 99–102 (quotations, 100, 101, 102); *DGFP*, D, vol. I, 764.

[20] *Documents diplomatiques belges 1920–1940. La Politique de sécurité extérieure*, vol. V, (hereafter *DDB*), no. 1; *DDF*, vol. VII, no. 287; John E. Dreifort, *Yvon Delbos at the Quai d'Orsay. French Foreign Policy during the Popular Front 1936–1938* (Lawrence, 1973), 177–80, 197.

Ciano believed alliance with Germany would reduce the possibility of western appeasement of Italy.[21]

Strain between Vittorio Emanuele III and the dictators during Hitler's May visit increased rumours of a monarchical–Fascist rift. In response, the Duce pressured the king into an unprecedented pilgrimage to Mussolini's birthplace in June. The visit represented a not-too-subtle humiliation of the monarchy. In July, the regime initiated increasingly vicious anti-Semitic propaganda. While creating closer ties with the Nazis, these attacks were also aimed at the king. Unlike other monarchies, the Casa Savoia had displayed philo-Semitism since the *Risorgimento*. This was designed to contrast the Liberal Kingdom of Italy with the intolerant Roman Church. Italy had been distinguished by several Jewish prime ministers, foreign ministers, and disproportionate numbers of Jewish generals and admirals. Close ties bound the monarchy and Italian Jews. But that summer, Mussolini began pressuring the king to end this tradition.[22]

In mid-August 1938, warnings about German–Czech friction reached Rome. Ciano began worrying that Hitler was planning war. Soon, Italy's ambassador and military attaché in Berlin confirmed this. Nonetheless, it took weeks of diplomatic prodding before Hitler admitted he would attack the Czechs if they 'provoked' him. Throughout September, the likelihood of war fluctuated. By 10 September, however, Mussolini decided that if general war erupted Italy would fight alongside Germany. A week later, he told Ciano that war was virtually certain. Mussolini announced his Axis solidarity in six north-eastern Italian cities. Doing so in the area near 1915–18 battlefields and threatened by the *Anschluß*, emphasised his pledge. The Duce swore that if the West endangered Hitler's regime, Italy would fight to defend Nazism and, by extension, Fascism.[23]

Some have insisted Mussolini wanted peace. But the Duce revealed his intentions to just a few subordinates. These included army chief of staff General Alberto Pariani. By September 8 and probably earlier, Pariani's records indicate that Mussolini was expecting war between the Axis and

[21] *DDF*, vol. XI, no. 105; Ciano, *Diario*, 133 (quotation); Gerhard L. Weinberg, *The Foreign Policy of Hitler's Germany*, 2 vols. (Chicago, 1970–80), vol. II, 295–9.

[22] Giovanni Artieri, *Cronaca del regno d'Italia*, 2 vols. (Milan, 1977–8 ), vol. II, 552–3; Cannistraro and Sullivan, *Il Duce's Other Woman*, 26, 502–3, 511–13; Meir Michaelis, *Mussolini and the Jews. German–Italian Relations and the Jewish Question in Italy 1922–1945* (Oxford, 1978), 151–69.

[23] Ciano, *Diario*, 166–86; Sergio Pelagalli, *Il Generale Efisio Marras adetto militare a Berlino (1936–1943)* (Rome, 1994), 34–8, 409–14; Hungarian National Archives, K100, Foreign Ministry Archives, Laszló Szabó, Military Attaché Papers (hereafter SP), 1938, report 671/443; *OO*, vol. XXIX, 146, 158, 164; De Felice, *Mussolini il duce. II*, 515–19.

France, while hoping for British neutrality. Since Mussolini knew the French would not attack, such expectation reveals his aggressive intentions. On 25 September, Mussolini ordered partial mobilisation. But the African and Spanish wars had devoured army and air force resources. The navy was better prepared but faced overwhelming odds against the combined Western fleets. After this news reached upper government levels, panic spread. The Casa Savoia, many generals, and some Party leaders viewed Mussolini's unequivocal commitment to Hitler as suicidal. Nonetheless, Mussolini remained firm. While he had no alliance with Hitler, he had abandoned balancing between Germany and the West.[24]

However, on 28 September, worried by his military unreadiness, Mussolini answered Western appeals to restrain Hitler. He told Hitler Germany probably could gain the Sudetenland peacefully. Still, Mussolini stressed his unconditional solidarity. The Führer's reluctant agreement led to convocation of the Munich conference. Besides settling the Sudeten issue, the conferees discussed Polish and Hungarian territorial claims against Czechoslovakia. Mussolini backed Magyar demands. Secret politico-military agreements linked Italy and Hungary. Mussolini hoped Hungary could replace Austria to block German Balkan expansion. On 2 November, Italian–German arbitration awarded Hungary southern Slovakia. Three weeks later, Magyar dishonesty nearly involved Italy and Germany in proxy war. Claiming Berlin approved, the Hungarians received Mussolini's approval for Italian-piloted aircraft to help invade Ruthenia. Ciano prevented take-off, after discovering Magyar duplicity. The episode alienated Ciano but not Mussolini.[25]

[24] Weinberg, *Starting World War II*, 452–7; De Felice, *Mussolini il duce. II*, 520–7; Rosaria Quartararo, *Rome tra Londra e Berlino. La politica estera fascista dal 1930 a 1940* (Rome, 1980), 395–9; G. Bruce Strang, 'War and Peace: Mussolini's Road to Munich', in Igor Lukes and Erik Goldstein (eds.), *The Munich Crisis, 1938: Prelude to World War II* (London, 2000); Caviglia, *Diario*, 190–1; Bottai,*Diario*, 135; Ciano, *Diario*, 179–84; Carte Pariani, Civiche Raccolte Storiche di Milano, (hereafter CP), quaderno 28, Pariani to Ciano, 8 Sept. 1938, Pariani to Tripiccione, 10 and 13 September 1938; ibid., q. 29, Pariani to Mussolini, 27 September 1938; Mario Montanari, *L'esercito italiano alla vigilia della 2a guerra mondiale* (Rome, 1982), 224–5; Franco Fucci, *Emilio De Bono, il Maresciallo fucilato* (Milan, 1989), 282; Dorello Ferrari, 'La mobilitazione dell'esercito nella seconda guerra mondiale', *Storia contemporanea* (Dec. 1992), 1006–7; Nino Arena, *La Regia Aeronautica 1939–1943*, 4 vols. (Rome, 1981–5), vol. I, 50–1, 75–92; Franklin D. Roosevelt Library, Hyde Park, NY, Presidential Special File, 'Estimate of Potential Military Strength', Documents D, Naval Attaché Rome, vol. I, 'Material Readiness and Efficiency of the Italian Air Force', 25 October 1938; Giorgio Giorgerini, *Da Matapan al Golfo Persico. La marina militare italiana dal fascismo alla Repubblica* (Milan, 1989), 399–401; Robert Mallett, *The Italian Navy and Fascist Expansionism 1935–1940* (London, 1998), 119–20. While Pariani's records cited above indicate that Ciano was privy to Mussolini's intentions, Ciano's diary does not reveal such information.

[25] Ciano, *Diario*, 184–5, 191, 207, 214–15; *DGFP*, D, vol. II, nos. 641, 661, 669, 674, 675; ibid., vol. IV, nos. 99, 118, 122, 127–34, 139; Pirelli, *Taccuini*, 208–9; Anfuso, *Roma Berlino Salò*,

During the Czech crisis, the royal family had prepared Mussolini's overthrow to prevent disaster. Crown Prince Umberto, Crown Princess Maria José, and Marshal Pietro Badoglio, Mussolini's francophile military adviser, formed the core conspirators. Other plotters seem to have included Marshal Rodolfo Graziani, resentful over recent dismissal as Viceroy of Ethiopia; Dino Grandi, former foreign minister and then ambassador to Britain; Margherita Sarfatti, Mussolini's ex-mistress and adviser; Aldo Castellani, physician to the king and Duce, and Italian Church leaders. The latter suggests involvement of the dying anti-Nazi Pius XI. The conspirators hoped to persuade the king to reject general mobilisation, order Mussolini's arrest and abdicate, with Maria José as regent for her infant son.[26] But Mussolini did not request full mobilisation on 27 September. The Munich conference was arranged, the conspirators dispersed. Was the Duce aware of this plot? Given his efficient security system, probably so. But Mussolini could not seize the royal heirs and two of the army's marshals without provoking revolt. That Mussolini could not crush a real conspiracy indicates the limits of his power. His combined knowledge and impotence provoked mounting rage and frustration, finding release only in June 1940. This was also so for his foreign policy.

Since the 1920s, Italians employed by foreign embassies had routinely opened safes therein, allowing Italian military intelligence to photograph the contents. Information so obtained gave Mussolini immense diplomatic advantages. The French discovered the security breach only in April 1939; the British, not until 1944. If his agents ever enjoyed similar success with the Germans, Mussolini banned it after Hitler came to power. Once the Italians resumed anti-German spying in mid-1934, they could not penetrate Germany's embassy. Formation of the Axis seems to have ended Italian illegal intelligence gathering in Germany. Pariani, who controlled such intelligence activities in

82–3; Giordano Bruno Guerri, *Galeazzo Ciano. Una vita 1903/1944* (Milan, 1979), 335–7; Gyula Juhász, *Hungarian Foreign Policy 1919–1945* (Budapest, 1979), 82–4, 104–5, 117; Ignác Romsics, *István Bethlen: A Great Conservative Statesman of Hungary, 1874–1946* (New York, 1995), 223–30.

[26] *DBFP*, vol. II, no. 362; Donatella Bolech Cecchi, 'Un colpo di stato antifascista di Maria José nel settembre 1938?', *Il Politico* (Dec. 1979); Giovanni Artieri, *Umberto II e la crisi della monarchia* (Milan, 1983), 682–90; Dino Grandi, *Il mio paese. Ricordi autobiografici*, ed. Renzo De Felice (Bologna, 1985), 445–50; Ugo Guspini, *L'orecchio del regime. Le intercettazioni telefoniche al tempo del fascismo* (Milan, 1973), 158; Alessandro Cova, *Graziani. Un generale per il regime* (Rome, 1987), 200–2; Luciano Regolo, *La regina incompresa. Tutto il racconta della vita di Maria José di Savoia* (Milan, 1997), 179–81; Cornwell, *Hitler's Pope*, 181–4, 189–92, 201–3.

1936–9, was pro-Nazi and cooperated closely with the Abwehr from mid-1938.[27]

The opposite was hardly true. From at least late 1936, a well-placed Italian diplomat spied for the Germans. He reported extremely sensitive information, including conversations between Mussolini and Ciano. No later than February 1940, the Germans broke Italy's diplomatic code. These sources provided Hitler with extraordinary insights into Italian foreign policy. He could manipulate Mussolini to the breaking point of patience and pride – but never beyond. Mussolini understood what he could extract from London and Paris but knew little about German support for his initiatives. But Hitler knew Mussolini's secrets, and also Italian intelligence on foreign governments. This information flow helps to elucidate Italian–German relations between 1936 and 1940.[28]

Before Munich, Mussolini had offered Hitler full support. Afterwards, he expected the same. To prove his worthiness, Mussolini enthusiastically introduced anti-Semitic legislation in early November. After Pariani retired all Jewish officers, some shot themselves. Even high-ranking Fascists considered the decrees deplorable. Popular opinion reflected bewildered disapproval. Vittorio Emanuele III complained bitterly to Mussolini, but otherwise kept silent.[29]

Three weeks later, Mussolini authorised an intimidation campaign to extract concessions from France. During Ciano's speech to the Chamber on 30 November, his mention of national aspirations elicited shouts of 'Tunis, Jibuti, Corsica, Nice!' Thereafter, Paris and Rome initiated threatening military movements that continued for months. The Duce used his good relations with Chamberlain to gain British 'understanding' of Italian demands. Mussolini enjoyed considerable success,

[27] Anthony Adamthwaite, 'French Military Intelligence and the Coming of War 1935–1939,' in Christopher Andrew and Jeremy Noakes (eds.), *Intelligence and International Relations 1900–1945* (Exeter, 1987), 201; David Dilks, 'Flashes of Intelligence: The Foreign Office, The SIS and Security Before the Second World War', in Christopher Andrew and David Dilks (eds.), *The Missing Dimension. Governments and Intelligence Communities in the Twentieth Century* (Chicago, 1984), 106–18; Giuseppe De Lutiis, *I servizi segreti in Italia. Dal fascismo alla seconda repubblica* (Rome, 1998), 30–1; NA T-78, reel 365, frames 6326680–81; David Alvarez, 'Axis–Sigint Collaboration: A Limited Partnership,' *Intelligence and National Security* (Spring 1999), 5–6.

[28] *DGFP*, C, vol. VI, nos. 14, 193; D, vol. I, nos. 129, 745, 769, 795; vol. IV, nos. 452, 458 vol., no. 153; vol. VI, nos. 86, 536; vol. VII, nos. 226, 438; David Irving, *Breach of Security* (London, 1968), 124–5.

[29] Michele Sarfatti, *Mussolini control gli ebrei. Cronaca dell'elaborazione delle leggi del 1938* (Turin, 1994), 16–40; Cannistraro and Sullivan, *Il Duce's Other Woman, 513–17*; Michaelis, *Mussolini and the Jews*, 169–205 and 'Mussolini's unofficial mouthpiece: Telesio Interlandi – *Il Tevere* and the evolution of Mussolini's anti-Semitism', *Journal of Modern Italian Studies* (Fall 1998), 227–37; Ciano, *Diario*, 217–18.

receiving Chamberlain in mid-January 1939, when Italian–French relations threatened conflict. The Duce insisted he sought comprehensive settlement with the French. Chamberlain refused to mediate. But after secret Italian–French talks collapsed, the British began pressuring Paris to re-open discussions. This strengthened Mussolini's conviction gained after meeting Chamberlain face to face in Munich and Rome: British leaders were weaklings.[30]

Meanwhile, Hitler had attempted to retard French rearmament. Ribbentrop had visited Paris in early December to insist that Germany would never fight 'for Italian questions'. This ploy suited Hitler's purposes but undermined Mussolini's. Still hoping for German diplomatic support, on New Year's Day 1939 the Duce authorised Ciano to sign the alliance Hitler wanted. But Ribbentrop's futile search for Japanese adherence caused delay, and lack of reciprocal German guarantees caused increasing anxiety in Rome. Mussolini wanted no immediate conflict with France despite his bluster but worried that his threats might provoke war.

In December 1938, he had approved Pariani's proposal to reduce forty-six army divisions from three infantry regiments to two, but to give each proportionately greater firepower and mobility. Surplus regiments from old divisions would form new ones, adding twenty-three new but weak divisions to the army. Pariani believed the increased numbers would enhance Italian influence. But the army would remain disorganised until late 1940, lacking necessary equipment for at least two years longer. Finally, on 30 January, Hitler declared that if Italy was forced into war, Germany would march at its side. Three days later, a French emissary made secret colonial offers to Ciano. But after Ribbentrop leaked news to the French press, Paris suspended the talks. In greater secrecy – even from the British – the French renewed contacts, continuing through the spring. However, Premier Edouard Daladier knew of Mussolini's dishonesty and unwavering hostility. He sanctioned the talks only to retain support from men like Pierre Laval and satisfy the British.[31]

[30] *DDF*, vol. XIII, nos. 1, 9, 26, 36, 52, 57, 130, 159, 194, 215, 282, 313, 377, 423, 426, 434, 459; vol. XIV, nos. 6, 75, 124, 138, 176, 196, 240; vol. XV, nos. 128, 162, 166, 175, 193; *DBFP*, vol. III, no. 490; vol. IV, nos 309, 317, 319, 323, 326, 327, 346, 353, 354, 356; vol. V, nos. 79, 85, 235, 242; *DGFP*, D, vol. IV, nos. 412, 421, 435, 447; Ciano, *Diario*, 187–8, 218–21, 235–40, 244, 271, 275; David Dilks (ed.), *The Diaries of Sir Alexander Cadogan 1938–1945* (New York, 1972) (hereafter *Cadogan Diaries*), 134–9, 176–7; Shorrock, *From Ally to Enemy*, 240–51; Martin Thomas, 'At the Heart of Things? French Imperial Defence Planning in the Late 1930s', *French Historical Studies* (Spring 1998), 347–8.

[31] *DDI*, 9, vol. I, no. 226 (Ribbentrop quotation); Ciano, *Diario*, 223, 233, 244–8, 252–3, 268–9, 289, 295; *DBFP*, vol. III, no. 484; vol. V, no. 255; *DDF*, vol. XIV, no. 46; *DGFP*, D, vol. IV, nos. 421, 447; Guerri, *Galeazzo Ciano*, 342–3; Ubaldo Soddu, 'Memorie e riflessioni di un generale

After last-minute warnings to the Italians, the Germans occupied Prague on 15 March, destroying the Munich settlement. Any semblance of equality between Mussolini and Hitler vanished. Still, the Duce gained some solace. The Spanish war ended in Nationalist victory two weeks later. He backed Hungarian seizure of Ruthenia from newly independent Slovakia. To offset growing German influence in the Balkans, Mussolini ordered the invasion of Albania on 7 April. British–French guarantees to Romania and Greece followed six days later.[32]

About two weeks earlier, Hitler had ordered preparations to attack Poland. From a high-ranking army informant in Berlin, Hungarian intelligence soon learned that war was anticipated for late summer. Hungarian information from London indicated that Britain – and therefore, France – would only protest. Successful German aggression would render worthless Western guarantees to Romania and Greece. The Hungarian Regent Miklós Horthy perceived an opportunity to recover Transylvania, authorising army chief of staff Col.-Gen. Henrik Werth to plan accordingly. Since Berlin had sold southern Slovakia and Ruthenia to Budapest for costly concessions, Horthy did not want German help, especially if it required war with Poland. He preferred Italian assistance. In Rome, Hungarian military attaché Lt-Col. László Szabó received instructions to meet Mussolini.[33]

Szabó had served in Rome since early 1932. Despite their different stations and the attaché's deference, Mussolini had befriended him. On 1 May, Szabó revealed German plans and begged Mussolini's veto if Hitler demanded Hungarian assistance to attack Poland. The Duce pledged protection in a localised conflict. But if the West made war on Germany, Mussolini insisted that Italy and Hungary must join hostilities. They would make the Balkans an Axis resource area, even by force. Italy's priority would be an offensive from Albania on Greece, Britain's gateway

(1933–1941)', part 2, 44–6; Dorello Ferrari, 'Dalla divisione ternaria alla binaria: una pagina di storia dell'Esercito italiano', in *Memorie storiche militari 1982* (Rome, 1983), 69–77; François Bédarida, 'La 'gouvernante anglaise,' in René Rémond and Janine Bourdin (eds.), *Edouard Daladier, Chef de gouvernement, avril 1938–septembre 1939* (Paris, 1977), 236–7; Pierre Guillen, 'Les relations franco-italiennes (avril–juin 1940)', in David Wingate Pike (ed.), *The Opening of the Second World War* (New York, 1991), 299; G. Bruce Strang, 'Once More into the Breach: Britain's Guarantee to Poland, March 1939', *Journal of Contemporary History* (Oct. 1996), 734–5; *Verbali delle riunioni tenute dal capo di SM Generale*, 4 vols. (Rome, 1983–5), (hereafter *Verbali SM Generale*), vol. 12, 7–8; Shorrock, *From Ally to Enemy*, 252–5; Weinberg, *Starting World War II*, 507–9, 522–3, 528–9.

32 Ciano, *Diario*, 264–300; *DGFP*, D, vol. IV, no. 243; Weinberg, *Starting World War* II, 563–8.

33 *FRUS, 1939*, vol. I, 85–6; Weinberg, *Starting World War II*, 559–61; *DDI*, 8, vol. XII. no. 582; 9, vol. II, no. 215; C. A. Macartney, *October Fifteenth. A History of Hungary*, 2 vols. (New York, 1956), vol. I, 347–8; Juhász, *Hungarian Foreign Policy*, 160; Thomas Sakmyster, *Hungary's Admiral on Horseback. Miklós Horthy* (New York, 1994), 232–4.

to Eastern Europe. After recent inspections of Tripolitania's fortifications, Badoglio had reported that Libya would be secure from French invasion by autumn. With their western frontiers sealed from the Alps to the Sahara, the Italians could overrun the Balkans.[34]

The next day, the Duce told Ciano that Germany might invade Poland soon, igniting general war. On 6 May, while the foreign minister was conferring with Ribbentrop in Milan, Mussolini telephoned to order agreement to an alliance with Germany. Mussolini had intended to form one eventually. Presumably he had gained corroboration of Szabó's information and decided the moment had arrived.

Leaving Mussolini responsibility for the consequences, Ciano unenthusiastically accepted Ribbentrop's proposals. He did ensure the pact required 'continuous contact' regarding European security and consultations if conflict threatened. The treaty obliged each party to enter hostilities if the other did. Entitled the Pact of Steel, it was ratified in Berlin on 22 May, ending the pretence of Italian neutrality. Past Nazi treachery soon gave Mussolini pause. On 30 May, he sent Hitler a memorandum. He described war with the democracies as inevitable but stressed Italian unreadiness before 1943. Meanwhile, the Duce could overcome Italian anti-German attitudes and Hitler could improve German–Vatican relations. But on 23 May Hitler had told his generals he would attack Poland as soon as possible.[35]

Historians have carefully analysed subsequent events; repetition is pointless.[36] Nonetheless, newer information illuminates the May–September 1939 period. Ciano's diary indicates that he first received credible intelligence on 19 July that Hitler planned to attack Poland and on 21 August of the imminent Nazi–Soviet agreement. In fact, he knew by late May that Hitler had ignored Italian warnings and was concealing his plans from them. The Nazi leadership sought a Soviet

[34] *Annuario diplomatico del Regno d'Italia* (Rome, 1937), 616; *DDI*, 9, vol. I, no. 77; Lajos Kerekes (ed.), *Allianz Hitler–Horthy–Mussolini* (Budapest, 1966), 230–2; Antonello Biagini and Fernando Frattolillo (eds.), *Diario Storico del Comando Supremo* (Rome, 1986-), vol. I (*11.6.1940–31.8.1940*), vol. II, *Allegati* (hereafter *Diario Storico*), 18.

[35] Anfuso, *Roma Berlino Salò*, 108; *Holy See*, no. 18; *DDI*, 8, vol. XII, no. 59; *DGFP*, D, vol. VI, nos. 341, 426 (quotation 562), 459; Guerri, *Galeazzo Ciano*, 407–14; De Felice, *Mussolini il duce. II*, 614–43.

[36] Brian R. Sullivan, 'The Impatient Cat. Assessments of Military Power in Fascist Italy, 1936–1940,' in Williamson Murray and Allan R. Millett (eds.), *Calculations. Net Assessment and the Coming of World War II* (New York, 1992), 97–135; Quarta raro, *Rome tra Londra e Berlino*, 461–625; De Felice, *Mussolini il duce. II*, 643–842; MacGregor Knox, *Mussolini Unleashed 1939–1941. Politics and Strategy in Fascist Italy's Last War* (Cambridge, 1982), 42–125; Militärgeschichtliches Forschungsamt (ed.), *Germany and the Second World War*, vol. III. (Oxford, 1995), 5–126.

alliance and imminent destruction of Poland. Hans von Herwath of the German Moscow embassy first warned an Italian colleague on 6 May. Within three weeks, Ciano accepted the reports. This helps explain the Duce's late-May clarification memorandum to Hitler. Of course, Szabó had already advised Mussolini about German plans. By early June, Mussolini was telling Ciano 'war was now inevitable and would explode in August'. Ciano accepted this evaluation. Soviet chargé d'affaires (and NKVD *rezident*) Leon Helfand apparently substantiated Herwath's information, in his frequent meetings with Ciano. On 13 June, Mussolini and Ciano told German Ambassador Mackensen they knew of 'certain steps' Berlin was taking with Moscow, warning that this could endanger the Axis. By mentioning Schulenburg, Germany's representative in Moscow, and Helfand, Mussolini provided clear indications of his sources and their accuracy. By late June, rumours of impending Nazi–Soviet agreements, including Polish partition, circulated within informed circles. Contrary to later assertions, the Hitler–Stalin pact was not unexpected.[37]

Despite knowledge of Nazi treachery, neither Mussolini nor Ciano attempted to restrain the Germans for months. Given their rage when Hitler revealed his intentions in mid-August, this seems inexplicable. But the Italians had been preparing aggression, too. Mussolini anticipated eventual partition of Yugoslavia. Until 21 May, however, he and Ciano valued it as a temporary barrier against German expansion. On 26 May, they decided to demolish the Serb barricade. Herwath's warning explains the turnabout. Mussolini and Ciano must have agreed that a Polish crisis would provide the opportunity. If they delayed, Germany might place Yugoslavia under protection. Presumably, the Duce had considered such a step since Szabó had revealed Hitler's plans.

In late March, the Italian army staff had prepared *Progetto C* to occupy Croatia. The contingency plan involved a surprise attack from Istria by twelve divisions to occupy the main towns, allowing the Croats to revolt for independence. Italian intelligence estimated that the Yugoslav army would number thirty-three infantry divisions, three

[37] Ciano, *Diario*, 310, 320–36, 452; Hans von Herwath and S. Frederick Starr, *Against Two Evils* (New York, 1981), 144–59; *DGFP*, D, vol. VI, nos. 211, 341, 523, 536, appendix I, no. III; vol. VII, no. 79; Giorgio Petracchi, 'Pinocchio, the Cat, and the Fox. Italy between Germany and the Soviet Union, 1939–1940', in Bernd Wegner (ed.), *From Peace to War. Germany, Soviet Russia and the World, 1939–1941* (Oxford, 1997), 505–10; Pirelli, *Taccuini*, 217, 223; *Holy See*, nos. 57 (Mussolini quotation 159), 58, 276 (387–8); Bottai, *Diario*, 149; *DDI*, 8, vol. XII, nos. 201, 489; *DBFP*, vol. VI, nos. 211 (259), 258; *FRUS, 1939*, vol. I, 221; NA, RG 59, Visa Division, General Visa Correspondence, 1940–45, box 39, Reed to Hull, 22 July 1940, Enclosures nos. 1–2.

cavalry divisions and two mountain brigades, seven to eight days after mobilisation. Unlike new Italian formations, each Yugoslav division contained three infantry regiments. To counter this superior force, *Progetto C* required ten German and three to four Hungarian divisions as reinforcements.[38] By May 1939, Yugoslav security had deteriorated due to the Italian invasion of Albania and Germany's occupation of Yugoslavia's Czech ally. However, stiffening Western resolve made justification for Italian destruction of Yugoslavia advisable. Mussolini decided to attack in the autumn, before Belgrade also received Western guarantees. Rome would annex Kosovo and Dalmatia, forming a territorial link with Greater Albania; the Magyars would also acquire territory. Hungary would become an Italian satellite and Croatia an Italian protectorate. However, subversion promoting Croat revolt – the hastily invented pretext for intervention – encouraged Croat–Serb reconciliation. Few Croatian separatists envisioned their nation as another Bohemia–Moravia.[39]

Hitler's destruction of the Munich settlement infuriated the Duce. German interference in Croatia alarmed him. He responded by invading Albania. The approaching German–Polish conflict encouraged Mussolini to conquer more, without Hitler's involvement or interference. The Duce had conceived 'parallel war' that he would develop more fully in early 1940. Consequently, unknown to Ciano, Mussolini adopted other schemes: imminent subjugation of Greece and Romania. Such compartmentalisation of information typified Fascist government. For example, when Marshal Pietro Badoglio, chief of the general staff, inquired about Mussolini's conversations with Chamberlain in January 1939, he was informed that the details did not concern him.[40]

On 27 May, Pariani and Szabó discussed recent events. Pariani revealed that Italy and Germany would share food and raw materials to facilitate war preparations. The general responded positively when Szabó suggested that Hungary join the consortium. Occupying Albania had isolated Yugoslavia, Pariani argued. But Western guarantees to Poland,

[38] Salvatore Loi, *Le operazioni delle unità italiane in Jugoslavia (1941–1943)* (Rome, 1978), 37–40; Teodoro Zurlo, 'Emergenza "E,"' in *Memorie storiche militari 1979* (Rome, 1980), 372–7; NA T-821, reel 145, frames 211–12; reel 107, frames 167–71; Minniti, 'Profilo dell'iniziativa', 1143–5; Ciano, *Diario*, 293, 298–302.

[39] Ciano, *Diario*, 302–4, 306, 308, 311–12, 321; Bottai, *Diario*, 149; Pirelli, *Taccuini*, 218; J.B. Hoptner, *Yugoslavia in Crisis 1934–1941* (New York, 1962), 151–5.

[40] *DGFP*, D, vol. VI, nos. 15, 45, 55, 86, 87, 94, 140, 144, 150, 170, 171; Ciano, *Diario*, 263–80; Knox, *Mussolini Unleashed*, 53–4, 88–9; ACS, Carte Badoglio, busta 5, Anfuso to Gandin, 6 February 1939.

Romania, and Greece, the British–Turkish security agreement, and Western–Soviet talks threatened the Axis. Claiming that he expressed personal views, Pariani said that if general war began, Germany should attack Poland. Italy, Hungary, and possibly Bulgaria, should simultaneously assault Greece, then Romania. Hungary would regain Transylvania; Bulgaria, Southern Dobrudja. Repeating Mussolini's recent arguments, the general claimed his army could seize Corfu and Salonika, blocking Western aid through Greek ports, conquering Romania's oilfields and preventing Soviet advance into the Balkans. But he invited Magyar participation. Pariani concealed Italy's need for assistance in conquering Yugoslavia. The Hungarian hid his greater knowledge of the strategic situation. Instead, Szabó stressed Romanian forces outnumbered Hungary's. Pariani preposterously proffered twenty Italian divisions and an air corps as reinforcements. The general lied about prearranged German assistance of another ten divisions and a Fliegerkorps. Szabó argued that these matters required diplomatic agreements. But both countries' representatives moved slowly and gossiped widely. Pariani said he would approach the Duce; Szabó should inform Col.-Gen. Werth. If both concurred, Szabó and Mussolini could complete arrangements. Then, both army staffs could initiate planning. Within three weeks, Szabó received orders to continue discussions with Pariani.[41]

They met on 16 June. The attaché reported Werth's eagerness to enter the Italian–German raw materials agreement. Werth also hoped Axis forces would assist Hungary to conquer Transylvania. Pariani replied that this required Hungary joining the Pact of Steel and promised to discuss this with the Duce. Still, the colonel worried that Pariani seemed more intent on attacking Greece and Yugoslavia than Romania. This coincided with Mussolini's views four weeks earlier. But Magyar need for Italian reinforcements determined the issue. Their assembly on the Hungarian–Romanian border required transit through Croatia, necessitating Yugoslavia's prior destruction. Horthy agreed to higher-level discussions. Werth would visit Rome starting on 18 July.[42]

On 7 June, Mussolini had received a letter from Chamberlain, warning that a German attack on Poland would prompt British intervention.

[41] SP, report 528/1/39, 'Promemoria. About my conversation with LtGen Pariani, Undersecretary of War, on May 27, 1939'; ibid., handwritten notes to 528/1/39, 14 pps., numbered 17–30 and report 609/39, Szabó to Ujszászy, 10 June 1939; *DGFP*, D, vol. VI, nos. 341, 459; Loi, *Le operazioni*, 36–42.

[42] SP, Szabó to Werth, 16 June 1939; ibid., 'Promemoria no. 2, 1939.VI.16', Szabó to Pariani; ibid., report 665/39, Ujszászy to Szabó, 19 June 1939.

Mussolini rejected the threat, telling British ambassador Percy Loraine that Italy would back Germany. Meanwhile, Mussolini had ordered Ciano to press Hungary and Bulgaria to join the Axis, thinking that a mobilisation by three German allies against their Balkan neighbours would deter the West.[43] Apparently assuming Ciano would oppose Italian–Hungarian arrangements, Mussolini kept him uninformed. Since November, Ciano had discouraged Hungarian irredentism, while Mussolini supported it. The Duce envisioned the Pariani–Szabó project creating Italian Balkan hegemony. Ciano believed Hungarian–Romanian conflict would trigger German intervention.

The terminal illness of Ciano's father distracted him from late June to early July. He then visited Spain, returning on 19 July. Ciano learned of high-level visits between Sofia and Budapest, and Hungarian requests for British neutrality regarding Magyar claims to Transylvania. He also noted importunate Bulgarian and Hungarian requests for Italian and German weaponry, and Szabó's shuttling between Rome and Budapest, but the full implications escaped him.[44]

Badoglio's further inspections of Tripolitania and Albania brought Mussolini worrying information. The marshal reversed earlier optimism, reporting in mid-June that shortages had stalled fortification work west of Tripoli. The vital port would be vulnerable to French attack for eighteen months. Two weeks later, Badoglio described Albania as an excellent base for seizing Dalmatia, Serbia, Macedonia, and Salonika, and assisting Bulgaria, but said that extensive infrastructure expansion was necessary. However, German moves goaded Mussolini towards action. On 5 July, Berlin agreed to barter 100 Bf 109 fighters and 370 ex-Czech anti-aircraft and anti-tank guns for Yugoslav minerals. Three days later, the Germans pledged an exchange of 30 He 112B fighters and 250 Skoda howitzers for Romanian petroleum. Delivering and integrating these into Yugoslav and Romanian forces would take months. But Italy, let alone Hungary and Bulgaria, had no equivalent aircraft and little matching artillery. Better invasion sooner rather than later.[45]

43 *DDI*, 8, vol. XII, nos. 60, 100, 463, 505; *DBFP*, VI, nos. 234, 261; *DGFP*, D, vol. VI, 629; Ciano, *Diario*, 303–4, 308.

44 *DDI*, 8, vol. XII, nos. 7, 277, 286, 287, 325, 336, 343, 350, 368, 557, 582, 584, 644; *DGFP*, D, vol. VI, nos. 476, 480, 500, 566, 617, 618, 656, 659; SP, document 43681, handwritten notes on conversations with Pariani and others, 18 July–3 September 1939, 44 pps., 9; Ciano, *Diario*, 216, 226, 238, 243, 291, 298, 311–20.

45 *Diario Storico*, 38–9, 53; Ciano, *Diario*, 319; *DGFP*, D, vol. VI, nos. 52, 117, 620, 632, 738; M. Axworthy, C. Scafe and C. Craciunoiu, *Third Axis, Fourth Ally. Romanian Armed Forces in the European War, 1941–1945* (London, 1995), 29, 278; William Green, *The Warplanes of the Third Reich* (New York, 1986), 314, 543.

Circumventing diplomatic channels impeded Italian–Hungarian communications. By mid-July, military planning had stalled. Exasperated, Szabó arranged to meet the Duce. When they spoke on 14 July – scheduled for Ciano's absence – Mussolini rejected Hungarian membership in the Pact of Steel. Such a formality could alert enemies (and Ciano): better the Duce's verbal promise and covert Hungarian declaration of pro-Axis alignment. Then, Pariani and Werth could formulate broad plans. Italian and Hungarian staffs would develop details under cover of attendance at early-August Po valley military manoeuvres. Horthy agreed.[46] Starting on 18 July, Pariani and Werth conferred in northern Italy. Werth gave advance warning that Hungarian sympathies prevented helping an attack on Poland. This precluded German involvement in Balkan operations as a *quid pro quo*, as Mussolini surely anticipated. Pariani persuaded Werth to proceed in the operational sequence Mussolini proposed. As compensation, the Italians promised more aircraft to the Hungarians. Pariani's staff had completed planning to concentrate forces along the Italian–Yugoslav frontier. Combined operations plans would be complete by early August; only Italians and Bulgarians would assault Greece. Clearly, Mussolini had informed neither Budapest nor Sofia about likely Nazi–Soviet accords. Nor, when Hitler and Mussolini received identical 24 July notes pledging Hungary's loyalty but refusal to attack Poland, did Ciano realise their meaning.[47]

Meanwhile, the Germans had inadvertently encouraged Italian–Hungarian cooperation. Berlin had accepted Hungarian membership in the Axis raw materials agreement only in principle. The Germans insisted on prior bilateral accords, the type of deal Horthy sought to avoid. When Werth visited Berlin in early July, the Germans rebuffed his arms requests. Yet they were bartering weapons for Jugoslav and Romanian resources. A week later, the Hungarian government sought additional Italian warplanes and the closest possible military ties to Rome.[48]

When Pariani and Werth met again in northern Italy on 3 August, however, no operations plans were ready. Nor had Pariani contacted the

[46] NA, T-973, reel 15, frames 328–30; *DDI*, 8, vol. XII, nos. 557, 582, 584.

[47] SP, document 43681; NA T-821, reel 108, frames 695–713; *DGFP*, D, vol. VI, no. 712; *DDI*, 8, vol. XII, no. 664; Ciano, *Diario*, 321–2; CP, q 39, Pariani to Viscontini, 11 August 1939; ibid., Pariani to Tripiccione, 12 August 1939; ibid., q. 40, 'Riunioni 17-8-39,' ibid., Pariani to Soddu, 17 August 1939; ibid., 'Riunioni 19-8-39'; Juhász, *Hungarian Foreign Policy*, 160–1; Roberto Gentilli, *L'aviazione da caccia italiana 1918–1939*, 2 vols. (Florence, 1977–82), vol. II, *Tecnica, stemmi, esportazioni*, 134–5; George Punka, *Hungarian Air Force* (Carrollton, TX, 1994), 5, 20–1, 37–8; *Diario Storico*, 101–48.

[48] *DGFP*, D, vol. VI, nos. 578, 595, 641, 706; *DDI*, 8, vol. XII, no. 426, 557, 582.

Germans. He described Pact of Steel matters as diplomatic responsibilities. Although Pariani had met the Duce the previous day, he claimed the dictator had ignored the issue. In fact, Pariani believed Mussolini and Ciano had never discussed the question. Yet Pariani insisted that he had informed Berlin of Italy's Balkan intentions. Actual planning could wait until he visited Germany in October–November. Pariani opposed a priori operational planning. Politics could quickly render plans obsolete. Better to defer them to the last minute. However, Axis forces would assuredly fight together. Italy had ten divisions ready for offensive deployment against France, Romania, or Greece, depending on the circumstances. Responding to Werth's question, Pariani insisted that Germany would provide troops to attack Romania. Likewise, the Hungarians must be ready to attack Yugoslavia. When Werth asked if this should be put in writing, Pariani argued that the West might discover such agreements: better a verbal understanding. The Germans would not demand that Hungary attacked Poland, since they could crush the Poles alone. Common action – against France or Romania – would be decided at an autumn tripartite conference. Pariani's lies and evasions echoed German treatment of the Italians.[49]

Did the Duce expect Western toleration of attacks on Greece and Romania? Neither he nor Pariani had mentioned precise dates to the Hungarians. That lapse and the concepts he and Pariani had propounded, suggest that Mussolini intended to wait until Hitler invaded Poland. If the West accepted such aggression, their other security guarantees would be worthless. Italy, Hungary, and Bulgaria could proceed to revise Balkan borders. Did Mussolini and Pariani think their army of infantry, horses, and mules could conduct three separate Balkan offensives within months? The rugged peninsula stretches over 700 miles east–west and 800 miles north–south, is intersected by numerous deep rivers, and traversed by few roads, bridges and railways. Balkan geography presented more challenges than Spain's, where victory had required over two years of hard fighting by motorised forces. In mid-1939, the punishing lessons inflicted by the 1940 Greek and North African campaigns had not yet taught Mussolini how inadequate were his army's logistics. Nonetheless, the Ethiopian and Spanish wars had already revealed how important trucks and fuel were for rapid operations.[50] Evidence

[49] *DDI*, 8, vol. XII, no. 584; SP, document 43681, 'Conversation with Gen Pariani from 1800 on Aug. 3', 19–24.

[50] Servizio Informazioni Militare, *Jugoslavia. Preparazione militare alla frontiera giulia* (Rome, 1938) and *Jugoslavia. Preparazione militare all frontiera albanese* (Rome, 1939); SP, '*Promemoria No. 2*, 1939.VI.

suggests that Mussolini expected Balkan conquests would require more threat than conduct of major operations. Since 1934, Pariani had developed a two-stage war planning concept: concentration plans, based on semi-permanent factors like geography, transport systems, and physical objectives, could be developed in advance for unit assembly and deployment. Operational planning, dependent on variables like political–strategic aims and contending forces, would be delayed until the eve of conflict. Superficially logical, this approach only rationalised Mussolini's strategic fantasies.

Since 1934, Mussolini had required readiness for war in East Africa, North Africa, Spain, southern France, the Austrian-Bavarian region, and throughout the Balkans – often simultaneously. Such demands would have severely challenged even the best army. For the threadbare Italian forces, such tasking proved wildly unrealistic. However, Mussolini had retired Pariani's predecessor for insisting that the army's means did not match the Duce's aims. Pariani avoided addressing the problem altogether by developing concentration plans to defend Italy's frontiers. Remaining forces would assemble for the offensive in one sector. Based on 1935–6 events, he preferred an advance from Cyrenaica on the Nile Delta. The First World War had convinced Badoglio that all offensives were risky and Europe was more important than Africa. He advised Mussolini to secure Italian borders, wait and then pounce on a vulnerable Balkan victim. Pariani's discussions with Szabó and Werth combined his concentration concept with Badoglio's geographic focus.[51]

The material unreadiness of the army was largely irrelevant to Mussolini and Pariani. The general had designed his two-regiment divisions to attack. He believed Fascism had toughened Italians. By throwing enough force at an opponent's weakest point, it would break. Thereafter, mobile Italian divisions would surge into the enemy's rear. Better to do so with the tanks, artillery, and trucks soon to be produced. But the army of 1939 should suffice against Balkan armies.

The Duce had laboured for a generation to create *homo fascistus*, whose willpower could overcome any obstacle. Still, Mussolini's memories of 1915–17 frontal assaults tempered his enthusiasm for such tactics. His

16'; Ferruccio Botti, 'La logistica dei poveri: Organizzazione dei rifornimenti e amministrazione dell'esercito nel 1940', *Studi storico-militari (1992)* (Rome, 1994), 429–38.

[51] ACS, Segretaria Particolare del Duce, Carteggio Riservato (hereafter SPD, CR), busta 41, Farinacci to Mussolini, 13 September 1939; Fortunato Minniti, 'Piano e ordinamento nella preparazione italiana alla guerra degli anni trenta', *Dimensioni e problemi della ricerca storica*, 1 (1990), 136–58.

confidence arose from misreading Clausewitz: war was a continuation of politics by similar means. Fascist–Nazi successes since 1935 had sprung far more from threats and manipulation than fighting. So it would be with Poland and the Balkans. Perhaps they would capitulate, perhaps resist. Either way, German and Italian forces would subjugate them. But the mobilisation of totalitarian armies would overawe the West as in September 1938. After the Axis had digested its latest prey, in three or four years it could devour the bloated pluto-democracies.[52]

As his plans proceeded, Mussolini asked Hitler to meet in early August. In a letter written on 22 July, Mussolini stressed that Italy would always back Germany in war – an odd pledge given German promises of years-long peace – but stressed that Italy would be even better prepared in 1940. They should propose a European conference. Germany could obtain Danzig, probably more, from the frightened West. Ribbentrop responded evasively. A week later, Mussolini repeated his request through Ciano, who noted pointedly: 'In a month's time [the conference] will force itself upon us of its own accord.'[53] Mussolini began receiving unsettling intelligence from the final week of July. Reliable sources indicated Western determination to back Poland by force. If Italy and Bulgaria intervened, the British, French, Greeks, and Turks would seize the Dodecanese, defend Salonika against Italian attack, overrun Bulgaria, attack Libya, and even invade northern Italy. The Romanians were mobilising against Hungary. The Franco regime, charmed by French ambassador Marshal Philippe Pétain, was no longer reliable. The Germans were ignoring Hungarian protests over arms sales to Yugoslavia and Romania. The West knew Hitler was concealing his Polish plans from Mussolini. After continued German silence, Mussolini insisted on August 7 that Ciano and Ribbentrop meet immediately.[54]

Ciano was invited to meet Ribbentrop and Hitler from 11 to 13 August. Meanwhile, Mussolini received more bad news. Marshal Emilio De Bono reported that the Western Alpine defences were gravely deficient. Pariani's Po valley manoeuvres of 1–7 August had revealed a poorly led, badly trained, wretchedly equipped army. The scenario had been a French invasion of north-western Italy, followed by counterattack

[52] NA T-821, reel 107, frames 63, 77, 112; Minniti, 'Profilo dell'iniziativa', 1153, 1157–60 and 'Piano e ordinamento', 151; Cannistraro and Sullivan, *Il Duce's Other Woman*, 133–51; Sullivan, 'The Impatient Cat', 134–5.

[53] *DGFP*, D, vol. VI, nos. 718, 737 (Ciano quotation); *DDI*, 8, vol. XII, nos. 640, 647, 662, 677, 678, 687, 717.

[54] *DDI*, 8, vol. XII, nos. 673, 690, 699, 745, 750, 757, 767, 759, 772, 784, 788, 797, 820; *DGFP*, D, vol. VI, no. 777; Bottai, *Diario*, 154–5.

by armoured and motorised units of the new Armata Po. But snarled railroad lines, mechanical breakdowns, lack of radios, and incompetent officers fragmented the army into a bewildered mob. Foreign observers chortled with amusement. The king departed enraged and humiliated. More seriously, all had witnessed Italian incapacity to defend the Po valley. When Ciano met Ribbentrop, the assumptions underpinning Mussolini's Balkan 'parallel war' had been demolished.[55]

Mussolini had insisted that Italy would back Germany unconditionally because he had thought the West would not fight over Poland. Trusting Mussolini, Hitler had proceeded accordingly. The Duce realised his error too late. Hitler would allow no *Schweinehund*, Chamberlain or Mussolini, to stop his war again through diplomacy.[56] Ciano's meetings with Ribbentrop and Hitler proved more theatrical than diplomatic. Before departing, Ciano had secretly informed the British of his implacable anti-German stance. He neither expected to dissuade Hitler nor to be persuaded that Italy should back Germany. He only sought proof of German indifference to Italian interests.[57]

Ciano's and – especially – Mussolini's subsequent anger sprang not just from brazen German admission of lies the Italians had long penetrated. It arose from envy, frustration, humiliation, and fear. Hitler could seize new booty, they could not. Hitler would invade Poland regardless of consequences. Either Italy could remain neutral, revealing Fascist bellicosity as bluster, or it could declare war and fall under concentrated attack. Germany lay safe behind the *Westwall*, Italian frontier fortifications offered little defence. Yet Mussolini's lust for conquest tormented him, leaving Hitler unaware how much he had wounded his ally. By keeping Ciano ignorant of his schemes, Mussolini had also prevented Germany's foreign ministry informant from learning of his plans. On 12 August, Hitler had suggested to Ciano that Italy dismember Yugoslavia after Poland had fallen. To Mussolini, this was like throwing some dog a bone.[58]

Thus, while agreeing that Italy could not enter general war, on 16 August the Duce ordered Badoglio to obtain plans from the chiefs of

[55] NA T-821, reel 107, frames 218–19, 229; reel 384, frames 377–411, 422–59; Ciano, *Diario*, 325–6; Bottai, *Diario*, 153; *DDI*, 8, vol. XII, nos. 809, 810; Fucci, *Emilio De Bono*, 285–7; Sullivan, 'The Impatient Cat', 114.

[56] *DGFP*, D, vol. VII, no. 192 (quotation 204); Weinberg, *Starting World War II*, 611.

[57] *DBFP*, vol. VI, no. 617; *DDI*, 8, vol. XIII, nos. 1, 4, 21; *DGFP*, D, vol. VII, nos. 43, 47; Ciano, *Diario*, 326–8; Anfuso, *Roma Berlino Salò*, 121; Guerri, *Galeazzo Ciano*, 416–23; Ray Moseley, *Mussolini's Shadow. The Double Life of Count Galeazzo Ciano* (New Haven, 1999), 72–9.

[58] *DGFP*, D, vol. VII, nos. 43 (42), 438; Grandi, *Il mio paese*, 513–15; Ciano, *Diario*, 327.

staff for attacks on Greece and Yugoslavia. Ciano thought such localised conflicts might be practical. That seems to explain his 19–20 August inspection of Albania. News that Mussolini was preparing to fight the West brought him back to Rome. While insisting the army was in fine shape, Pariani admitted that it could not conquer Greece or Yugoslavia without foreign assistance. Yet he ordered preparations to attack Greece with Italian forces alone. The king warned that recent manoeuvres had revealed an army in a shambles. Badoglio stressed Italian vulnerability to French attack, the dangers in relying on German military aid and Hungarian and Bulgarian weakness. For once, technical arguments overcame the Duce's Fascist ideology. Nonetheless, it took Ciano until late on 25 August to dissuade Mussolini from war. But until the last, the dictator tried arranging a second Munich to acquire some Balkan territory. Only undeniable evidence of Italian impotence finally forced Mussolini's reluctant declaration of non-belligerence on 1 September. Three days later, he talked again of smashing Yugoslavia and seizing Romanian oil.[59]

Thereafter, Mussolini tolerated Ciano's anti-German policies. They supported Mussolini's short-term goals. Ciano hoped to provoke a break with Germany. The Duce remained loyal to the Axis. But first he wanted Hitler to acknowledge his value as an ally. These different goals explain why Ciano proposed – and Mussolini agreed to – forming a neutral Balkan bloc.[60] The Romanians had offered Hungary a non-aggression pact on 24 August, which Budapest rejected. Five days later, the British informed Bucharest that their guarantee excluded Bessarabia. These rebuffs worried the Romanians. Soviet invasion of Poland on 17 September terrified them. Encouraged by London, the Romanians sought the formation of a neutral Balkan bloc. Simultaneously, the Germans pressured Hungary to permit the transit of Wehrmacht forces. Furthermore, the Hungarians feared that Yugoslav and Romanian mobilisation heralded an Allied Balkan campaign via Salonika. If French forces from Syria entered Bulgaria, it would prompt German and Soviet countermoves. After the Red Army invasion of Poland established a common Hungarian–Soviet border, the Magyars begged Mussolini for protection.[61]

59 *Diario Storico*, 107–14, 132, 135, 138, 145, 150; CP, q. 40, 'Riunione 17–8–39'; Pariani to Soddu, 17 August 1939; 'Riunione 22–8–39-XVII'; 'Riunione pomeriggio 22-8-39'; Vincenzo Gallinari, *Le operazioni del giugno 1940 sulle alpi occidentali* (Rome, 1994), 27–30, 64–73; *DDI*, 8, vol. XIII, nos. 162, 186; Ciano, *Diario*, 328–42; Grandi, *Il mio paese*, 505–16; Guerri, *Galeazzo Ciano*, 429–42; Moseley, *Mussolini's Shadow*, 79–85; Minniti, 'Profilo dell'iniziativa', 1159–60.

60 André, 'La non belligeranza', 157–9.

61 *DDI*, 9, I, nos. 7, 104, 124, 216, 238, 585; SP, typed notes marked '1939.IX.5'; ibid., handwritten notes marked 'IX.9', '1939 IX.10', '1939.IX.11', 'IX.17', 'IX.18'; Dov B. Lungu, *Romania and the*

Unable to conquer Balkan resources, Mussolini considered controlling them to strengthen Italy before intervention in the war. Throughout September 1939, Hungarian and Romanian appeals reinforced other reasons for the Duce to form a Danube–Balkan neutrals group. Italian intelligence confirmed Allied planning for a Balkan campaign but also of Turkish opposition if the peninsula remained peaceful. The Yugoslavs also asked Rome for support against Germany. Responding to Mussolini's request, Hitler stopped pressuring Budapest and Belgrade, and approved a neutral bloc, if anti-British. In turn, Yugoslavia, Romania, and Hungary partially demobilised. The Germans, Soviets and French all opposed increased Italian Balkan influence at their expense. No regional states except Hungary and Bulgaria welcomed possible Italian hegemony. (But the Magyars offered support for the neutral bloc only in exchange for still more Italian aircraft and artillery.) Nonetheless, Italian predominance was preferable to German or Soviet. The British promoted the bloc after contacts between Ciano and Chamberlain persuaded London it would be anti-German. Assurances between Rome, Athens, and London led to Greek support in mid-October. The Soviets retaliated by ending oil sales to Italy. This only strengthened Mussolini's desire for Balkan predominance, as Romanian petroleum became essential for Italian war preparations.[62]

But as the neutral bloc neared realisation, Mussolini backed away. Neutrality repelled him. Worse, Turkey allied with the West on 19 October. The Turks agreed to defend Greece, Romania, and Allied Mediterranean territory. This made Italian bloc membership pointless, especially after Hungarian intelligence reported that the French had doubled their intervention force in Syria. Under German pressure and at Mussolini's order, Ciano denounced the initiative, repeatedly reassuring Berlin of his opposition. With British and Romanian assistance, however, he secretly encouraged formation of the bloc for two months. Only on 9 December did he acknowledge that Mussolini's hostility had stymied the project. The following week, in a thinly veiled anti-German speech justifying recent Italian foreign policy, Ciano formally rejected the

*Great Powers, 1933–1940* (Durham, 1989), 200–4; Keith Hitchens, *Rumania 1866–1947* (Oxford, 1994), 444.

[62] *DDI*, 9, vol. I, nos. 76, 175, 258, 385, 394, 407, 523, 634, 736, 761, 772, 792, 807; vol. II, no. 547; *Cadogan Diaries*, 226–7; ACS, Ministero dell'Africa Italiana, b. 9, *Verbali della XVIII Sessione della Commissione Suprema della Difesa* (hereafter CSD), 80; SP, handwritten notes marked 'IX.18', 'IX.28'; Ciano, *Diario*, 342, 344–7, 349, 351–3; Lungu, *Romania*, 205-6; Hoptner, *Yugoslavia in Crisis*, 167–71; John O. Iatrides (ed.), *Ambassador MacVeagh Reports. Greece, 1933–1947* (Princeton, 1980), 171, 174, 179; Bottai, *Diario*, 165.

neutral bloc proposal. Since August, he had not acted from pro-Allied sentiment, nor Mussolini from pro-German feelings. Indeed, Ciano hoped cooperation with the West would allow Italy to dismember Yugoslavia. Instead, Mussolini and Ciano had proceeded from their differing assessments of who would win the European war.[63]

After a decent interval, in late October–early November, Mussolini dismissed Pariani and others as scapegoats for his own failure to match military means to strategic ends. This, however, was a tactical move for domestic political reasons, not a sign of diplomatic reorientation. The Duce glumly accepted Hitler's veto on Balkan aggression to preserve German access to raw materials and avoid provocation of Allied intervention in south-east Europe. He even surrendered to Berlin much production from Italian-owned nickel mines in Greece, despite Ciano's objections. Save for those in northern Finland – presently under Soviet threat – the Lokris mines were the only European source of nickel, essential for armour plate. Nickel and copper, abundant in Yugoslavia, were among the metals especially essential for Italian arms manufacture. Given Mussolini's determination to subjugate Yugoslavia and Greece, these concessions implied expectation of future Balkan rewards from a victorious Germany.

Mussolini rebuffed Western reconciliation attempts. To speed war preparations, he rejected lucrative Allied offers for Italian arms. He temporised over Romanian and additional Hungarian requests, finally granting them in early 1940. He did sell Finland and Sweden armaments – more evidence that he knew of the Hitler–Stalin Pact's secret protocol – to divert the Soviets from the Balkans and remind Hitler that Italians could be helpful allies but dangerous opponents. The Duce sought general negotiations after Poland collapsed. After learning in late December of Germany's aggressive intentions in the west, Mussolini let Ciano warn the Low Countries of an impending German attack – subsequently cancelled. He allowed Belgium to purchase forty fighter planes. On 3 January 1940, he explicitly asked Hitler to make peace with the democracies, then let their inner rot destroy them. But Mussolini only intended to delay Hitler's offensive until Italy could participate. As the

[63] *DDI*, 9, vol. II, nos. 142, 212, 225, 278, 282, 307, 321, 374, 510, 530; *DGFP*, D, vol. VIII, nos. 266, 358, 372, 478; Ciano, *Diario*, 353, 358–60, 364, 374–5; Anfuso, *Roma Berlino Salò*, 127–8; NA T-821, reel 107, frames 161-3; Pirelli, *Taccuini*, 249; Lungu, *Romania*, 206-7; Knox, *Mussolini Unleashed*, 50–2, 62.

Duce privately assured Col. Szabó on several occasions, he remained committed to the Axis.[64]

Meanwhile, various Italian groups sought true neutrality. Most leading Fascists, worried that war could destroy the regime, supported Ciano's efforts. Many diplomats concurred, believing intervention would wreck Italy. Bankers, industrialists and landowners favoured trade rather than conflict with the West. Given their impoverished forces, military leaders preferred peace. To his intimates, Badoglio expressed pro-French and violently anti-German sentiments. Middle-class majorities, officers included, expressed open anti-Soviet and covert anti-German attitudes. These stances hindered Mussolini. For workers and peasants, another war meant death and taxes. But Fascism had reduced that majority to passive obedience. Only king or pope could rouse their defiance. But Vittorio Emanuele III and Pius XII preferred *coups* to revolutions.[65]

The pontiff supported Wehrmacht plots against Hitler between November 1939 and April 1940. Pius XII relayed messages from the conspirators to Britain's Vatican mission embassy. Evidence suggests he simultaneously backed conspiracy against Mussolini. But both intrigues ultimately depended on internal military revolt.

Ciano had gained royal support against war in late August 1939. Especially after the Hitler–Stalin Pact, Vittorio Emanuele III loathed the idea of fighting alongside Germany. Over the following months, Ciano, Prince Umberto, and Crown Princess Maria José met frequently. A Vatican representative contacted Ciano in early September, stressing papal desire for Italian neutrality. In late December 1939, Ciano presided over unprecedented visits between Pius XII and the notoriously

[64] *DDI*, 9, I, nos. 77, 122, 211, 240, 328, 817, 827; vol. II, nos. 335, 490, 491, 527, 563, 637, 764; vol. III, nos. 44, 74, 196, 221, 236, 264, 636; *DGFP*, D, vol. VIII, nos. 504, 551, 553, 557; *DDB*, no. 208; *OO*, vol. XXIX, 312–13; vol. XLIII, 17, 19–20; SP, Ujszászy to Szabó, 10 and 12 December 1939; ibid., Ministry of Industrial Affairs to Szabó, 12 December 1939; *FRUS, 1940*, I, 26; Soddu, 'Memorie' part 3, 'Un anno di sottosegretaria alla guerra', 3, 23; Ciano, *Diario*, 374, 377, 383; ACS, CSD *XVII*, 123; Fortunato Minniti, 'Gli aiuti militari italiani alla Finlandia durante la guerra d'inverno', *Memorie storiche militari 1979* (Rome, 1980); Arena, *La Regia Aeronautica*, vol. I, 47–8; Gentilli, *L'aviazione da caccia*, 135; Charles Burdick and Hans-Adolf Jacobsen (eds.), *Halder Diary* (Novato CA, 1988), 85–91; Knox, *Mussolini Unleashed*, 52–7, 68–9; André, 'La non belligeranza', 159. The Italian Air Force possessed only eighty metal mono-wing fighters in October 1939. Mussolini sold thirty-five to the Finns.

[65] Pirelli, *Taccuini*, 228–48; ACS, SPD, CR, busta 63, 'Badoglio', report of 8 February 1940; *Holy See*, nos. 57, 151, 191, 211, 276; *DGFP*, D, vol. VIII, nos. 505, 612; Sumner Welles, *The Time for Decision* (New York, 1944), 83, 143, 146; Petracchi, 'Pinocchio, the Cat, and the Fox', 513–16; Brunello Vigezzi, 'Mussolini, Ciano, la diplomazia italiana e i problemi della politica di potenza all'inizio della seconda guerra mondiale' in Brunello Vigezzi, *L'Italia unita e le sfide della politica estera. Dal Risorgimento alla Repubblica* (Milan, 1997); Mimmo Franzinelli, *I tentacoli dell'OVRA. Agenti, collaboratori e vittime della polizia politica fascista* (Turin, 1999), 229–360, 376.

anti-clerical king to establish mutual trust. Soon after, Ciano told Maria José Hitler planned to invade her native Belgium. The pope sent similar warnings. In early 1940, princess, pope, and foreign minister drew military and Fascist leaders into the conspiracy. Many feared where Mussolini led. Friendship between Maria José and Pius XII facilitated communication. Nonetheless, all depended on the king. Only his army could overthrow Mussolini.[66]

Mussolini discovered the intrigue. Anxiety burdened him, increased by Hitler's silence. He vented his feelings on 10 February. After Szabó inquired about Axis solidarity, the Duce bellowed his response. He alone had saved the alliance, despite German actions! Germany's economy would survive blockade. Neither side could pierce the other's fortifications (the king and Ciano agreed). Victory would be won in the air and at sea. Thus, Italian air and naval intervention would prove decisive. His navy would be ready by summer. But Mussolini did not mention that the air force needed longer, and the army still more time.

Hints of negotiations raised Mussolini's spirits, then dashed them when proven unfounded. Roosevelt's emissary Sumner Welles met the Duce on 26 February. Mussolini appeared 'fifteen years older than his actual age'. Still, he defended Hitler vehemently. Several days later, Mussolini called those anticipating German defeat 'criminals and imbeciles'. The next week he insulted Ciano as stupid to expect British victory.[67]

Ribbentrop finally delivered a letter from Hitler on 10 March. The Führer would crush the Allies, invited the Duce's participation, and requested talks. Mussolini agreed to meet. On 11 March, after Ribbentrop revealed German plans to attack the West in June or July, Mussolini promised to join Hitler's offensive. Within forty-eight hours, Mussolini claimed to regret his rashness. He assured Ciano modification of his position at the 18 March conference. Yet Mussolini displayed exuberance. When Welles saw him on 16 March, Mussolini appeared relieved

[66] Ciano, *Diario*, 333, 343, 366–7, 375–8, 396, 398–9; *Holy See*, nos. 221, 230, 237, 241, 243, 244, 276; *Cadogan Diaries*, 227; Cornwell, *Hitler's Pope*, 234–40; John H. Waller, 'The Double Life of Admiral Canaris', *International Journal of Intelligence and Counterintelligence* (Fall 1996), 278–9; PRO FO 371/23820 Italy 1939 R8007, Biondani to Foreign Office, 19 September 1939; Paolo Puntoni, *Parla Vittorio Emanuele III* (Bologna, 1993), 5; Caviglia, *Diario*, 215, 234–6, 243; Artieri, *Umberto II*, 699–701; Regolo, *La regina incompresa*, 188–99; André, 'La non belligeranza', 159; Bottai, *Diario*, 150–1, 153–8, 164–76; Cesare Maria De Vecchi, *Il Quadrumviro scomodo. Il vero Mussolini nelle memorie del pi monarchico dei fascisti*, ed. Luigi Romersa (Milan, 1983), 234–35; Fucci, *Emilio De Bono*, 291–4; Egidio Ortona, *Diplomazia di guerra. Diari 1937–1943* (Bologna, 1993), 83, 86; Ubaldo Soddu, 'Memorie', part 3, 40–45; *FRUS, 1940*, vo. I, 115.

[67] *Holy See*, nos. 274, 335; SP, report 288/1940; *FRUS, 1940*, vol. I, 28 (quotation); Caviglia, *Diario*, 218–21, 225–6; Ciano, *Diario*, 399–400, 403–4.

of 'some great weight'. Rumours of Mussolini's commitment spread. On 14 March, the king had informed Ciano that *coup* preparations were complete.[68]

At the Brenner in plenary session, Mussolini promised intervention – when opportune. He persuaded Ciano that this left Italy free. However, the dictators spoke privately. Hitler trusted Mussolini with secrets. He may have revealed plans for the Scandinavian and French campaigns. Writing to the king, the Duce stressed that the talks proved 'more important than ... expected'. Thereafter, Mussolini displayed increasing determination to join Hitler. Yet previous deceits made him wary. He ordered Badoglio to make war preparations independently, avoiding entanglement with German plans. In late March, Mussolini completed a strategic directive, proposing only air and naval offensives. He doubted that the Wehrmacht could or even would try to smash the Maginot Line. 'Only in the case, in my opinion, very improbable, of a complete French collapse' would he order ground operations. Mussolini retained the paper for a week.[69]

The king's moment had arrived. But throughout March doubts had afflicted him. About 1 April, after deciding he lacked sufficient support, Vittorio Emanuele III informed Ciano the time 'was not ripe'. In turn, Mussolini considered, then rejected, dismissing his son-in-law. On 4 April, having apparently ascertained that it was prudent, Mussolini sent Vittorio Emanuele III his memorandum. After a favourable reaction from the king, Mussolini then passed a copy to Badoglio two days later. The marshal considered it reasonable but assumed it applied to 1941 or later. Reassured, Mussolini distributed the memorandum to the other military leaders and Ciano. After Badoglio convoked the service chiefs on 9 April, however, they rejected Mussolini's concepts. Even the air and navy chiefs insisted offensives were impossible in the near- or midterm. That day, the Wehrmacht invaded Denmark and Norway.[70]

Mussolini gradually regained authority. First privately, then publicly, he sounded increasingly bellicose. Italian newspapers echoed him. In mid-April, Badoglio argued that Italy was so weak only Allied

[68] Ciano, *Diario*, 404–08; *DGFP*, D, vol. VIII, nos. 663, 665, 667, 669, 670; Welles, *The Time for Decision*, 137–8 (quotation 138); *FRUS, 1940*, I, 100–2.

[69] *DGFP*, D, vol. VIII, no. 384, 442; vol. IX, no. 1; *Holy See*, no. 276; *Halder Diary*, 100-6; *OO*, vol. XLIII, 31–2 (Mussolini quotation, 31); Ciano, *Diario*, 408–16; *Diario Storico*, 176–9; Minniti, 'Profilo dell'iniziativa', 1150–1; Petracchi, 'Pinocchio, the Cat, and the Fox', 519. In editing his original draft, Mussolini replaced 'very improbable' with just 'improbable'. Minniti, 'Profilo dell'iniziativa', 1151, n. 6.

[70] *FRUS, 1940*, vol. I, 96; *Holy See*, no. 276; Ciano, *Diario*, 412, 419; *Diario Storico*, 174–6, 180–9.

collapse would permit grabbing some easy 'success'. But Germany's Scandinavian victories impressed diplomats, government, and Party leaders, and, especially, the king. Vittorio Emanuele III had accepted the logic of Mussolini's March directives as 'geometric'. Consequently, the military's resistance diminished. By early May, they grudgingly accepted Mussolini's idea of attacking Yugoslavia in September. The Duce himself had already decided to attack the Allies as soon as practical. Then, on 10 May, Hitler ordered his Western offensive. Pius XII and Maria José had futilely warned the victims three days earlier.[71] Ciano retreated from resignation to acceptance to qualified enthusiasm for intervention. Contrary to his and most other Italian leaders' expectations, the Germans pressed forward, avoiding a repetition of 1914. Once the Wehrmacht bypassed the Maginot Line, Italians began supporting involvement. As Mussolini moved towards war, the king again considered a *coup*. But Vittorio Emanuele III realised that the French army was broken and his own military was increasingly converted to supporting intervention. He reluctantly decided that removing Mussolini would provoke civil war and bring Hitler to Mussolini's support. For several weeks he procrastinated. But on 20 May, German forces reached the Channel, trapping Allied mobile forces to the north. Belgium capitulated on 28 May. The next day, the king granted Mussolini's wish.[72]

Special intelligence strengthened Mussolini's resolve. In October 1939, an American embassy clerk in London began passing codes and hundreds of cables to Italy's assistant military attaché. These included messages between Roosevelt and Churchill. Those extant form two groups: exchanges until March 1940, while Churchill was First Lord of the Admiralty, and four from May, after he became prime minister. Earlier correspondence revealed Anglo-American naval cooperation and Roosevelt's unneutral sympathies. Mussolini provided some copies to Hitler.[73]

[71] Ortona, *Diplomazia di guerra*, 80–2; Bottai, Diario, 183–91; *OO*, vol. XXIX, 378–81; *Diario Storico*, 192–212, 223 ('geometric' quotation); Minitti, 'Profilo dell'iniziativa', 1162–5; De Felice, *Mussolini il duce. II*, 700; SP, report 815/1940, 'Air cooperation etc. Rome. May 9'; Puntoni, *Parla Vittorio Emanuele*, vol. III, 7; *Holy See*, nos. 291, 293–5, 307; *FRUS*, *1940*, vol. I, 701–2; PRO, FO 371/24947/8771 Loraine to Halifax, May 28, 1940; Regolo, *La regina incompresa*, 200.

[72] Ciano, *Diario*, 419–36; Bottai, *Diario*, 192; Anfuso, *Roma Berlino Salò*, 145–55; Caviglia, *Diario*, 205–6; Puntoni, *Parla Vittorio Emanuele III*, 7-9; Soddu, 'Memorie', part 3, 35–6, 51, 60–2; *FRUS, 1940*, I, 105; Guerri, *Galeazzo Ciano*, 457–60; André, 'La non belligeranza', 160–1; Regolo, *La regina incompresa*, 201–3; Denis Mack Smith, *Italy and its Monarchy* (New Haven, 1989), 287–92. Mack Smith's judgement of Vittorio Emanuele III seems overly harsh.

[73] Warren F. Kimball (ed.), *Roosevelt & Churchill. The Complete Correspondence*, 3 vols., (Princeton, 1984), vol. I, 23–37; *DGFP*, D, vol. IX, no. 305; Martin Gilbert, *Finest Hour. Winston S. Churchill 1939–1941*

Mussolini and Churchill had long admired each other. Churchill was a rare Briton who impressed Mussolini as determined and courageous. Thus, the May Churchill–Roosevelt messages Mussolini read must have impressed him. Churchill obviously worded his 15 May letter for maximum effect. But he seemed sincere when predicting to Roosevelt massive German air attacks, followed by an airborne invasion of Britain. He pleaded for American arms. Roosevelt replied the next day. Congress would never approve; as President, he could supply but meagre means and that could arrive only in July. On 17 May, Mussolini received an appeal from Churchill urging peace but pledging merciless war if attacked. Churchill claimed forthcoming American aid in 'increasing measure'. On 18 May, Churchill sent Roosevelt a desperate-sounding plea, stressing determination to persevere 'to the very end'. After reading that, no wonder Mussolini rebuffed another Churchillian peace missive received that day. The Duce received a final purloined letter sent on 20 May. Churchill wrote to Roosevelt that the RAF was succumbing to the Luftwaffe. His successor might have to surrender the Royal Navy. Thereafter, frantic French offers of territory, plus inducements and veiled threats from Roosevelt, only increased Mussolini's certainty of Allied defeat. On 30 May, he notified Hitler of intervention in five days, then postponed war to avoid diverting French forces from planned Luftwaffe strikes.[74]

On 10 June, the Duce delivered his historic announcement from the balcony fronting the Palazzo Venezia. By despoiling the pluto-democracies, Italy would escape poverty and Mediterranean imprisonment, he insisted. The crowd's roaring approval signified the magnitude of Mussolini's achievement. Rarely has an individual so shaped a nation's history. Hitler's deeds had surpassed Mussolini's determination in converting Italians to belligerence. Nonetheless, the Duce's struggle towards world power had created, then saved the Axis. What perverse and ironic triumph of the will that proved. Six months later, Churchill would blame 'one man, and one man only' for the catastrophes visited upon Italy. He did not overly exaggerate the fruits of Mussolini's accomplishment.[75]

(London, 1983), 341–68, 485–6; Ray Bearse and Anthony Read, *Conspirator. The Untold Story of Tyler Kent* (New York, 1991), 3, 59, 148, 277–92; David Stafford, *Roosevelt & Churchill. Men of Secrets* (London, 1999), 40–43.

74 *Roosevelt & Churchill. The Complete Correspondence*, vol. I, 37–41 (Churchill quotations, 39, 40); Ortona, *Diplomazia di guerra*, 91–4; Ciano, *Diario*, 436-42; *DGFP*, D, vol. IX, nos. 356, 357, 373, 406, 410; Sullivan, 'More than meets the eye', 191–2; Enrica Costa Bona, *Dalla guerra alla pace. Italia-Francia 1940–1947* (Milan, 1995), 27–36.

75 *OO*, vol. XXIX, 404–5; Soddu, 'Memorie', 10–12; Gilbert, *Finest Hour*, 960–1.

CHAPTER 6

# *Treaty revision and doublespeak: Hungarian neutrality, 1939–1941*

*Tibor Frank*

Hungary's neutrality between 1939 and 1941 was a very precarious exercise in balancing between three powers. By paying lip-service to Nazi-Germany and, simultaneously, courting the West, particularly Great Britain, Hungary tried to restore its pre-First World War borders and maintain its non-belligerency. At the same time, no active Hungarian politician thought in terms of dealing with the Soviet Union, which they dreaded. They thought in terms of border revision without considering the cost they would have to pay for it.

## 'THE UNWILLING SATELLITE'?

In a book published in 1947, America's longest-serving pre-Second World War minister to Hungary, John Flournoy Montgomery, erected a monument to Hungary's claim to have been an 'unwilling satellite' of Nazi Germany and urged that 'the true story of Hungary's nazification' be 'presented to Americans'.[1] Underlining the reluctant nature of official Hungary's friendship with Nazi Germany, Montgomery not only echoed official Hungarian opinions but spoke of his personal experience from 1933 to early 1941.[2] Through his long years of increasingly intimate friendship with Hungarian political leaders such as Regent Admiral Miklós Horthy, former Prime Minister Count István Bethlen, members of the government and the diplomatic corps, Montgomery seemed to have agreed with former Foreign Minister Kálmán de Kánya in mid-1940 that 'Hitler at this moment [was] the undisputed master

[1] John Flournoy Montgomery, *Hungary, The Unwilling Satellite* (Morristown, 1993, Ist edn, 1947).

[2] 'Diplomatic Images of Admiral Horthy: The American Perception of Interwar Hungary, 1919–1941', in Waldemar Zacharasiewicz (ed.), *Images of Central Europe in Travelogues and Fiction by North American Writers*, Transatlantic Perspectives, vol. VI (Tübingen, 1995), 192–211; 'Unlikely Friendship: U.S. Minister John F. Montgomery and Hungary's Regent Miklós Horthy', in Attila Pók (ed.), *The Fabric of Modern Europe: Studies in Social and Diplomatic History* (Nottingham, 1999), 183–99. Reproduced in Tibor Frank, *Ethnicity, Propaganda, Myth-Making* (Budapest, 1999).

of the European continent, and much as it distressed him and other Hungarians, if Hungary was to exist and to get any satisfaction in the way of revision it would be at the will of Mr. Hitler.'[3]

The US minister made an important point in quoting de Kánya's statement. By 1940 Hungary was trapped. On the one hand, there was an uncompromising eagerness to bring about the revision of the Peace Treaty of Trianon (1920) and regain the territories lost to Romania, Czechoslovakia, and Yugoslavia. On the other hand, reasonable circles of the Hungarian political establishment, such as those around Counts István Bethlen and Pál Teleki, found it increasingly dangerous to serve unreservedly the interests of Nazi Germany and Fascist Italy in the hope of redrawing the political map of Central Europe. This paper sets out to examine the trap into which the Second World War led Hungary, and investigates the period when the country was balancing between the mirage of regaining lost territories and the foreseeable tragedy of total war on the side of Adolf Hitler's Germany.

## TRIANON, 1920

To understand the position of Hungary in the early war years one should go back to the Paris peace treaties of 1919–20 and to the Treaty of Trianon (1920) in particular. As a member of the Central Powers in the First World War, Hungary was severely punished, losing over two-thirds of its territory and some three-fifths of its total population, including 28 per cent of the native speakers of Hungarian. Out of the pre-war total population of close to 21 million 7,615,000 people were left in the country.[4] Redressing these immense losses became the single most important driving force of Hungarian politics in the entire inter-war period. Cutting deep into ethnically compound blocks of Hungarians, these huge territories were transferred, almost overnight, to the new republic of Czechoslovakia and the Kingdom of the Serbs, Croats, and Slovenes (later to become Yugoslavia), as well as to the much-expanded Romania. Transylvania, the region attached to Romania, was actually

[3] John F. Montgomery to Kálmán de Kánya, Coversation, Budapest, 19 June 1940, Confidential Conversations, vol. 11, MS. Transferred from the Minister's family to Budapest, to be published by Tibor Frank (ed.), *Dreaming Peace, Making War: The Budapest Conversations of John F. Montgomery, 1935–1941* (forthcoming).

[4] Tibor Hajdú and Zsuzsa L. Nagy, 'Revolution, Counterrevolution, Consolidation', in Peter F. Sugar, Péter Hanák, and Tibor Frank (eds.), *A History of Hungary* (London, 1990), 314; Henry Bogdan, *From Warsaw to Sofia. A History of Eastern Europe* (Santa Fe, 1989), 179; Szekfű Gyula, *Három nemzedék és ami utána következik* (Budapest, 1934), 384.

bigger than what was left as the newly independent Kingdom of Hungary. The Treaty of Trianon became a national rallying cry for all possible social classes, political parties, and religious denominations to centre around for nearly a quarter of a century, a symbol and a household name for subsequent generations of Hungarians. 'Trianon' – or rather the *Grand Trianon,* actually one of the small châteaux of Louis XIV in the royal park behind the Palace of Versailles where the Treaty with Hungary was signed on 4 June 1920[5] – came to assume a distinct political meaning, just as 'Versailles' did for Germans. 'Trianon' became the ultimate cause, the arch-reason for the sufferings and humiliations of the Hungarian nation, and subsequent Hungarian governments knew only one *raison d'être:* revision and revisionism. Trianon became a call for unity, for action, for struggle.[6]

Hungary was transformed from being half of a huge, multinational empire into a small 'nation-state'. Apart from European Jewry, 'Trianon' created probably the second biggest global diaspora, that of Hungarians, and the single biggest ethnic minority in Europe, that of Transylvanian Hungarians in Romania, which is still the case today. Life and thought, history and philosophy, political strategy and foreign policy revolved around revisionism in inter-war Hungary. Territorial changes and the transformation of the ethnic composition of the new, post-First World War countries of Central Europe drastically changed the course of Hungarian politics, the national economy, and social developments. The conversion of the Austro-Hungarian monarchy into a new Central Europe based on the Treaties of Paris left an unparalleled imprint on the mind of every generation in the area since 1920.[7] Millions of Hungarians had to accept a new identity as citizens of different states, typically hostile to what was left of the Kingdom of Hungary. To make the new situation worse, a political alliance of Romania, Czechoslovakia and Yugoslavia was brought about mainly as a barrier against Hungary.[8] A tool of French foreign policy, the Little entente was destined to consolidate the new borders of Hungary by

5 Gerald van der Kemp and Daniel Meyer, *Versailles* (Paris, 1981), 114.

6 Based on Tibor Frank, 'Nation, National Minorities, and Nationalism in Twentieth-Century Hungary', in Peter F. Sugar (ed.), *Eastern European Nationalism in the Twentieth Century* (Washington, 1995), 205–42.

7 For Hungarian national minorities see Martin L. Kovacs, 'National Minorities in Hungary, 1919–1980', in Stephan M. Horak (ed.), *Eastern European National Minorities 1919–1980. A Handbook* (Littleton, 1985), 160–74; and N. F. Dreisziger and A. Ludanyi (eds.), *Forgotten Minorities: The Hungarians of East Central Europe, Hungarian Studies Review,* 16/1–2 (Spring–Fall 1989).

8 Piotr Wandycz, 'The Little Entente: Sixty Years After', *The Slavonic and East European Review,* 59/4 (1981), 548–64.

providing international control and supervision of Hungary's potential political ambitions.

The Treaty of Trianon is a fundamental turning point in modern Hungarian history and also a watershed in the history of Hungarian nationalism. The only reaction post-war Hungarians could possibly give to Trianon was *Nem, nem, soha* (No, no, never), the semi-official slogan all children in Hungarian schools were brought up with through the entire inter-war period. For these generations '[m]utilated Hungary was no country, while the whole of [original] Hungary was Heaven', as a widely quoted propaganda verse put it, or as proclaimed in Mrs Elemér Papp-Váry's popular *Magyar Hiszekegy* (Hungarian Credo), both deeply ingrained into the public mind, particularly in schools. A new kind of nationalism was born.

After the shock of World War I and the series of major social and political upheavals in 1918 and 1919, Trianon gave birth to a defensive, protective interpretation of nation and nationhood. All political parties and factions (even Béla Kun's government, which organised a 200,000-man Red Army and tried to defend the country against Czechoslovakia and Romania in 1919) accepted the notion that Trianon's stipulations were unacceptable and forced upon Hungary only by the overwhelming military and political power of the Great Powers assembled at Paris. The nation felt that the treaty had to be reversed and virtually any means or tool seemed suitable to achieve this purpose. 'Treaty revision' became the official Hungarian government policy, the utmost national ambition through the 1920s and 1930s, which resulted in a treaty with Mussolini's Fascist Italy in 1927 and in immediate contacts at the highest level with Adolf Hitler from the summer of 1933, a fellow revisionist of the most ferocious sort.

## THE FOREIGN POLICY OF HORTHY'S HUNGARY

The foreign policy of Hungary in the immediate post-First World War period had a number of different priorities. It had to make sure that the Bolshevik experiment of 1919 would never be repeated in Hungary and, to boot, that the country could become a bulwark against the ideas of Communism in the Danube valley. Second, it was supposed to guarantee that the restoration of the Habsburg house would not become feasible in Hungary, a threat that all the surrounding 'post-Trianon' countries with former ties to the Austro-Hungarian monarchy dreaded and emphatically fought against. Third, it started to build friendly relations with some or all of the Great Powers in an attempt to create confidence in Hungary's economic, political, and military 'usefulness', and its role as a potential anti-Bolshevik counterweight in Central Europe. To achieve this intricate combination of foreign policy objectives, Hungary's new political regime had to devise a series of different approaches, methods, and sponsors that were supposed to help subsequent Hungarian governments build a more favourable climate of foreign opinion for an eventual revision of Trianon.

The regency of Admiral Miklós Horthy (1920–44) was built upon the notion of 'order' that held out the promise of a successful fight against revolutions in general and against another Soviet experiment in particular. Horthy's political friend Miklós Kozma quoted the Regent from 1923 'We must have order in this country and I will make sure of that. Whatever is disturbing the peace will be shot at, and if the disturbance comes from the right, the only difference for me is that I will order fire with an aching heart, whereas I would order shooting at possible disturbers of peace from the left with passion.'[9] 'It seemed,' explains historian Gyula Juhász, 'that upon the slogan of "order" successes could be built in foreign policy.'[10] Throughout, the Horthy regime turned towards a variety of different foreign policy options, trying to balance them and shifting the emphasis always to the solution desired and made possible by the changing political momentum.

Before the treaty was signed in June 1920, Horthy himself and his first governments thought in terms of British support, both economic and political. Their expectations were justified by the British role in helping Horthy's regime come to power in 1919. At this time the British seemed the most likely among the Powers to be of some assistance: the French were hostile, the Italians weak, and the United States disinterested. In January 1920 Horthy made it quite clear to British envoy Sir Thomas Beaumont Hohler that 'it is Great Britain alone who enjoys his own full confidence and that of his country'.[11] Hungary at this point was thought of as a potential barrier against the Bolshevik menace, but London did not consider this of sufficient importance to justify changing the content of the future peace treaty. A group of French industrialists and financiers also showed interest in French investment and economic control in Hungary. In return, again, the Hungarian government tried to get French support for the idea of revising the pending peace treaty.[12]

[9] Quoted by Ignác Romsics, *István Bethlen: A Great Conservative Statesman of Hungary 1876–1946* (Boulder, CO, 1995), 196.

[10] Gyula Juhász, *Magyarország külpolitikája 1919–1945* (3rd edn, Budapest, 1988), 61.

[11] Ibid., 61. [12] Ibid., 61–4.

Though Hungary's longest-lasting inter-war prime minister, Count István Bethlen (1921–31), did not speak of treaty revision until 1927, he looked into the possibilities of finding potential allies of Hungary. As a *Realpolitiker*, however, he increasingly realised that he had to integrate his country into the gradually consolidating political system of Europe. 'Reconciliation and integration' were the watchwords of Count Bethlen's foreign policy between 1923 and 1927 when he came to realise that Hungary had no suitable partners available for its revisionist plans.[13] Hungary was accepted as a member of the League of Nations in the autumn of 1922 and discussions were started on a substantial loan from the League that materialised in 1924. However, the road to international recognition proved to be bumpy, and the appreciation of the West was halted by disturbing episodes. The manufacturing of false French francs revealed the willingness of some of the highest circles in the country to produce enough money for their revisionist aims.[14] Yet Hungary was granted the benefit of escaping the strict financial (1926) and military supervision (1927) of the League of Nations and found its way out of the near total international isolation of the post-war era.

Late in 1926 Bethlen started a more active foreign policy. This was based on the willingness of Italy, one of the Big Four, to cement a political treaty with Hungary just at the time when Hungary was trying to come to terms with Yugoslavia. Italy was trying to isolate Yugoslavia and a treaty with Hungary was to serve that purpose. It offered the friendship of a major European power which was also unhappy with the results of the Paris Treaties and was trying to change the territorial structure of Europe. The Bethlen government eagerly accepted Mussolini's hand and by April 1927 a treaty was signed pledging 'constant peace and permanent friendship' between the two countries. The agreement, destined to serve as a pivot of Hungarian foreign policy until Germany emerged as a much stronger power, gave Hungary the hope of counteracting the policies of the Little entente countries.[15]

Mussolini's support encouraged the government and the press of Hungary to launch a major international campaign for the revision of Trianon. Soon after the treaty with Italy was signed, Mussolini received the well-known British conservative media mogul, Lord Rothermere,

[13] Ignác Romsics, *István Bethlen*, 171–2.

[14] Mária Ormos, *Magyarország a két világháború korában (1914–1945)* (Debrecen, 1998), 108–10, 120–1.

[15] Juhász, *Magyarország külpolitikája*, 104–8.

who committed his papers to a major fight against Trianon. Introducing the campaign, The *Daily Mail* published its first article on 21 June 1927, under the promising title of 'Hungary's Place Under the Sun'.[16] The article unleashed a tremendous response. In Hungary, it 'affected the easily excitable fantasy of local public opinion with such tremendous force as if it contained the official declaration of the imminent revision of the peace treaty'.[17] A counter-campaign was launched in France and the Little entente countries, and the episode contributed to the growing influence of France in the region.[18] The British government found the Rothermere campaign harmful and Foreign Secretary Austen Chamberlain made representations to the Hungarian Prime Minister to that effect in December 1927.[19]

## THE FIRST VIENNA AWARD

The Munich Agreement of 30 September 1938 is a part of every modern history textbook. It is often forgotten, however, that the German attack on the integrity of Czechoslovakia and the transfer of the Sudeten–German territories to Germany was followed, almost immediately, by the concerted action of the Hungarian government to try to benefit from the apparent dissolution of its northern neighbour. The German government had a vested interest in pretending that the dismantling of Czechoslovakia was an international affair and that just as its western parts belonged to Germany, the eastern parts were appropriately claimed by another country, Hungary. Before 1939, Berlin was eager to cultivate Hungarian friendship and readily set up a self-styled international court of arbitration in Vienna, where, together with Fascist Italy, it 'awarded' the southern part of Slovakia to Hungary. The 1st Vienna Award (2 November 1938) divided the former Hungarian Uplands between Hungary and Slovakia, returning 11,927 km$^2$ from Czechoslovakia to Hungary, with a large group of 869,299 people of whom 86.5 per cent were Hungarians and 9.8 per cent Slovaks.[20]

The return of the 'ancient land' had peculiar social and political consequences. The incoming new Hungarian administration was represented by a number of old-fashioned gentry bureaucrats who tried to teach

[16] Ibid., 109–10.
[17] Austrian Minister (Budapest) to Federal Chancellor Ignaz Seipel, 28 June 1927, cited in Miklós Vásárhelyi, *A lord és a korona* (Budapest, 1977), 81.
[18] Juhász, *Magyarország külpolitikája*, 109. [19] Ibid., 109–10.
[20] Kálmán Benda (ed.), *Magyarország történeti kronológiája* (Budapest, 1982), vol. III, 960.

the 'old' Hungarians a lesson on 'gentlemanly' behaviour and authority. After twenty years in the democratic republic of Czechoslovakia this was a tall order and met with understandable resistance.[21] Even the government had to deal with this issue that signalled the conflict of values old and new.[22]

Hungary was grateful for this first, tangible step towards treaty revision, and responded to the Award with an almost unanimous outburst of exaltation and national satisfaction. Even moderates were enthusiastic: the great, pacifist poet Mihály Babits greeted the event with a poem. Hitler's decision, however, not to return territories inhabited by non-Hungarians added a measure of frustration to the public display of excitement.[23] On 11 April Foreign Minister Count Csáky declared that Hungary would leave the League of Nations.

## PRIME MINISTER COUNT PÁL TELEKI

Prime Minister Count Pál Teleki (1879–1941), a learned Transylvanian aristocrat, university professor of geography, and internationally acclaimed cartographer with a historical name and family, was a resolute opponent of Hungary's participation in the Second World War.[24] As prime minister after 16 February 1939, Count Teleki maintained Hungary's official friendship with both Italy and Germany, and was a dedicated champion of racism. But he did not want to join Germany in any war and was unwilling to subscribe to German notions of anti-Semitism. He did not believe in a potential German victory and despised the Nazis. When meeting Hitler in Berlin in late April and early May 1939, Teleki was almost completely silent and simply listened to the Führer's endless diatribe. Teleki offered his assistance to discuss and resolve the German–Polish conflict, an offer which of course Hitler firmly refused to accept. Somewhat later, on 21 July, Teleki wrote to Hitler and Mussolini assuring them of Hungary's loyalty but insisting that it did not wish to participate in a war against Poland. As historian Mária Ormos rightly notes in her new survey of inter-war Hungary,

[21] Gyula Juhász, *Uralkodó eszmék Magyarországon 1933–1944* (Budapest, 1983), 62–3.

[22] Minutes of the government meeting of 23 May 1939, cited in Loránt Tilkovszky, *Revízió és nemzetiségpoltika* (Budapest, 1968), 81.

[23] Ignác Romsics, *Hungary in the Twentieth Century* (Budapest, 1999), 198–9.

[24] The best presentation of Teleki's war years in English is still C. A. Macartney's *October Fifteenth: A History of Modern Hungary 1929–1945* (2nd edn, Edinburgh, 1961), chapters 13–19.

'Teleki wanted to keep the country out of war at all costs.'[25] In fact, Teleki did keep Hungary out of the war as long as he could, and committed suicide once he realised he could not. Any discussion of Hungarian neutrality between 1939 and 1941 must acknowledge the sincere patriotism of this sensitive, erudite, somewhat uncertain, elderly gentleman who tried to save his country and the *ancien régime* as long as he lived. It is not by chance that Hungary entered the war within a few months of his death on 3 April 1941.[26]

The Teleki government was conservative and cautious in its policies but went along steadfastly with anti-Semitic legislation and treaty revision. Teleki inherited the idea of a second anti-Semitic bill from his predecessor Béla Imrédy, whose bill was introduced just before Christmas 1938, and papers such as *Pesti Napló* certainly had all the details of the bill on 24 December.[27] Ironically, Imrédy's opponents used his own alleged Jewish ancestry against himself when trying to get rid of him: he had to leave office in early 1939. The bill was postponed until the spring and was left to Teleki to introduce in parliament. 'Had I brought here a bill of my own,' Teleki declared in the debate of the bill in the Upper House on 15 April 1939, 'that would have been stricter than the present one.'[28] Teleki explained that his racist thinking was motivated by his own scientific persuasion and was not influenced by 'the alien ideology of race and blood'.[29] 'The bill to limit the domain of Jews in public life and the economy' was indeed a much stricter extension of the first anti-Semitic act (1938: XV) which limited the number of Jews in the professions to 20 per cent and considered people Jewish only if they belonged to that denomination. This time anybody with a Jewish father or mother or with two Jewish grandparents was considered a Jew. The percentage permitted in the professions was much lower (6 per cent) and no Jewish person was to be employed by the state. No papers could hire Jewish publishers or editors.

The bill provoked a mixed reception in parliament. The debate in the Upper House was an interesting and significant contribution to the history of the Jewish question in Hungary.[30] It showed the dissolution of

[25] Ormos, *Magyarország*, 219.

[26] Churchill believed that Teleki 'was by no means convinced that Germany would win the war', and considered that his suicide 'clears his name before history'. Winston S. Churchill, *The Second World War*. Volume III: *The Grand Alliance* (Boston, 1951), 167–8.

[27] 'Az új zsidótörvény alapelvei, rendelkezései és indoklása', *Pesti Napló*, 24 December 1938.

[28] Gróf Pál Teleki, *országgyűlési beszédei* (Budapest, 1938–1941), vol. II, 120. [29] Ibid., 122.

[30] *Az 1935. évi április hó 27ére hirdetett Országgyűlés Felsőházának Naplója* (Budapest, 1939), vol. IV, 153–99.

the liberal legacy of the political élite and the erosion of the spirit that had once welcomed the emancipation of the Jews in the nineteenth century. Liberal-minded Conservatives such as former cabinet minister Loránd Hegedüs opposed the bill. Hegedüs warned the House to avoid seeming as though it 'acted under any foreign pressure'.[31] 'The Hungarian race is needed in Europe only as long as it remains faithful to the idea of freedom, and because this bill attacks that idea, I am not going to vote for the bill in general or in detail.'[32] Right-wing members such as Aladár Szluha, on the other hand, rejected the bill's assumption that the Jews were a denomination rather than a race, and demanded a new bill 'that would declare at least the minimum of what are known as the Nuremberg norms in terms of race'.[33] As a characteristic response to the bill, former Prime Minister Count Bethlen renounced his membership of parliament next day, whereupon the regent awarded him with a lifelong membership in the Upper House. On 5 May 1939, the bill became law.

Teleki's foreign policy was based on a combination of cooperation with Germany and, simultaneously, the upholding of favourable relations with the West. German support proved its worth on 15 March 1939 when Hitler finished off Czechoslovakia and created an 'independent' puppet regime under Jozef Tiso in Slovakia. Hitler offered the sub-Carpathian Ukraine as a booty to Hungary, but the land of the Ruthenes was simply subjugated by Hungary, which sent troops to take over the former north-eastern corner of the Kingdom of Hungary. One successful further step had been made towards the revision of the Treaty of Trianon, and the weekly Hungarian newsreel programmes repeatedly showed episodes of the 'retaking of the ancient land of Hungary'. On 17 March the Hungarian papers proudly proclaimed that 'the common Hungarian–Polish frontier had become a reality', while the *Manchester Guardian Weekly* soberly noted: 'The common frontier with Hungary may seem to be, if only temporarily, a holiday from German pressure eastwards, but, it is asked, for how long?'[34]

For the second time, Hungary's revisionist claims were satisfied with Nazi assistance. At a reception in honour of the Hungarian delegation visiting Hitler in Berlin, Teleki declared on 30 April 1939, that 'the

[31] Loránd Hegedüs, in *Az 1935*, 185. Parts of Hegedüs's long address were published by László Karsai, *Befogadók. Irások az antiszemitizmus ellen 1882–1993* (Budapest, 1993), 134–6.

[32] Loránd Hegedüs, in *Az 1935. évi április hó 27ére hirdetett Országgyűlés Felsőházának Naplója*, 191.

[33] Aladár Szluha, in *Az 1935. évi április hó 27ére hirdetett Országgyűlés Felsőházának Naplója*, 163.

[34] I am most grateful to my old friend Éva Kerekes, who presented me with her valuable collection of wartime newspaper clippings.

Hungarian government tenaciously returns the confidence placed in it by the German government'.[35] Teleki and his political friends knew, however, that a German war might end disastrously and that Hungary should keep out of it. The lessons of 1920 were well remembered and the ultimate goal was the survival of Hungary as a potentially strong nation in the Danube valley.[36]

Before the Second World War broke out, Teleki's foreign policy was built upon the notion of 'armed neutrality' and an effort to avoid further commitment to Germany. The government therefore stepped up its military preparations against Romania on its own, hoping to win back Transylvania without being sucked into a major European war. Typically, Teleki sent letters to both Hitler and Mussolini on 24 July guaranteeing that 'in case of a general conflict Hungary will bring her policy in line with that of the Axis, as we have shown our willingness to this effect so far'. Nevertheless, he went on to add, 'it cannot be doubted, however, that our adherence to this policy could in any way jeopardise our sovereignty which is embodied in our constitution, and it cannot build a barrier to hinder the fulfilment of our national goals'.[37] To make sure his point was not missed, Teleki sent what seemed to be a mere afterthought to the Führer the same day: 'Unless circumstances change significantly, Hungary from moral considerations is not in a position to start military operations against Poland.'[38] Count Galeazzo Ciano, Mussolini's foreign minister, quickly realised what the two letters meant when noting in his diary the same day: '[Hungarian Minister Baron Frigyes] Villani brings the Duce two letters from Teleki. The first to confirm the absolute adherence of Hungary to the Axis; the second raises some reservations as regards a conflict with Poland. I vaguely suspect that the first letter was written in order to launch the second.'[39]

The letters remained unanswered until 8 August, when Foreign Minister Count István Csáky visited Berchtesgaden. Hitler's response was stormy. Csáky was received by the Führer and von Ribbentrop and was told what an 'impossibility' Teleki's letters were after Hungary had regained so much of her lost territory with exclusively German support.

[35] Otto von Erdmannsdorff to Joachim von Ribbentrop, Berlin, 1 May 1939, in György Ránki, Ervin Pamlényi, Loránd Tilkovszky, and Gyula Juhász (eds.), *A Wilhelmstrasse és Magyarország. Német diplomáciai iratok Magyarországról 1933–1944* (Budapest, 1968), 392.

[36] Juhász, *Magyarország külpolitikája*, 217–18.

[37] Count Pál Teleki to Adolf Hitler, Budapest, 24 July 1939, in László Zsigmond (ed.), *Magyarország és a második világháború. Titkos diplomáciai okmányok a háború előzményeihez és történetéhez* (Budapest, 1961), 242.

[38] Ibid., 243. [39] Malcolm Muggeridge (ed.), *Ciano's Diary 1939–1943* (London, 1947), 118.

Hungarian territorial demands could no longer be met, the Führer said in no uncertain terms, and added: 'If Germany loses a war, that would also put an end to the Hungarian dreams of revision.'[40] Count Csáky was so intimidated that, later that day, he renounced Teleki's letters to Hitler and Mussolini and promised to have them withdrawn. He took full responsibility for his action and suggested to von Ribbentrop that he would tender his resignation should the government object to his procedure.[41] The letters were officially withdrawn on 9 August.[42]

Teleki, however, stood firm. At the end of August he sent a note to British Foreign Secretary Lord Halifax stating that Hungary would not cooperate with Germany in a war against Poland and would remain neutral without actually declaring it officially. British indifference to the problems of the region was revealed by Prime Minister Neville Chamberlain's broadcast on 27 September 1938 when he said, 'How horrible, fantastic, incredible it is that we should be digging trenches and trying on gas-masks here because of a quarrel in a faraway country between people of whom we know nothing.'[43] Not only did London support the 1st Vienna Award but it expressed its appreciation to the Hungarians for not attacking Czechoslovakia before the Munich agreement was signed, thereby enabling Chamberlain to 'save peace'. That the Hungarian government did not declare its neutrality was not only the result of German pressure: once again, the exigencies of Hungarian revisionist ambitions also advised caution. Double-dealing in Hungary's foreign policy continued into the war period.[44]

## HUNGARY AND THE OUTBREAK OF THE SECOND WORLD WAR

Even after the German attack on Poland Hungary continued planning an offensive on Romania. Teleki and his government hoped that the circumstances would be appropriate to resolve the Transylvanian question and expressed their hope in a letter on 2 September 1939 to Benito Mussolini. The idea of an international conference of arbitration that would include the Hungarian claims in Romania was, however, extremely short lived. Berlin did not require Hungarian participation in

[40] Note by German Minister Otto von Erdmannsdorff, Obersalzberg, 8 August 1939, in Ránki, Pamlényi, Tilkovszky, and Juhász (eds.), *A Wilhelmstrasse és Magyarország*, 418, 419.
[41] Ibid., 423.
[42] Hungarian Legation in Berlin to German Foreign Ministry, Berlin, 9 August 1939, in Zsigmond (ed.), *Magyarország és a második világháború*, 247.
[43] *The Times*, 28 September 1938. [44] Juhász, *Magyarország külpolitikája*, 221, 196.

the Polish war, though demanded on 9 September that they use the railway line through Hungary to transport their troops to Poland. The Germans also vaguely hinted at the chance of a border revision *vis-à-vis* Romania when warning Hungary against attacking Romania. Late on 9 September Horthy received the prime minister, the foreign minister, the minister of defence and the Chief of the General Staff and concluded that Hungary should not participate in any military measure connected with the war against Poland.[45] There was fear in the air, declarations of war were expected from Britain, France, and Poland in case of complying with the German demand. Next day, von Ribbentrop was informed of the Hungarian decision. Ciano noted in his diary on 11 September, 'I believe that this refusal will not be forgotten by the Germans and that at some time or other the Hungarians will have to pay for it.'[46] The shrewd Italian had observed two days earlier 'the Germans were using the same language to the Hungarians that they had used six months previously to Poland'.[47]

Recognising Hungary's neutrality, Britain and France maintained a certain understanding towards Hungary even after the war was started. Economic gestures helped ease the problems of production and even the prospects of border revisions were treated with a measure of tact – unaccompanied, however, by any gesture of firm commitment.

Perhaps the single most important gesture that helped build the image of Hungary as a pro-Western country was the warm welcome given to the Polish army and particularly to its officer corps that took refuge in Hungary in large numbers after suffering a humiliating defeat at the hands of Germany. This programme was developed under the auspices of the Ministry of the Interior, where József Antall, Sr., a cabinet minister after the war and father of József Antall, Jr., future prime minister of Hungary (1990–93), was put in charge of the operation.[48] The number of Poles who entered Hungary has been hotly debated, with estimates varying, according to the political circumstances of the time, from anything between 110,000 to the more realistic figure of 45,000 to 50,000. Probably some 25,000 to 30,000 Poles left for the West, of whom about 10 per cent were officers. One fact was never questioned: at least the better half of the Polish troops in Hungary were recruited by the Polish military attaché

[45] 'Wir können an aktiven Kriegshandlungen nicht teilnehmen.' Minutes of the meeting of the Hungarian Government, 10 September 1939, cited in Zsigmond (ed.), *Magyarország és a második világháború*, 253.

[46] *Ciano's Diary 1939–1943*, 150. [47] Ibid., 149.

[48] I am indebted to Tamás Salamon-Rácz for his personal communications on the Polish rescue operations.

in Budapest for further fighting in the West.[49] The traditional Polish–Hungarian friendship and the Hungarian government's eagerness to maintain a pro-Western attitude meant that Budapest maintained its sympathy, if one which was increasingly veiled, for the Polish refugees until 1942.[50] Later during the war, after 1942, a number of escaped French prisoners were also given sanctuary in Hungary.[51] Nonetheless, the Hungarian government went on with its cherished plans of border revision *vis-à-vis* Romania, possibly before the war had come to an end.

Italy, and somewhat later Romania, suggested the creation of a neutral bloc in Central Europe based on the Balkan pact of 1934, comprising of Yugoslavia, Greece, Romania, and Turkey, to which Bulgaria and Hungary would be added, with the political support of Italy as guarantor.[52] This bloc was also to serve as a bulwark against the Soviet Union. As György Barcza, Hungarian minister in London, argued: 'In the judgement of the British, the neutrality of Italy and the safekeeping of the neutrality in the south-eastern countries of Europe are not only important in the current situation but for the later checking of the Soviets.'[53] Although the Hungarians themselves had considered 'some form of federation' with its neighbours possible before the start of the war, it flatly refused the idea of the neutral bloc in November 1939, by demanding border revisions in exchange for its participation.[54] That a regional

[49] József Antall, Sr., *Lengyel menekültek Magyarországon a világháború alatt* (Budapest, 1946); István Lagzi, 'Adatok az 1939 (Őszán Magyarországra menekült lengyel katonák evakuációjának történetéhez (1939–1941))', *Hadtörténeti Közlemények*, 20/4 (1973), 691–719; Ágnes Godó, *Magyar-lengyel kapcsolatok a második világháborúban* (Budapest, 1976), 81–228. Ágnes Godó (Ibid., 156–7) put the overall figure of Poles in Hungary at 45,000 to 50,000, Gyula Juhász (*Magyarország külpolitikája*, 224–5) at 70,000, while Romsics (Hungary, 200), more recently, suggests 100,000. István Lagzi (Adatok az 1939', 692) had the highest possible (and least likely) figure of 140,000, in 1973.

[50] The number of Poles going to Romania was estimated at about 90,000, although a more realistic number would be certainly lower. It is thought that the number of Polish troops who actually left for the West through Romania was around 22,000. Anita Prazmowski suggests that some 34,000 Poles reached France from Romania and Hungary. *Britain and Poland, 1939–1943. The Betrayed Ally* (Cambridge, 1995), 13.

[51] Endre Bajomi Lázár (ed.), *Ego sum gallicus captivus. Magyarországra menekült francia hadifoglyok emlékezései* (Budapest, 1980), *passim.*

[52] Juhász, *Magyarország külpolitikája*, 228–9.

[53] Quoted by Juhász, *Magyarország külpolitikája*, 229. Cf. the memoirs of György Barcza, *Diplomataemlékeim 1911–1945. Magyarország volt vatikáni és londoni követének emlékirataiból* (Budapest 1994), vol I., 435–507.

[54] When his sceptical minister in Washington questioned the plan, Count Teleki repeated emphatically to John Pelényi: 'Yes, Hungary is ready to join a federation with *all* his neighbours.' John Pelényi, 'The Secret Plan for a Hungarian Government in the West at the Outbreak of World War II', *Journal of Modern History*, 36/2 (1964), 171.

plan was on the minds of the Hungarian political élite to counteract the Germans was, however, shown by the journey of Tibor Eckhardt, member of Parliament and head of the Smallholders' Party, to Yugoslavia, apparently with the aim of discussing the possibility of forming a Yugoslav–Hungarian–Italian bloc in the Adriatic.[55]

As for the Soviet Union, diplomatic relations with Hungary were restored on 24 September 1939, and Moscow expressed its willingness to develop political, economic, and cultural relations. For some time, the Soviet–German non-aggression treaty of 23 August 1939 destabilised the traditionally pro-German and anti-Soviet spirit of the Hungarian ruling élite and weakened the influence of the extreme right wing among the lower classes.

Though Hungary remained neutral throughout 1940, the question of border revision at Romania's expense continued to be a tempting issue. Neutrality and the friendship of the Western Powers was just as inviting as the return of Transylvania to Hungary with Nazi support. Confidentially the Regent spoke bitterly about Hitler to US Minister John F. Montgomery:

> He spoke of Hitler in terms of contempt and said everybody hated him. He told me again in detail how the Poles, the Czechs, and everybody else in this country had despised him, and said that if somebody came to him and said that Hungary would be better off if he would quit he would do so in a minute; however, no matter how much his country might suffer, Hitler would never quit.[56]

Yet the Teleki government was continuously vacillating between Germany and the West. To make sure that the country could maintain its integrity and sovereignty, in the spring of 1940 Teleki made arrangements to establish a government-in-exile and sent $5m to the Hungarian minister in Washington, János Pelényi, for use in the event of an 'emergency situation'.[57] Soon, however, the money was returned to

[55] Report of Otto Braun, Director of the Transdanubia Co., Berlin, 23 November 1939 in György Ránki, Pamlényi, Tilkovszky and Juhász (eds.), *A Wilhelmstrasse és Magyarország*, 461. The Romanian plan, raised in November 1939 after consultation with the governments of their Balkan allies, included a declaration of neutrality, a non-aggression pact, neutrality in case of an attack against any of the member-states, and economic cooperation among member-states. With regard to Hungary and Bulgaria, the plan did not guarantee the *status quo* nor did it include a mutual assistance pact. It was hoped that the Balkan countries would first sign a pact, ask Hungary and Bulgaria to join, and finally call on the support of Italy.

[56] John F. Montgomery to Miklós Horthy, Budapest, 7 May 1940, Confidential Conversations, vol. II, MS. published by Tibor Frank, 'Unlikely Friendship,' in Pók, *The Fabric of Modern Europe*, 192.

[57] Pelényi, 'The Secret Plan for a Hungarian Government,' 170–7. See also John Pelényi to Count Pál Teleki (Washington) 28 November 1940, John Pelényi to Count Miklós Bánffy (Washington) 11 January 1941: Janos Pelenyi Papers, Box 1, Hoover Institution on War, Revolution and Peace.

Hungary: the government proved unable to transfer its authority and maintained its allegiance to the Axis powers to the bitter end.[58]

July 1940 brought significant changes in the German attitude towards treaty revision between Hungary and Romania. Hitler made his final decision to start preparations against the Soviet Union and tried to eliminate prospective disturbances on the way to the potential Soviet front. He tried to balance the repeated Hungarian threats of an armed attack and the lack of flexibility on the part of Romania. Berlin had a vested interest in appearing, once again, as an arbiter of peace, since a suitable agreement would make both Hungary and Romania even more dependent on Germany. Direct negotiations produced no tangible results and brought the dangers of war closer than ever. Romania decided to ask the Axis powers to arbitrate, resulting in the 2nd Vienna Award on 30 August 1940.[59] Transylvania was divided between the two neighbouring countries in an apparent attempt to make both of them loyal to Germany; 43,591 $km^2$ were returned to Hungary in Northern Transylvania, with 2,185,546 people, of whom 51.4 per cent were Hungarians and 42.1 per cent Romanians.[60]

For a third time, Hungarian demands to revise the map of Central Europe were satisfied through the active support of Nazi Germany, but left Hungary's claim to neutrality as weak as ever. Hungary was the first state to join the Tripartite pact, on 20 November 1940. Only one member of parliament, the Smallholders' leader, Endre Bajcsy-Zsilinszky,

John Pelényi published some of the critical documents in English translation in 1964; more documents were published by Gyula Borbándi in original Hungarian, 'A Teleki-Pelényi terv nyugati magyar ellenkormány létesítésére', *Uj Látóhatár* 9/2 (1966), 155–70. Cf. Mario D. Fenyo, *Hitler, Horthy, and Hungary: German-Hungarian Relations, 1941–1944* (New Haven and London, 1972), 110; Juhász, *Magyarország külpolitikája*, 233; Nándor Dreisziger, 'Bridges to the West: The Horthy Regime's "Reinsurance Politics" in 1941,' *War & Society*, 7 (1989), 1–23.

58 To a considerable extent, Teleki's anti-Nazi stand was also served by the American publication of Domokos Kosáry's *A History of Hungary* in 1941. Frank, *Ethnicity, Propaganda, Myth-Making*, 292–3.

59 Protocol and Resolution of the 2nd Vienna Award, 30 August 1940, in Gyula Juhász (ed.), *Magyarország külpolitikája a nyugati hadjárattól a Szovjetunió megtámadásáig 1940–1941* (Budapest, 1982), 527–30.

60 Kálmán Benda (ed.), *Magyarország történeti kronológiája* (Budapest, 1982), vol. III, 975–6. After signing the treaty, Hitler suggested to Teleki and Csáky that Hungary conciliate Yugoslavia. The Hungarian leaders interpreted the Führer's words as a wish to conclude a Hungarian–Yugoslav treaty, thereby 'appeasing' the southern border of Hungary. On 10 December Csáky was already in Belgrade where he signed the treaty two days later. Csáky was however double-dealing: for the Yugoslavs he painted the agreement in vivid anti-German colours, while sending the text of the treaty to Ribbentrop for his approval. There was nothing new in these double-dealing policies: already a year earlier a member of the US legation in Budapest was told that, 'the only thing [that] could save Hungary would be a two-faced game to try to prove to the Germans that they were friendly'. Conversation of Mr. Travers with Dr. Antal Ullein-Reviczky, Budapest, 9 April 1940, John F. Montgomery Conversations, vol. II MS.

opposed the decision. Teleki, on the other hand, spoke of the 'spiritual approbation' of the Hungarian nation on 3 December 1940, while Foreign Minister Count István Csáky, in a Hungarian German-language magazine, made it quite clear that joining the pact was a 'direct consequence of the foreign policy Hungary pursued for the previous twenty years'.[61] Be this as it may, the gesture paved the way towards Hungary's catastrophic cooperation with the Fascist powers.[62] Very soon, the British government warned the Hungarian minister in London that adherence to the Tripartite pact would make Hungary a *de facto* enemy of Britain. 'Hungary has thus played away every right to be treated in case of an Anglo-American victory in any other way than as Britain's open enemies.'[63]

## THE WAR AND THE MEDIA

The German attack on Poland and the quick spread of Nazi barbarism in Europe invited sharp though clandestine criticism in the liberal papers. Indeed, it was the press that showed best the ambivalence of Hungarian society and politics in the early war years. Sándor Pethő's *Magyar Nemzet*, Károly Rassay's *Esti Kurír*, Ákos Dutka's *Friss Újság*, and József Balogh's *The Hungarian Quarterly* were among the notable liberal papers and journals that made a special effort to preserve their free, democratic spirit and anti-German stance in the increasingly intolerant early war years and managed to survive until the German occupation of the country. Not all liberal papers were so successful: the markedly liberal *Pesti Napló* was forced to stop publication on 31 October 1939, *Az Est* soon afterwards on 17 November.

The anti-German message appeared often in a covert way, hidden 'between the lines'. The liberal daily *Magyar Nemzet* published a lengthy article by János Lénárd discussing the study of Goethe's drama *Egmont* in a high-school class. In an evidently symbolic way the teacher talks about the message of *Egmont* in no uncertain terms when he declares: 'Being a fanatic, Philip II did not want to think of a country or a people that would seek its fortune in a way different from his. Material power, the army, the fleet, preparation were all on whose side? On that of the Spanish. What was on the side of the Dutch? Their confidence in their own right.

[61] Elek Karsai, *A budai Sándor-palotában történt 1919–1941* (Budapest, 1963), 433.
[62] Gyula Juhász, *A Teleki-kormány külpolitikája 1939–1941* (Budapest, 1964), 244–6.
[63] Hungarian minister to Britain, György Barcza, quoted by Gyula Juhász, *A Teleki-kormány külpolitikája 1939–1941*, 282.

And yet, which party wins over our compassion, our empathy, and whose final success do we trust? Well, of course, the Dutch.' Concluding the article, a student quotes Egmont saying at the end of the drama: 'Defend your property. To save those dearest to you, fall with joy, as I give you an example in myself.'[64]

On the anniversary of the German armistice at the end of the First World War, an article with the characteristic title 'Humanism and Christianity' in *Magyar Nemzet* first seemed to argue that 'we Hungarians cannot make our destiny more difficult through any emotional stance . . . when history is rushing, when terrible forces that are independent from us, turn the cube of fate to "six or nix".' The author continued, however, on a completely different note when commenting on an address of French Finance Minister (and noted anti-Nazi leader) Paul Reynaud: 'France, the land of Gothic domes . . . the land that produces saints, is today the most unpardoning, as it finishes off any sort of anti-Christianism in an inner, spiritual way, just as it put an end to the Communist threat overnight.' At the end of his article the well-known anti-Nazi journalist Jenő Katona[65] saluted France 'as the last escape of intellectual freedom, social justice, and human solidarity, a cliff where any human conceit, arrogance, and coercion smashes itself with bloody forehead'.[66] This was very clearly an emotional demonstration of the values represented by France and a warning for Germany.

A perfect example of the pro-Western, anti-German spirit of a distinguished section of Hungary's political élite was provided by *The Hungarian Quarterly*. Originally conceived as a revisionist device in 1934 by former Prime Minister Count István Bethlen, members of the business oligarchy such as Ferenc Chorin, Pál Fellner, Béla Imrédy, Baron Frigyes Korányi, Baron Móric Kornfeld, Baron Marcell Madarassy-Beck, Lajos Reményi-Schneller, Tibor Scitovszky, Fülöp Weiss, and György Wolfner launched the *Quarterly* in 1936 and kept it alive up until the German occupation of Hungary on 19 March 1944. The *Quarterly* was first intended as a vehicle of Hungarian revisionism built upon the spirit of

[64] János Lénárd, '"Egmont" a VIII./b-ben' (Egmont in Class VIII/b), *Magyar Nemzet*, 16 November 1933. Cf. *Egmont*, by Johann Wolfgang von Goethe. In Goethe, *Auswahl in drei Bänden* (Leipzig, 1956), vol. I, 378. Newspaper clippings of Éva Kerekes.

[65] Jenő Katona (1905–78) was an important contributor to Catholic journals in the 1930s and a brave figure of the anti-Nazi movement in Hungary before and during the Second World War. A leading member on the staff of *Magyar Nemzet* (1938–44), he was imprisoned toward the end of the war, but emerged later as a member of parliament, influential editor and a member of the Presidential Council of Hungary (1949–53).

[66] Jenő Katona, 'Humanizmus és kereszténység', *Magyar Nemzet*, 11 November 1939.

Bethlen's 1933 lectures at the Cambridge University League of Nations Union, the Near and Middle East Association in London, the Royal Institute of International Affairs, and the Balkan Committee. They were published in both London and Budapest in the following year as *The Treaty of Trianon and European Peace* and *Bethlen István angliai előadásai.* Contemporary British critics of Bethlen, such as R. W. Seton-Watson, warned against a 'none too scrupulous propaganda' and reminded the British public of the former Prime Minister's 'governing in intelligent anticipation of Nazi methods'[67] since 1921. Increasingly, however, as the Nazi menace rose and approached Hungary, the *Quarterly* became an instrument of pro-British, anti-German Hungarian cultural diplomacy in the English-speaking world, carefully edited by the noted classical scholar and cultural diplomat József Balogh with the active support of the pro-Western group around Count Bethlen and the tacit approval of the Hungarian foreign policy establishment. Balogh was a great editor.[68] He was extremely proud of the national, non-partisan status of his journal. '*The Hungarian Quarterly* is not the organ of official Hungarian foreign policy', he explained to Count Bethlen in the spring of 1941, 'it is a social establishment and as such a synthesis of the national foreign policy'.[69] This was a proud statement in Hungary in 1941 when Balogh knew all too well that the censor might not want to let him publish articles in English that were still considered acceptable for the Hungarian public. Balogh was skilful enough to ask for constant advice from the circle around the *Quarterly*. In early 1939, for example, he visited György Barcza, the Hungarian minister in London, and asked for directives for his journal in the new situation after Munich and the first Vienna Award. Barcza urged him to continue to discuss 'the requirements of Hungarian justice' but underlined that 'just as in the previous twenty years, only the arguments based on democratic and ethnographic, perhaps economic principles' should be offered, rather than 'the construction of Saint Stephen['s crown], cultural superiority and similar slogans that may harm rather than serve our cause in the public opinion of England'. After some hesitation, the foreign ministry sternly warned the minister 'not to write about the idea of St Stephen, the holiest

[67] R. W. Seton-Watson, *Treaty Revision and the Hungarian Frontiers* (London, 1934) quoted by Tibor Frank, 'Luring the English-Speaking World: Hungarian History Diverted', *The Slavonic and East European Review,* 69/1 (1991), 61.

[68] Tibor Frank, 'Editing as Politics: József Balogh and The Hungarian Quarterly', *The Hungarian Quarterly,* 34/129 (1993), 5–13.

[69] József Balogh to Count István Bethlen, Budapest, 6 March 1941, OSzK: József Balogh Papers, Fond 1/322. Quoted by Tibor Frank, 'Editing as Politics', 10.

tradition of the Hungarian state and the basis of its existence, in such a way'.[70]

CENSORSHIP

Censorship during the early war years was in the hands of Antal Ullein-Reviczky. Educated in Vienna, Ullein got his first major job in the ministry of foreign affairs, immediately after the dissolution of the Republic of Councils in 1919. Together with other young men such as István Csáky and László Bárdossy he was to change the antiquated 'Kaiserlich und Königlich' (Imperial and Royal) spirit in the new Hungarian ministry of foreign affairs bringing along 'national' and 'Christian' ideas and ideals. In the 1920s and 1930s Ullein served in Paris, Geneva, Ankara, and Zagreb before he returned to the ministry in Budapest to head the press and cultural department with the title of 'ambassador extraordinary and minister plenipotentiary'. The merger of the two departments under Ullein meant the centralisation of Hungarian propaganda in one hand.

At a dinner party of the foreign policy establishment in the autumn of 1939, Ullein gave a talk on 'The Press of the Neutral Countries', which was published in the *Külügyi Szemle* (Foreign Affairs Review) in January 1940. Reflecting on the declaration of Teleki, Ullein announced: 'The press of a neutral country is allotted the great and noble role to try, as well as she can, to prepare for what is bound to follow the war: peace.'[71]

Ullein's role was unique in the foreign policy of Hungary during the war. He considered the press of the nation as a huge orchestra which he conducted in a regal way. He embodied the typical Hungarian government official of the period, yet he was different from the norm. His thinking was based on the idea of treaty revision, but he opposed complete siding with the Germans and tried to use the wise tactics of waiting. He married the daughter of a British diplomat and was also a professor of international law at Debrecen University.[72]

By early 1939 this clever and ambitious man realised that the essential qualities and directions of Hungarian propaganda should be

[70] Instruction from the Foreign Ministry to Minister György Barcza, 30 March 1939, György Barcza to the Foreign Ministry, London, 25 February 1939, László Márkus, Miklós Szinai, Miklós Vásárhelyi, (eds.) *Nem engedélyezem! A cenzúra bizottság dossziéj ából* (Budapest, 1975), 331–2.

[71] Antal Ullein-Reviczky, 'A semleges országok sajtója,' *Külügyi Szemle*, January 1940, 112, in Márkus, Szinai, and Vásárhelyi (eds.), *Nem engedélyezem!*, 26–7. See also 25–6. Cf. the memoirs of Antal Ullein-Reviczky, *Guerre Allemande, Paix Russe. Le drame hongrois* (Neuchâtel, 1947); Hungarian translation: Budapest, 1993).

[72] Márkus, Szinai, and Vásárhelyi (eds.), *Nem engedélyezem!*, 26.

changed and adjusted to the situation after the dissolution of Czechoslovakia. While previous Hungarian arguments were based mostly on the effort to convince the former Great Powers of how unjust Trianon had been and were directed mostly towards Britain and France, 'this type of propaganda could no longer be used after Munich, the return of the Hungarian part of the Uplands [of former Hungary], the enormous accomplishment of the Axis Powers, and strengthening of Hungary's ties with them'. Ullein, however, made sure that 'a cultural propaganda with skilful tact' complemented the press campaign, 'particularly in countries where political propaganda would not serve our interests in the current foreign political circumstances. The peoples of these countries, I think of England and France in the first place, could be kept warm through a tactful and not transparent cultural propaganda without our being politically committed.'[73]

Upon the outbreak of the war, the foreign ministry instructed the papers to discuss 'the moral victory of the Germans. The question of responsibility for the future of Europe is not weighing upon the Germans.'[74] By a declaration of the prime minister on 2 September,[75] censorship was immediately introduced under the auspices of a Committee for Press Control reporting to the Prime Minister's Office and located in the parliament building in Budapest. The relevant documents of the Committee perished in the Second World War, but copies survived in the files of the Hungarian Legation in Berne, Switzerland and among the papers of the ministry of justice and the foreign ministry. The papers reveal the highly centralised and strict nature of censorship during the 'neutral' years, when 'any multiplied text (even if multiplied on a typewriter) had to be censored'. Apart from the military news reports, 'any other news, going out or coming in, should be considered political in nature and belongs to the competence of the Hungarian Royal Foreign Ministry'.[76]

Loyal to the cause of the Axis as he was, Ullein was in touch with all political forces in Hungary and listened to opposition leaders such

[73] Antal Ullein-Reviczky's directives for foreign press propaganda, 3 February 1939, in Márkus, Szinai, and Vásárhelyi (eds.), *Nem engedélyezem!*, 325, 330.

[74] Foreign Ministry directives for the press, 1 September 1939, in Márkus, Szinai, and Vásárhelyi (eds.), *Nem engedélyezem!*, 333.

[75] *Budapesti Közlöny*, 2 September 1939; Otto von Erdmannsdorff to the German Foreign Ministry, Budapest, 2 September 1939, in Ránki, Pamlényi, Tilkovszky, and Juhász (eds.), *A Wilhelmstrasse és Magyarország*, 434.

[76] Note by Miklós Illés-Illyasevics (Foreign Ministry) on the distinction between military and political censorship, 18 February 1941, Editors' Preface, and Jenő Zilahi-Sebess to Viktor Sztankovics, 26 September 1940, in Márkus, Szinai, and Vásárhelyi (eds.), *Nem engedélyezem!*, 49, 340–1.

as Endre Bajcsy-Zsilinszky, who was most anxious to stop the extreme right-wing articles of the paper *Magyarország*, directed against President Franklin D. Roosevelt and Prime Minister Winston Churchill.[77]

After the entry of Hungary into the war in the summer of 1941, Ullein had a key role in the Hungarian government, trying to expand the policy of double orientation. Continuing to be pro-German on the surface but increasingly looking for Western ties, this new Hungarian policy aimed at securing the survival of Horthy's regime and a favourable territorial settlement, regardless of the war's final outcome.

## THE SUICIDE OF TELEKI: THE END OF NEUTRALITY

The end of neutrality actually came to Hungary before the war did. Before the ring of the Axis powers closed around his country, Teleki tried to keep the only remaining option open and approached Anglophile Yugoslavia with a view to maintaining relations with the West. 'It is impossible to live surrounded by enemy nations alone on our borders', Teleki declared when arguing in the Committee on Foreign Relations for an agreement with Yugoslavia. The treaty 'of peace and eternal friendship' was negotiated in October and November and was finally signed in Belgrade on 12 December 1940.[78] Though the idea of the treaty was supported in Berlin and Rome, the treaty itself was received with mixed feelings. Germany was well on its way to preparing an attack on Greece, and taming Yugoslavia, one way or another, would obviously assist in these plans. Hitler signed the order for an attack on Greece on 13 December 1940, but the Wilhelmstraße was anxious lest an 'eternal friendship' between Hungary and Yugoslavia might disturb its plans for south-eastern Europe.

Teleki was more than anxious to secure the understanding of the British government for a Hungary that, the Prime Minister suggested to British Foreign Secretary Anthony Eden, was 'constantly fighting German demands'.[79] The British response was unyielding and made it quite clear that Britain would consider Hungary an enemy should it allow German troops to cross its territory in an attack against a foreign country.

[77] Endre Bajcsy-Zsilinszky to Antal Ullein-Reviczky, 4 May 1941, in Márkus, Szinai, and Vásárhelyi (eds.), *Nem engedélyezem!*, 350–7.

[78] Juhász, *A Teleki-kormány külpolitikája 1939–1941*, 254–65.

[79] Pál Teleki to György Barcza, 12 March 1941, quoted in *A Teleki-kormány külpolitikája 1939–1941*, 284–5.

This 'country', Teleki knew full well, was Yugoslavia. The original German plans were founded on Yugoslavia joining the Tripartite Agreement, which it eventually did on 25 March 1941; two days later, however, an anti-German *coup* dismissed the government and left Berlin with only one possible course of action. The attack on Yugoslavia on 6 April 1941 necessitated the use of Hungarian territory. Teleki, who was desperately trying to defend Hungary's integrity and his own, committed suicide on 3 April 1941. 'He had to understand that it was impossible to continue that unfeasible and senseless policy which hoped to maintain Hungary's sovereignty by constantly giving way to fascist Germany in both foreign and domestic policies'. For a long time to come, Teleki was to have an excellent reputation in Britain. Even the BBC, and more particularly its chief spokesman for Hungary, C. A Macartney, zealously emphasised that 'Up till the time when Hungary actively joined Germany's war on Russia there was nothing wrong with her official policy. Count Teleki as prime minister pursued a successful policy in the interest of the Hungarian nation.'[80] Count Teleki's suicide brought the theory and practice of political 'doublespeak' to an end. This bitter end came quickly under Teleki's successor, László Bárdossy, who ultimately led the country into war.

The new prime minister was a staunch defender of the idea of border revision. His entire diplomatic and political career was built on the assumption that treaty revision was inevitable. When asked, during his trial in 1945, about the connection between revisionism and Hungary becoming a Nazi satellite country, Bárdossy admitted, 'I hoped that revisionist policies would attract the attention of the whole world towards Hungary. This did not succeed, we failed. This was the point when Hungarian politics got into the situation the consequences of which I had to draw.'[81]

Germany's invasion of Russia was almost immediately followed by Hungary's entry into the war. Hungary's attack on the Soviet Union was initiated at the implicit instigation of the German government and the high command. They wanted to avoid an outright, official solicitation on their part, and they could easily rely on the support and willingness

[80] Juhász, *A Teleki-kormány külpolitikája 1939–1941*, 310. On Teleki's suicide see Macartney, *Teleki Pál*, 213–35; Barcza, *Diplomataemlékeim 1911–1945*, 484–502; Ullein-Reviczky, *Német háború*, 86–90. Ullein-Reviczky called Teleki 'an idealist professor'. Notes and Suggestions on BBC Broadcasts in Hungarian, March 1942 Confidential. Published by the Association of Hungarian Journalists and Authors of Czechoslovakia in Great Britain, p. 5, as well as Enclosure 7, Macartney's broadcast on 31 August 1941, p. 16.

[81] Pál Pritz (ed.), *Bárdossy László a népbíróság előtt* (Budapest, 1991), 132.

of the Hungarian military leaders to start the war on their own initiative, without direct, open German coercion.[82] The trick they used was the alleged Soviet bombing of the city of Kassa (Košice), then in Hungary, formerly in Czechoslovakia, on 26 June 1941, which the Hungarian government immediately declared an act of aggression. Less than a week after the German attack of 22 June, Bárdossy's government provoked war with the Soviet Union. Careful research on the subject has shown that the provocation was invented in order to give the Hungarian troops a good and 'patriotic' excuse to launch an attack on the Soviet Union the next day, 27 June 1941.

An attack on the Soviet Union seemed like a good cause to many in the Hungarian leadership, one that they cherished even though they despised the Nazis. Horthy suppressed the Republic of Councils in 1919 and was an arch-enemy of Communism. He spoke of a potential war against Russia with delight, and as early as 1937 informed John F. Montgomery, that

> the greatest danger today was subversive activities of the Bolshevists. He said you could fight a foe you could see and meet, but all this undercover business was difficult to deal with [,] that the nations should get together and go in and simply whip the Bolshevists. He was in hearty sympathy with Hitler's ideas on this subject.[83]

Anti-Communism in inter-war Hungary was more important than avoiding Nazi Germany. It seems that the country was trapped between her own eagerness to revise the borders established at Trianon and the fact that only Nazi Germany was willing to grant this possibility. In her desperation to revise Trianon, Hungary became a German satellite, however reluctantly, without realising the awesome price she was to pay for the friendship of Adolf Hitler. Manoeuvring between the Axis and the West for several years, Hungary was simply unprepared to meet the challenge of the Soviet Union and the ideas it represented. Hungary's neutrality had come to an end.

[82] Hungary's entry into the German–Soviet war was encouraged by the Hungarian high command, which was blindly confident of a final German victory. General Henrik Werth, head of the Hungarian high command, argued that the results of the revisionist foreign policy would be jeopardised by Hungary's neutrality, whereas 'loyal policies' (i.e. loyal to Hitler's Germany) would result in 'the safe return of the complete territory of historical Hungary'. Lóránd Dombrády, *Hadsereg és politika Magyarországon 1938-1941* (Budapest, 1986), 226. Contrary to popular belief, the German military leaders did not send an official invitation to Hungary to join the war effort, instead, a low-ranking German general suggested 'voluntary' participation. Romsics, *Hungary*, 205.

[83] John F. Montgomery to Miklós Horthy, Conversation, Budapest, 2 February 1937; John F. Montgomery, Confidential Conversations, vol. 1, MS.

CHAPTER 7

# *Romanian neutrality, 1939–1940*

*Maurice Pearton*

In all but the exceptional cases where neutral status is internationally defined or recognised, how we define 'neutrality' depends on how we define 'war' and arguments about that fall, broadly, into two categories. If we regard 'war' as a violation of some kind of system which gives value to and constrains the behaviour of the constituent states, such as a *res publica Christiana* or a League of Nations, then war is, in some sense, a criminal act against the community of states and 'neutrality' is logically excluded if one of its members flouts the rules. Justice demands that one cannot be neutral towards crime. If, however, we regard 'war' as a natural recourse of states in the pursuit of their objectives, then 'neutrality' is, equally, a legitimate option. It does not discriminate between 'just' wars and their opposite. War is war, and staying out is a right. But if that right is absolute, the resultant practice is highly contingent. A claim to neutrality formally obliges the neutral state to observe impartiality and abstention in its relationships with belligerents. Equally, it automatically confers rights on belligerents – specifically in regard to 'un-neutral conduct' arising from any failure to observe impartiality and abstention. This makes unilateral neutrality a precarious option. Its scope and limits were worked out in international law from the late seventeenth century, that is, *after* the era of religious conflicts in Europe and the effective abandonment of a *civitas maxima* constraining state behaviour. International law did not pronounce on the legality of war as such but sought to regulate its conduct, including particularly the role of neutrals. In so doing, it evolved the framework and the vocabulary in which conflicts of interest are fought out by belligerents and neutrals alike.

Experience shows, however, that, as a conflict develops, the legal protocols do not cover all that actually happens because 'the rules' are, in essence, derived from the previous upheaval. This has been the case since industrialisation created an international economy which fractured the carefully argued formulae of eighteenth-century legalists and turned neutrals into formal or informal 'co-belligerents'. They were no longer insulated from the combat – but neither were they just dragged into it by being components in the industrial system. The record in two world wars shows that they had, *for their own reasons*, a positive political and economic interest in keeping intact the circuit of requirements of the contending states, irrespective of their formal status in international law.[1] Hence, neutrality became not an internationally recognised device for passively sitting out the storm, but a means to allow the state to continue to pursue its objectives in the changed international circumstances. In these terms, of course, the practical chances of success rest largely on the strategic irrelevance of the neutral to the belligerents. Thus, a neutral's policies have to be carefully shaped so that a belligerent does not have an excuse to procure for itself a more amenable government or collect physically whatever it needs, be it raw materials or strategic real estate, or move to deny them to its enemy. In principle, however, when war is regarded as a legitimate enterprise, a declaration of neutrality gives notice of the rubric governing a state's foreign policy in wartime. This was the option chosen, on 6 September 1939, by the Council of Ministers in Bucharest when it 'unanimously decided upon the strict observance, as regards the belligerents in the present conflict, of the rules of neutrality laid down in International Conventions'. The 'rules' referred to were those laid down by the Hague Convention of 1907. They had been much modified by the experience of the First World War, but the lessons to be drawn were still unresolved by international lawyers, much less accepted by governments. By 1939, it was widely recognised that the 'rules' contained many uncertain and hence debatable provisions and that Romania's position was precarious. For that reason, 'neutrality' could have widely differing entailments.

Since 1919, Romania's foreign policy objectives could be reduced to one simple proposition, namely, to maintain the gains of the peace settlements intact. These involved Transylvania, which had accrued from Hungary; the southern Dobrudja, from Bulgaria; Bukovina, from Austria and Bessarabia, from Russia. The first three acquisitions had been recognised by international treaty, though had generated demands for revision; the last, however, had been acquired unilaterally in more contentious circumstances and had not been similarly secured. Romania

[1] See Maurice Pearton, *The Knowledgeable State: Diplomacy, War and Technology since 1830* (London, 1982), part 4 and 'The Theory and Practice of Neutrality in the First World War – The Romanian Contribution 1914–1916', in G. Buzatu and S. Pascu (eds.), *Anglo-Romanian Relations after 1821* (Iasi, 1983), 111–25.

had to solicit recognition, point by point. Though some states gave it, Russia remained implacably opposed and during the inter-war decades, negotiations on the issue repeatedly broke down. The continuing symbol of Russo-Romanian relations was the wrecked railway bridge over the river Dniester on the only track directly connecting the two states.[2]

Romania's policy of refusing any concessions in regard to the post-war frontiers made sense so long as its external guarantor, France, was a strong presence in Eastern Europe and Titulescu who, as foreign minister, conducted Romania's foreign policy largely from Geneva, was adept at using the League of Nations to frustrate any revisionist initiatives from that quarter. From the middle of the 1930s, that was no longer the case.[3] In March 1936, the reoccupation by German forces of the Rhineland deprived French forces of unimpeded access to Central and Eastern Europe and thereby eviscerated the alliances built up since the last days of the First World War. That encouraged Romania's leaders to think of some 'rapprochement' with a resurgent Germany and even to contemplate making some more positive move towards Russia. Nazi Germany was considered a threat only if it chose to support Hungarian demands for the return of Transylvania. The obvious tactic was to get closer to the German government to ensure that it did not. So, within six months of the march into the Rhineland, Romanian policy began to shift towards Germany.[4] The shift, however, did not preclude friendly relations with France and Czechoslovakia, where Romania was buying armaments with funds supplied by the French.

Russia was far more problematical. In June 1933, in direct response to Hitler's 'Machtergreifung', Romania resumed diplomatic relations with Russia, and in September duly voted for Russia's admission to the League of Nations. A year later, the Romanians joined the Poles and the Russians in guaranteeing each other's frontiers and, subsequently, signed in London – along with the Russian government – the London

[2] Denis Deletant, 'A Shuttlecock of History: Bessarabia', *South Slav Journal*, 10/4 (Winter 1987/88), offers a succinct guide to the complexities of the Bessarabian problem.

[3] During Romania's neutrality, France, although party to the Guarantee and to schemes for depriving the Reich of oil, was not as important as its historical position in Romanian politics and culture would lead one to expect. The failure to attack in the west when the Reichswehr was overrunning Poland cost France much of the influence it had traditionally exercised and it never recovered the lost ground before May/June 1940. Its importance to Romanian policies, therefore, narrowed considerably. An examination of the reasons and an analysis of Romanian responses would exceed the limits required for this chapter.

[4] Rebecca Haynes analyses the shift in detail in *Romanian Policy towards Germany* (London, 2000). I am grateful to Dr Haynes for allowing me to see her book, before publication. See also Dov B. Lungu, *Romania and the Great Powers* (Durham/London, 1989).

pact defining 'aggression'. This act the Romanians viewed hopefully as a tacit recognition of their acquisition of Bessarabia. The Dniester bridge was repaired. So far, so good. But the Soviet government failed to return the Romanian gold stock, transferred there 'for safe keeping' in 1916, and continued to depict Bessarabia on maps as Russian, 'under Romanian military occupation'. In Bucharest, such instances were freely interpreted in terms of a not-always-latent Russophobia and a fear of Panslavism. That posture and the sheer discrepancy in power deployable by the two states helped to maintain a profound mistrust of Russian intentions. Romanians were apt to recall lengthy occupations by Russian troops of Moldavia and Wallachia, the core of the modern Romanian state, in the previous century. In August 1936, Titulescu, long identified with an anti-German policy, was forced out of office because he was considered to have gone too far in promising the Czechs that Romania would allow Russian troops through its territory, should Czechoslovakia be attacked by Germany. (Romanian governments feared that once Soviet troops crossed into Bessarabia, not all of them would leave.) Among the elites, suspicion of Russia had a cultural dimension; Romania had been open to the civilising influence of Rome; Russia had not. It represented a basically untamed barbarism, which, given the chance, would submerge Latinate Romania in a sea of Slavs.

In accounting for Romanian behaviour in the Thirties and down to 1941, it is vital to recognise that Russia was regarded on many levels as *the* supreme threat to the independent existence of the Romanian state and that this attitude governed its relationships with *all* other powers, including Germany. From the Romanian point of view, the chances that bargains struck would be kept were reckoned far higher with the Third Reich than with Stalin's Russia. Pro-German opinion apart, this assessment relied not on the good faith of the government of the Third Reich, whose record in that respect was extremely dubious, but on the fact that Romania had assets which enabled it to appeal to German self-interest, principally oil. It was also important in Romanian calculations that, after the occupation of Prague in March 1939, the German government was willing to fulfil contracts for arms' deliveries originally signed with the Czechs. The trade balance with the Reich itself was becoming an increasingly important factor in Romania's trading account, particularly as a market for Romanian agriculture.[5] That Germany had no direct frontier with Romania, had no territorial claims against it and was militantly

[5] See details in David E. Kaiser, *Economic Diplomacy and the Origins of the Second World War* (New Jersey, 1980) and, for a contemporary analysis, A. Basch, *The Danube Basin and the German Economic Sphere*

anti-Bolshevik into the bargain also featured prominently in appreciations in Bucharest. If any Romanian Government found itself forced to choose between Germany and Russia – though it hoped it would not have to – it would choose Germany.

Nevertheless, the historical orientation towards France still exercised its attraction and, with that, the hope that French power could offset any German designs on Romania. This was not entirely implausible, since, even after 'Munich' finally negated the French alliances in Central and Eastern Europe, France continued to concern itself in Romania's defences and to send military missions and supply arms to Romania's neighbours, Poland and Yugoslavia, with both of whom Romania enjoyed good, though not untroubled, relations. And behind France stood Britain, perceived more dimly through the fogs of the North Sea, but with immense imperial resources, its naval power and, through the international trade in oil and wheat, its important contribution to Romania's balance of payments in 'hard' – that is, freely transferable – currency. In Romanian thinking, Britain's actual policies remained more problematic; they had resulted in the cession of Central Europe to Germany and, in regard to Romania itself, the British were considered tediously insistent on the settling of outstanding trade and payments problems and unpaid bonded debt, and were conspicuously unwilling to make the broad economic arrangements which – the Romanians argued – would offset the German trade drive and underwrite the country's security, while underpinning Britain's position in the Near East. The British construed this argument as an attempt to get a privileged position in the sterling area and were, in any case, reluctant, on grounds of principle, to engage in 'political' trading, for which, in any case, they lacked the appropriate mechanisms.[6] In addition, they remained extremely sceptical of the alleged strategic benefits, especially as, in that respect, Romania could offer nothing for which Turkey was not more suitably placed. In their pre-war planning, the military had discarded Romanian oil on the unimpeachable grounds that the Germans could get to Ploesti first. Nevertheless, in circumstances which are still controversial among

(London, 1944). See also G. Ranki, *Economy and Foreign Policy. The Struggle of the Great Powers for Hegemony in the Danube Valley, 1919–1939* (Boulder/New York 1983).

[6] On 'political' trading, see M. Pearton 'British Policy towards Romania 1939–41', in R. Haynes (ed.), *Occasional Papers in Romanian Studies*, No 2. (School of Slavonic and East European Studies, London, 1998) and M. J. Rooke, 'The Concept of Political Trading in Peacetime. The British Government and Trade with South-Eastern Europe 1938–39', *Revue des Etudes Sud-Est Européennes*, 22/2 (1984). Also the papers of Sir Frederick Leith-Ross; Public Record Office, London, T188–244 and his memoirs, *Money Talks* (London, 1968) chs. 16 and 17.

historians, Britain, with France, guaranteed Romania's frontiers on 13 April 1939. This, although solicited by the Romanians, was made to appear unilateral, so as not to complicate Romania's relations with Germany – against whom it was aimed – or with Poland, about whose anti-German stance by that time the Romanian leadership had serious doubts. Moreover, the Guarantee was qualified to exclude Russia. Later, Russia was included, but only provided Turkey allowed access through the Straits. This *caveat* was required by international law and practical logistics, but it effectively put the operation of the Guarantee in Turkish hands and the Turks stated they were willing to intervene against Russia only if the Red Army crossed the Danube. Evidently, they were not going to war for Bessarabia.

In the inter-war period, Romania's foreign policy encompassed two other sets of relationships. The Little Entente, with Czechoslovakia and Yugoslavia, was designed to prevent a Habsburg restoration in Austria and guarantee to the member-states their gains from Hungary after the First World War. 'Better Hitler than the Hapsburgs' – a phrase used variously by Beneš and Titulescu – expresses a bizarre and ultimately fatal fixation on a dead issue. Moreover, the Entente was never keyed into French strategic planning, *as a system*. Instead, the constituent states each had bilateral military arrangements covering security objectives which diverged from those of their partners. The German take-over of Czechoslovakia in March 1939 and the increasing tendency of Yugoslavia to rely on Germany to offset the threat from Italy, effectively dissolved the Entente.

From February 1934, the Balkan Entente with Yugoslavia, Greece, and Turkey had seemed to offer Romania better prospects in an area where her military contribution could have greater efficacy. The main problem was Bulgaria and the terms on which she could be persuaded to join, and here Romanian possession of the southern Dobrudja, recognised by the Treaty of Neuilly in 1919, was at issue.[7] To outsiders, the retrocession of an area in which ethnic Romanians formed only 12 per cent of the population would be a minor territorial readjustment, but Romanians defined it as a vital interest. The Entente also suffered from the divergent objectives of its members. Romanian policy was not so anti-Italian as that

[7] The Treaty of Neuilly merely confirmed Romania's possession of Southern Dobrudja ceded by Bulgaria by the Treaty of Bucharest, 1913, after the Second Balkan War. Transylvania was annexed by Romania on 11 January 1919, ahead of the Peace Conference. The annexation was recognised by the Treaty of Trianon, 4 June 1920. The union of Bessarabia was formally recognised by treaty in October 1920.

of Yugoslavia; Turkey had made it clear that it would not go to war on behalf of Romania against Russia, while Greece stipulated that it would not be bound to participate in any war against a major power, meaning Italy, and was consistently hostile to Bulgaria, mainly over Macedonia. Albania was too firmly under Italian influence to join, and Bulgaria refused to join any arrangement which did not settle *all* Bulgaria's claims against neighbouring states. So the Entente fell far short of being a Balkan security system. Among the participants, projected highest-level security negotiations became, successively, conversations between general staffs and then, further down the hierarchy, meetings between military attachés. In these conditions, the Entente largely dissipated any capability for coherent action. Again, an external impulse from France was lacking; the Entente was not effectively tied in to French security arrangements. In September 1939, Romanian suggestions of a joint démarche were not followed and the Entente's members announced their neutrality separately. Grigore Gafencu, the Foreign Minister (December 1938–May 1940), nevertheless persisted in trying to put together, successively, a 'Balkan bloc' or a 'bloc of neutrals' under Italian leadership. Both failed, partly by reason of French objections, but, basically because, even in wartime, the declared interests of the intended member-states were irreconcilable. In the next eighteen months, the carefully worded loopholes in their treaties with one another helped Germany to pick them off one by one.

The collapse of the League security system left the Romanian government to claim neutrality unilaterally, with all the attendant risks. It knew that Romania was not strategically irrelevant to the combatants, but that the likelihood of intervention depended on the development of the conflict. Its problem was to establish how far Romanian policy could influence the respective intentions of the belligerents – a judgement in which the vital element was the uncertainty of *Soviet* intentions. At the outbreak of war, this was the essence of Romania's predicament.

The government which took the decision was a royal autocracy but King Carol ruled only by striking bargains with specific interests and with the remnants of the old party structure he had formally abolished in February 1938. Foreign policy, however, remained very much in his hands. His nomination of ministers were taken to indicate the tendency of state policy. Armand Calinescu as minister president would denote that Romania's interest lay with the Allies; a cabinet under Ion Gigurtu would indicate a preference for Germany. Nevertheless, until September 1939, the policy followed was officially defined as one of 'equilibrium' between the Axis partners and the 'western' states. After the outbreak of hostilities, 'equilibrium' shaded easily into 'neutrality'. At that juncture, Calinescu was firmly in place. The British minister, Sir Reginald Hoare, judged him as 'entirely fearless and having some of the characteristics of the best type of highwayman'. Gafencu was also identified as 'pro-Ally', not least because his wife was a 'desperately loyal, frenziedly garrulous Frenchwoman'.

The domestic political scene, however, was far from settled. Communism, which was irretrievably associated with Russia and with the Comintern line demanding the return of Bessarabia to the Soviet Union, was represented by a small faction-ridden party, most of whose leaders were in jail or in Russia. Romania's indigenous Fascist party – the Iron Guard – posed more of a threat and was partly financed by Germany. Carol's crackdown on its leadership in November 1938 had left it sullenly acquiescent. Perhaps the greatest weakness, however, was the existence of minorities – principally Hungarian, which official policies since the 1920s had failed to reconcile to Romanian rule, and ethnic German, which, in spite of enjoying better relations with Romanian authority, remained susceptible to *Grossdeutschland* propaganda – particularly its younger members. Additionally, there were the Ashkenazi Jews in Moldavia, Bukovina, and Bessarabia who, deeply orthodox and speaking Yiddish and Russian, were widely regarded in Romanian society as *Russians* and, as such, a stalking-horse for the Soviet Union. In the given situation, all these could be manipulated by either Germany or Russia and thus were hostages to fortune who could make the claim to neutrality difficult to sustain.

The day after the declaration of neutrality, Calinescu told Hoare that he considered it 'a purely juridical formula which changed nothing in Romania's intention to afford all practicable support to the Allied cause'. Gigurtu, apparently, considered it 'but a step towards alliance with Germany'. Calinescu, however, had qualified his statement by adding that the only thing which could change that policy would be 'a series of German successes and Allied failures'. This proved a prescient forecast of events over the next year, by the end of which Allied military failures had proved both Calinescu and Gigurtu, in their different ways, right. The rapid invasions and subsequent partition of Poland between Germany and Russia set a new context for Romanian policy. Poland's government and remnants of its army took refuge in Romania – thus posing the first major questions about 'neutral' behaviour and its converse, now made the more acute by the fact that the occupation of Galicia gave Germany a direct frontier with Romania. The German government severely pressed the Romanians over the admission of the Polish government and Polish troops and refugees, and the transit of the Polish gold stock – on all of which the Romanian government held its ground, making only minor concessions. Soviet declarations that, in Poland, the Red Army had retaken territories of their 'blood brothers, Ukrainians and Byelorussians' lost in 1921, were ominous and, coupled with the *de facto* take-over of the Baltic States, inevitably raised questions in Bucharest about the security of Bessarabia, if not about a possible partition of the whole country, on the Polish model. Iron Guard terrorism flared up; among its victims was Calinescu. It was suppressed, but had it been a *German-sponsored* attempt to get a pro-German government in Bucharest, or not?[8] The Romanian government promptly denied that Calinescu's death resulted from any plot hatched abroad, or that it had any international significance – which tended only to substantiate the speculations. From then on, Hoare detected in some quarters a subtle tendency towards regarding Germany as the only possible counterpoise to Russia. The alternative, more optimistic, view was that the conflicting interests of these two states would preserve the country's neutral status.

Right from the outset, there was no question of the Romanian government's trying simply to distance itself scrupulously from the belligerents, within the framework of 'the rules', however inconclusive they might be. No-one was starting from a *tabula rasa*. Instead, the government adopted a policy of balancing concessions to each side to secure what it believed to be Romania's interest. These could be on quite minor issues. In September 1939, it forbade all demonstrations in cinemas when Hitler and Molotov (catcalls and hissing) or Chamberlain and Daladier (cheers and applause) appeared on newsreels – both regarded as 'un-neutral behaviour,' but, at the same time, sponsored parties of schoolchildren to see 'Goodbye Mr Chips' which was drawing packed houses in Bucharest. However, the belligerents' practice of 'economic warfare' raised problems of a different order.

Experience of the First World War had shown that the capacity of a state to sustain industrialised war related to its access to or command

[8] Since Calinescu, as Minister of the Interior, had been in charge of the action against the Iron Guard in November 1938, the Guardists had ample reason for revenge for the killing of Codreanu. But their connections with Nazi Germany were well known, and their behaviour after the killing, i.e. of broadcasting from the radio station, was widely interpreted as having been intended to provoke chaos which would give the Germans an opportunity to enter the country to restore order and install a government responsive to their own wishes. This the Romanian government's prompt retribution had negated. Subsequently, an official investigation concluded that the assassins had been trained in Germany by the SS and had returned to Romania among the refugees from Poland, whose admission only four days previously was thought to have 'triggered' the murder.

of raw materials and manufacturing capacity, from sources which by that time were part of the international economy.[9] The inter-war period had generated a vast literature on the subject. In 1939, the German policy in Romania was to offset the existing position of the British and French (principally in oil, heavy industry, and Danube shipping) by making comprehensive arrangements with the Romanian government which then would allow Germany to acquire direction or control of particular economic assets. This process was in train before the war, most notably in the 'Wohlthat Agreement' of 23 March,[10] but continued into the period of neutrality. In trading, Germany enjoyed two advantages – its economy (unlike Britain's) was largely complementary to that of Romania and its operation of clearing agreements left the Romanians with Reichsmark balances which could only be used to purchase German goods, and therefore with an in-built incentive to buy from German sources. The level at which the RM/leu exchange rate was set determined the volume of trade between the two states. Indeed, in 1940, a Romanian government's decision to change these levels, thus reducing the incentive, provoked accusations of 'un-neutral behaviour' from Germany.

The British approach was different and more consistent with 'neutrality' in its formal sense. It followed from a general strategic appreciation of south-east Europe as a whole – which was to avoid involving states which could easily be overrun until the Allies could support them; otherwise, they were a tempting invitation to the Germans. This regard for form could lead to some bizarre outcomes. The British found that delivering goods, military or otherwise, to Romania from ports on the Aegean was acceptable if they went in separate lorries but was in breach of neutrality if the lorries went in convoy. Nevertheless, the British government could not afford to forgo the exercise of the rights conferred on a belligerent, in order to prevent the Romanian government from succumbing to German pressure. In this context, the vital instruments were widely held to be the British- and French-capital companies operating in the Romanian economy. These, being directly or beneficially owned by their respective nationals, had managements which could be reckoned to be

[9] Pearton, *The Knowledgeable State*, 155–64.

[10] See R. Haynes, *Romanian Policy towards Germany*, ch. 3 and Ranki, *Economy and Foreign Policy*, ch. 11. The agreement represented the convergence of Romanian ideas for a reorganisation of the economy and the Four Year Plan's estimates of Germany's needs. Romania's bargaining position was weakened by external events, namely, the concentration of Hungarian troops on the border to march into Ruthenia. Noting that the force was too large for police and garrison duties and that Ruthenia enlarged the area from which an invasion of Romania might be mounted, the Romanian government mobilised six divisions and appealed to Berlin for mediation. Pointedly, the appeal fell on deaf ears. The Romanians took the hint and signed.

responsive to Allied policies as devised in London and Paris and, therefore, inimical to 'neutrality'. The crucial fact, however, was that they were *Romanian* registered institutions, subject to Romanian jurisdiction. That gave the Romanian authorities a lien on the companies, if they cared to exercise it. Accordingly, Allied policies sought to avoid giving the authorities any excuse for doing so, at the behest of the Germans. Assets 'on the ground', so far from conferring *control*, could turn out to be hostages for good behaviour. Hoare cautioned London that Romanian opinion would be increasingly hostile to foreign enterprises if it felt that they were waging economic war in such a way as to endanger the country's neutrality.

Reliance on the judicial system was a demonstrably 'neutral' way in which the Romanian government could secure its interest – however that was defined. In November 1939, it tried to control the movement of shares in heavy industry by requiring them to be registered (traditionally, shares in Romania were 'bearer') and threatening to cancel any remaining unregistered. Applying this law revealed one particular problem which conveniently demonstrates how 'neutrality' translated into practice. In the 1930s, the Czech arms works at Brno, with the consent of the Romanian government, had acquired shares in Romanian armament firms, on its own account and on account of the Skoda works and the Czech state. After March 1939, these firms passed under German control. The Germans' problem was to secure their interest in the Romanian firms by securing the appropriate shares; otherwise, they could not be recognised in Bucharest as legal owners. However, they found that the shares had been deposited in the Westminster Bank, in London. Consequently, they applied to the Bucharest court for their cancellation and replacement by duplicates. The British were wholly unwilling to see their enemies gain legal control of additional arms' manufacturing capacity. They passed the existing shares to the Custodian of Enemy Property and sought to oppose the application. Opinion in Whitehall was that such action would probably fail in the courts – against which the British government represented to the Romanian government that, while it was perfectly entitled to legislate for Romanian firms, any issue of duplicate shares would amount to the confiscation of property rights now vested in His Majesty's government. This would, the British reckoned, at least lead to a prolonged diplomatic dispute, which would delay indefinitely the acquisition of the firms by the Germans and which the Romanians might easily welcome. The issue vanished with the collapse of Romanian neutrality, but it does show that, as long as the Romanian government considered it had any room for manoeuvre at all, it was an active, not passive, participant in a *triangle* of relations in which it could lay down the rules. The belligerents' problem was to persuade it not to change them to their disadvantage. For this reason, the Romanian government could insist on the fulfilment of pre-war export contracts, even though, in the state of trade, this meant that 'Allied' companies would have to supply Germany or German-controlled destinations. The Allies' response was, naturally, to try to limit such obligations but their arguments had to recognise the legal competence of the Romanian government. This was particularly evident as regards oil.

For the Romanian government, oil policy, under 'neutrality', had three facets: oil was a commodity which the Germans wanted and was the most significant medium of exchange for the arms which Romania badly needed; conversely, the Western Allies, Romania's guarantors, sought to diminish, if not deny, deliveries to Germany, which they attempted to do through commercial action; trading on the international oil market could bring to the Romanian economy much-needed foreign exchange in hard currency – principally sterling and dollars.[11] Alongside these was a strategic preoccupation; a threat to destroy oilfields and installations could be used to counter any German intention to make sure of these resources by invading the country. This was a separate matter, insofar as putting it into effect would demonstrate that 'neutrality' had already broken down. Immediately before the outbreak of hostilities, contingency measures had been negotiated between the Romanian and British governments, who continued to work on them during 1939 and 1940. However, in all these respects, what was attempted or achieved stemmed from decisions made by Romanian governments as to the best option for the country in the changing circumstances of the war. 'Neutrality' does not imply stasis; judgement of 'the best option' on 1 September 1939 was not necessarily the same eighteen days later, with Poland overrun and no effective Allied measures to inhibit Germany. This was even more the case after the invasion of Norway, which, for the Romanians, was a test case of Allied effectiveness in protecting a small state. It had been an *Allied* initiative which the Germans had decisively defeated.[12] Shifting strategic evaluations affected day-to-day policies; German military success altered the terms of the political and economic competition in Bucharest. In January 1940, Hoare summed up the dilemmas of the government to which he was accredited in trying to elaborate a coherent

[11] See Maurice Pearton, *Oil and the Romanian State* (Oxford, 1971), chs. 7–8.
[12] M. Pearton, *Oil and the Romanian State*, ch. 9.

policy: 'The Romanians will make promises to us, not really believing that they can keep them but hoping that something will turn up to enable them to do so, whereas they make promises to the Germans hoping that circumstances will break them for them or that in a month or two they will themselves dare to evade or break them.'[13]

The general sea-going export trade via Constança, although an earner of hard currency, had to be compatible with the Allied blockade of Germany, but the Allies had an interest in ensuring that it continued, if only to diminish supplies which might otherwise become available to the Reich. German requirements, paid for through the clearing, went by the Danube and by rail.[14] These routes could not be blockaded and presented the Germans and the Allies with opposing policies, respectively, to maximise or minimise their use. Control of the railway was, and remained, effectively in the hands of the Romanian government, as owner and manager of a large proportion of the physical assets: control of the Danube was shared with two commissions, the International Danube Commission and the European Commission of the Danube. Romanian neutrality required British and German officials on their management boards to sit round the table at meetings, even though the states they represented were at war. In practice, the Danube trade relied upon a number of shipping companies, owned by British, French, German, Dutch, Italian, and Yugoslav enterprises. The Allies and the Germans competed over the use of these assets,[15] but their competition had to take account of Romania's rights and interests in the waterway.

From September 1939, the Romanian government was engaged in managing its requirements between embattled states who were, at the same time, important contributors to the country's economy and who had reasons of their own for wishing to 'observe the rules', as long as they did not completely work out to the advantage of the enemy. Romania's ability to maintain this position was threatened by its over-riding need for one commodity – weapons – for which, in the given circumstances, there was only one supplier – Germany. The German government used this dependence to gain substantially increased and cheaper oil deliveries. Currently, tonnages exported to

[13] Letter to Lord Halifax, 26 January 1940, Public Record Office, London. Halifax papers, vol XIV, FO 800/332. For Romanian evaluations of the country's situation, see the symposium 'La Roumanie en 1940', *Revue Romaine d'Histoire*, 34/3–4 (1995).

[14] In 1939, 59 per cent of oil exports went by sea, 17 per cent by rail and 24 per cent via the Danube. The rail/river traffic was predominantly to Germany, including Austria and the Protectorate of Bohemia and Moravia.

[15] See Pearton 'British Policy towards Romania 1939–41'.

the Reich were running below contracted levels, in consequence of successful Allied action in the market and the Germans' failure to provide adequate rail transport. Negotiations opened in March 1940. The Germans consciously exploited Romania's fear of Russia and, at one stage, dramatised the country's vulnerability by simultaneously stopping arms deliveries from the Reich, cancelling talks on the supply of Polish weapons and abruptly repatriating representatives of German heavy industry. The final 'Oil pact' was signed on 27 May. Basically, it guaranteed supplies of oil against armaments, at price levels which negated the Anglo-French tactic of raising open market prices and led the companies to withdraw from pre-emptive purchasing. The Wehrmacht was now assured of the fuels with which to overrun France. It was also, from the German point of view, particularly satisfactory that meeting the tonnages stipulated required the Romanian government to compel 'Allied' companies to export to Germany. Whether this *coup*, by itself, could have marked the beginning of the end of neutrality, thus fulfilling Gigurtu's prediction, is impossible to say. The Germans *did* negotiate, that is, they still conceived their interest to be served by a neutral Romania. In fact, neutrality collapsed not because of any vital Romanian failure to curb internal meddling by belligerents but because of developments in *Soviet* policy.

Ribbentrop's sudden visit to Moscow on 21 August 1939 and the conclusion of a Pact of Non-Aggression and Friendship two days later caused rapid revaluations of policies in all the states situated between the new allies. Calinescu noted: 'Have they come to an understanding to effect a partition of Poland and Romania?' By 16 September, the first had been effected. What neither Calinescu nor anyone else knew was that, under the Secret Additional Protocol to the Agreement of 23 August (systematically denounced as a forgery by Soviet historians), Germany had acquiesced in Russia's interest in Bessarabia. The first public evidence of that interest followed on 21 September, when Molotov told M. Saraçoğlu, the Turkish foreign minister, that he wanted to restore the frontiers of 1914. At much the same time, the journal *Communist International* suggested that the Soviet Union should conclude a Mutual Assistance Pact with Romania on the lines recently concluded with the Baltic States. On 30 November, the Red Army attacked Finland. To the Romanian government, these moves loomed somewhat larger than the assurances of the Soviet chargé d'affaires in Bucharest that Russia had no aggressive designs on Bessarabia and also than the denial, communicated by Tass, that the *Communist International* article represented the views of the Soviet government. As late as April 1940, the British Ambassador in Moscow reported public assurances by Vishinsky, the deputy foreign minister, to the Romanian minister that the Soviet government had no claims on Romania and suggesting a quick and sympathetic settlement of all frontier questions. Presumably, in Vishinsky's mind, Bessarabia was excluded from Romania, by definition, but his approach was interpreted as an attempt to foster anti-German attitudes in Bucharest. The German government, however, warned that it would not intervene in any Russian policy designed to restore the 1914 frontiers but renewed its offers of weapons as an inducement to Romania to align itself with the Axis. King Carol expressed to Lord Lloyd, an envoy whose friendship with the king dated from 1920s, the wish that Germany might be defeated, but not too soon – a sentiment which was beginning to be shared even by his pro-western subjects. Lloyd reported that Carol had stressed 'the comparative unimportance of the German, as against the Russian, danger' – arguing that every great war was succeeded by a lesser one, that Britain and France, having beaten Germany, would be too war weary and therefore disinclined to further operations, but that Russia would not. 'Neutrality' allowed Romania time to provide against the contingent danger by renovating its forces and strengthening the defences along the river Prut. That required German arms and training expertise, which, in turn, meant Romania's delivering more materials than the British would approve.

On 27 May 1940, the Crown Council reversed its decision of September 1939 and decided to veer towards the Axis, since only Germany could offer support against Russia. Neutrality, therefore, had to be abandoned and the Anglo-French Guarantee scrapped – otherwise, the risk was of partition between Germany and Russia. It was the day German forces reached Calais. Belgium capitulated during the night 27/28 May and the Dunkirk evacuation began on the 29th. In the evening of that day, the Romanian Government informed the German government that it would renounce the Guarantee and follow a policy of 'open and conspicuous collaboration' with Germany. The announcement, made public only on 5 June, initiated an increasing identification with German policies formally completed by Romania's joining the Tripartite pact on 23 November.[16] In this process, the government was quickly reconstructed to get rid of those too identified with 'the West' and, as a more positive

[16] For the political manoeuvres taking Romania fully into the German orbit, see Lungu, *Romania and the Great Powers*, part 3, and Haynes, *Romanian Policy towards Germany*, chs. 5 and 6.

sign, Iron Guardists were admitted to office. On 6 September, General Antonescu became prime minister.[17]

Earlier in the year, Romanian ministers had talked of a probable Soviet move against Bessarabia in the spring of 1940, but in fact, the ultimatum demanding its return – in the Soviet definition – was made only on 26 June – the day after the French armistice with Germany. The German government advised acceptance. The loss of Bessarabia provoked action by the other claimants to territories lost in 1919/20. Bulgaria and Romania agreed on the transfer of the Southern Dobrudja on 21 August 1940. Hitler, already considering the invasion of Russia and finding two strategically important states, Hungary and Romania, too obdurate to reach an agreement on territory, imposed a solution, dividing Transylvania between them, on 29 August.[18] These adjustments having been made, the next day he guaranteed the territory of Romania as it then stood. Changes which triumphalist nationalism had rejected in the 1920s and early 1930s were forced on Romania in 1940. Manoilescu, the foreign minister, pronounced the epitaph of neutrality: 'The Axis powers have offered absolute safety to the Romanian state . . . By this guarantee, we tie ourselves indissolubly to the Axis powers.' The immediate quid pro quo was that Romania became a base for Wehrmacht operations eastwards or, as events soon showed, southwards[19] and one from which

[17] For King Carol's relations with Antonescu, see Larry Watts, *Romanian Cassandra. Ion Antonescu and the Struggle for Reform 1916–1941* (Boulder/New York, 1993).

[18] By the partition of Transylvania, Hungary received only 45,000 sq kms of the 123,000 lost in 1919 but in the acquired area Hungarians were still in a minority. The arbitration is still execrated in Romanian historiography as a 'Diktat' but there are some indications that Romania preferred an imposed to a negotiated solution. (A negotiated solution implies consent and can create a precedent; an imposed solution avoids these entailments and creates a politically useful grievance.) See Woermann (Director, Political Department), memo, 21 August 1940, *Documents on German Foreign Policy 1918–1945*, Series D, vol. x, no. 375. It was the *scope* of the decision a week later that caused, and causes, so much offence. Soviet pressures – naval operations between the mouths of the Danube and the Prut, minor troop incursions across the frontier – contributed to Romanian acquiescence. They sharply underlined the need for a territorial guarantee, which only Germany could provide, whatever the cost.

[19] Keitel (Hitler's Chief of Staff) explained the German priorities in a directive of 20 September 1940: 'To the world, the tasks (of German instructors and instruction troops) will be to guide friendly Romania in organising and instructing her forces. The real tasks – which must not become apparent to the Romanians or our own troops – will be (a) to protect the oil districts against seizure by third powers or destruction; (b) to enable the Romanian forces to fulfil certain tasks . . . with special regard to German interests; (c) to prepare for deployment from Romanian bases of German and Romanian forces in case a war with Soviet Russia is forced on us.' International Military Tribunal, Nuremburg 1946, quoted in J. Lukacs, *The Great Powers and Eastern Europe* (New York, 1953). At that juncture, German planners were, evidently, not thinking about intervention in the Balkans – which reinforced the preference for Romania's neutrality. For German planning and operations in south-east Europe see Gerhard Schreiber, Bernd Stegemann, and Detleff Vogel, *Germany and the Second World War* (Oxford, 1995), vol. III, parts II and III.

such operations could be fuelled. Conversely, German forces could defend the oilfields from air attacks which the British were expected to mount from Crete.[20]

From then till June 1941, the Romanian government had lined up with Germany; it had ceased to be neutral but had not yet entered the war. This circumstance has led Romanian historians to prolong 'neutrality' till that date – which unwarrantably stretches the notion well beyond accepted juridical limits to mean, only, non-participation *de facto* in military operations. In terms of the traditional requirements of 'impartiality and abstention', Romania was, of course, no longer neutral; it had become the ally of one of the belligerents. Neutrals cannot have strategic alliances. Attempts to limit German influence at the level of *haute politique* were jettisoned – to pass to the bureaucracy, a body with a long experience of administrative obstruction. Nevertheless, the change in policy did not immediately foreclose the rights of western states with whom Germany was at war. In this diplomatic limbo, they still were represented in Bucharest. They were, however, not accredited to the same regime. The frontier losses – regarded as amputations from the living body of Romania – provoked internal chaos – in which, successively, King Carol was obliged to abdicate and was expelled. The monarchy formally continued but dictatorial power was exercised by Marshal Antonescu as 'Conducator' in a 'National Legionary State' in which the Iron Guard was the sole legal political group. The Soviet government was the first to recognise his new regime. From October 1940, German forces arrived in the country in large numbers. The Guardists were, perhaps, the only genuinely pro-German movement in Romania. Their leader, Horia Sima, praised 'the spiritual unity of the Romanians under the auspices of the Greater German Reich' but the latter was not prepared to tolerate 'an isolated revolutionary laboratory' in Romania, and when Antonescu tried to disarm the Guard, stood back during the ensuing days of street fighting in January 1941. Thereafter, Romania supported Germany on military and political rather than ideological grounds, as the strongest external power able to guarantee its interests – and perhaps

[20] This seems to have been a favoured argument of Hitler's. Presumably, no-one told him that the RAF had no bombers in the area with the range to mount an attack on the oilfields from Crete and that those which had the range were too few in number to be deployed anywhere but in western Europe. It was only on 12 June 1942 that aircraft with the requisite range and payload, Liberators of the USAAF, could raid Ploesti, when they suffered heavy losses for minimal damage. The second raid took place only on 1 August 1943, when a far larger force of Liberators inflicted significant though not decisive damage, but 54 out of 166 aircraft reaching the target area were shot down and 31 failed to get back to base. Ploesti resumed production in a matter of weeks. Only in 1944 could repeated strikes cause adequately extensive damage.

get back Bessarabia and the lost areas of Transylvania. In June 1941, it joined in the invasion of Russia. By that time, the British had withdrawn their diplomatic representation from Bucharest. The French, however, remained, representing Vichy.

In the First World War, Romania was neutral while trying to pick the winner; in the Second, it adopted neutrality as the option which might ensure that the state, with its complex and unresolved minority and economic problems, held together under external pressures which were already identifiable. This option was under threat even before the policy was announced, by the German–Russian Agreement of 23 August 1939. What finally destroyed Romania's policy was the swift elimination of France and Britain in the summer of 1940, which prompted the abandonment of neutrality in recognition of 'the new constellation' in European politics. The trouble, from the Romanian point of view, was that 'the new constellation' included Russia. Germany's sweeping victory in the West opened the way for the cession of Bessarabia. One can argue that the Romanian state structure could, perhaps, have withstood that particular loss, had it been the only one and had the country been domestically stable. It was not, and the further drastic frontier revisions under German auspices in August and September 1940 produced internal political chaos. Nevertheless, the record shows that, until the *sauve qui peut* following the collapse of France and the non-appearance in the Balkans of Weygand's army in Syria – the repository of both official and popular hopes[21] – the Romanian government conducted a skilful defence of its interests. In the prevailing conditions, 'neutrality' served it reasonably well till the interaction of external pressures with unresolved internal discontents led to its being abandoned, in favour of alliance with Germany, as less damaging than the alternative of partition between Hitler's Germany and its Soviet ally.

[21] This was, perhaps, the last evidence of Romanian faith in French power. Weygand had 'saved' Warsaw in 1920; he could 'save' Bucharest twenty years later. The hope ignored the formidable logistic problems of moving the army to Salonica; also that the Germans were unlikely to wait while Weygand solved them. Additionally, the experience of 1915 to 1918 in penetrating the terrain north of Salonika was not encouraging.

CHAPTER 8

# *Bulgarian neutrality: domestic and international perspectives*

*Vesselin Dimitrov*

Bulgaria was one of the most unlikely neutrals in the Second World War. The country had been on the losing side not only in the First World War but also in the Second Balkan War, and had territorial grievances against all four of its neighbours. Her revisionist aspirations should have driven her willingly into the arms of Nazi Germany, the continent's leading revisionist power. At the same time, the lessons of the two defeats had sunk deep in the psyche of the country's small and vulnerable political élite. Their overwhelming priority was to avoid yet another military defeat and the social disturbances that were bound to follow in its wake. As King Boris, the effective ruler of the country in the late 1930s and early 1940s, confided to one of his closest confidants in October 1939: 'I can still remember the roar of the rebel guns at the very gates of Sofia (in 1918) . . . I know what it feels to be faced with a discontented nation.'[1] Bitter experience had left Bulgarians with both an abiding distrust and a resigned helplessness towards the Great Powers. As Boris put it in one of his homely proverbs, 'when the horses start kicking each other, it is better for the donkeys to stand aside'.[2] He had little faith in the judgement of the upstart 'corporal' ruling Germany and regarded him as 'a showcase in hysteria' and yet felt powerless to stand in his way.[3] Impressed by the staying power of Britain, the king was far too pragmatic not to realise that British and Bulgarian interests would rarely coincide and that even if they did, Britain would not be in position to help his small Balkan country. More in desperation than in hope, he kept Bulgaria neutral for nearly a year and a half after the outbreak of the war, before finally succumbing to Hitler's threats and blandishments in March 1941.

Bulgarian foreign policy in the period of neutrality has not as yet been studied in the English-language literature on the basis of primary

[1] Diary of L. Lulchev, 15 October 1939, quoted in S. Rachev, *Churchil, Bulgariia i Balkanite, 1939–1944* (Sofia, 1995), 22.
[2] S. Moshanov, *Moiata Misiia v Kairo* (Sofia, 1991), 14. [3] Ibid., 16–17.

Bulgarian sources. The author who has given the subject most attention, Marshall Lee Miller, in his monograph on the history of Bulgaria during the Second World War, has based his work on secondary Bulgarian literature and the diplomatic documents of the Great Powers. Other authors who have examined the topic include Britain's foremost historian of Bulgaria, Richard Crampton, and the Israeli-American historian Nissan Oren. The use of primary material from the Great Powers has helped to highlight important factors influencing the formation of Bulgarian foreign policy, but could not provide a reliable insight into the core of the policy-making process. The indirect inferences that could be made from these sources often point in divergent directions. The German representatives in Sofia, as well as Hitler and Ribbentrop, for instance, generally believed Boris' assurances that Bulgaria was faithful to the 'comradeship-in-arms' from the First World War and had taken her natural path alongside the Reich. German diplomatic documents can therefore be easily used to demonstrate the pro-Axis credentials of Bulgaria's ruler. British sources, on the other hand, produce a rather different picture. George Rendel, the active British minister in Sofia, was prepared to give credence to the king's professions of respect for Britain and his unwillingness to plunge his country into a war. The Foreign Office was more sceptical, although Halifax did seek, on a number of occasions, to draw Bulgaria into a British-led Balkan bloc. Whilst partly stemming from Boris' undeniable wish to curry favour with whoever he was meeting at the time, the contrasting impressions he made on foreign diplomats and statesmen were also a real reflection of the different and often contradictory strands of his policy.

The difficulty of disentangling the king's underlying motives is increased by his preference for appointing ambassadors who were generally sympathetic towards the policy of the country to which they were accredited. The Bulgarian minister to London Momchilov, for instance, sincerely believed in the desirability of closer cooperation between his country and Britain. The Germanophile Prime Minister Filov considered him 'more English than Bulgarian' in his allegiances.[4] Momchilov was unable to stomach Bulgaria's accession to the Tripartite pact and submitted his resignation in March 1941. Draganov, the minister to Berlin, on the other hand, whilst never blindly pro-German, considered almost fatalistically that his country's destinies were linked to those of

[4] B. Filov, *Dnevnik* (Sofia, 1986), 265.

Germany. The two ambassadors naturally tended to tell their hosts what they wanted to hear, whilst not necessarily representing the policy of the king.

On the basis of the limited sources used, the three historians mentioned above have formulated contrasting views on the nature of Bulgarian foreign policy. Oren concludes that Boris was basically oriented towards Germany even if his natural caution prevented him from open commitment at too early a stage.[5] Miller and Crampton, on the other hand, maintain that the king's preferences were firmly on the side of neutrality.[6] As Crampton puts it, 'Boris believed Bulgaria's best interests were served by peace, or failing that, neutrality without commitment to any great power . . . for months he remained deaf even to the most alluring of siren calls.'[7]

In Bulgaria itself, primary sources were made available to selected historians, but interpretation had to conform rather strictly to the political imperatives of the period. For several decades after the war, the dominant official doctrine portrayed neutrality as nothing more than a convenient cover for a policy of deliberate and purposeful commitment to Nazi Germany.[8] One of the main factors which fostered this interpretation was the determination to saddle the deposed wartime governments with exclusive responsibility for the shameful legacy of collaboration. The legitimacy of the Communist regime which came to power in 1944 was based critically on the claim that it had overthrown a pro-German 'Fascist' dictatorship. Nearly all wartime ministers, half the parliamentary deputies and thousands of other civilian and military officials met a gruesome death in the quasi-judicial 'people's trials' that swept the country in the winter of 1944–5. The ideological fervour waned with the passage of time, but the condemnation of the communists' predecessors remained in place until the very end of the regime.

Partly as a reaction to what was seen as the regime's deliberate misinterpretation of Bulgaria's 'real' history, a minority of historians began to argue in the late 1960s that the king had pursued a policy of genuine neutrality, and had joined the Axis camp only when he had had no

[5] N. Oren, *Revolution Administered: Agrarianism and Communism in Bulgaria* (Baltimore and London, 1973), 55.

[6] M. L. Miller, *Bulgaria During the Second World War* (Stanford, 1975), 1.

[7] R. J. Crampton, *A Concise History of Bulgaria* (Cambridge, 1997), 169.

[8] To cite two representative examples, D. Mashev, 'Progermanskata Orientatsiia na Bulgarskoto Pravitelstvo v Navecherieto na Vtorata Svetovna Voina', *Godishnik na Sofiiskiia Universitet, Iuridicheski Fakultet* (Sofia, 1964), vol. 1, 31; I. Paunovski, *Vuzmezdieto* (Sofia, 1988), 180–1.

other realistic choice.[9] The emergence of this view was stimulated by a slow process of nationalist revival, which gathered pace in the following decades. After the collapse of Communism in 1989, this interpretation crystallised into a new orthodoxy, part of the broader effort to 'prove' the democratic credentials of Boris' regime.

The politicised nature of Bulgarian historiography has meant that it has been unable to make full use of the primary sources in the country. Instead of guiding investigation, they were employed selectively to support preconceived conclusions. This chapter makes an attempt to use the available primary sources which include the records of the ministry of foreign affairs and the diaries of prominent Bulgarian statesmen and close advisers of the king, to produce a full and balanced examination of the rise and fall of the policy of neutrality. First, I shall look briefly at the factors that shaped the country's domestic and international position on the eve of the war. Having set the context, I shall then focus my attention on the evolution of Bulgarian foreign policy from the pre-war crises of 1938–9 to the decision to join the Tripartite pact in March 1941.

## BULGARIA ON THE EVE OF THE WAR: INTERNATIONAL AND DOMESTIC FACTORS

Bulgaria's policy in the Second World War was shaped powerfully by the impact of previous military defeats and the international and domestic legacies of the inter-war period. For Bulgaria, the First World War had begun not in August 1914 but in September 1912 when she joined Serbia, Greece, and Montenegro in attacking the decrepit Ottoman empire. What was intended as a short victorious war ended up by dragging the country into a series of military conflicts which lasted, with short interludes, for the next six years. The successes of the First Balkan War only served to set the erstwhile allies against each other, and in the Second Balkan War Bulgaria lost most of the territories that she regarded as belonging to her by right. The largest losses were in Macedonia, most of which was shared between Greece and Serbia, but a particularly unpleasant blow was the loss to Romania of southern Dobrudja that had belonged to Bulgaria since her creation as an independent state in 1878. The First World War provided an opportunity to redress those grievances, and after sitting on the fence for more than a year, Bulgaria

[9] N. Genchev, 'Vunshnopoliticheskata Orientatsiia na Bulgariia v Navecherieto na Vtorata Svetovna Voina (Septemvri 1938-Septemvri 1939)', *Godishnik na Sofiiaskiia Universitet, FIF* (Sofia, 1968) vol. LXI, part III, 171.

decided to ally herself with the central powers which promised most and appeared to be winning the war. In 1918, after three years of fighting, Bulgaria found that she had made the wrong choice. By the Treaty of Neuilly (1919), she lost western Thrace and her access to the Aegean to Greece, whilst several border territories went to the new Serbo-Croat–Slovene kingdom (Yugoslavia). Strict limitations were imposed on the Bulgarian army and the country was required to pay substantial reparations.

The country's position in the Versailles peace settlement severely restricted her choices in the inter-war decades. Bulgarian governments had to choose between two equally unpalatable options: to establish good relations with the victorious powers but renounce any territorial aspirations, or retain revisionism but remain in international isolation. The chances for escaping the unpleasant dilemma were minimal. In contrast to Germany, Bulgaria was not sufficiently important for Britain and France to at least make an effort at reconciliation. Furthermore, Bulgaria's position was complicated by the fact that any change was dependent on the dubious willingness of her insecure Balkan neighbours to make concessions to a country they regarded as their historic enemy.

In the first few years after the war, Alexander Stamboliisky, a reforming agrarian prime minister, made great efforts to overcome the legacy of militant nationalism. He sought to improve Bulgaria's relations with the Versailles powers, starting with a comprehensive understanding with Yugoslavia. He went a long way towards appeasing Belgrade, promising in an agreement signed in March 1923 to respect the new frontier and to restrain the activities of the Macedonian bands which attacked Yugoslav Macedonia from Bulgarian territory. His experiment, however, suffered from two fundamental weaknesses. First, the Yugoslav politicians did not prove sufficiently receptive to his approaches and his efforts brought little apparent success. More importantly, he could conduct his conciliatory policies only as long as he could suppress the powerful nationalist forces at home, most notably, the Macedonian exiles of the Internal Macedonian Revolutionary Organisation (IMRO) who were violently opposed to Yugoslav rule. Stamboliisky did not prove equal to this task. He showed himself an extraordinarily bad tactician and managed to antagonise virtually all the powerful interests in the country, thus paving the way for the bloody overthrow of his government in June 1923 by a coalition of the Macedonians, the military and the great majority of traditional political leaders.

The victory of the anti-Stamboliisky coalition meant, among other things, that the Macedonians achieved a position of prominence which they were to keep for eleven years. The strength of the Macedonian lobby effectively blocked all attempts to achieve understanding with Bulgaria's Balkan neighbours and hence with Britain and France. The only exceptions to Bulgaria's state of international isolation were extensive links with Italy, which in the 1920s emerged as an organiser of the discontented countries in Europe. Italy's resources, however, were fairly limited and thus her support could not take Bulgaria very far.[10]

In October 1931 the right-wing Democratic Alliance which had governed since 1923 was defeated in one of the few genuinely free elections in the country's history by the People's Bloc, a coalition of several liberal parties and moderate agrarians. The new government made persistent efforts to improve relations with the neighbouring states, but was prevented from making any significant progress by its inability to control the Macedonians. Despite some encouraging signs such as the meeting of Boris and King Alexander of Yugoslavia in September 1932, Bulgaria's isolation was confirmed when Romania, Yugoslavia, Turkey, and Greece created the Balkan entente in February 1934. The main purpose of the entente was to safeguard the *status quo* on the Balkans against threats from within the peninsula, that is, from Bulgaria.[11]

In May 1934, the People's Bloc government was overthrown by a military *coup* organised by Zveno, a small authoritarian group aiming to clean up the perceived corruption of parliamentary democracy. One of the unintended benefits of what was in most respects a disastrous undertaking was the government's success in destroying the power of IMRO. In foreign policy, Zveno sought to improve relations with Yugoslavia and through her, with France, the dominant Versailles power in the Balkans. As with Stamboliisky, the attempt to break away from the traditional revisionist agenda was undermined by ineptitude in domestic politics. Lacking popular support, Zveno was easily outmanoeuvred by the king who after decades of staying on the sidelines decided to take the reins of power into his own hands.

By the mid-1930s, he had succeeded in making himself the pivotal figure in Bulgarian politics. All other political actors have been decisively weakened by the events of the 1920s and the early 1930s.[12] Political parties had almost ceased to function, due as much to their internal weakness as to Zveno's formal ban on organised political activity. Instead of relying on parties, Boris based his rule on the state bureaucracy

[10] Oren, *Revolution Administered*, 50–1.

[11] R. J. Crampton, *A Short History of Modern Bulgaria* (Cambridge, 1987), 109, 120.

[12] Ibid., 116.

and on the support of what he believed was the silent majority of the nation.

The various opposition groupings ranging from quasi-Fascist organisations on the extreme right to the communists on the extreme left, were not able to offer a common alternative to Boris' regime. As far as domestic policy was concerned, they could agree only on the demand for the restoration of parliamentary democracy and disagreed about everything else. In foreign policy, while all accepted the justice of Bulgaria's revisionist claims and most agreed (with the possible exception of the extreme right) on the need for caution and non-involvement in any serious conflict, there was profound disagreement on the choice of the Great Power which could serve as Bulgaria's patron. The extreme right insisted on active cooperation with Germany, the liberal parties and most of the agrarians were inclined towards Britain and France – never, however, going as far as to suggest an actual alliance – and the Communists and a minority of agrarians advocated closer links with the Soviet Union.

The opposition did not succeed in overcoming their internal differences and by March 1938 the king felt sufficiently confident to restore some vestiges of democracy by calling the first general election since 1931. The government, helped by intensive propaganda, gerrymandering, and police measures, won a majority in the new national assembly, although the opposition also did well, gaining 60 of the 160 seats.[13] The new assembly was not sufficiently pliable and in December 1939 the government held a new general election, this time reducing the number of opposition deputies to a mere twenty.[14]

King Boris' domestic position had three important consequences regarding foreign policy. First, although the elections were clearly rigged, it seems that the king's moderate policies did gain at least the passive acceptance of the majority of Bulgarians. In one sense, this made Boris a prisoner of the image he had chosen to create for himself – one of moderation and avoidance of any extremes. Even if he had wanted to undertake any drastic action in foreign policy, which is doubtful, it would have been difficult for him to do so since that would run the risk of damaging the very basis of his popularity. Secondly, the consolidation of his personal regime gave him enough power to push through the foreign policy he desired without being unduly worried that any single political group would be able to impose upon him any particular orientation. At the same time, however, he preferred to conduct his policies not directly

[13] Ibid., 118. [14] Miller, *Bulgaria*, 20.

but through the government, by appointing and then manipulating suitable ministers. In cases where he was uncertain about the policy to be pursued, he sought to transfer the conflict to the cabinet, allowing and even encouraging ministers to act in different directions. Thirdly, the king was careful not to antagonise irrevocably any powerful interest and to tailor his policies to what he perceived to be the majority view in the country. Given the virtually unanimous agreement on the legitimacy of Bulgaria's revisionist goals, this meant that the king could never renounce the commitment to changing the country's borders when in his estimation the balance of risks was favourable.

One important factor which restricted Boris' options was the country's pattern of trade. From at least the early 1930s Germany began to emerge as Bulgaria's main economic partner. By 1936, Germany took 47 per cent of Bulgaria's exports and supplied 61 per cent of her imports.[15] The trade dependence on Germany, as well as the fact that Germany was the main supplier of weapons for the rearmament of the Bulgarian army in the late 1930s, meant that any Bulgarian government, irrespective of its convictions, had to take great care not to disturb relations with Germany. Whilst acknowledging these constraints, Boris' own personal preferences seemed to point away from any premature commitment.

Unlike many other Bulgarians, the king did not seem to have a sentimental attachment to any Great Power. As he once put it to a visiting diplomat, 'My army is pro-German, my wife is Italian and my people are pro-Russian. I am the only pro-Bulgarian in this country.'[16] Other significant features of Boris' personality were his natural caution and deep scepticism. The bitter defeats of Bulgaria in the Second Balkan War and the First World War, the latter bringing, with the abdication of his father, the turmoil of the post-war years, the radical Stamboliisky government, the attempts on his life in 1925, the military *coup* in 1934 – all these undoubtedly made a big impression on Boris and could have only made him deeply unwilling to involve the country in risky foreign undertakings which could easily end in defeat, generate social unrest and endanger his position and that of his dynasty.

On a more personal level, Boris had a strained relationship with his father, king Ferdinand who had ruled Bulgaria from 1886 to 1918. By most accounts, Ferdinand was excessively critical and domineering and did not hesitate to point out Boris' real or imagined weaknesses even

[15] N. Genchev, 'Bulgaro-Germanski Diplomaticheski Otnosheniia (1938–1941)', in *Bulgaro-Germanski Otnosheniia i Vruzhki* (Sofia, 1972), vol. 1, 20.

[16] Miller, *Bulgaria*, 1.

after the latter had taken the throne. Perhaps in reaction to that, Boris was often inclined to act in a way deliberately different from the pattern set by his father. In particular, he was unwilling to follow in his father's footsteps in constructing grand and ambitious plans in foreign policy and in allying Bulgaria unambiguously with the 'brothers-in-arms' from the First World War.[17] On the other hand, Ferdinand's criticisms and the revisionist tasks he had left unfinished motivated Boris to show that he could be a better king by fulfilling the country's nationalist aspirations.

Boris' personal preferences, as well as the domestic context within which he operated, pointed to a policy of neutrality combined with a commitment to the recovery of Bulgaria's lost territories. Which one would become dominant depended largely on the development of the international situation. Combining the two aims was feasible only as long as no Great Power became sufficiently interested in the Balkans to be prepared to use force to drag Bulgaria into a war, or offer the country territorial rewards no Bulgarian ruler would dare to refuse. If a Great Power was able to do both, the choice became practically non-existent. As the war progressed, the possibilities for independent action, in spite of Boris' desperate manoeuvres, became increasingly tenuous.

## THE RISE AND FALL OF NEUTRALITY

Boris' preference for the revision of the most unjust features of the Versailles system through peaceful negotiations between the revisionist states and the upholders of the system seemed to have materialised with the Munich agreement of September 1938. Indeed, he took a direct, if a rather modest part in the preparations of the meeting. Visiting London at the beginning of September 1938, he was asked by Neville Chamberlain to go to Berlin and try to persuade Hitler to come to terms with Britain and France. The king went straight to Berlin and did his best to convince the Führer that it would be in Germany's own interests to reach a settlement, warning him that a failure to do so would result in a world war which could be extremely dangerous for Germany.[18]

The more immediate impact on Bulgaria came in the form of the removal of the military restrictions of the Treaty of Neuilly through an agreement with her Balkan neighbours. The agreement was inspired by the British, with the eventual aim of bringing Bulgaria into

[17] Filov, *Dnevnik*, 209. [18] Moshanov, *Moiata Misiia*, 14–16.

the Balkan entente. The Bulgarian government, however, was not fully satisfied with these concessions, and cautiously tried to sound out the Great Powers on their attitude towards the country's territorial claims.[19] The replies received were not very encouraging and the government did not take the matter any further. The continuing rapprochement with Yugoslavia symbolised by the meeting between the Bulgarian Prime Minister Kioseivanov and the Yugoslav Premier Stoyadinović in October 1938 also failed to bring any significant results.

With the gradual eclipse of the spirit of Munich, Germany began putting pressure on Bulgaria to declare herself more openly in favour of the Axis powers. The Germans decided to use as a means of pressure the Bulgarian request for an armaments credit submitted in November 1938. On the orders of Goering, in January 1939 the head of the Economic Staff in the War Ministry, General Thomas, told the Bulgarian minister in Berlin that Germany would not grant the requested credit if Bulgaria did not declare that she would join the anti-Comintern pact. The minister objected to the proposal, trying to convince the Germans that such a declaration would be both unnecessary and provocative. His position was eased when it became clear that the military had made the proposal on their own initiative and had not consulted the Foreign Ministry. What the diplomats objected to, however, was not so much the substance as the form of the proposal. On 24 February, Weizsäcker, State Secretary of the German Foreign Ministry, told the Bulgarian minister that whilst there was no specific link between the requested credit and the pact, Germany did not expect Bulgaria to pursue a line different from her own. In similar vein, the German ambassador in Sofia advised Kioseivanov in March that he should assume a more openly pro-German line. Although the prime minister claimed that he was conducting a policy sympathetic to Germany, he was not prepared to commit himself in any open way. In the end, the Germans, perhaps aware that they did not yet have the means to put enough pressure on Bulgaria, decided to settle for Kioseivanov's vague declarations and for some Bulgarian economic concessions, and granted the credit in April 1939.[20]

The episode demonstrated the vulnerable position in which economic and military dependence on Germany had placed Bulgaria, but also the room for manoeuvre that was still available to her. The basic premises of the policy which the Bulgarian government was pursuing in the spring

[19] Miller, *Bulgaria*, 14. [20] Genchev, 'Bulgaro-Germanski Diplomaticheski Otnosheniia', 401–3.

of 1939 were laid out in the Directive Number 19, which was sent by Kioseivanov to all Bulgarian representatives abroad in April 1939. In this directive, although noting that Bulgaria was not satisfied with the existing frontiers and thus could not join the Balkan entente which guaranteed the *status quo*, the government emphasised that the country 'is conducting and would continue to conduct, as long as it is possible, an independent foreign policy without committing herself to anyone'. At the same time, it acknowledged that 'our economic links with Germany, which absorbs 75 per cent of our exports, make it impossible for us to position ourselves on the side of the democratic states against the totalitarian ones. Our attempts to buy weapons on credit (from other states) did not succeed and we are forced to get weapons solely from Germany. Thus there is a danger that Germany might attempt to set political conditions on us.'[21] As this revealing document shows, the Bulgarian government had already all but cancelled out the option of an alliance with Britain and France. Of the two choices left – alliance with Germany or neutrality, the government clearly preferred the latter, although it was evidently not certain that it would be able to carry out this policy if Germany decided to put pressure on it. As the document concluded, the best policy was to 'wait and see'.

The outbreak of war in September 1939 did not bring any immediate threats to the country's security, and the policy of neutrality was formalised with an official declaration on 15 September 1939. Germany was absorbed by the war against Poland and the potential conflict on the western front, and was only interested in the Balkans as a source of valuable raw materials. Of more immediate concern to Bulgarian policy makers was the significance of the Nazi–Soviet pact of 23 August 1939.

The pact had several important effects on Bulgaria. First, by making Germany and Russia appear allies, it made it easier for many Bulgarians to reconcile closer association with Germany with their traditional affection for Russia. The king did not share in the wave of relief that swept most of the country. A few days after the pact, he told the British ambassador in Sofia that he had 'hoped that you would come to an agreement with Germany, but instead Russia did that . . . Does it really make sense for you to destroy each other?'[22] Apart from his displeasure at the demise of appeasement, Boris was worried that Germany

[21] Tsentralen Durzhaven Istoricheski Arhiv (TsDIA) (Central State Historical Archive, Sofia); fond (f.) 176, opis (op.) 7, arhivna.edinitsa (a.e.) 877, list (1.) 19; This and all subsequent citations from TsDIA based on D. Sirkov, *Vunshnata Politika na Bulgariia, 1938–1941* (Sofia, 1979).

[22] TsDIA, f. 95, op. 1, a.e. 1, 1. 48.

might have conceded Bulgaria to the Soviet zone of influence, and repeatedly sought assurances from the Germans that that was not the case.[23] The Germans reassured him, but also hinted that they would not be able to support Bulgaria if she came into conflict with the Soviet Union.

Even without the German warning, Boris recognised and adjusted to the new power structure by improving Bulgaria's relations with the Soviet Union. While rejecting the Soviet offer in October 1939 of a friendship and mutual assistance pact, he did authorise several less significant measures, such as not criticising the USSR for its war against Finland and concluding a trade agreement with the Soviets in January 1940. As he told the British press *attaché* in January 1940, he would never repeat his father's mistake of appearing to be a Russophobe in a Russophile country.[24]

In the first few weeks of the war, the Bulgarian government was concerned by the question of whether the war between Germany and Poland would remain a localised one or whether it would develop into a European conflict. The Bulgarian minister to Berlin, Draganov, considered that the conflict would remain confined to the east,[25] a view shared by his superiors in Sofia. This was all the easier to believe as it coincided with the king's own dearly held wishes. He still retained the hope that a conflict between Germany and the Western Powers could be averted. Italy's decision to stay neutral seemed to indicate that not all avenues for compromise had been closed. On 2 September he told Filov, the minister of education and a future prime minister, that he did not believe in Germany's victory and could not understand why the Germans had launched the war. On numerous occasions, he pleaded with British and French diplomats to stop the war and to come to an agreement with Germany if they wished to avoid 'universal destruction'.[26]

It was Britain rather than Germany that first became diplomatically active in the Balkans and seemed, in the eyes of the government in Sofia, to be planning to bring Bulgaria into the war by trying to entice her into an ostensibly neutral bloc with her neighbours. Lord Halifax, the foreign secretary, recognised the strategic importance of Bulgaria, regarding her as the 'key to the Balkans'.[27] He considered that Bulgaria's attitude towards a neutral Balkan bloc aimed at restraining both German and

[23] Miller, *Bulgaria*, 15–16. [24] Ibid. [25] TsDIA, f. 321, op. 1, a.e. 3244, 1. 74–6.
[26] TsDIA, f. 95, op. 1. a.e. 1, 1. 58, 60. Filov, *Dnevnik*, 190.
[27] E. Barker, *British Policy in South-East Europe in the Second World War* (London, 1976), 55.

Soviet interference in the region was dependent on the satisfaction of at least some of her territorial aspirations, and in mid-September the British ambassador in Bucharest was instructed to encourage the Romanian government to make some concessions on Dobrudja.[28] Gafencu, the Romanian foreign minister, proved unwilling to accept any compromise, suggesting that the bloc should be created on the basis of the already existing Balkan entente, and only then should be enlarged to include Bulgaria.[29] His intransigence was motivated not so much by concern for Dobrudja as by the fear that concessions to Bulgaria might set an unwelcome precedent and re-open the much more important question of Transylvania. A similar British attempt in Athens also ended in failure, with the head of the Greek government, General Metaxas, declaring that giving Bulgaria an outlet to the Aegean would ultimately benefit Germany and the Soviet Union, and might encourage Yugoslavia to push her demands of Salonika.[30] The hopes placed on Yugoslavia as an intermediary, in view of the rapprochement between Sofia and Belgrade in the years before the war, were undermined by the implacable and almost personal distrust of Boris entertained by the Regent, Prince Paul, who had taken full control of Yugoslav foreign policy after the resignation of Stoyadinović in the spring of 1939.[31]

Bulgaria herself was not officially approached by the Foreign Office, although the government was aware of the British plans through the information it was receiving from its ministers abroad. Predictably, it was not attracted by the idea, both because of the risk of war and because Britain could not offer any territorial rewards. By the end of November 1939 the Foreign Office realised the futility of their endeavours, and shelved the plans for a Balkan bloc. British diplomacy focused its efforts on maintaining Bulgaria's declared neutrality, against both German and Soviet threats. The government in Sofia continued to suspect the British, as late as the spring of 1940, of planning to spread the war to the Balkans.

Scrupulously neutral in foreign policy, Boris was prepared to accept some increase in German influence in Bulgaria itself. The parliament elected in December 1939 had far fewer pro-Allied members than its predecessor. In February 1940, the neutral Kioseivanov was replaced at

[28] Public Record Office, London, FO 371/23731.
[29] E. Campus, *Intelegerea Balcanica* (Bucharest, 1972), 320.
[30] Z. Avramovski, 'Pokusaj Formiranija Neutralnog Bloka na Balkanu (Septembar–Decembar 1939)', *Vojnoistorijiski Glasnik*, 1, (1970), 164.
[31] Barker, *British Policy*, 56.

the head of government by Professor Filov, a fervent admirer of Germany. Gabrovsky, a Germanophile with anti-Semitic tendencies, was given the ministry of the interior. Boris was careful, however, to maintain a balance in the cabinet, placing the critical foreign and war ministries in the hands of men who, whilst not pro-Allied, were deeply suspicious of Germany. The first telegram of the new foreign minister Popov to Bulgarian ministers abroad stated that 'the foreign policy of Bulgaria, wisely adopted by my predecessor, continues without change.'[32] This hid uncertainties both on the likely course of the war and the possibility of pressing some of Bulgaria's revisionist demands. According to the information coming from Bulgarian ministers in March, Germany was planning to launch an offensive on the western front in the spring of 1940 and would thus not be interfering directly in the Balkans even though she considered them part of her Lebensraum. Britain and France, on the other hand, were seen as intending to broaden the conflict into the Caucuses and the Balkans.[33]

The start of Germany's offensive in Scandinavia and in the west removed some of the anxieties in Sofia. At a meeting of the Bulgarian ministers in Sofia in April 1940, Draganov noted that for the time being Britain and France would be kept busy and would not have the resources to attack the Balkans. Whilst the diversion of the war was welcome, at the same time there was unease at the thought that the chances of realising Bulgaria's territorial ambitions were diminishing.[34] The resolution adopted at the end of the meeting noted the possibility of putting Bulgaria's demands to the attention of the Great Powers not only at the eventual peace conference but 'possibly even before that'.[35]

Some steps in that direction were taken even without waiting for the outcome of the great battles raging in the west. At the beginning of May, the government sent instructions to the ambassadors in Berlin, London, and Paris, to bring the Dobrudja question to the attention of the respective governments.[36] A decision was precipitated much sooner than expected by an intervention from the one power that was not approached, the Soviet Union. Stung by Hitler's successes, Stalin moved to consolidate his position in Eastern Europe and on 26 June presented the Romanian government with an ultimatum demanding the immediate secession of Bessarabia. Deprived of French and British support, and

[32] TsDIA, f. 316, op. 1, a.e. 273. [33] TsDIA., f. 176, op. 8, a.e. 17, a.e. 855, 1. 5–7, 15, 22, 23.
[34] TsDIA, f. 176, op. 8, a.e. 17a, 1. 23. [35] Ibid., 1. 12.
[36] TsDIA, f. 176, op. 8, a.e. 931, 1. 37–8.

faced with Germany's reluctance to interfere in a dispute over a territory she had recognised as belonging to the Soviet sphere of influence (although the Germans did restrain Soviet demands on Bukovina, which had not been included in the Molotov–Ribbentrop pact), Romania was forced to back down. This naturally aroused the hopes of Bulgaria and Hungary. Hungary was the more daring, mobilising its army on 2 July. The government in Sofia, less confident in their own strength, preferred to act through Berlin. At first, their demands were deflected, as Germany was unwilling to destabilise her most important trading partner in the Balkans. The Bulgarians sought to impress upon Berlin that if Germany was unable to do anything they might be forced to accept Dobrudja from the hands of the Soviet Union.[37] The plausibility of that threat was reinforced by the fact that the Soviet government indicated in early July that it supported Bulgaria's claims. In a meeting with Richthofen, the German minister to Sofia on 29 June, the king noted the danger of a 'forcible *coup*' which would establish a pro-Soviet government in Sofia.[38] In Berlin, Draganov insisted on the need to 'solve the Dobrudja question with Germany's assistance before the conclusion of the war, which will remove any danger of a communist conspiracy and will strengthen the position of the government'.[39]

On 16 July, Popov was finally notified by Richthofen that Hitler had 'advised' the Romanian king to reach a friendly understanding with Bulgaria and Hungary.[40] The Bulgarian government was not satisfied, and on 27 July Filov and Popov visited Hitler in Salzburg to emphasise the Russian danger and to express their distrust of the Romanians' assurances.[41] The fears seemed to come true when the talks between Bulgaria and Romania came to a halt less than a fortnight after they started. On 4 September Popov instructed Draganov to tell the Germans yet again that Bolshevik propaganda would use public dissatisfaction for its own 'sinister aims'.[42] The warning seemed to have an effect, as Berlin warned the Romanians the following day not to delay the negotiations any longer.[43]

Faced with a seeming blind alley, Filov decided to mobilise the army and invade Romania. The king was forced to intervene and restrain his impatient prime minister who was threatening to bring the country

[37] *Akten zur deutschen auswartigen Politik* (hereafter *ADAP*) (Baden-Baden), Series D, vol. x, 32.
[38] *ADAP*, vol. x, 46.
[39] TsDIA, f. 316, op. 1, a.e. 273, 1. 258.
[40] *ADAP*, vol. x, 183.
[41] Filov, *Dnevnik*, 194–5.
[42] TsDIA, f. 316, op. 1, a.e. 273, 1. 111.
[43] Ibid., 1. 148.

into yet another disaster.[44] The episode demonstrated the dangerously growing confidence of the amateur prime minister, but also the king's ultimate ability to restrain him.

The Romanians finally gave way and on 7 September 1940 conceded Dobrudja to Bulgaria along the 1913 frontier. In the noisy celebrations that followed, the government gave all public credit to Germany. This gave a tremendous boost to Axis prestige among the nation at large and made it more receptive to future calls for closer association. For the first time, pro-Axis deputies called in the national assembly for an alliance with Germany. As one of the king's closest confidantes wrote in a letter to Boris, 'virtually everyone has given up on neutrality'.[45] In private, Boris was careful to thank both Britain and the Soviet Union for their approval of the Bulgarian claims. Whilst this ensured that alone of the Nazi-sponsored territorial changes in Europe, the return of Dobrudja was not reversed at the end of the war, it paled in comparison with the fact that Bulgaria had effectively, if not formally, departed from her neutrality and had actively solicited German help in order to impose herself upon a vulnerable neighbour.

This left Bulgaria in a much weaker position to resist German demands when in the autumn of 1940 Germany began to change her policy towards the Balkans. The failure of the air war against Britain prompted Hitler to consider other alternatives. One option, strongly urged by foreign minister Ribbentrop, was to create a global anti-British alliance. The Tripartite pact between Germany, Italy, and Japan was a step in that direction, and its extension to the Balkans could serve to deny that vital region to the British. For Hitler, whose own preferences were moving increasingly in the direction of war with the Soviet Union, the pact could also serve an anti-Soviet purpose.[46] In October 1940, Germany began putting pressure on the Balkan countries to join the pact. Hungary, Romania and Slovakia complied, becoming members on 20, 23, and 24 November 1940.

On 16 October 1940, Ribbentrop sent a telegram to the Bulgarian government requesting it to join the pact, warning that a failure to do so would have serious repercussions on the attitude of the Axis powers towards Bulgaria, and requesting a reply within three days.[47] The anxiety and confusion in Sofia was increased by a letter from Mussolini

[44] TsDIA, f. 95, op. 1, a.e. 1, 1. 107.
[45] Letter from L. Lulchev to Boris, 24 June 1940; cited in Sirkov, *Vunshnata Politika*, 238.
[46] A. Bullock, *Hitler and Stalin: Parallel Lives* (London, 1991), 755–6.
[47] TsDIA, f. 176, op. 8, a.e 17, 1. 31.

the following day informing the king of his intention to attack Greece and noting that that created an opportunity for solving Bulgaria's 'legitimate demands' in Thrace. In contrast to Ribbentrop, however, Mussolini did not set any specific demands or a deadline. The king was encouraged by the discrepancy, which he took to imply a lack of unity between the two Axis powers. On 19 October he wrote to Mussolini wishing him success in his 'inspired aims' but pleading that Bulgaria could not act because of the weakness of her army and encirclement by hostile neighbours.[48] Hitler received a similarly flattering letter, thanking him for 'the unforgettable discussions' the king had had with him and for his 'constant and benign attention to the Bulgarian people'. Whilst assuring him that 'Bulgaria's interests coincide and will continue to coincide with those of the great German Reich', the king sought to persuade him that Bulgaria was not capable of joining the pact. Indeed, Boris claimed that the country's current 'unambiguous' position already held in check Germany's enemies in the Balkans, and any change in that position risked creating complications, for instance pushing Turkey and the Soviet Union into each other's arms. The king pointed to Bulgaria's economic collaboration with Germany as an example of how his country was already fulfilling her 'tasks' in the new European order, and offered to send his prime minister and foreign minister to Berlin to discuss any outstanding issues.[49]

The king's emphasis on the weakness of the Bulgarian army, which was to become a recurrent theme in his exchanges with the Germans, was not merely a diplomatic ploy. It reflected the genuine concerns of the Bulgarian general staff over the country's inability to fight a war against her better-armed neighbours. Under the Treaty of Neuilly (1919), Bulgaria had been restricted to a volunteer army of 33,000 men. The country had been left with only 219 artillery pieces (out of a total of 1,484), 38,065 rifles (out of a total of 391,306) and 355 machineguns (out of a total of 1,971).[50] The rearmament efforts of the middle and late 1930s bore little fruit, as Britain and France were unwilling to sell arms to a former and perhaps future enemy, and Germany, whilst favourably disposed, had few arms to spare and used her position as Bulgaria's main supplier to impose economic if not, at that stage, political conditions (barring the half-hearted attempt in January 1939). It was only in the late summer of 1939, just before the outbreak of the war, that Germany began to send substantial quantities of armaments to Bulgaria, most of

48 Cited in I. Dimitrov, *Bulgaro-Italianski Politicheski Otnosheniia 1922–1943* (Sofia, 1976), 388–9, 384.
49 *ADAP*, vol. XI, 1, 310–11.
50 L. Spasov, *Bulgariia, Velikite Sili i Balkanskite Durzhavi, 1933–1939* (Sofia, 1993), 112–13.

them from the captured Czechoslovak and Austrian arsenals. Even that flow was insufficient to make up for the shortages that had accumulated over the years. As late as 1 December 1939, the Bulgarian general staff estimated that the country was unable to equip a wartime army, with even basic items such as rifles in short supply.[51]

Boris' tactic was rather similar to the one followed at the time by Franco's Spain and might have succeeded had Germany's interests in the Balkans remained purely political. Mussolini's adventure in Greece, however, undertaken against the wishes of the Germans, began almost immediately to run aground. In spite of, or rather because of being a miserable failure, the invasion had a number of important consequences. Hitler could not allow Mussolini to lose the war, especially after the British intervened in the conflict in early November by sending a couple of squadrons to the Greek islands. It became a priority for Germany to prevent a possible strengthening of Britain's strategic position in the Balkans and on 12 November 1940, in War Directive No. 18, Hitler instructed his generals to begin drawing up plans for a war against Greece.[52]

Without replying directly to Boris' letter, Hitler invited the king to visit him in the Berghof on 18 November. No minutes of the meeting have survived, but its essentials can be reconstructed from other sources. Filov noted in his diary that Hitler had not asked for Bulgaria's direct participation in the war and had limited his demands to joining the Tripartite pact. The king had declined the offer, noting Bulgaria's military unpreparedness and the threat from her neighbours and Russia. According to Filov, Hitler had accepted the king's objections.[53] Boris' rejection, couched as it was in terms of immediate dangers rather than on grounds of principle, was, however, open to modification if these dangers were overcome. In a conversation with von Papen, Germany's ambassador to Turkey, on 21 November, Boris noted that 'the military situation would probably make Bulgaria's accession to the pact necessary only in the spring and by that time he would definitely get rid of the Russians, without antagonising them'.[54]

Up to November 1940, the Russians had provided Boris with a convenient excuse with which to fend off the Germans rather that cause him any sleepless nights. By the time of his visit to Hitler, however, the Soviet threat had turned from a distant possibility into an actual and rather frightening reality. Following his take-over of Bessarabia, Stalin began

[51] Ibid., 134–6. [52] Bullock, *Hitler and Stalin*, 758, 756.
[53] Filov, *Dnevnik*, 199. [54] *ADAP*, vol. XI, 2, 547.

to entertain grander territorial ambitions in the Balkans, the only part of Eastern Europe which had not been explicitly divided into spheres of influence by the Molotov–Ribbentrop pact. He anticipated a lengthy bargaining process with the Germans who, in spite of their earlier protestation of disinterestedness, had moved into Romania in October 1940. He expected Molotov's visit to Berlin in mid-November 1940 to set the scene for these negotiations. Bulgaria was the one country in which Stalin was particularly interested, as underlined in the instructions the Soviet foreign minister received on the eve of his departure to the German capital. Bulgaria was to be regarded as 'the central question' in the negotiations, and was to be placed, with the agreement of Germany, 'in the USSR's zone of influence'.[55]

The Soviet demands came as a surprise to the Germans. For Ribbentrop, the Berlin meeting was an opportunity to build upon his success in August 1939 and draw the Soviet Union into a grand continental alliance with Germany, Italy, and Japan. Hitler was less sanguine, and had already instructed his generals to prepare plans of war against the Soviet Union. He may have been, however, prepared to see whether Soviet ambitions could be deflected away from Eastern Europe. Molotov's rapacious demands, therefore, struck the German dictator as particularly offensive. With regard to Bulgaria, Molotov asked for nothing less than the kind of security guarantees that Germany had offered Romania a month earlier. Hitler stalled angrily, asking whether the Bulgarians had actually approached the Soviet government with such a demand. The talks ended in complete failure and were instrumental in confirming Hitler's decision to attack the Soviet Union.

At his meeting with Hitler, Boris was informed of the Soviet plans for his country. Any potential scepticism Boris might have harboured was dissolved by a direct approach from Moscow a few days later. For Stalin, the inauspicious end of the talks in Berlin did not as yet signify that the time for bargains had passed. On 25 November he sent Hitler a letter indicating that he was prepared to go as far as joining the Tripartite pact provided that the Germans in their turn were prepared to accept a Soviet-Bulgarian treaty of mutual defence and a Soviet military base on the Turkish Straits. Without awaiting for the German reply (none eventually came), the Soviet leader decided to take matters into his own hands and apply direct pressure on Bulgaria. On the day the letter was sent

[55] 'Direktivy I. V. Stalina V. M. Molotovu pered poezdkoi v Berlin v noiabre 1940 goda' (Memorandum from Stalin to Molotov, 9 November 1940), published in *Novaia i Noveishaia Istroiia*, 4 (1995), 76–9.

to Berlin, the general secretary of the Soviet Commissariat for Foreign Affairs, Arkadi Sobolev, descended on Sofia with barely a few hours' warning, brandishing an offer of a mutual assistance pact. The Soviet note demanded the granting of naval facilities on Bulgaria's Black Sea coast and in exchange offered to support some of Bulgaria's territorial claims on European Turkey.[56]

In the eyes of Boris, the Soviet offer constituted a grave threat to Bulgaria. The Soviet government had not approached any other Balkan country with a similar proposal, and it was clear that its special interest in Bulgaria could lead to a take-over of the country. The Baltic states of Latvia, Lithuania and Estonia had been forced to accept similar pacts in the autumn of 1939, only to find themselves occupied by the Soviet army. The king scarcely hesitated in rejecting the offer, his only concern being to find a diplomatic enough language not to offend Soviet *amour-propre.* His position was made even more uncomfortable by a massive propaganda campaign launched by the Communist Party on instructions from Moscow. As Boris told Mushanov, the last democratically elected prime minister before the 1934 *coup*: 'Whilst Hitler has threatened me with his forces, Stalin is putting pressure on me through my own people.'[57]

Stalin's precipitate actions undermined Boris' resolve to defend Bulgarian neutrality against pressure from Berlin. However distasteful, Germany now appeared to be the only power that could guarantee Bulgaria against the Soviet ambitions. The Germans were not slow to profit from Boris' discomfort. On 23 November Hitler pointed out to Draganov that had Bulgaria joined the pact from the beginning, she would not have had her present problems with Russia. The Russian pressure did not ease through December 1940, with two further notes sent to Sofia on 6 and 18 December.[58]

Boris' other major objection to the pact, the threat from Turkey, began to lose its importance. On his return to Ankara after his meeting with Boris, von Papen realised the reality of Turkey's concerns about Bulgaria's possible membership of the pact, and in a telegram to Ribbentrop supported Boris' views. The ambassador then acted to reassure the Turkish government that neither Germany nor Bulgaria had aggressive intentions towards Turkey, and that Bulgaria herself felt threatened by her southern neighbour. The Turks acted quickly, with their minister in Sofia contacting Filov on 25 November with an

[56] Cited as Doc. No. 6, in D. Sharlanov and P. Meshkova (eds.), *Suvetnitsite na Tsar Boris* (Sofia, 1993), 183.

[57] Cited in Rachev, *Churchil, Bulgaria*, 100–1.

[58] *ADAP*, vol. XI, 2, 673, 757, 542, 563.

offer of a non-aggression pact.[59] Given the fact that it had just declined a Soviet offer of a pact, the Bulgarian government was not prepared to agree a pact with Turkey, fearing a strong reaction from Moscow. The danger of that was quite real, since one of the Soviets' main aims in offering the pact to Bulgaria was to safeguard themselves against hostile Turkish action. Whilst shelved for the time being, the offer was not declined and could be taken up when the Bulgarians decided to do so.

By December 1940, Boris was running out of options. On the negative side, the German decision to intervene militarily in Greece, formalised on 13 December as Operation Marita,[60] meant that with the coming of spring Bulgaria would be used as a corridor for the passage of the German armies. In the winter of 1940–1, troops began massing on the country's northern borders, reaching some 680,000 by February 1941. Bulgaria could no longer maintain her neutrality: she could either resist, which meant an inevitable war, or she could allow German forces to pass through peacefully which would effectively end her neutrality. Given Boris' almost pathological fear of war, and the inability of Britain to offer substantial military help, the first option was ruled out almost from the start. Indeed, no Balkan country, not even traditionally pro-Allied states such as Yugoslavia, Greece, or Romania, was prepared to challenge Germany. On the positive side, Boris appears to have been persuaded that Germany would win the war. In a conversation with Mushanov on 13 December 1940, the king ridiculed the phoney power of France and Britain in unprecedentedly harsh terms: 'Your great France could not withstand the German attacks for a single month ... My colleague and friend George (VI) is fortunate in having the Channel between Belgium and the British shore ... Otherwise he would have to sail the seas on some old Dreadnought.' He told Mushanov that 'only your prejudices against Nazism prevent you from seeing the future' and accepting Germany's victory as inevitable. That victory offered Bulgaria a chance to realise some of her national aspirations. Any attempts to resist the Germans would bring about a brutal occupation without benefiting the country in any way. It was only as a loyal ally of Germany that he could preserve the Bulgarian people from the fate of other occupied nations.[61]

[59] Filov, *Dnevnik*, 199. [60] Bullock, *Hitler and Stalin*, 764.

[61] Cited in Rachev, *Churchil, Bulgariia*, 100–1. For Bulgarian relations with Greece see, X. Stefanidis, 'Greece, Bulgaria and the approaching tragedy, 1938–1941', *Balkan Studies* (1991), 293–307.

Boris' mind might have been made up, but he wished, as was his custom, to put responsibility for the momentous decision on the shoulders of his government. On 24 December 1940, Draganov was instructed to organise a secret visit of the prime minister to Berlin between 3 and 10 January.[62] The very fact that Boris chose to send Filov to Berlin, instead of going there himself or sending the hesitant Popov, indicates that the king was preparing the ground for an acceptance of the German offer. He was fully aware of Filov's almost blind admiration for Germany as well as of his inability to stand his ground in diplomatic negotiations. The gullible prime minister was perfectly suited to bow to Germany's demands, and serve as a potential scapegoat if the alliance ended in a disaster.

In his meeting with Hitler on 4 January, Filov recited the old objections to joining the pact, but was easily convinced that Turkey would not be prepared to fight German troops, the Soviet Union would be forced to accept the situation and that Yugoslavia was going to join the pact herself and might even forestall Bulgaria by grabbing Salonika. On his return to Sofia, he informed the king that 'we have no choice but to accept the German advice and sign the pact'. Boris reacted 'incredibly strongly', threatening to abdicate and even throw himself into the hands of the Russians rather than ally his country with Germany. He refused to subject his people to the horrors of war; they had absolutely no wish to fight, and would revolt if forced to do so. Filov, a desk-bound former university professor, was forced to play the warrior, telling the king that a nation must be prepared to fight and make sacrifices for its ideals. It was the government that was to blame for the people's defeatism. As the war was inevitable, the government's task was to secure the best possible conditions for the country. A British victory would do nothing for Bulgaria since the destruction of German power would mean immediate 'Bolshevisation'. The option of embracing Bolshevism was 'always available', but would be fraught with danger, as the example of Hungary in 1919 demonstrated. The king gradually calmed down and 'accepted the force' of Filov's arguments.[63]

Boris' fundamental insecurity no doubt made him prone to doubt at a time when the fate of his country, and his dynasty, was being decided, but the exaggerated nature of his outburst makes it probable that this was a staged theatrical performance for the benefit of the prime minister. His closest adviser at the time had no doubt that the king had

[62] TsDIA, f. 316, op. 1, a.e. 273, 1. 15. [63] Filov, *Dnevnik*, 200–10.

reached a decision beforehand and his behaviour was not due to any real hesitation.[64] Had he been in need of persuasion, the rigid prime minister would have been the last person he would have called upon. One indication of Boris' commitment to the new policy was the fact that he never subsequently wavered from it, and even helped Filov to overcome the objections of Popov and the sceptical war minister. The council of ministers formally endorsed the decision on 20 January 1941.

Once the decision had been made, last-minute interventions from the Americans and the British could have little effect. President Roosevelt's personal representative, Col. Donovan, met Boris on 19 January, to inform him of the United States' firm commitment to Britain and warn him of the consequences an Axis defeat will have for his country. Without telling the forceful American of the decision he had made, Boris responded with a tired complaint that it was always small countries that were being blamed when Great Powers could not resolve their differences. As Miller noted, 'uncertain threats from a faraway country could not compensate for overbearing presence of a Great Power with troops on the Bulgarian border'. Britain was in a similar position since it had the power neither 'to bribe or to threaten'.[65] A non-aggression declaration with Turkey was finally signed on 17 February, putting an end to the only realistic means available to Britain of exerting pressure on Bulgaria.

The formal accession of Bulgaria to the Tripartite pact took place on 1 March 1941 in Vienna. The Bulgarian government wanted the accession to take place with as little pomp and ceremony as possible and suggested that the pact should be signed by Draganov.[66] The Germans rejected that option, insisting on the presence of the prime minister, and the foreign minister. Popov, who had agreed to the pact with extreme reluctance, did not want to be present at the ceremony and pretended that he was ill. Thus it was the prime minister, Filov, appropriately enough, who signed the pact. In his declaration after the signature, Filov emphasised that Bulgaria would continue to maintain friendly relations with the Soviet Union and Turkey. Later that day, the Germans and the Italians gave Filov an official letter promising Bulgaria an outlet on the Aegean between the Struma and Maritsa rivers.[67]

[64] *Suvetnitsite na Tsar Boris*, 106. [65] Miller, *Bulgaria*, 42, 43.
[66] Genchev, 'Bulgaro-Germanski Diplomaticheski Otnosheniia', 430.
[67] Filov, *Dnevnik*, 254–5, 250.

The German troops entered Bulgaria the very next day. On 5 March, Britain broke diplomatic relations in response not only to Bulgaria's accession to the pact, but also to a series of provocations against British Embassy officials. The Soviet Union issued a sharply worded protest, but did not take matters any further.

The government's control of the National Assembly ensured that the pact would be ratified by 140 to 20 votes. There was little enthusiasm for the pact, however, as even Hitler recognised: 'I have been struck to learn that after the conclusion of the Tripartite pact the Bulgarian prime minister was scarcely acclaimed by the population of Sofia, despite the major importance of the Pact to Bulgaria.'[68]

The Belgrade *coup* of 27 March 1941 and Hitler's decision to invade Yugoslavia made it certain that in addition to the Aegean outlet Bulgaria would also gain Macedonia. She was able to occupy both territories soon after the Germans crushed the Greek and Yugoslav armies in April 1941. The seeming realisation of the country's national aspirations and the escape from a direct participation in the war produced a feeling of euphoria which affected all shades of opinion. With even anglophile politicians such as Mushanov supporting the 'liberation' of Macedonia and Thrace, the king threw caution to the wind and irrevocably associated himself with the triumphant nationalism by assuming the title of a 'Tsar Unifier', thus placing himself on par with the founding father of the modern Bulgarian state, the Russian emperor Alexander II who was credited with the title 'Tsar Liberator'.

## CONCLUSION

From the viewpoint of Bulgaria's immediate interests, it is possible to see the decision to abandon neutrality and join the Tripartite pact as the best possible choice in the existing circumstances. At the very least, it allowed the country to escape the destruction that wrecked neighbouring Greece and Yugoslavia. By granting the Germans their minimum request for a formal alliance and later issuing a declaration of war against Britain and the United States, the king was able to avoid making more substantial concessions and succeeded in keeping Bulgaria out of direct military conflict. More problematically, accession to the pact and the subsequent German victories in the Balkans enabled Bulgaria to occupy territories which she had long regarded as her own.

[68] Miller, *Bulgaria*, 45–6.

In the long term the abandonment of neutrality was to have fateful consequences for Bulgaria. By linking his country's fate with that of Germany, Boris progressively lost the capacity to direct her policies. As long as he lived, there remained the hope that he might execute a *volte-face* at the convenient moment and extricate Bulgaria from the war. That, however, was rather unlikely. His limited achievements, both domestic and international, had been the result of manipulating, if rather adroitly, forces greater than his own. He had shown no evidence of an ability to seize the moment and act boldly without regard to the immediate risks. His reputation with the Allies, especially the British, had been sullied beyond repair, and they could hardly be expected to look favourably on a change of course under his leadership. The decision to accept territories from Nazi Germany, and to use them as the main ideological prop for the regime meant that any abandonment of the 'national unification' would have been politically suicidal. Finally, Boris' unwillingness to tolerate strong political leaders around him and elevations of pro-Germans into the cabinet meant that after his sudden death in August 1943, power remained in the hands of men who neither wished nor had the capacity to change course. The democratic politicians who alone could have had the courage to risk a change of course had been marginalised, both by their own failures and by Boris' deliberate exclusion. It was Germany's change of plan in November 1940 which ultimately doomed Bulgarian neutrality; and yet the failure to defend it also had roots in the internal divisions and unbalanced nationalism of Bulgaria's own leaders.

CHAPTER 9

# *Yugoslavia*

*Dragoljub R. Živojinović*

Internal instability and international confusion determined Yugoslav's approach to the events that led to war in September 1939. The Regency headed by Prince Paul Karadjordjević endeavoured to solve numerous problems, internal as well as external, in order to maintain Yugoslavia in the constantly deteriorating international situation. A pronounced anglophile, Prince Paul had to hide his innermost feelings and adjust his policies to ever-changing realities. The feelings within the country were also deeply divided: the Croats looked to Italy and Germany for support, while the Serbs expected help from Great Britain and France. Besides the Croatian demands, which in essence amounted to the granting of complete autonomy, the Regency had to cope with an economic crisis, a dearth of capital, rivalry between Germany and Great Britain for control over Yugoslavia's mineral resources, problems of rearmament, as well as others.[1]

It was Italy that initially posed the greatest threat to Yugoslavia, since Rome claimed the Balkans, especially the Adriatic, as her zone of special interest. The Fascist government had persistently tried to destabilise Yugoslavia by protecting extreme Ustashi elements and supporting Croatian separatism. The Italians also demanded the demilitarisation of the Dalmatian coastline, encouraged Hungarian revisionism, and finally attacked Yugoslavia's southern neighbour, Albania, and her ally, Greece. Belgrade blamed Italy and the Ustashi for the assassination of King Alexander in Marseilles in October 1934, and there is evidence to suggest that their suspicions were not misplaced. Soon afterwards however, the pro-Fascist prime minister, Milan Stoyadinović, set out to woo Italian sympathies. Stoyadinović's policy culminated in the signing of the Italo-Yugoslav Treaty of Friendship in March 1937.

[1] Ž. Avramovski, 'Sukob interesa Velike Britanije i Nemačke na Balkanu uoči drugog svetskog rata', *Istorija XX veka. Zbornik radova II* (Belgrade, 1961), 8–49.

The rapprochement which this created between the two countries has been seen by the historian Alfredo Breccia as a recognition of the regency's determination to adopt a policy of neutrality. To the Axis, it represented a tactical step, promising them a benevolent neutrality and economic cooperation in return for German protection against Italian aggression. To the Allies, it represented a strategic move, an assurance that Yugoslavia would join their ranks if they could eliminate Italy from the war and acquire control over the Mediterranean and especially the Adriatic.[2]

Yugoslavia's Italian policy began to unravel, however, early in 1939. In January 1939, Ciano visited Belgrade to secure Stoyadinović's consent for the forthcoming Italian action in Albania, by offering Yugoslavia a share in the spoils. Prince Paul rejected the agreement since there were, in his words, 'already too many Albanians living within Yugoslavia'.[3] The event led to Stoyadinović's resignation and replacement, in early February, by a new government headed by Dragiša Cvetković. Prince Paul was determined to stabilise the internal situation and reestablish Yugoslavia's international position. Externally, while confirming its policy of neutrality, it nevertheless decided to lean more heavily on Germany in the forthcoming days. Economic cooperation between the two countries was substantial even before Hitler's accession to power in 1933. Under the Nazis, however, Germany became a major trade partner of Yugoslavia. Walter Funk, minister of economy, argued that Germany was the best market for Yugoslav mineral and agrarian products, and in the summer of 1936 German Finance Minister Hjalmar Schacht visited Yugoslavia in order to confirm Germany's interest in economic cooperation.[4] Internally, Cvetković tried to resolve the Serbo-Croatian conflict through the creation of the *Banovina Hrvatska* in August 1939, and bringing the Croatian Peasant Party into the government. The Peasant Party's leader, Vlatko Maček, became the deputy prime minister.[5] At first glance, then, it seemed that on the eve of the Second World War

[2] A. Breccia, 'La potenze dell'Asse e la neutralità della Jugoslavia alla vigilia della II guerra mondiale (febbraio-settembre 1939)', in *The Third Reich and Yugoslavia 1939–1945* (Belgrade, 1977), 108; for a detailed discussion, A. Breccia, *Jugoslavia 1939–1941. Diplomazia della neutralità* (Rome, 1978), *passim*. This is the best study on the subject to date.

[3] V. Terzić, *Slom Kraljevine Jugoslavije 1941*, 2 vols. (Belgrade/Ljubljana, 1982), vol. I, 242.

[4] For an extensive analysis of German and British economic rivalry see Ž. Avramovski, 'Sukob interesa Velike Britanije', 5–26.

[5] J. B. Hoptner, *Jugoslavija u krizi 1934–1941* (Rijeka, 1973), 167–71. English original *Yugoslavia in crisis 1934–1941* (New York, 1962); Breccia, 'La potenze dell'Asse', 108–11, argues that it was done in order to strengthen the unity of the country and remove any chance of foreign interference.

the consolidation of Yugoslavia's internal political situation had been achieved.

During the mid-1930s German revisionism had not been considered a threat to Yugoslav interests. The *Anschluß* with Austria in March 1938, however, challenged these assumptions. At a stroke, Germany became Yugoslavia's neighbour and was able to exert strong pressure over the Danube basin and support pro-Fascist groups and the revisionist ambitions of Hungary, Bulgaria and Yugoslavia. Moreover, Berlin's control of Austrian foreign investments made her a creditor of Yugoslavia. Despite the evident threat to Yugoslavia, Stoyadinović heartily greeted Hitler's moves.[6] Prince Paul, on the other hand, did not approve of such closeness between Germany and Yugoslavia, believing that it was too dangerous for his country. It was no wonder that Prince Paul decided to dispense with Stoyadinović's services.[7]

Although an important factor in the preservation of the Versailles settlement, Britain's interest in the Balkans, and Yugoslavia in particular, was inconsistent. After the assassination of King Alexander, London threatened to withhold its support from Yugoslavia if Belgrade publicly accused Italy of connivance in the murder. There were even moments when the British government advised Prince Paul to improve relations with Berlin.[8] British capital investment gave London significant leverage over the Yugoslav government. In 1937, the value of British investments was second only to those of the French; by 1938, British capital moved to first place.[9] Britain used its position to lobby in favour of the creation of the *Banovina Hrvatska*, and gave full support to Prince Paul's decision to jettison Stoyadinović and abandon his pro-Axis policies. However, Chamberlain's appeasement of Hitler created enormous problems for Prince Paul and his government and provoked great concern amongst the general public and military circles.[10] By the spring of 1939, with the dissolution of Czechoslovakia and Italy's occupation of Albania, London's approach to the Balkans began to change. Nevertheless, while London was anxious to prevent Germany's expansion into the Romanian oil fields, it was not prepared to commit itself to providing military aid to either Yugoslavia or Greece. In such circumstances it made sense for Prince Paul to

[6] Ibid., 21–6. [7] Hoptner, *Jugoslavija u krizi*, 142.

[8] I. Jukić, *Pogledi na prošlost, sadašnjost i budućnost hrvatskog naroda* (London, 1965), 113; V. Kazimirović, *Srbija, i Jugoslavija 1918–1945*, 4 vols. (Kragujevac, 1995), vol. II, 391.

[9] H. Bötner, *England greift nach Südost Europe* (Vienna, 1939), 31, 140.

[10] Kazimirović, *Srbija*, vol. II, 390–5.

resist the British initiatives and insist on the preservation of strict neutrality.[11]

Subsequent events provided the Yugoslav leadership with plenty of opportunities to prove their commitment to neutrality. In the forthcoming months and years Belgrade was to be repeatedly tested, while the room for manoeuvre became increasingly narrow. Such a balancing policy required substantial skill, persistence, courage, and a capacity to devise proper answers; in a word, the art of politics. Divisions within the country, lack of military equipment and Yugoslavia's long-exposed frontiers clearly restricted Belgrade's foreign policy options over subsequent years.

The entry of the German troops into Czechoslovakia on 15 March 1939 was Belgrade's first major test. When the British inquired as to Belgrade's attitude towards collective security, Prince Paul replied that Germany's small neighbours – Romania, Poland, Yugoslavia – should stay out of such alliances. If not, according to Prince Paul, German aggression was inevitable.[12] A similar approach governed Yugoslav actions after Italy's invasion of Albania in April 1939. Cvetković made no protest to Rome, but demanded that no further moves be made in the direction of Kosovo. Ciano accepted Cvetković's demand. However, the Yugoslav army chiefs were more sombre in their assessment of Italian actions, believing that the invasion of Albania was a direct threat to Kosovo and Macedonia. The Chief of General Staff, General Dušan Simović, advised the government that no military actions in Albania should be planned or undertaken. But the damage was done. By moving to Albania, Italy became a military factor in the Balkans.[13]

These events clarified Yugoslavia's approach to neutrality. Alexandar Cincar-Marković, the foreign minister, explicitly explained it in such terms. During conversations with Hitler and Joachim von Ribbentrop, the German foreign minister, in Berlin in April 1939, he insisted that Yugoslavia would not take sides in any hostile action against the Axis powers. That was an advance on the definition of neutrality.[14]

[11] Kazimirović, ibid., vol. II, 39–6; E. Barker, *British Policy in South-East Europe in the Second World War* (London, 1976), 351; N. Balfur and S. Mekej, *Knez Pavle Karadjordjević. Jedna zakasnela biografija* (Belgrade, 1990), 111–12.

[12] Terzić, *Slom Kraljevine Jugoslavije*, 247–8.

[13] Memo, no date. Arhiv Vojnoistorijskog Instituta (hereafter AVII). Reg. no. 51–2, box 20. The students of Belgrade University published a declaration in which they castigated the Cvetković government for its behaviour.

[14] He also assured Ciano that Yugoslavia would not accept guarantees from the Western Powers and would pursue a policy of 'benevolent neutrality'. Terzić, *Slom Kraljevine Jugoslavije*, 244–6.

Prince Paul's visit to Italy in May 1939 proved to be another step in Belgrade's evolving policy of neutrality. Prince Paul was told that Yugoslavian neutrality was desirable in case the Axis powers decided to go to the war. Mussolini and Ciano proposed the conclusion of the treaty of non-aggression, but Prince Paul adamantly refused to entertain the proposal, since it obviously contradicted Yugoslavia's claim to neutrality. Unbeknown to his Italian hosts, Prince Paul was taking active steps towards securing Yugoslavia's position in a future war. During his visit to Naples, he took the salute of the Yugoslav navy training ship which had transported two-thirds of Yugoslavia's gold reserves to Britain for safe keeping.

Prince Paul's visit to Berlin in early June 1939 appeared to be marked by Hitler's efforts to bring Yugoslavia under closer German influence. Hitler insisted that Yugoslavia demonstrate its friendship by either concluding an agreement or joining the anti-Comintern pact. Ribbentrop also suggested that Belgrade leave the League of Nations and cooperate with Germany in reviving the Balkan pact. Hitler argued that the relationship between the two countries was well settled, and informed his guest that Germany would continue to pursue friendly relations with Yugoslavia. He ominously added that this would in addition help stabilise Yugoslavia's internal situation and promote peace with Croatia. Hitler's fine-sounding words and promises did not, however, move Prince Paul, and both he and Cincar-Marković resisted Germany's demands to the end. Prince Paul informed Hitler that he and his government shared Hitler's sentiments and sought close cooperation with Germany, even though the Western states made it difficult for him to do so. But Yugoslavia would neither leave the League of Nations, nor adhere to the anti-Comintern pact. This made Hitler furious with the regent, and he did not hide his disappointment with the outcome of the visit. For his part, Prince Paul left Berlin with an impression that war was imminent, and also with the distinct impression that Hitler was secretly negotiating with the Soviet Union.[15]

An invitation from King George VI brought Prince Paul and his wife, Olga, to London in July. Besides festivities and receptions, Prince Paul held numerous conferences and discussions in Downing Street and the Foreign Office. He was an interesting guest since he could comment on numerous subjects. He told Chamberlain and his ministers that Hitler

[15] Terzić, *Slom Kraljevine Jugoslavije*, 249–51; Hoptner, *Jugoslavija u krizi*, 165–6; Balfur and Mekej, *Knez Pavle Karadjordjević*, 114–15.

believed that Britain was about to collapse, that he was in negotiations with the Soviets. Prince Paul's suggestion, that Britain ought to clinch a deal with Moscow without delay, was not taken seriously. The British voiced no doubt about Prince's loyalty to Britain, but the position of Yugoslavia was not discussed.[16]

On the eve of the conclusion of the Molotov–Ribbentrop pact and the German invasion of Poland, the highest German officials expressed the opinion that the Yugoslav army and government were loyal to their country's policy of neutrality. According to General Simović, Prince Paul was greatly alarmed by the news of the imminent signing of the pact and the forthcoming attack on Poland. He instructed Cvetković to conclude an immediate agreement with the Croats, even at the cost of accepting some extreme Croatian demands and conceding some Serbian territory. The initiative came not a moment too soon: Cvetković secured an agreement between the Serbs and Croats on 23 August, the very same day that Ribbentrop finalised his historic pact with Molotov.[17]

The confusion caused by Germany's attack on Poland was palpable and ubiquitous; it seemed that everything was possible. Although Germany devoted its full attention to the Soviet Union and Poland, Hitler and Ribbentrop did not forget Yugoslavia. Before the invasion of Poland, Hitler, still angry at the failure to extract some formal obligations from Prince Paul, expressed his doubts about Yugoslavia's neutrality. He believed that Yugoslav neutrality would not last long and advised Ciano that Yugoslavia ought to be crushed. Ribbentrop even suggested that Italy use Germany's attack on Poland to seize Dalmatia and Croatia. Fortunately, Marshal Pietro Badoglio, Chief of the Italian General Staff, and Ciano refused to act. Contrary to Hitler's expectations, Belgrade proclaimed its neutrality on 5 September, and declared that it would follow such policy in all conflicts which did not involve Yugoslavia's independence or political integrity.[18]

The defeat of Poland and its subsequent partition caused an enormous shock in official Yugoslav circles as well as amongst the population. Prince Paul and the government had good reasons to be worried. Italian ambitions were one of them; Rome posed a major threat so long as

[16] Balfur and Mekej, *Knez Pavle Karadjordjević*, 116–18.

[17] Simović, *Memoari, Dušana T. Simovica, 1–2, popisnik* XVI. Archiv Vojnoistorijskog instituta (AVII), Belgrade, vol. II , p. 45; Hoptner, *Jugoslavija u krizi*, 167–70.

[18] *Politika*, 5 September 1939, Belgrade. The Yugoslav government informed Hitler that it was ready to defend Yugoslav independence if Italy decided to enter the war and move towards Salonika. Terzić, *Slom Kraljevine Jugoslavije*, 257–8; Hoptner, *Jugoslavija u krizi*, 180–1.

Germany was tied up elsewhere. Italy's declaration of non-belligerency was welcomed, but Prince Paul did not trust Mussolini. Prince Paul assured Lord Halifax that Yugoslavia would fight if attacked, but that the outcome of the conflict would depend on the British ability to interrupt the Italian lines of communications in the Mediterranean. In an effort to calm tensions, Cincar-Marković claimed that peace in the Balkans was of the greatest importance for Germany while she was busy in Poland. General Simović believed that Hitler's quick success in Poland had disturbed the Regent so much so that he permitted German propaganda in the country and the activities of the Fifth Column.[19]

German and Italian assessments of Yugoslavian intentions and internal situation confirmed the state of excitement. A German intelligence report, written in mid-October, noted the strong impression created by the success of the German army and claimed that Yugoslavian armaments were so poor that the current army was a less potent force than the Serbian army in 1914. It was vital, therefore, for the country to remain neutral and at peace to allow the army to rearm. The re-emergence of the Soviet Union only added to the sense of alarm. Prince Paul and the ruling elite saw great danger in the popular attraction to ideas of Slavic solidarity and Bolshevism. After repeating that Yugoslavia wanted to defend her neutrality, one German confidant noted that the number of the troops had increased. He mentioned, however, that in Croatia there were numerous cases of disobedience. His conclusion was that Yugoslavia acted to maintain the neutrality of south-east Europe. Victor von Heeren, the German Minister in Belgrade, even made the surprising claim, after a meeting with the Croatian leader Maček, that the Croatian people and politicians fully approved of the policy of neutrality. The invasion of Poland and the outbreak of war had unified the country and armed forces and aggravated the substantial latent anti-German sentiments found in many sections of Yugoslavian society.[20]

It was obvious that Yugoslavia found herself in an unenviable situation – encircled by Germany, Italy, and several smaller states whose commitment to neutrality was doubtful, to say the least. Such a situation forced Prince Paul and the government to play for time: draw out any negotiations, conclude worthless agreements, but above all win time necessary for rearmament.

19 Simović *Memoari*, vol. II, p. 46; Terzić, *Slom Kraljevine Jugoslavije*, 260.
20 Terzić, *Slom Kraljevine Jugoslavije*, 260–2.

In retrospect it is clear that during this period Yugoslavia came close to abandoning its neutrality. With German operations in Poland in full swing, Prince Paul opened a series of conversations with French and British emissaries about the supply of the arms for the Yugoslav army. During these discussions he suggested that Allied forces be dispatched to the Balkans, while, with the French minister, he even proposed the landing of the French troops at Salonika so as to secure Yugoslavia's access to the Mediterranean and prevent the Axis extending the war into the Balkans. Prince Paul stated that so long as the port of Salonika was open for traffic, Yugoslavia would be able to preserve its neutrality and possibly even join the Western Powers. The regent was clearly ready to go to considerable lengths to secure French and British support for his country. However, the French government and military chiefs were unwilling to accept the proposal. The British, meanwhile, were openly hostile to it, since it conflicted with Foreign Office hopes of keeping Italy out of the war by promoting an Italian-led neutral bloc in the Balkans. The proposal thus came to nothing. Failure to bring the French and British troops to Salonika was a defeat not only for France but also for Prince Paul, who was firmly of the belief that if the Axis gained control of the Greek port, Yugoslavia would be forced to make an agreement with Germany.[21]

Up to March 1940, numerous conferences were held in which problems relating to the Balkans were discussed. No agreement could, however, be reached. The permanent Council of the members of the Balkan Entente met in Belgrade on 2 February, but could only agree to recommend that their governments pursue a policy of peace, stay together and foster closer trade relations. Bulgaria shunned the proceedings, on account of her claims over the Romanian province of Dobrudja. The question of neutrality was not discussed. Despite his failure to persuade Western Powers to station troops in Salonika, Prince Paul continued to negotiate with the French. He and his ministers kept them informed about German troop movements and armament shipments to Bulgaria, and allowed French officers to inspect Yugoslav airfields. These efforts produced no concrete result other than to alert Germany to Belgrade's pro-western sympathies.

Over the spring of 1940, Yugoslavian neutrality was again menaced by her Italian neighbour. Numerous acts had indicated that Italy was

[21] Breccia, *Jugoslavia*, 206–10; Hoptner, *Jugoslavija u krizi*, 183–4; Terzić, *Slom Kraljevine Jugoslavije*, 261–3; Balfur and Mekej, *Knez Pavle Karadjordjević*, 124–6.

preparing to attack Yugoslavia in order to secure possession of Dalmatia and guarantee access to Yugoslavia's raw material and mineral resources (principally copper, zinc, bauxite, iron) which were badly needed for her military production. Nothing came of Mussolini's plans, however, as Hitler told him to keep his hands off the Balkans. Winston Churchill, familiar with Mussolini's intentions, argued against Britain declaring war on Italy in case she attacked Yugoslavia.[22] Unable to act militarily, Mussolini and Ciano were nevertheless ready to support the activities of Ante Pavelić's Ustashi, stationed in Italy. Aware of Mussolini's plan, Cincar-Marković informed the British Foreign Office on 23 April that Yugoslavia was determined to defend herself against any violation of her neutrality and territorial integrity. Lord Halifax praised Yugoslavia's determined stance, since it contributed to the preservation of peace in the Balkans. In a conversation with Carl Clodius, a high-ranking official of the German Foreign Ministry, on 3 May, Prince Paul stated that Yugoslavia was intent on preserving her economic neutrality and was ready to offer Germany full guarantees about mutual trade.[23] In retrospect, these proposals and statements appear dangerous and largely futile, and only reveal how fragile Yugoslavia's position had become.

The swift collapse of France and the Low Countries in May/June 1940 opened a new phase in the European crisis, and created an enormous shock in Yugoslavia, especially amongst the Serbs. Italy's long delayed attack on Dalmatia and Slovenia could now be expected at any moment. On 27 May Cincar-Marković told the Italian Minister in Belgrade, Francesco Mamelli, that 'Yugoslavia was absolutely neutral and intent on defending herself against anyone'; the activities of the Yugoslav troops, he added, were 'negligible'. Cincar-Marković's words did not, however, have the desired effect. Ciano informed Italy's ambassador in Berlin, Dino Alfieri, that Yugoslavia was carrying out a policy of 'double standards' and described Yugoslavia as a 'potential enemy of the Axis'. These remarks were duly passed on to Ribbentrop. In fact, Mussolini was all set to launch an attack on Yugoslavia, and was only prevented from doing so by Marshall Rodolfo Graziani, the Chief of the General Staff, who told him that the army was not yet ready for action. In a fit of exuberance following the victory over France, Ribbentrop instructed von Heeren to inform Cincar-Marković that Yugoslavia must end all exports to France and instead direct all her mineral resources, especially copper, to Germany and

[22] W. Churchill, *Their Finest Hour* (Boston, 1949), 128–9.
[23] Terzić, *Slom Kraljevine Jugoslavije*, 265–9.

Italy. It was an ultimatum that confirmed the new bullish Axis attitude to Yugoslavia. Although the British could be of no practical help, they nevertheless encouraged Prince Paul to maintain his policy of neutrality.[24]

The danger emanating from Italy did not disappear. Throughout the summer months, Mussolini, Ciano and the generals plotted to finish off Yugoslavia, 'that anti-Italian and the Versailles product' (Mussolini). By 19 August the plan was ready, but Hitler's failure to crush Britain led to renewed postponement. The final German word came on 19 September, when Ribbentrop informed Mussolini and Ciano that military action in the Balkans was undesirable since all resources had to be concentrated against Britain. Mussolini had no other option than to accept Germany's advice. Despite evident excitement in the country, Yugoslavia was spared from the trial of invasion. Her neutrality was preserved, although the events over the summer months had noticeably reduced her room for manoeuvre.[25]

Faced with a growing Italian menace on one hand and British impotency on the other, Prince Paul was forced to look to the Soviet Union for support. The decision was far from easy, not the least since Belgrade had no diplomatic relations with Moscow. Nevertheless, Italian bellicosity made some kind of decision imperative. Germany's agreement with Bulgaria and Hungary, and the transportation of the German troops across Hungary to Romania, forced Prince Paul to act. In making this decision, he hoped to exploit differences between Berlin and Rome as well as traditional Russo-German rivalry in the Balkans. Although the danger of the Soviet involvement in the Balkans was great, Yugoslavia was eventually able to play off the competing sides against each other. In July 1940, Yugoslavia's first accredited Minister to the USSR, Milan Gavrilović, the leader of the Serbian Agrarian Party, arrived in Moscow. In establishing diplomatic relations with Yugoslavia, the Soviets hoped to demonstrate that no power had the right to play the dominant role in the Balkans. The German government on the other hand, fearing that the two countries might come to a military agreement, judged the move as an attempt by Moscow to involve itself in Balkan politics, and an unpleasant and unwelcome intrusion in the Axis sphere of interests.[26] Nevertheless,

[24] Terzić, *Slom Kraljevine Jugoslavije*, 272–3; Balfur and Mekej, *Knez Pavle Karadjordjević*, 131–2.

[25] Terzić, *Slom Kraljevine Jugoslavije*, 278–9; Breccia, *Jugoslavia*, 323–6.

[26] G. Roberts, *The Soviet Union and the Origins of the Second World War. Russo-German Relations and the Road to the War, 1933–1941* (New York, 1995), 131–4. V. K. Volkov and L. J. Gibjanskij (eds.), *Vostočnaja Evropa meždu Gitlerem i Stalinem, 1939–1941 gg.* (Moscow, 1999), 241–96, 405–501, discuss the problems on the basis of the newest archival materials from the Soviet, Polish, and Romanian archives.

Ribbentrop informed the Soviet Foreign Minister, Vyacheslav Molotov, that Germany and Italy were ready to promote peace in the Balkans, since they were interested solely in trade and not territorial expansion. The real reason was, of course, very different. Peace in the Balkans served Hitler's long-term ambitions and preparations for war against Russia: any outbreak of fighting in the region threatened to disturb his timetable for war in the east.

In his conversations with the Soviets, Hitler assumed that he spoke for the Italians. Mussolini, however, had different ideas. On 15 October, despite being fully aware of Hitler's views, Mussolini decided on an attack against Greece to start in eleven days-time. Italy's assault on Greece inevitably undermined Yugoslavia's position. Greece was a friendly state, and closely related to the regent's family. The beginning of the invasion found the government uncertain as to what action to take. After waiting to hear about the attitude of Germany, Russia, Bulgaria and Turkey, the Crown Council met on 1 November and decided to strengthen defences on the southern border and do everything possible to prevent the Italians reaching Salonika. Over the following two months, however, the government arranged for the secret dispatch of substantial quantities of armaments, ammunition, food, and horses to the Greek side. Naturally, this did not remain unnoticed, and in retaliation Ribbentrop promptly suspended the delivery of material which had been ordered for the Yugoslav airforce. Clearly, Yugoslavia departed from its policy of strict neutrality in its attitude towards the Italo-Greek war. Despite this however, on 1 November Cincar-Marković informed London that Yugoslavia would remain neutral and defend her frontiers in case of the attack. Such a decision was motivated by the desire to prevent the spread of the conflict to the rest of the Balkans.

Italy's attack on Greece exposed for the first time serious divisions within the Yugoslav government on the question of neutrality. General Milan Nedić, minister for the army, forwarded to the prime minister a memorandum outlining the weaknesses of the army and the country and recommending that the government should cease wavering and join the Axis. The proposal provoked great consternation and after a meeting with the regent and prime minister on 2 November Nedić was forced to resign. He was replaced by General Petar Pešić. The same day, the government publicly affirmed its commitment to neutrality, a policy which was devoted to the preservation of peace in the Balkans and the Danube basin. The communiqué expressed deep regret that two states, Italy and Greece, found themselves at war with each other, and expressed the hope that Yugoslavia's interests would not be disregarded by the warring sides.

The conflict confronted Yugoslavia with the danger of complete political, economic and military isolation. Salonika became the symbol of Yugoslavia's salvation, the only exit to the Mediterranean and link with the Western states.[27] Its fate was of immense importance for Belgrade. The military attaché in Berlin, Col. Vladimir Vauhnik, was instructed to test German attitudes by asking for a response to Belgrade's declaration of 2 November. The Germans were non-committal in their reply, stating that the issue lay within Italy's sphere of interest. On 5–6 November when Italian planes bombarded the town of Bitolj, Belgrade immediately warned the warring parties, through the British Foreign Office, that any such attack in the future would be met with a swift response. With the war turning against them, the Italians adopted a cooperative attitude and promised to pay damages. Ciano insisted that Italy had no designs on Salonika and proposed that the two countries conclude a new treaty of cooperation. Prince Paul nevertheless refused the proposal, as he considered it too binding.[28]

Since Italy and Yugoslavia could not resolve their differences, the ultimate decision was thrust into Hitler's hands. Hitler's view on the situation is revealed in a discussion held with Ciano at Obersalzburg on 18 November. His description of the situation in the Mediterranean was a bleak one: the British occupied Crete and other Greek islands and were in the process of constructing bases and airfields. Germany was not ready to attack the British; the Soviets had shown a strong interest in the Balkans, while the attitude of the small states was unclear. Hitler therefore proposed that Italy should try to neutralise Belgrade, politically and militarily, by offering guarantees for her territorial integrity and promising her Salonika once hostilities came to an end. Hitler also expressed the belief that German intervention in the Balkans would not be possible before March 1941, and then only if Yugoslavia was neutralised. In the meantime, 'any threatening move against her will make the situation more difficult': Mussolini reluctantly accepted the Führer's suggestions.[29]

Hitler's direct interest in Yugoslavia did nothing to improve Belgrade's chances of survival. On 23 November, the day Romania and Hungary joined the Tripartite pact, Hitler invited Prince Paul to visit him at Fuschl. On the same day, Cvetković dispatched Danilo Gregorić, the

[27] Breccia, *Jugoslavia*, 347–9; Terzić, *Slom Kraljevine Jugoslavije*, 289–91.
[28] Hoptner, *Jugoslavija u krizi*, 193–6.
[29] Hoptner, *Jugoslavija u krizi*, 197; Terzić, *Slom Kraljevine Jugoslavije*, 295–7.

editor-in-chief of the Belgrade daily, *Vreme*, and well known for his pro-German sympathies on a mission to Berlin. Gregorić carried a message for Ribbentrop, in which Cvetković expressed his desire to preserve peace and enhance economic and political cooperation with Germany, if Berlin, for its part, would offer guarantees about Yugoslavia's frontiers and recognise her interest in securing access to the Aegean Sea. In response, however, Ribbentrop warned Gregorić that Germany could no longer tolerate any further equivocation on Yugoslavia's part and proposed instead that she should join the Tripartite pact. While accepting the validity of Yugoslavia's ambitions towards Salonika, Ribbentrop asked that Cincar-Marković visit him at Fuschl.[30]

Yugoslavia was slowly, but irresistibly, becoming a part of Germany's political game. With no change in the anti-German sentiments of the population, Prince Paul had his hands tied and had little choice other than to continue his policy of formal neutrality. By this stage however, it was Hitler who set the rules of the game. The Crown Council met in Belgrade on 27 November and resolved to send Cincar-Marković to meet Hitler. On 29 November the foreign minister was received in the Berghof. In a lengthy monologue, Hitler told Cincar-Marković that the preservation of Yugoslavia was of great importance for Germany and that there should be no differences between them. Hitler accused the Italians of committing serious political mistakes in the Balkans. Nevertheless, in order to secure and regulate Yugoslavia's ill-defined position, Hitler proposed that she joined the Tripartite pact. This, he claimed, was the only way for her to achieve her various goals – access to Salonika, peace with the Croats and protection from Italy. Hitler even promised to waive the right of German troops to pass across Yugoslavian territory. The suggestion was clear: Yugoslavia's neutrality was no longer appropriate. Hitler cleverly used Salonika as bait to win Yugoslavia's consent for his proposals. Before Cincar-Marković's departure, Hitler extended an invitation to Prince Paul or Prime Minister Cvetković to visit him at Berchtesgaden. The Yugoslavs were given three months to decide. After that time, the proposal could be different.

The members of the Yugoslav government and Prince Paul examined Hitler's proposals closely. They refused to enter the Tripartite pact, but instead proposed a Yugoslav–German non-aggression pact, which would guarantee Yugoslavia's frontiers. Ribbentrop rejected the proposal outright, and relations were further strained when Belgrade refused to

[30] Terzić, *Slom Kraljevine Jugoslavije*, 301–2; Breccia, *Jugoslavia*, 389–90.

allow a convoy of 1,000 lorries to pass across the country for Italian forces in Albania. On 1 December, in a speech on Radio Belgrade, Prince Paul reminded his listeners that while Yugoslavia enjoyed peace the majority of other European nations were at war. Yugoslavia's success in this regard was to be explained, he said, by the policy pursued by his government and by the friendly cooperation of other powers. He pointed out however that the war created innumerable difficulties for Yugoslavia's policy of neutrality.[31]

In order to strengthen its diplomatic position, on 13 December the Yugoslav government brought to a conclusion a series of long negotiations with Hungary for a Pact of Eternal Friendship. The Germans did not like it, especially after they learnt that Prince Paul had told the American minister in Belgrade, Arthur Bliss Lane, that the purpose of the pact was to stop further German expansion into the Balkans. Unexpectedly however, the pact also created difficulties with the British and Soviets. Although Prince Paul saw the pact as an anti-German measure, London feared it would merely result in Yugoslavia coming into closer alignment with German wishes.[32] The Soviet reaction was more drastic. Moscow took it as a sign that Belgrade was deliberately demoting their relations with Russia in favour of closer ties with Berlin, and promptly suspended delivery of military equipment which had been promised long before.[33]

At the same time as Belgrade's talks with the Hungarians were reaching their conclusion, Hitler finalised his plans for an attack on Greece and Russia: Operation Marita was accepted on 13 December, while Operation Barbarossa was signed eight days later. These decisions set in motion a series of events which made it essential for Germany to resolve the remaining questions in the Balkans without delay. Hitler was clearly anxious to settle his problems with Greece, Bulgaria, and Yugoslavia through diplomacy. Against this, however, Britain and the Soviet Union did everything in their power to prevent these states from signing the Tripartite pact.[34] This struggle was to last until the German invasion of Yugoslavia in April 1941.

31 *Politika*, Belgrade, 1 December 1940. The reply of the Yugoslav government came five days later. It confirmed its readiness to work jointly with Germany and Italy, adding that relations with the former were good.

32 C. Fotich, *The War We Lost. Yugoslavia's Tragedy and the Failure of the West* (New York, 1948), 39.

33 Hoptner, *Jugoslavija u krizi*, 203–4.

34 D. Lukač, *The Final Stage in the German–British Diplomatic Struggle for the Balkans (November 1940–March 1941). The Third Reich and Yugoslavia 1933–1945* (Belgrade, 1977), 46–9.

On 22 December Ribbentrop turned up the heat on Belgrade and once again repeated the suggestion that Yugoslavia should join the Tripartite pact. The problem remained unresolved. The dispatch of German troops to Romania, and Berlin's blatant efforts to extract similar concessions from Sophia inevitably raised Yugoslav unease about Germany's ultimate intentions. Von Heeren insisted that German actions were designed to promote peace and order in the Balkans, but Belgrade could hardly avoid being worried by a move that brought Axis forces to her every frontier. One day she would have to decide whether to go along with Germany or go against her. Her 'formal' neutrality had become all but worthless. By the end of 1940, it was obvious that Yugoslavia found herself in a very grave situation: economically, militarily, and politically the country was isolated; her traditional allies, Britain and Russia, were incapable of offering any serious assistance.

Yugoslav neutrality was of crucial strategic importance to German preparations for the attack on Greece. If hostile, Yugoslavia could pose a problem for German divisions moving through Bulgaria to Greece. Moreover, with planning against Russia in full swing, it was equally imperative for Germany to eliminate any real or potential threat to the southern flank of its invasion forces. In short, the entire Balkans had to be neutralised in some way or other. Greece had to be defeated and the British troops ejected from the Balkans. Clearly, therefore, it was undesirable for Hitler to complicate matters further by making war against Yugoslavia. Instead, he decided to win her to Germany's side. During the three following months, Hitler used every means at his disposal to bring Yugoslavia into the Tripartite pact.[35]

On 29 January 1941, Hitler invited Cvetković and Cincar-Marković to visit him in Berchtesgaden. Before leaving Belgrade, a secret meeting was held to define Yugoslavia's negotiating position, attended by the two emissaries, Prince Paul, and several other ministers. After an extensive discussion the meeting concluded that it was above all 'necessary to preserve the neutrality of the country and avoid entering into the conflict between the two sides'.[36] The discussion with Ribbentrop was held in Fuschl on 13–14 February. Asked about Yugoslavia's readiness to join the Tripartite Pact, Cvetković replied that Yugoslavia preferred to stay neutral, although she was ready to cooperate closely with Germany. Yugoslavia was prepared to conclude agreements with Bulgaria and Turkey and expected the

[35] R. L. Krimper, 'The Diplomatic Prelude to the Destruction of Yugoslavia, January to April 1941', *East European Quarterly*, 7/2 (1973), 127–9.
[36] Terzić, *Slom Kraljevine Jugoslavije*, 341–2.

quick ending of the Greek–Italian war. Ribbentrop was not impressed. On the afternoon of 14 February the Yugoslav ministers were received by Hitler at Berchtesgaden. After a lengthy monologue touching on a host of different subjects, Hitler stated that 'a unique heroic occasion has arrived for Yugoslavia to definitely fix her place in Europe for all time. She had to take a clear position now regarding the New Order in Europe and that was, to be sure, in her interest. That meant in other words, she had to take her place in the order envisaged by Germany and Italy, by immediately joining the Tripartite pact.' Hitler brushed aside Cvetković's arguments and counter-proposals. Hitler even expressed his readiness to make certain concessions: Yugoslavia would have no military obligations during the war, no demands for the transiting of the troops from the Tripartite pact states would be made and Germany would guarantee Yugoslavia's territorial integrity and recognise her 'rights' over Salonika.[37] Since the ministers could not assume the responsibility for the decision, they promised to report Hitler's proposals directly to the regent.

For their part, Britain and the United States made persistent efforts to persuade Prince Paul to keep Yugoslavia out of the pact. Paul was undoubtedly receptive to their views, not least since he was well aware that the majority of the Serbs and army officers were pro-British. Yet, he was ultimately not prepared to jeopardise his country's security and independence by following the course of action proposed by the British. On 12 January, for example, Minister Sir Ronald Campbell passed on to Prince Paul a suggestion made by Winston Churchill that, since a front was shortly to be opened up in Greece, Yugoslavia ought to renounce her neutrality and throw in her lot with the Allied cause. Prince Paul was taken aback by the suggestion, since the landing of British troops was bound to trigger a German attack on the Balkans, which in the current circumstances would only result in Yugoslavia's defeat and occupation. Prince Paul's refusal to entertain Churchill's proposal, prompted the following remark from the British prime minister: 'Prince Paul's attitude looks like that of an "unfortunate man in a cage with a tiger, hoping not to provoke him while steadily dinner-time approached".'[38]

In their desperation to force Yugoslavia to relinquish her neutrality, the British requested American diplomatic support. On 23 January Col. William Donovan, a special envoy of the president, arrived in Belgrade

[37] Krimper, 'Diplomatic Prelude', 129; Terzić, *Slom Kraljevine Jugoslavije*, 345–59; Lukač, *The Final Stage*, 53–4.

[38] Balfur and Mekej, *Knez Pavle Karadjordjević*, 141; Barker, *British Policy in South-East Europe*, 87.

for meetings with the regent, his senior politicians and army generals. In conversation with Prince Paul, Donovan announced that it was 'the definite policy of the USA to give every possible assistance to those states willing to fight for independence'. Prince Paul was restrained. The ministers who met Donovan expressed their fear for the unity of the country and the inability to defend herself. Maček informed his American guest that the government had little choice but to try to postpone military operations; only in the case of a German–Soviet conflict, he added, might Yugoslavia have a chance of survival. General Simović was more encouraging. He informed Donovan that Yugoslavia was in a dangerous situation, the army was unprepared for war and would value American military supplies. But when Donovan bluntly asked him which side Yugoslavia would fight on in the event of war, Simović immediately replied, 'our people would never betray their friends and allies from the last war'. The Americans repeated their interventions in Belgrade after Donovan's return to Washington.[39]

With the deadline for Germany's attack on Greece set for late March, German pressure on the Yugoslavs became intense. On 16 February, a day after Cvetković and Cincar-Marković had briefed the Crown Council on their discussions in Fuschl and Berchtesgaden, Prince Paul received an invitation from Ribbentrop to visit Hitler without delay. The Council approved the regent's trip: Yugoslav efforts to remove the German pressure through Italian mediation produced no result, and according to the army minister, General Pešić, whom Prince Paul consulted shortly before departing for Germany, the only salvation [for the country] was accession to the Tripartite pact.' On the other side, the British and Americans were anxious that Yugoslavia enter the war, but offered little in the way of tangible assistance. King George VI and Roosevelt made personal appeals to the regent to assume a clear position against the Axis threat, but the regent was reluctant to commit either himself or his country. He asked for comprehension for Yugoslavia's position, demanded stable political neutrality, and emphasised Yugoslavia's powerlessness in the absence of outside assistance. His arguments evoked little sympathy in London and Washington.[40]

[39] Simović, *Memoari*, II, 39–40; A. C. Brown, *The Last Hero. Wild Bill Donovan* (New York, 1983), 156–7; R. Nenadović, 'Američka javnost i 27. mart 1941 u Jugoslaviji', *Istorija XX veka*, vol. II (Belgrade, 1987), 55–6, discusses the correspondence between Washington and Belgrade.

[40] Prince Paul assured them that Yugoslavia would defend herself and that she would not permit the passage of the German troops across Yugoslavia; he also promised not to conclude a political agreement with Germany that would threaten independence and sovereignty of Yugoslavia. Breccia, *Jugoslavia*, 469–72.

Prince Paul became increasingly unhappy with British policy. When, in the middle of February, Churchill dispatched his new foreign secretary, Anthony Eden, and Chief of Imperial General Staff General Sir John Dill to Cairo with a brief to send help to Greece and to 'make Yugoslavia and Turkey fight', the rift between London and Belgrade became insurmountable. When Eden invited him to talks in Athens, the regent refused to go, and sent an army officer instead. His reply to Eden's letter was considered unsatisfactory. The regent recapitulated his earlier arguments, but left unanswered the question as to how Yugoslavia would respond to the entry of German troops into Bulgaria. It was clear from British questions that London wanted Yugoslavia in the war, come what may, regardless of whether she had been the victim of a German attack or not.[41]

As Prince Paul's trip to Berghof approached, the situation in the Balkans became increasingly hectic. Mussolini was anxious to conclude a treaty with Yugoslavia before she joined the Tripartite pact. The Duce was far from happy about Yugoslavia's accession to the Pact and was desperate to settle the Italo-Greek conflict prior to German intervention. Prince Paul refused Mussolini's proposal, rightly sensing that any involvement in Italy's war with Greece would inevitably destroy Yugoslavia's neutrality. By contrast, Hitler's offer was infinitely more attractive: its guarantees over Yugoslavia's future freedom, unity, and independence appeared to offer Belgrade a chance of remaining out of the war and maintaining its formal neutrality. On 25 February von Heeren informed Ribbentrop that Prince Paul would arrive at Berghof in the strictest secrecy in early March. In the meantime, on 26 February, Yugoslavia had ratified the pact of Eternal Friendship with Hungary. On 1 March Bulgaria joined the Tripartite pact and the following day German troops began entering the country. At the ceremony marking Hungary's accession to the Pact, Ribbentrop pointedly remarked that he hoped other states would follow Bulgaria's example. His thinly disguised allusion to Yugoslavia provoked immediate excitement and agitation in Belgrade.

It was in these circumstances that Prince Paul and Cincar-Marković arrived in Berghof on 4 March. The discussion was open, as both sides tried to explain their particular standpoint and proposals. Hitler made it clear that accession to the Pact would stabilise Yugoslavia's position in the New Order and enable her to fulfil her long-held desire to secure access to the Aegean through the port of Salonika. He pledged that Germany

[41] Barker, *British Policy in South-East Europe*, 87–8; Hoptner, *Jugoslavija u krizi*, 217.

would be a reliable partner and would defend Yugoslavia's territorial integrity. Finally, Hitler declared that he did not expect Yugoslavia to enter the war. Though visibly impressed by Hitler's offer, Prince Paul nevertheless set out the obstacles preventing him from putting his signature to the Pact. Among other reasons, he mentioned his sympathy for Britain and public hostility towards any closer alignment with Germany. At this point the discussion came to a close. The regent took leave of his host, promising to make a final decision in due time. The Germans assumed that the decision would be reached within two weeks.[42]

The debates which followed, especially within the Crown Council, revealed deep divisions among the Yugoslav policy-making élite. The majority of the members of the Council were inclined to meet Hitler's demands, one spoke out against the proposal (R. Stanković), while the remainder felt that additional guarantees and assurances ought to be obtained before a final decision was made. Over the next three weeks, numerous improvements were made to the text and Germany's demands and rights further clarified. Hitler and Ribbentrop even accepted certain obligations. As the negotiations between Belgrade and Berlin progressed, public protests against any capitulation to Germany became more vociferous. On 7 March the US minister handed Prince Paul a message from Roosevelt in which the President expressed the hope that Yugoslavia would reject Hitler's proposals. The Regent once again reiterated the dangers of resisting German demand: namely, the death of hundreds of thousands of people and the occupation and partition of his country. He had to decide what was the best interest of all his countrymen and put aside his own personal feelings and sympathies. Prince Paul later remarked that during his conversation with Ambassador Lane he felt like someone being cross-examined on the charge of heresy. Dissatisfied with Prince Paul's response, Sumner Welles, the deputy secretary of state, let it be known that Washington would 'freeze' Yugoslavia's gold reserves held in America.[43]

At the sixth meeting of the Crown Council, held on 20 March, the documents on the Yugoslav accession to the pact were read and agreed upon by all present. Maček and Kulovec, as representatives of the Croats and the Slovenes, gave their approval. General Pešić told the Council

[42] Terzić, *Slom Kraljevine Jugoslavije*, 360–6; Krimper, 'Diplomatic Prelude', 130–1; Breccia, *Jugoslavia*, 501–6. Breccia claims that during the meeting Hitler informed the Regent that he had decided to invade Russia.

[43] Terzić, *Slom Kraljevine Jugoslavije*, 379–80; Hoptner, *Jugoslavija u krizi*, 234. The British intervention had no effect.

that, with the exception of Zagreb, the commanding officers of all garrisons in Yugoslavia were in accord with government policy. In drawing the meeting to a close, Prince Paul pointed out that, although joining the pact was contrary to his deepest beliefs, he was not ready to take his country into a war in which there was only one possible result: defeat. His dilemma was tremendous.

On 25 March 1941, in the Belvedere Palace in Vienna, Cvetković and Cincar-Marković put their signatures to the Protocol of the Accession of Yugoslavia to the Tripartite pact. The great test of conscience was over; the awesome task of carrying out its provisions lay ahead. The country was divided internally and its leaders in open conflict with the British and Americans. Both conflicts appeared to be unavoidable. The question immediately arose: why had it happened? The decision to join the pact hinged on a traditional approach to international affairs. The Serbian dynasty had abandoned its traditional allies and protectors, Great Britain, France, and America, and from that moment sought the protection and cooperation of Germany and Russia. Both of these powers had been 'knocked out' during the First World War, suffered military defeat, revolution, and civil war. But by the late 1930s both had recovered and were playing an active role in Balkan politics. The decision to join the pact was a victory for those ethnic groups in Yugoslavia, the Croats and Slovenes, which had historically looked towards Germany. At the critical moment Serbia's traditional allies let her down. Consequently, the masses of the Serbs and the army officers, grown up and educated in anti-German tradition, could not understand or accept the turn towards Germany; they interpreted it as a betrayal of the Western Allies.

Those who led Yugoslavia into the pact firmly believed that the decision would preserve Yugoslav neutrality and protect her independence. Moreover, it appeared that they were prepared, at least to some extent, to take Hitler's words and promises at face value. Debate over the rights and the wrongs of Yugoslavia's foreign policy began almost as soon as the war came to an end, with powerful arguments being deployed on both sides. Participants in the events, such as the former prime minister, Dragiša Cvetković, insisted that Yugoslavia's accession to the pact had been dictated by dire necessity. Foreign Minister Cincar-Marković echoed these sentiments, adding that given the circumstances no other policy could have provided for Yugoslavia's salvation. Not everyone, however, shared these views. General Simović believed that the decision to join the pact compromised the future of the nation, and destined it to servitude. No more of a consensus could be found amongst historians. J. B. Hoptner was inclined to share Cincar-Marković's opinion: the decision to join the pact was realistic in view of the evident weakness of the West. Nevertheless, immediately after the war, Ferdo Čulinović, a historian from Zagreb, claimed that signing the pact was an act of capitulation for which the most prominent leaders of the Yugoslav kingdom were responsible. He insisted that Yugoslavia had surrendered herself to the Axis. Terzić, on the other hand, argued that Prince Paul had agreed to join the Tripartite pact under pressure, but concluded that the regent should have refused to sign. The most recent analysts reflect these sentiments: Lukač insists that only the subsequent armed resistance against German occupation made up for Prince Paul's treasonable activities. B. Petranović likewise criticises Yugoslavia's policy-making élite for pursuing a policy of neutrality which was too one-sided and static, and which deprived the country of its freedom of manoeuvre; its creators believed that it could stay out of the conflict.[44]

It is of course possible to address this enormous dilemma from a slightly different perspective. What would have happened if the Yugoslav army officers had stayed in their barracks, not deposed Prince Paul and his government and provoked German retaliation a week later? This author's answer would be the following: there would have been no *coup d'état* of 27 March 1941, no German invasion and no capitulation of Yugoslavia. In these circumstances, it is likewise possible to speculate that Yugoslavia would have been spared from occupation, spared from partition, and perhaps, too, spared from the creation of an Independent State of Croatia, which immediately set about annihilating the Serbian population and the other former nations of Yugoslavia. There would also have been, at least initially, no civil war between the two contending factions, the Royalists and the Communists. In short, it is possible to suggest that the destiny of the monarchy in Yugoslavia might have been different. Of course, had Operation *Barbarossa* been successful in crushing Soviet resistance, it is reasonable to assume that Hitler might have decided upon occupying Yugoslavia, especially once Anglo-American forces landed in Southern Europe. But by then, the effects of occupation would have been far less painful and far-reaching: Yugoslav's traumatic history would have been very different.

44 B. Petranović, *Istoriografske kontroverze* (Belgrade, 1998), 412.

# PART III

## *The 'long-haul' neutrals*

CHAPTER 10

# *Spain and the Second World War, 1939–1945*

*Elena Hernández-Sandoica and Enrique Moradiellos*

The foreign policy of Spain under Franco during the Second World War has been the source of much historiographical controversy. The interpretations have swung between the following alternatives: either it can be defined as a policy of voluntary neutrality between the two belligerent sides, the aim of which was to avoid participation in the war at all costs; or it can be seen as a policy of qualified neutrality, imposed by the circumstances and subject to the temptation of intervention in favour of the Axis powers. A brief review of the opinions of various witnesses and historians will allow us to appreciate this difference in interpretation.

According to Willard L. Beaulac, the United States Counsellor of Embassy in Madrid between 1941 and 1944, Franco had been the Allies' 'silent ally', and the objective of his foreign policy was to 'keep out of active participation in the war'. In contrast, in the opinion of Sir Samuel Hoare, the British ambassador in Madrid between 1940 and 1944, 'Spanish non-belligerency did not mean Spanish neutrality' and 'if Franco did not come into the war, it was for no love of us or doubt about an ultimate German victory'.[1]

This difference of appreciation is mirrored in the differing opinions of two Spanish protagonists. For José María Doussinague, the general director of foreign policy in the Spanish foreign ministry during the conflict, Spain had followed 'a clearly marked policy of peace' and its 'objective was to reach the end of the war without being drawn into the turmoil'.[2] On the other hand, Ramón Serrano Suñer, brother-in-law and confidant of Franco and foreign minister between 1940 and 1942, recognised that 'we maintained a completely benevolent policy towards

[1] Sir Samuel Hoare, *Ambassador on Special Mission* (London, 1946), 285–6. Willard L. Beaulac, *Franco. Silent Ally in World War II* (Carbondale, 1986), viii.

[2] José María Doussinague, *España tenía razón* (Madrid, 1949), 355, 359–60.

the Axis' and that 'the attitude of each and every one of us was a real and sincere reflection of Franco's disposition'.[3]

In the historiographic sphere, the contrast in interpretations concerning Francoist foreign policy during the conflict is equally apparent. Scholars who are ideologically in tune with the Francoist regime confidently argue that Spain remained neutral due to Franco's desire to avoid taking part in the war.[4] According to Suárez Fernández, Franco 'allowed Spain to survive unscathed the terrible effects of the war'. 'The assumption that Franco wished to enter the war but that circumstances changed this intention', he adds, '... has never been proven by documents. There is however, fairly abundant evidence that could be used to prove the contrary.'[5]

In opposition to these pro-Franco historians, over a long period a new historiographic tendency has taken shape, which, on the strength of new documentary evidence available in Spain and abroad, is much more critical in its analysis. The following words of Javier Tusell can synthesise this point of view:

> If Spain under Franco did not enter the World War, it certainly did verge on this possibility repeatedly and of its own free will, and was very far from strict neutrality during a large part of the conflict.[6]

Political sympathies apart, the differences among historians stem to a large extent from two concurrent factors. Firstly, it is a result of the serious documentary shortages that affect the official Spanish archives. The lengthy duration of the Franco dictatorship permitted a systematic purging of material considered to be compromising. There is, for instance, no trace of the wartime correspondence between Franco and Mussolini in either the presidential or foreign ministry archives. This makes the consultation of foreign archives obligatory to know *de facto* the

[3] R. Serrano Suñer, *Entre Hendaya y Gibraltar* (Madrid, 1947), 133 and 138. (New expanded edition, 1973.)

[4] See Ricardo de la Cierva, *Historia del franquismo. Orígenes y configuración* (Barcelona, 1975); Brian Crozier, *Franco. A Biographical History* (London, 1967); Ramón Salas Larrazábal, 'La División Azul', *Espacio, Tiempo y Forma. Historia Contemporánea*, 2 (1989), 241–69; Luis Suárez Fernández, *Francisco Franco y su tiempo* (Madrid, 1984), 8 vols.

[5] Luis Suárez Fernández, *España, Franco y la Segunda Guerra Mundial* (Madrid, 1997), 14 and 169.

[6] J. Tusell, *Franco, España y la Segunda Guerra Mundial* (Madrid, 1995), 13. See Antonio Marquina, *España en la política de seguridad occidental* (Madrid, 1986); Víctor Morales Lezcano, *Historia de la no-beligerancia española durante la Segunda Guerra Mundial* (Las Palmas, 1980); Paul Preston, *Franco. A Biography* (London, 1993); Javier Tusell and Genoveva García Queipo de Llano, *Franco y Mussolini. La política española durante la Segunda Guerra Mundial* (Barcelona, 1985); Angel Viñas, 'Factores comerciales y de aprovisionamientos en la neutralidad española en la Segunda Guerra Mundial', in *Guerra, dinero y dictadura* (Barcelona, 1984), 239–64.

Spanish conduct and determine their intentions. And this, in turn, throws an inevitable degree of uncertainty on the historical interpretation of Spanish foreign policy during that period.[7] The second factor relates to the changes in the legal and political position adopted by Spain during the conflict. In fact, one must not overlook that over the duration of the war, Spain was successively 'neutral,' 'non-belligerent,' 'moral belligerent,' and once again 'neutral.' This diversity of official postures hinders a global characterisation and imposes the necessity of a strict periodic precision.

In any case, specialised historiography agrees on one unavoidable starting point. It is impossible to understand Spanish foreign policy without paying due attention to the fact that when the conflict broke out, Spain had just emerged from a bloody civil war, lasting from July 1936 to April 1939.

## THE LEGACY OF THE CIVIL WAR

The result of the civil war[8] had been the defeat of the democratic and socially reformist project inaugurated in April 1931, with the proclamation of the Second Republic, and restarted in February 1936, after the electoral victory of the 'Popular Front', a coalition of Left-wing republicans, socialists, and Communists with tacit anarchist support. Once the military uprising in July 1936 turned into a civil war, the weakened republican government had to confront threats of internal revolution during the first months and was never able to achieve a high degree of domestic political unity. From the outset, the republic also suffered serious reverses in its search for military and diplomatic support abroad. In virtue of the Non-intervention Agreement it was deprived of vital help from the western democracies and had to depend on costly and insufficient Soviet military assistance.

Victory had belonged to an ultra-nationalist, Catholic fundamentalist, fervently anti-Communist, and anti-liberal military uprising. The rebel generals counted on the support of the right-wing political groups: pro-Alfonso monarchists (in favour of the restoration of King Alfonso XIII), Carlists (supporting a rival dynasty), the Falange (until then a tiny Spanish Fascist party), and the political Catholics (up to then the dominant group). In the course of the war, the insurgent camp gradually evolved into a

[7] On the situation of the Spanish archives see A. Viñas, 'La historia de la contemporaneidad española y el acceso a los archivos del franquismo', *Sistema*, 78 (1987), 17–36.

[8] Paul Preston, *A Concise History of the Spanish Civil War* (London, 1996).

personal dictatorship under Francisco Franco, the most prestigious of the generals and renowned for his political opportunism. Franco eventually concentrated in his hands undisputed and arbitrary power over the three pillars of what was to become the Francoist regime: head of state and 'Generalísimo' of the armed forces by choice of the insurgent generals: 'Caudillo' of the 'Falange Española Tradicionalista', a party created in 1937 after the forced unification of the right-wing political groups: and defender and protector of the Catholic Church, in the role of crusader and divine envoy to save the religion and the Patria.

In Franco's victory, the military, diplomatic and financial aid lent by Fascist Italy and Nazi Germany had been vital. As a result, the official ideology, the institutional structure and the line of internal and external conduct of the new Spanish regime had undergone a visibly pro-Fascist transformation between 1936 and 1939. In the diplomatic sphere, the relations with the Axis powers were firm and constituted the reference point of foreign policy. Spain had signed secret treaties of friendship and collaboration with Italy (28 November 1936) and Germany (31 March 1939). The civil war over, the regime also publicly announced its adhesion to the Anti-Comintern Pact of Italy, Germany and Japan (7 April 1939) and its withdrawal from the reviled League of Nations (8 May 1939).[9]

Thus, in the tense atmosphere in Europe leading up to the Second World War, the Francoist dictatorship had aligned itself with the Axis in opposition to France and Great Britain, the democratic powers that safeguarded the territorial *status quo*. Reinforcing this alignment, the repudiation shown by the Spanish regime of liberalism and democracy was mixed with patriotic aspirations shared by all the political groups. These aspirations took on an anti-British character (due to the colonial presence in Gibraltar) and also anti-French (because of rivalry in the Protectorate over Morocco and dispute over the control of the international city of Tangier).

However, any attempt by Franco radically to revise its foreign policy was limited by Spain's internal and geo-strategic situation. Above all, the population (25.8 million in 1940) was decimated and exhausted after a devastating war. At least half the population could be classified as hostile to the regime. The war had brought about a demographic drain of more than 300,000 dead, another 300,000 exiles, and 270,000 political prisoners in 1940. The destruction had seriously affected the

[9] Hispano-Italian treaty in *Ciano's Diplomatic Papers*, ed. M. Muggeridge (London, 1948), 75–7. Hispano-German treaty in *Documents on German Foreign Policy, 1918–1945* (hereafter *DGFP*), Series D (1937–45), vol. III (Washington, 1950), document 773.

productive infrastructure and created acute shortages of food, services, and industrial material. A large proportion of the railway system and rolling stock had been destroyed (30 per cent of engines and 40 per cent of freight wagons), as well as a considerable part of the road network and maritime ports, a quarter of the merchant fleet, and a high percentage of livestock. At the same time, agricultural and industrial production had fallen by 22 per cent and 14 per cent respectively from pre-war levels (1935).[10] Moreover, with gold reserves exhausted during the conflict, the financial situation was desperate and insufficient to carry out independently (or with Italian or German support) urgent post-war economic reconstruction. This obliged Franco to resort to the well-stocked market of Anglo-French (and North American) capital in search of loans to effect the essential imports of grain, industrial equipment, and fuel.

If the economic situation was dramatic, the geo-strategic front was hardly a cause for optimism. In spite of the victory, the Francoist army lacked the necessary material and logistical resources to meet possible Anglo-French action in Spanish Morocco, on the exposed coasts and island possessions (Canaries and Balearics), or along the Pyrenees and Portuguese border. In fact, during the Munich crisis, Franco, with resigned regret, had announced his neutrality in an eventual war between the hated democracies and the admired Axis. According to his pragmatic analysis, shared by the Italians and Germans, there was no alternative but to try to isolate the Spanish War from the general European crisis to avoid a total defeat. As a senior foreign ministry official had pointed out in a confidential report in May 1938:

> One need only open an atlas for any doubt to disappear. In a war against Franco-British forces, one can safely say, without the slightest exaggeration, that we would be totally surrounded by enemies. From the word go we would find them on every perimeter of our territory, on all the coasts and all the borders. We could hold them back in the Pyrenees; but it seems little short of impossible to prevent an invasion at the same time along the Portuguese border . . . Germany and Italy could only lend us help that was insufficient for the defence of a weak Spain, and nothing they may offer us could compensate the risk involved in fighting by their side.[11]

[10] Jordi Catalán, *La economía española y la Segunda Guerra Mundial* (Barcelona, 1995), 40–59. For the decline of agricultural and industrial production in Albert Carreras, 'Depresión económica y cambio estructural durante el decenio bélico (1936–1945)', in J. L. García Delgado (ed.), *El primer franquismo. España y la Segunda Guerra Mundial* (Madrid, 1989), 3–33; *Anuario Estadístico de España. 1944–1945* (Madrid, 1946), 1093.

[11] Conde de Torrellano, 'Consideraciones sobre la futura política internacional de España,' 20 May 1938. Archivo del Ministerio de Asuntos Exteriores (Madrid) (hereafter AMAE), serie 'Archivo Renovado', vol. 834, document 31.

In short, although the Francoist ideology was anti-democratic, francophobic, anglophobic, and called for the re-conquest of Gibraltar and imperial expansion in Africa, the reality imposed a period of peace and internal recuperation which could not be financed without resorting to loans from these democratic powers. During the summer of 1939, Franco and his foreign minister, Colonel Juan Beigbeder, warned Rome and Berlin of Spain's need for peace given its internal difficulties and military vulnerability. On 19 July, during the visit to Spain of Count Ciano, Mussolini's foreign minister, Franco explained the reasons for Spanish neutrality were a European conflict to break out:

> He spoke of his gratitude to the Duce and to Italy in terms which allow no doubt as to his sincerity ... Franco considers that a period of peace of at least five years is necessary, and even this figure seems to many observers optimistic. If, in spite of what is foreseen and in spite of goodwill, a new and unexpected fact should hasten on the testing time, Spain repeats her intention of maintaining very favourable – even more than very favourable – neutrality towards Italy.[12]

## ENFORCED NEUTRALITY

This was the critical situation in Spain when, on 1 September 1939, the German invasion of Poland drew a declaration of war from Great Britain and France. Franco's reaction was the only one that could be expected; on 4 September he decreed 'strict neutrality' in the conflict. After all, his admired political model Mussolini had opted for 'non-belligerency'.[13] The German ambassador in Madrid was informed by Beigbeder of the declaration of neutrality and received guarantees that Spain was nevertheless 'willing to assist [Germany] as far as she possibly could'.[14]

The French and British governments favourably received the decision taken by Spain as a lesser evil, given the circumstances. Their first reaction was to apply a naval blockade on the peninsula to interrupt commercial traffic with Germany and reestablish their lost hegemony over Spanish foreign trade. As was to be expected, one result of the special relations between Franco and the Axis during the civil war was that the

[12] *Ciano's Diplomatic Papers*, 290–1.

[13] As proof of his goodwill, Franco informed Mussolini of his declaration of neutrality in advance. *I Documenti Diplomatici Italiani* (hereafter *DDI*), ninth series (1939–43), vol. I (Rome, 1954), documents 47 and 63.

[14] German ambassador (Madrid) to Berlin, 1 September 1939. *DGFP*, vol. VII, 524. On Spanish–German relations, Rafael García Pérez, *Franquismo y Tercer Reich* (Madrid, 1994) and Christian Leitz, *Economic Relations Between Nazi Germany and Franco's Spain, 1936–1945* (Oxford, 1996).

Western Powers had been replaced by Germany and Italy as the primary recipients of Spanish goods: in 1938 Germany had absorbed 40.7 per cent of Spain's exports (basically, iron ore and ferrocopper pyrite destined for the war industry), followed by Italy (15.3 per cent), the USA (13.5 per cent), Britain (11.7 per cent), and France (0.3 per cent).[15]

As a complement to this blockade, with a view to softening its devastating effects, both powers also agreed to finance the post-war reconstruction programme and supply Spain with the corn, industrial products, and fuel that it desperately needed. A few weeks after the outbreak of the war, a British delegation arrived in Madrid to negotiate a War Trade Agreement. The Spanish authorities had decided, not without some reservations, that 'the negotiations with Great Britain must be treated and studied with preference, given the volume of traditional Hispano-British trade and the difficulties involved, due to the war, in commerce with other countries.'[16]

The fruit of this pragmatism was the signing of a preliminary commercial agreement with France in January 1940 and, two months later (18 March), a commercial and financial agreement with Great Britain. According to this, Spain received a loan of £2m for purchases of raw material in the sterling area, as well as an advance of almost £2m to be paid on outstanding Spanish debts. By these agreements, the Western Powers put into practice a peculiar policy of carrot and stick that bordered on economic appeasement.[17] Not surprisingly, if on the one hand this policy allowed Spain to acquire vital alimentary and industrial products, on the other it meant the continuing of the strict vigilance of the coasts and Spanish merchant traffic and strict rationing of imports to prevent the possible re-exportation of this merchandise or others to Germany via Italy.

The reason for these Allied precautions was none other than the public identification of the Francoist regime with the German cause.

[15] García Pérez, *Franquismo y Tercer Reich*, 60. Angel Viñas, Julio Viñuela, Fernando Eguidazu, *et al.*, *Política comercial exterior de España, 1931–1975* (Madrid, 1979), vol. I, 239–40.

[16] Minutes of the inter-ministerial commission of treaties, 20 October 1939, cited in Viñas, 'Factores comerciales y de aprovisionamientos', 248. Cf. David Eccles, *By Safe Hand. Letters of Sybil and David Eccles, 1939–1942* (London, 1983). Eccles was the representative of the Ministry of Economic Warfare in Madrid.

[17] Denis Smyth, *Diplomacy and Strategy of Survival. British Policy and Franco's Spain, 1940–1941* (Cambridge, 1986). 'Appeasement, once more' is from Henry Pelling, *Britain and the Second World War* (London, 1970), 91–2. Sir Llewellyn Woodward, *British Foreign Policy in the Second World War* (London, 1970), vol. I. On Hispano-French relations refer to Juan Avilés, 'Un país enemigo: Franco frente a Francia, 1939–1944', *Espacio, Tiempo y Forma. Historia Contemporánea* 7 (1994), 109–34.

Since 'strict neutrality' was of necessity rather than free choice, from the very beginning the Spanish authorities showed a clear bias towards Germany. Beigbeder, at that time a fervent Germanophile, made this explicit: 'I make an exception of you, not because we love you, but because the British Empire is our best market.'[18]

The official Spanish manifestations in favour of the German cause were varied. On the most visible level, the controlled press, dependent on Serrano Suñer (Interior Minister after 1938), was systematically pro-German. The Spanish police and army, great admirers of their German counterparts, allowed Nazi spies to operate throughout Spain, and also permitted Luftwaffe reconnaissance planes to fly into Spanish air space and the installation of a radio station in La Coruña. This freedom of action and logistical support was very efficient in the Straits of Gibraltar, with a view to controlling Allied merchant and military traffic. Furthermore, as from September 1939, with Franco's approval German warships and submarines were to receive all kinds of facilities for the supply of fuel, water, and food in several Spanish ports (Vigo, Ferrol, Cadiz, and Las Palmas de Gran Canaria). By the end of 1942 there were at least twenty-three cases of German submarines resupplied with Spanish assistance.[19]

This inclination towards Germany continued to be limited by the economic situation and military vulnerability. In March 1940, the prestigious General Kindelán (captain general of the Balearics) submitted a report on the military situation during a crucial meeting of the High Council of the Army which was approved by those present and was passed on to Franco. Any possibility of undertaking offensive operations was dismissed:

> We regret to report that we are in no way prepared for such a contingency (entry into the war): the air force and navy have lost efficiency over the year since the (Civil War) victory and on land the reorganisation has only just begun: our borders are still defenceless and the essential problems of fuel and explosives are yet to be resolved.[20]

Apart from these motives that called for neutrality, at the beginning of 1940 a new political factor arose to complicate the precarious

[18] Note of 17 March 1940. Eccles, *By Safe Hand*, 92.

[19] Charles B. Burdick, '"Moro": The Resupply of German Submarines in Spain, 1939–1942', *Central European History*, 3/3 (1970), 256–84. Ibid., *Germany's Military Strategy and Spain in World War II* (Syracuse, 1968). Donald S. Detwiler, 'Spain and the Axis during World War II', *Review of Politics*, 33/1 (1971), 36–53. Department of State, *The Spanish Government and the Axis* (Washington, 1946).

[20] Tusell and García, *Franco y Mussolini*, 97.

internal situation. Since 1937, Franco, with the collaboration of Serrano Suñer, had overseen a pro-Fascist change in the regime, in imitation of the Italian model. This orientation implied a growing predominance of the Falange within the regime and the adoption of its political proposals (press law, union legislation, programme of economic autarky, definition of the state as national-syndicalist, etc). This process gradually gave rise to a confrontation between Serrano Suñer and his Falangist support and the remaining political groups of the coalition. In fact, the prospect of a Falangist hegemony which would reduce their own share of power was intolerable for the other two pillars of the regime: the military leadership (those who had elected Franco as *primus inter pares* and in the midst of which was a growing number of supporters of a restoration of the monarchy in the form of don Juan de Borbón, the son of Alfonso XIII) and the Catholic hierarchy (in favour of the restoration and opposed to the Falangist control of cultural and educational life, an area they considered their own).

This internal political tension led to differing orientations in foreign policy, though both sectors understood the need for neutrality. The traditional Right-wing, Conservative, monarchic, and Catholic (dominant among the high-ranking officers, the most highly qualified civil servants, and the aristocrats), was much more prudent in its pro-German attitude and accepted the necessary tolerance towards the Allied Powers. In contrast, the Falangist sectors (well represented among the younger officers of the army, and the new political and administrative staff recruited during the Civil War) were fervent supporters of the Axis and were willing to risk a confrontation with the Allies. This increasing opposition between the two groups in aspects of internal and foreign policy, always under the watchful and arbitrating eye of Franco, would become more acute as the European conflict progressed and affected Spain more directly.

## NON-BELLIGERENCY BY FREE WILL

The sudden German victory against France in May and June of 1940, together with Italy's entry into the war (10 June), completely changed the European panorama and brought about a marked change in the Spanish attitude towards the conflict. France's fate was sealed (the armistice was signed on 22 June with the mediation of the Spanish ambassador in Paris) and with Britain isolated and expecting an imminent German assault, Franco was tempted to enter the war with a view to winning back Gibraltar and realising his imperial dreams in

Africa. Sure enough, the strategic situation had radically changed since September 1939: the German occupation of the French Atlantic coastline and the formation of the collaborating Vichy regime under Marshal Pétain eliminated any danger for Spain from that direction,[21] and the Italian intervention extended the war to the Mediterranean and limited the capacity of the British fleet, which could no longer use the metropolitan and North African ports belonging to France.

However, the essential problem for Franco remained unchanged: Spain could not stand a prolonged war effort, due to its economic and military weakness and the British naval control of its food and fuel supplies. Constrained by these limitations, but also encouraged by the prospect of a final Axis victory, during the month of June Franco deployed a cautious diplomatic strategy to make the fulfilment of Spanish territorial claims compatible with the economic situation and the military forces at his disposal.

Needless to say, the overwhelming German victories and the Italian intervention had reinforced public inclination and covert help for the Axis. The day Italy entered the war, the Caudillo wrote a revealing private letter to the Duce:

> Our moral solidarity will fervently accompany you on your mission, and as for economic help you can be sure that as much as we are able (as you know our situation well) we will willingly offer you it. You already know the reasons for our current position ... I emphasise the cordiality with which we will take advantage of any opportunity to help you with the means at our disposal.[22]

Franco was well aware that this hidden support would not be enough to allow him to carry out his expansionist programme. Therefore, he hoped to take part in the war on the side of the Axis powers but only when the worst of the fighting was over and Britain's defeat was assured, with a view to participating in the sharing out of colonial booty at the expense of France and Britain. In Serrano Suñer's words, Franco had the intention of entering the war 'at the moment of the German victory, when the last shots were being fired'. Spanish belligerency would always be 'more formal than real and would not cause us any real sacrifice.'[23]

[21] Matthieu Séguela, *Franco, Pétain. Los secretos de una alianza* (Barcelona, 1994). J. Avilés, 'Vichy y Madrid. Las relaciones hispano-francesas de junio de 1940 a noviembre de 1942', *Espacio, Tiempo y Forma. Historia Contemporánea*, 2 (1989), 227–39.

[22] *DDI* 4, 847.

[23] Comments by Serrano to *París-Presse*, 26 October 1945, cited in David W. Pike, 'El estigma del Eje', *Historia 16*, 115 (1985), 50–66 (54). Heleno Saña, *El franquismo sin mitos. Conversaciones con Serrano Suñer* (Barcelona, 1982), 193.

In short, Franco was ready to take advantage of the certain Axis victory over the Franco-British alliance to achieve Spain's territorial aspirations at a limited cost, one which was acceptable given the conditions.

Following this tempting strategy, on 13 June 1940 Spain abandoned 'strict neutrality' and officially declared its 'non-belligerency'. To the British government, just in case, Franco justified the change as a precautionary measure prompted by the extension of hostilities to the Mediterranean. But internally it was admitted that the step imitated Italy's earlier conduct and opened the door for future offensive action. As Doussinague wrote for Beigbeder, the declaration of non-belligerency 'is, in fact, a preparatory stage for entry in the conflict and this must exert a fearsome pressure on the countries who can assume to be threatened by our arms'.[24] The next day, as German troops occupied Paris, Spanish military forces 'provisionally' occupied the city of Tangier under the pretext of preserving order and neutrality. It constituted the first step, if a cautious and reversible one, towards the fulfilment of Franco's ambitious imperial programme.[25]

The final Francoist move took place on 16 June 1940. It was a Spanish initiative and did not respond to any German request (let alone pressure). That day, a special envoy of the Caudillo, General Juan Vigón, the Chief of the General Staff, had an interview with Hitler and his Foreign Minister, Joachim von Ribbentrop. On behalf of Franco, from whom he brought a private letter for the Führer (dated 3 June), Vigón offered Hitler Spanish belligerency in return for certain specified conditions: in particular the cession to Spain, after the victory, of Gibraltar, French Morocco, Orenesado (the western region of Algeria) and the expansion of Spanish possessions in the Sahara and Equatorial Guinea. The offer was also made conditional on the prior supply of sufficient German food, fuel, arms, and heavy artillery to alleviate the critical economic and military shortages in Spain. While these personal negotiations were taking place, Beigbeder informed Rome by telegraph of the Spanish conditions to join the Axis.[26]

Fortunately for Franco, though Hitler congratulated Vigón on the occupation of Tangier and expressed his desire that Gibraltar would soon become part of Spain, he refused to commit himself on the other demands, alleging the need to consult Italy over any modifications in

[24] Minute, 14 June 1940. AMAE R833/36.

[25] Charles R. Halstead, 'Aborted Imperialism: Spain's Occupation of Tangier, 1940–1945', *Iberian Studies*, 7/2 (1978), 53–71.

[26] 18 June 1940. *DDI* 5, 54. *DGFP* vol. IX, 456.

the Mediterranean. In fact, the Nazi leaders looked down on the costly Spanish offer, considering it unnecessary at the time when France was falling and Britain's defeat seemed assured. Mussolini made no effort to satisfy what he considered to be excessive demands, which moreover could give rise to a competitor in the Mediterranean and North Africa.[27]

The bilateral negotiations on Spain's entry into the war continued over the summer of 1940, without any German or Italian pressure and with a repeated Spanish insistence on its conditions. On 19 June the Spanish ambassador in Berlin presented a memorandum repeating Spain's offer of belligerency.[28] To Franco's obvious disappointment, the German answer was delayed until 25 June and when it eventually arrived it could not have been more ambiguous. It merely stated that the German government 'has taken cognisance of Spain's territorial desires with regard to North Africa' and, with regard to the demands for material help, 'Germany will at the proper time give them most sympathetic consideration.' The note finished with a clause that was particularly ominous for the future: 'As soon as the further military situation after conclusion of the French armistice can be ascertained, the Reich Government will again consult the Spanish Government.'[29]

This attitude of official reserve was emphasised by the reports on the Spanish situation. According to the German ambassador, 'Spain is economically unfit to carry through to the end a war lasting more than a few months' and 'the economic assistance requested of us could represent a great burden (especially with respect to nutrition)'. As for the Abwehr, they warned of the military vulnerability of the country: 'Because of many internal difficulties of the country now under reconstruction, Spain can *without foreign help wage a war of only very short duration.*'[30] Admiral Wilhelm Canaris, the head of the Abwehr, accurately summarised the nature and dangers of Franco's offer for the German general staff:

> Franco's policy from the start was not to come in until Britain was defeated, for he is afraid of her might (ports, food situation, etc.) ... Spain has a very bad internal situation. They are short of food and have no coal. The generals and the clergy are against Franco. His only support is Suñer, who is more pro-Italian than pro-German ... The consequences of having this unpredictable

[27] As early as 14 June 1939, during Serrano Suñer's visit to Rome, Mussolini confessed his doubts concerning these claims: see *Ciano's Diary*, 1939–1943, 105.

[28] *DGFP* vol. IX, 488. [29] For evidence of Spanish disappointment: *DGFP* vol. X, 3.

[30] Memo by German Ambassador (Madrid), 8 August 1940. Note of the High Command of the Army. 10 August 1940. *DGFP* vol. X, 313 and 326.

nation as a partner cannot be calculated. We shall get an ally who will cost us dearly.[31]

Spanish disappointment over the failure of their offer of belligerency was accompanied by a sudden worsening of the internal economic situation which intensified their dependence on Allied supplies. The British government under Churchill had understood, from the start of the German victories, Spain's new strategic importance and had hastened to take precautionary steps in case circumstances turned further against them. As part of these measures, on 1 June 1940 Sir Samuel Hoare arrived in Madrid as the new ambassador 'on special mission'. His task consisted of preventing Spain's entry into the war by means of persuasion, threats, or simple bribery.[32] The British secret service, although unaware of the negotiations of Vigón and those thereafter, did suspect Franco's temptation of 'picking up something cheap.'[33] To contain this temptation, the British authorities put into practice two complementary operations. On the one hand, foreseeing the worst, various strategic plans were drawn up for the eventuality of Spain declaring war against Great Britain or being invaded by Germany: Operation 'Challenger' (occupation of Ceuta), 'Blackthorn' (Anglo-Spanish resistance in Morocco), 'Puma' (occupation of the Canaries), etc.[34] The second line of action consisted of tightening the maritime blockade on the Spanish coasts and imposing a strict ration, with American help, on food and fuel imports so as to prevent the build-up of stocks in preparation for war or their re-exportation to Germany. The resulting 'policy of a controlled rhythm of supplies on a monthly quota basis' was very efficient in the case of petroleum products. In this matter, the defined and attained target was to authorise 'imports sufficient to permit normal consumption and the maintenance of stocks at two and a half month's consumption'.[35] This demonstration of naval strength was accompanied by offers of help and facilities for the import of essential products if Spain remained 'non-belligerent'. Together, as Hoare and his diplomatic team were pleased to point out, this policy 'proved a vital factor in convincing

[31] Report from Canaris, 27 August 1940 in *The Halder War Diary, 1939–1942*, ed. Charles Burdick and Hans-Adolf Jacobsen (London, 1988), 252.

[32] D. Smyth, '"Les Chevaliers de Saint-George": La Grande-Bretagne et la corruption des généraux espagnols (1940–1942)', *Guerres Mondiales*, 162 (1991), 29–54.

[33] Note 24 July 1940. WO 208/1868.

[34] Luis Pascual Sánchez-Gijón, *La planificación militar británica con relación a España* (Madrid, 1984).

[35] Memo by A. Yencken (HM Minister in Madrid, 1940–44), 5 January 1942. FO 371/31234 C514. Professor Atkinson, 'Anglo-Spanish Relations since the Outbreak of the War', 3 June 1942. FO 371/31230 C5659. All British sources used are in the Public Record Office.

Spain where her interests lay'. In fact, at the beginning of September the Spanish ministry of agriculture predicted a harvest shortfall of 1 million tons. The current Spanish harvest would yield no more than 2.6 million tons against a normal consumption of 4 million tons (of which 400,000 were normally reserved for seed). The evidence clearly showed that Spain was entering 'a period of intense internal hardship, verging on famine'.[36]

The deterioration of the Spanish internal situation from September 1940 coincided with the crucial moment of the Battle of Britain and the first German doubts as to the feasibility of invading the island. It was in this context that the German strategists started to turn their attention to Gibraltar, the conquest of which could help break British resistance and limit the activity of the Royal Navy in the Mediterranean. The result of this change in strategy was the invitation by Hitler to Franco to send a representative to Germany to negotiate the conditions for the entry of Spain in the war.

Leaving Beigbeder aside (as he was becoming increasingly convinced in the benefits of neutrality), Franco decided to send the man whom he most trusted; Serrano Suñer. Between 16 and 27 of September 1940, Serrano Suñer had several interviews with Hitler and Ribbentrop. During the conversations the disparity in criteria between the two sides and their differing perception of the importance of Spain in the conflict and the future New Order in Europe became clear.[37] Not surprisingly, the uncertainty concerning the Battle of Britain together with the relative freedom of the Royal Navy in the Mediterranean, had heightened Franco's caution and his wish to run only limited risks in exchange for large compensation.

Following instructions, Serrano Suñer insisted on the acceptance of the territorial claims and the previous shipment of material aid. He required a secret 'political protocol' which accepted Spanish demands and left the decision as to the optimum moment to enter the war up to Franco. In the words of Franco to his brother-in-law: 'It is better for us to be in the Axis but without rushing in.' And this because 'the alliance has no doubt', but there are many reasons 'which favour limiting the duration of our war' and it could not be overlooked that 'a long war is now a

[36] Report by A. Yencken, 5 November 1940. FO 371/24509 C12016. Smyth, *Diplomacy and Strategy of Survival*, 78 and ch. 6.

[37] German minutes in *DGFP* vol. XI, 63, 66, 67, 97, 104, and 117. R. Serrano Suñer, *Entre el silencio y la propaganda, la Historia como fue. Memorias* (Barcelona, 1977), 329–48.

distinct possibility'.[38] As for the material aid, Serrano Suñer maintained the volume at the levels determined in the first offer of belligerency and considered by the German authorities as impossible to meet: 400,000 tons of gasoline, about 700,000 tons of wheat, 200,000 tons of coal and at least 100,000 tons of diesel oil and 200,000 tons of fuel oil.[39] The military shipments consisted of planes, munitions as well as heavy naval and anti-aircraft artillery to protect the Spanish coasts and islands, and also to attack Gibraltar. According to Franco, this help, far from being excessive, was 'no more than what was essential for this mission'.[40]

However, to the disappointment of Franco and his emissary, the German reply was very different from the one they had expected. Though Hitler seemed willing to allow the cession of French Morocco, in exchange he requested from Spain one of the Canary Islands, bases in Agadir and Mogador (in Morocco), Guinea (for his proposed empire in central Africa), and important economic concessions in Morocco and Spain. Moreover, Serrano Suñer's German interlocutors reduced the volume of food and military aid since they considered the attack on Gibraltar as a limited operation within its overall anti-British strategy and not as an integral defence of Spain and its far-flung territories. As Ribbentrop highlighted on several occasions, 'the figures seemed to be too high, specially with regard to the gasoline, since . . . large-scale troop movements would not be involved'.[41] Serrano Suñer had imagined that he would be considered a valued ally and found himself treated as the representative of a virtual satellite state.

In view of these differences, the discussions were suspended pending a personal meeting between Franco and Hitler. Serrano Suñer left Berlin without having agreed any protocol for entry in the war and after attending the signing of the Tripartite pact between Germany, Italy, and Japan as a mere spectator. The interview between the Caudillo and the Führer took place on 23 October 1940 at Hendaya (on the Hispano-French border), taking advantage of a visit by Hitler to the south of France for a meeting with Pierre Laval, the vice-premier of the Vichy government (22 October), and Pétain (24 October). However, in the interval between the conversations in Berlin and the interview in Hendaya, the course of the war reaffirmed both

[38] Letters of Franco to Serrano, 21, 23, and 24 September. Serrano Suñer, *Entre el silencio y la propaganda*, 338, 340 and 342–3.

[39] Original Spanish request in *DGFP* vol. IX, 488, details in *DGFP* vol. X, 355 and 404.

[40] Note by Franco, 21 September. Serrano Suñer, *Entre el silencio y la propaganda*, 338.

[41] Conversation on 16 September 1940. *DGFP* vol. XI, 63, 90.

sides in their position and reduced the already narrow margin for agreement.

Firstly, Franco's enthusiasm for the war began to fade for two reasons: the British victory over the Luftwaffe (which ruled out a collapse of the British resistance and would lead to the cancellation of the planned invasion of Britain on 12 October); and the determination of the Royal Navy to maintain its hegemony against Italy in the Mediterranean (which convinced him that an occupation of the Suez Canal was an essential precondition before any attack on Gibraltar). Furthermore, the Spanish general staff, with the support of the monarchists and the church hierarchy, were increasingly opposed to the interventionist policy of the Falange; the extreme military vulnerability, the famine existing in the country (the winter of 1940/1 was the most dramatic) and the dependence on Anglo-American food and fuel supplies. In these conditions, in Franco's opinion, the implicit risks made the complete fulfilment of all demands necessary for Spain to join the Axis. His commitment to this policy was renewed on 17 October, when Serrano Suñer replaced Beigbeder as foreign minister.

As for Hitler, he was finding it more and more difficult to blend the Francoist demands into his overall strategy. A few days after receiving Serrano Suñer, the Führer had a meeting with Ciano in Berlin and confessed to him that Spanish belligerency 'would cost more than it is worth'. Ciano was also of the opinion that the Spanish 'have been asking for a lot and giving nothing in return'.[42] Moreover, a crucial new event had taken place: on 25 September 1940 the French colonial army, remaining faithful to the government of Vichy, had beaten back an attack on Dakar by the forces of General De Gaulle with British support. Its leaders had guaranteed the neutrality of its army provided Germany respected the integrity of the French North African empire. Under the impact of the events of Dakar, Hitler and Mussolini met at the Brenner on 4 October to discuss their response to Franco's demands on Morocco.[43] Hitler emphasised that the intervention of Spain 'was of strategic importance only in connection with the conquest of Gibraltar; her military help was absolutely nil'. However, the acceptance of Spanish demands would provoke two adverse phenomena for the Axis: 'firstly, English occupation of the Spanish bases in the Canaries, and secondly, the adhesion of North Africa to the Gaullist movement'. As a result,

[42] *Ciano's Diary*, 294–5. *DGFP* vol. XI, 124.

[43] Minutes of meeting in *DGFP* vol. XI, 149 and *DDI* vol. V, 677. *Ciano's Diplomatic Papers*, 395–8.

Hitler considered that 'at all events, it would be more favourable for Germany if the French remained in Morocco and defended it against the English'.[44] Mussolini expressed his agreement and his desire to reach 'a compromise . . . between the French hopes and the Spanish wishes' in order to align both countries against Britain.

In these conditions, during the interview in Hendaya on 23 October 1940, the possibility of a Spanish–German agreement had considerably diminished.[45] Franco refused to commit himself to a definite date to enter the war, as Hitler requested, unless the Spanish colonial claims were accepted. However, the Führer neither wished nor was able to agree to them. Anticipating his forthcoming meeting with Pétain, Hitler had concluded that the priority was to keep Vichy on his side. He refused to dismember the French territories, as such an act would push the authorities into the arms of De Gaulle and Britain. He could not risk the proven advantages of French collaboration for the costly and doubtful belligerency of a country like Spain that was hungry, defenceless, and dilapidated.

Despite the absence of agreement, in order to secure rights over the distribution of the post-war booty, Franco agreed to sign a 'secret protocol' at Hendaya which prescribed Spain's adhesion to the Tripartite pact and obliged her to 'intervene in the present war of the Axis Powers against England after they have provided her with the military support necessary for her preparedness, at a time to be set by common agreement of the three Powers'. The fifth article of the protocol recognised the handing over of Gibraltar to Spain and formulated the 'compromise' between 'French hopes and Spanish wishes' sought by Hitler and Mussolini:

> The Axis Powers state that in principle they are ready to see . . . that Spain receives territories in Africa to the same extent as France can be compensated, by assigning to the latter territories of equal value in Africa, but with German and Italian claims against France remaining unaffected.[46]

In this way, Spain became an as yet non-belligerent associate of the Axis. Mussolini accurately described the significance of the above document in his meeting with Hitler on 28 October: 'That Protocol represents the secret adhesion of Spain to the Tripartite pact.'[47]

[44] Hitler to Ciano on 28 September.

[45] P. Preston, 'Franco and Hitler: The Myth of Hendaye 1940', *Contemporary European History*, 1/1 (1992), 1–16. *DGFP* vol. XI, 220 and 221; Serrano Suñer, *Entre el silencio y la propaganda*, 283–308.

[46] On the circumstances surrounding the adhesion see Serrano Suñer, *Entre el silencio y la propaganda*, 300–5 and 311–24.

[47] *Ciano's Diplomatic Papers*, 404.

The subsequent course of the war, with Italian defeats in Greece and North Africa, convinced Franco that this was going to be a prolonged and exhausting conflict. As a result, he continued to postpone *sine die* Spanish belligerency, in spite of German demands that he fulfil the terms of the Protocol and fix a date for the joint attack on Gibraltar. At the end of 1940 these demands were particularly intense, to ensure Spanish collaboration in Operation Félix (the German attack on Gibraltar, planned for 10 January 1941). Canaris had a meeting with Franco on 7 December to obtain his final approval. However, the Caudillo refused, since Spain 'was not prepared for this. The difficulties in the way were not so much military as economic; food and all other necessities were lacking'. According to Franco, Spain's military weakness was so great that she 'would lose the Canary Islands and her overseas possessions upon entry into the war.' He therefore concluded that 'Spain could enter the war only when England was about to collapse.'[48]

These stalling tactics were reinforced by the deterioration of the economic situation (which heightened the dependence on supplies from abroad controlled by the Royal Navy). The critical situation deepened the conflict between the military and the Falange for control over internal and foreign policy. Taking advantage of the circumstances, the British and Americans ordered the shipment of corn and fuel essential to alleviate the hardship with the aim of underpinning the pro-neutrality tendencies within the regime. Churchill had written to President Roosevelt on 23 November favouring this benevolent policy on the basis that Spain 'is not far from the starvation point' and 'an offer by you to dole out food month by month so long as they keep out of the war might be decisive'.[49]

In order to force Spanish resistance and fix a date for her entry in the war, Hitler requested the mediation of the Duce. That was the origin of the meeting between Franco and Mussolini in Bordighera (on the Italo-French border) on 12 February 1941. In the course of this meeting, Franco again emphasised the 'conditions of real hunger and the absolute lack of military preparation' which forbade Spanish belligerency. Conscious of Spanish incapacity, Mussolini refrained from exerting pressure on Franco and submitted a report to Hitler which put an end to all German hopes: 'Spain, today, is in no state to initiate any offensive

[48] Canaris report in *DGFP* vol. XI, 476. Maximum pressure was exerted on 21 January 1941. *DGFP* vol. XI, 682 and 692.

[49] *Roosevelt and Churchill. Their Secret Wartime Correspondence*, ed. Francis L. Loewenheim, Horold D. Langley, and Manfred Jonas (London, 1975), 121.

action.'[50] From then on, Franco's regime maintained its alignment with the Axis without passing the threshold of war. Anti-British campaigns continued in the press; the covert help to German and Italian secret services was maintained; logistical support continued to be given to the navy and airforce of both countries; the exportation of products useful to the Axis war effort was encouraged, including wolfram, iron ore, and pyrites.

## MORAL BELLIGERENCY BY IMPOTENCE

The pinnacle of Spanish identification with the Axis occurred after Germany's invasion of the Soviet Union on 22 June 1941, and the shift of the war to the east. A few weeks earlier, Franco had confronted the first serious crisis caused by the conflict between Serrano Suñer and the military ministers in the government. Imposing his position as the undisputed arbitrator, the Caudillo had overcome this challenge by means of several appointments which underscored the power of the army while curtailing the influence of the Falange. General Galarza was appointed Interior Minister, whilst the frigate captain Carrero Blanco was named Under-Secretary of the Presidency. Carrero Blanco, as the virtual representative of military interests, would become the most influential adviser to the Caudillo.[51]

Franco and Serrano Suñer, their differences partially overcome, congratulated the Nazi government on its initiative and offered as a 'gesture of solidarity' the dispatch of Spanish volunteers to fight alongside the German army against Communism. On 2 July, Serrano Suñer defined the position adopted by Franco as 'the most resolute moral belligerency at the side of our friends'.[52] Immediately, under the slogan that 'Russia is responsible for our civil war', the recruitment of volunteers began. On 14 July 1941 the first contingent of the so-called Blue Division (because of the colour of the Falangist uniform) set off for the Russian front, consisting of 18,694 men at the orders of professional military commanders headed by General Muñoz Grandes. By the time the division was finally withdrawn in February 1944, a total of 47,000 Spanish had fought with

[50] Tusell and García, *Franco y Mussolini*, 124. *DDI* vol. VI, 568 and 577 (583). *Ciano's Diplomatic Papers*, 421–30. Ribbentrop suspended further pressure on Spain on 22 February: *DGFP* vol. XI, 73.

[51] J. Tusell, *Carrero. La eminencia gris del régimen de Franco* (Madrid, 1993).

[52] *DGFP* vol. XII, 671, vol. XIII, 12. Serrano's declaration was made to the German newspaper *Deutsche Allgemeine Zeitung* and reproduced in the Spanish press.

the German army in Russia (approximately 10 per cent of whom lost their lives).[53]

The political intention of the dispatch of the Blue Division was clear. With the contribution of Spanish blood to the war effort the Axis would have to recognise future territorial claims. In the words of Serrano Suñer: 'Their sacrifice would give us a title of legitimacy to participate one day in the dreamed-of victory and exempted us from the general and terrible sacrifices of the war.'[54] Nor can one dismiss the fact that it constituted a first tentative step (just in case there was no formal declaration of war against the Soviet Union) towards a larger intervention in the war at an opportune moment. According to the dispatches of the German and Italian ambassadors in Madrid, this was Serrano Suñer's objective, since he believed that 'Spanish unity could be restored only by a resolute entry into the war; the regime could be saved and the Spanish national aspirations be fulfilled only in this way.'[55]

The status of 'moral belligerency' reflected by the dispatch of the Blue Division was articulated most clearly in a resounding speech given by Franco before the National Council of the Falange on 17 July 1941. Carried away by his emotions, the Caudillo abandoned his proverbial caution and showed himself more favourable towards the Axis and more scornful of the Allies than ever before:

> The die is already cast. The first battles were joined and won on our soil . . . The war has taken a bad turn for the Allies and they have lost it . . . At this moment, when the German armies lead the battle for which Europe and Christianity have for so many years longed, and in which the blood of our youth goes to join that of our comrades of the Axis as a warm expression of our solidarity, let us renew our faith in the destinies of our country under the watchful protection of our closely united Army and the Falange.[56]

In keeping with these sentiments Franco signed an agreement with Germany on 22 August 1941 in which he promised to send 100,000 Spanish workers as a substitute for those mobilised for the war. Spain

53 Klaus-Jörg Ruhl, *Franco, Falange y Tercer Reich* (Madrid, 1986), 22–30 and 378, note 169. Gerald R. Kleinfeld and Lewis A. Tambs, *Hitler's Spanish Legion. The Blue Division* (Carbondale, 1979). R. Salas Larrazábal, 'La División Azul', 241–69.

54 Serrano Suñer, *Entre Hendaya y Gibraltar*.

55 German ambassador (Madrid) to Berlin 2 September 1941. *DGFP* vol. XIII, 273. Tusell and García, *Franco y Mussolini*, 131–2.

56 Cited in *Extremadura. Diario Católico*, 18 July 1941. The speech was reported widely in the international press. See Research Department, Foreign Office, 'Spanish Neutrality as Reflected in the Press', 6 December 1944. FO 371/31234 C514 and Conrado García-Alix, *La prensa española ante la Segunda Guerra Mundial* (Madrid, 1974).

thus followed the example set by Italy and the rest of the satellite states (Vichy, Bulgaria, Hungary, Romania, and Croatia) and became the only 'neutral' state to subscribe such an agreement of collaboration. In the end, due to difficulties in recruitment and transport, only 10,000 workers were dispatched.[57] Similarly, in the last days of November, Serrano Suñer travelled to Berlin and signed the extension of the Anti-Comintern pact.

However, as on previous occasions, the public alignment with the Axis did not mean a complete rupture with the Allies. The Anglo-Americans responded to Franco's speech by reinforcing the naval blockade and interrupting food and fuel supplies. On 24 July, Anthony Eden, the British foreign secretary, admitted to the House of Commons that the Caudillo's declaration showed that 'he does not desire further economic assistance for his country' and, therefore, British policy 'will depend on the actions and attitude of the Spanish government'. Five days later, the minister of economic warfare promised to employ 'the utmost vigilance to see that nothing should reach General Franco which would increase his power to go against us'. Meanwhile, following orders from Churchill, the British strategists prepared an expeditionary force of 24,000 troops to occupy the Canary Islands with a minimal delay in the event of the entry of Spain in the war. These emergency measures were only revoked in February 1942 after the danger had passed.[58]

Conscious of the vital dependence on Anglo-American supplies, the Francoist diplomacy hastened to deploy all its efforts to alleviate suspicions in London and Washington. The interruption of fuel supplies practically paralysed the transport system and placed the whole of the Spanish economy on the verge of asphyxiation. By the end of 1941 there were only stocks of 39,071 tons of petroleum, when the quarterly consumption had been 114,252 tons of oil and its imports in that same period had only reached 82,936 tons (compared with 285,208 tons imported in the last quarter of 1940). It was a demonstration of what Churchill had called the 'policy of limited supplies' to put a brake on Franco's belligerent impetus, a policy which Eden had privately described as 'turn[ing the] tap on but regulate it and be ready to turn it off'.[59]

[57] R. García Pérez, 'El envío de trabajadores españoles a Alemania durante la Segunda Guerra Mundial', *Hispania*, 170 (1988), 1031–65.

[58] Smyth, *Diplomacy and Strategy of Survival*, 230–8. Sánchez-Gijón, *La planificación militar británic*, ch. 3.

[59] Eden to Churchill, 14 February 1941. FO 371/26910 C1437. Churchill to Roosevelt, 16 December 1941. *Churchill and Roosevelt. The Complete Correspondence*, ed. W. F. Kimball (Princeton, 1984), vol. 1, 298.

To face up to British protests over the Blue Division, Franco elaborated a 'theory of the two wars' which would excuse his policy of 'moral belligerency'. According to this theory, Spain, continuing its Crusade during the civil war, was a belligerent in the fight against Communism, but continued to be non-belligerent in the conflict between Britain and the Axis in the west. From then on and almost until the end of the war, in spite of Anglo-American reservations, Francoist diplomacy would follow the principle that 'the struggle against the Bolsheviks was something quite distinct from the battle being fought in the west between civilised nations'.[60] The instrumental character of this theory is made quite clear in a report for Franco by Carrero Blanco on 12 December 1941:

> The Anglo-Saxon Soviet front ... is really the front of Jewish power where the whole complex of democracies, free-masonry, liberalism, plutocracy, and Communism raise their flags ... the Axis is fighting today against everything that is fundamentally anti-Spain.[61]

## RETREAT INTO NEUTRALITY

The entry of the United States in the war, together with the serious Italian defeats in Libya and the difficulties of the German offensive in Russia, gradually eroded Franco's belief in a final Axis victory. From then on, the Caudillo, as well as his advisers, understood that the war was going to be very long and that the strategic position of Spain had become more vulnerable due to the American military presence in the Atlantic, the continuing presence of the British in Suez, and the forced withholding of German troops on the eastern front.

In these circumstances, to ensure himself against possible hostile Allied action, Franco resorted to a trump he had kept in his hand: his close relation with the dictatorial regime of Salazar in Portugal, the traditional British ally in the peninsula who had supported him in the Civil War. A treaty of friendship had existed between the two dictatorships since 17 March 1939 and an additional protocol (of mutual consultation) had been added on 29 July 1940.[62] On Spain's initiative, Franco met Salazar in Seville on 12 February 1942. In the course of this meeting the previous

[60] Hoare, *Ambassador on Special Mission*, 139; L. Suárez, *España, Franco y la Segunda Guerra Mundial*, 324–5 and 331.

[61] Document from Carrero Blanco's private archives in J. Tusell, *Carrero*, 61 and 63, and Antonio Téllez Molina, 'España y la Segunda Guerra Mundial: los informes reservados de Carrero Blanco', *Mélanges de la Casa de Velazquez*, 29/3 (1993), 263–80 (267).

[62] Text of treaty and protocol in *Dez Anos de Política Externa (1936–1947). A Naçao Portuguesa e a Segunda Guerra Mundial* (Lisbon, 1967–74), vol. V, 1978, vol. VII, 1066.

agreements were ratified with a view to safeguarding the peace and territorial inviolability of the peninsula.[63] Hence the Iberian Bloc took shape (christened in December 1942, after the visit of the Spanish Foreign Minister to Lisbon), conceived by Franco as a tacit offer of neutrality towards the Allies and as a guarantee of Anglo-American respect towards the Spanish regime.

Within Spain, the tension between the military and the Falange reached critical levels on 16 August 1942 when a group of Falangists unsuccessfully attacked General Varela, the Minister of the Army, as he came out of a mass in Bilbao to honour the Carlists who fell in the civil war. The vigorous reaction of Varela, supported by the military commanders, brought about an immediate court-martial and execution of one of the guilty Falangists. The serious deterioration of the situation forced a decisive intervention by Franco. In an operation of calculated balance, on 3 September Franco satisfied the military demands by dismissing Serrano Suñer and appointing the veteran General Gómez-Jordana as foreign minister (the post he had occupied during the civil war). But he also significantly replaced the Royalist Varela with a new minister of the army, the more reliable General Asensio. Franco thereby put into practice a strategy that would allow him to remain as Head of State indefinitely: using the support of the most docile and anti-monarchic sectors of the Falange to counteract the military's demands for a transfer power to the pretender to the throne, don Juan de Borbón.[64]

The political crisis solved, Franco had to face up to a decisive event. On 8 November 1942 Allied troops landed in the French zone of Morocco and Algeria and thereby opened a second front against the Axis in the Mediterranean.[65] The US ambassador, Carlton J. H. Hayes, informed a surprised Gómez-Jordana of the news at 2 a.m. on the very day of the operation. The presence of Allied troops on the other side of the Straits of Gibraltar and along the Spanish Moroccan border was sufficient to put an end to Franco's interventionist airs. Apart from the inability of Spain to react militarily, Hayes handed over to Gómez-Jordana a personal

[63] *Dez Anos de Política Externa*, vol. x, 3131. M. S. Gómez de las Heras y E. Sacristán, 'España y Portugal durante la Segunda Guerra Mundial', *Espacio, Tiempo y Forma. Historia Contemporánea*, 2 (1989), 209–25. J. C. Jiménez Redondo, 'La política del Bloque Ibérico. Las relaciones hispano-portuguesas (1936–1949)', *Mélanges de la Casa de Velázquez*, 29/3 (1993), 175–201.

[64] P. Preston, 'Franco and his generals, 1939–1945', in P. Preston, *The Politics of Revenge. Fascism and the Military in 20th Century Spain* (London, 1995), 85–198.

[65] D. Smyth, 'Screening "Torch": Allied Counter-Intelligence and the Spanish Threat to the Secrecy of the Allied Invasion of French North Africa in November, 1942', *Intelligence and National Security*, 4/2 (1989), 335–56.

letter from Roosevelt to Franco in which the former assured that 'these moves are in no shape, manner or form directed against the Government or people of Spain ... Spain has nothing to fear from the United Nations.'[66]

As news arrived of the Allied victories in North Africa, Spanish diplomacy began to regain its neutralist complexion. Progressively, public identification with the Axis and abuse of the democracies gave way to a generic anti-Communist denunciation and the binding of Spain with the Vatican. As Gómez-Jordana recalled at the end of November 1942: 'It is not exactly that we are in favour of the Axis but rather against Communism.' Meanwhile, Franco began calling for peace between the Axis and Anglo-Saxon countries to avoid the propagation of Soviet influence over Europe. In a speech on 9 May 1943 he claimed: 'We think it foolish to delay peace. I say this because behind the façade lies something worse: Communism ... Russian barbarism waiting for its prey.'[67]

The invasion of Sicily and the fall of Mussolini in July 1943 hastened Spain's return to neutrality. Conscious of their powerful position, the Allies (particularly the US) began to press Madrid to cease all kinds of covert aid to Germany. At the end of September, Franco announced the disbanding of the Blue Division. The withdrawal came into effect in the middle of November (though one battalion of volunteers remained with the German army until February 1944). On 1 October 1943 Franco once again decreed 'strict neutrality' of Spain in the war. Seven days later he accepted, without protest, Portugal's decision to allow the Allies to use military bases in the Azores.

Anglo-American pressure intensified at the beginning of 1944. On 28 January, the US imposed an embargo on fuel until Franco's regime met the Allied demands. Shortly afterwards, the same measure was applied to the export of wool, causing a crisis in the Catalan textile industry. Confronted with the prospect of a total economic collapse, Franco gave way because 'Spain was in no condition to be intransigent.' By virtue of the agreement signed on 2 May 1944, the Spanish government promised to expel all German agents reported for espionage or sabotage; to halt all logistical support for German military forces in ports

[66] C. J. H. Hayes, *Wartime Mission in Spain, 1942–1945* (New York, 1945); Beaulac, *Franco. Silent Ally*, 19–20; C. R. Halstead, 'Historians in Politics: Carlton J. H. Hayes as American Ambassador to Spain, 1942–1945', *Journal of Contemporary History*, 7/3 (1975), 383–405; Herbert Feis, *The Spanish Story: Franco and the Nations at War* (New York, 1948).

[67] Reproduced in *Extremadura. Diario Católico*, 10 May 1943. Research Department, Foreign Office, *Spanish Neutrality as Reflected in the Press*, 6 December 1944. FO 371/49574 Z1063.

and airfields; and to virtually suspend wolfram exports (a total of 580 tons for 1944 as against 1,309 tons in 1943).[68] Nevertheless, Franco extended until the end of the war certain covert military facilities to Germany, as well as a profitable smuggling of wolfram and raw materials. By contrast, Spanish authorities slowly relaxed its restrictions on refugees and Jews entering the country, as Allied interest in their fate became more public. Probably 30,000 refugees passed through Spain during the whole of the war although only about 300 remained in the country.[69]

In short, at the close of the war, Franco bent to Anglo-American demands, determined to survive the collapse of the Axis. To this end he called on the anti-Communism and Catholicism of his regime and began a propaganda operation destined to portray himself as the 'sentry of the west' and 'the man who, with skilful prudence, had stood up to Hitler and preserved Spanish neutrality.' Simultaneously, the press began bedevilling Serrano Suñer, attributing to him sole responsibility for Spain's identification with the Axis during his ministerial term.

Guided by José Félix de Lequerica (foreign minister after Gómez-Jordana's death in August 1944), Francoist foreign policy concentrated on winning America's favour and sounding the alarm about the Soviet menace. With this aim, on 7 November 1944, in declarations to the United Press, Franco defined his regime for the first time as a Catholic 'organic democracy', adding that 'the international policy of the United States in no way contradicts the ideology of Spain'. He also stated that Spain had 'honourably maintained a policy of complete neutrality' and had never identified itself with the Axis because 'Spain could never identify herself ideologically with nations not guided by the principle of Catholicism.'[70] On 11 April 1945 the Caudillo severed diplomatic relations with Japan, a former partner in the Anti-Comintern Pact, using as a pretext a series of incidents that had previously happened in the Philippines.

In spite of the neutral façade, the defeat of Germany in May 1945 meant the beginning of a purgatory for the Francoist regime. Two months earlier, Roosevelt wrote to his ambassador in Madrid explaining that he could 'see no place in the community of nations for governments founded on Fascist principles'. While he had no intention of intervening

[68] James W. Cortada, *Relaciones España–USA, 1941–1945* (Barcelona, 1973). Memo by Sir Samuel Hoare, 1 May 1944. FO 371/49612 Z7075.

[69] See Antonio Marquina and Gloria Espina, *España y los judíos en el siglo XX. La acción exterior* (Madrid, 1987); Haim Avni, *España, Franco y los judíos* (Madrid, 1982).

[70] *Pensamiento político de Franco*, ed. Agustín del Río Cisneros (Madrid, 1964), 415–16.

in Spanish internal affairs, American political and economic aid was impossible while Franco remained in power. On 19 June, the founding conference of the United Nations Organisation (UN) in San Francisco (to which Spain had not been invited) approved without any opposition a Mexican proposal to forbid expressly the entry of Francoist Spain into the UN. Finally, when the Allied conference of Potsdam drew to a close, Stalin, Truman, and Attlee issued a joint declaration on the 'Spanish question' on 2 August which confirmed the condemnation of Francoist Spain to international ostracism 'in view of its origins, its nature and its close association with the Aggressor States'.[71]

The Caudillo hastened to confront this pressure from abroad with a 'policy of patience' disguised by an operation of cosmetic constitutionalism. The aim was to satisfy western democratic sensibilities and check the demands for an immediate monarchial restoration in Spain. Franco was convinced that antagonism between the United States and the Soviet Union would soon break out in Europe, and that the former would resort to the services of Spain because of its incalculable strategic value and firm anti-Communist stance. Until this situation arrived, he held the belief that the Anglo-Saxon powers would not take any serious measures against his regime, either militarily or economically, through fear of facilitating the expansion of Communism or a reopening of the civil war. Therefore, this policy of patience obliged a closing of ranks around the regime, either willingly or by force, and obsessive recall of the Communist danger and the possibility of the vengeful return of the defeated Republicans. In the words of Carrero Blanco to Franco on 29 August 1945:

> With the last shot in the Pacific has begun the diplomatic war between the Anglo-Saxons and Russia ... For this fundamental reason of *cold interest*, the Anglo-Saxons not only will not support, but will oppose anything that may bring about a situation of Soviet hegemony in the Iberian peninsula ... They are interested in preserving order and anti-communism over here ... The only formula for us can be none other than: *order, unity and endurance*.[72]

This political calculation turned out to be correct. The growing atmosphere of Cold War prevailing after August 1945 became the salvation of the Francoist regime. Not surprisingly, the British and American authorities, between the alternatives of supporting an inoffensive Franco or

[71] E. Moradiellos, 'The Potsdam Conference and the Spanish Problem', *Contemporary European History*, 10/1 (2001), 73–90. Florentino Portero, *Franco aislado. La cuestión española, 1945–1950* (Madrid, 1989).

[72] Report reproduced in Portero, *Franco aislado*, 105–6.

provoking political instability, resolved to bear his presence as a lesser evil and preferable to another civil war or a Communist regime in the peninsula. And that despite the profound personal and political displeasure that he caused in official spheres and their respective public opinions. The 'stigma of the Axis' as an 'original sin' condemned Franco's Spain to political and diplomatic isolation. However, it in no way justified the adoption of economic or military sanctions with a view to eliminating Franco's regime. In the end, it would not even prevent its formal reintegration into the western orbit, though it was as a junior partner, despised for its political structure and recent past. Franco was not wrong when he declared in September 1953, after signing the Hispano-American military collaboration Agreement: 'At last I have won the Civil War.'[73] He had also put an end to his brief sentence of toothless ostracism imposed on account of his less than neutral conduct during the Second World War.

[73] Cited by George Hills, *Franco. El hombre y su nación* (Madrid, 1969), 430.

CHAPTER 11

# *Portuguese neutrality in the Second World War*

*Fernando Rosas*

The purpose of this chapter is to analyse, in a summarised form, the conditions which made it possible for Portugal – a small and peripheral country – to declare and maintain its neutrality during the Second World War. We will analyse the structural conditions – or geo-strategic conditions – which lay at the basis of the Portuguese declaration of neutrality and its different phases of evolution throughout the conflict, and conclude with a brief examination of the factors which might have contributed to its success.

## THE LUSO-BRITISH ALLIANCE AS THE KEY STRATEGIC FACTOR IN PORTUGUESE FOREIGN POLICY

On the eve of the Second World War, Portugal was a country with the singular characteristic of being simultaneously at the edge of Europe, while being relatively dependent on the 'centre' of Europe's political and economic system, and of having a relatively large colonial empire in Asia, equatorial Africa, and especially in Southern Africa (Angola and Mozambique).

Portugal's peripheral situation was manifest in its special bilateral relationship with Britain and in the double dependency which resulted from this association. It was, firstly, a strategic dependency: as the principal maritime power and main imperial power in southern Africa, Britain historically provided security for the communications and trade routes between Portugal and its colonies. Britain also guaranteed the integrity and subsistence of these colonies. This was a situation which was founded in the terms of the 'old alliance' of 1386, and renewed by the Treaty of Windsor, in 1899. It has to be added that, quite apart from their – much debated – economic importance to Portugal, the Portuguese colonies were unanimously considered by the Portuguese political and intellectual élite as an essential precondition for the maintenance of Portuguese independence in the face of the traditional annexationist intentions of its powerful Spanish neighbour.

Secondly, there was an economic dependency on Britain which, by the end of the 1930s, could be observed in the fact that Britain was still the main importer, supplier, and foreign investor in the Portuguese economy.[1] This meant that for successive Portuguese governments in the first half of this century, the maintenance of the Luso-British alliance was beyond discussion, regardless of what kind of regime was in power. It was for Salazarism, as it had been for the first liberal Republic, and before that the constitutional monarchy, an unavoidable fact of political and economic life. For these governments, the maintenance of colonial and national sovereignty and the essential functioning of the domestic economy depended largely on British goodwill and on Britain's commitment to the alliance. If for London the alliance was a diplomatic instrument whose obligations were only taken seriously when Britain's vital interests were at stake, for Lisbon it was nothing short than essential for Portugal's survival as a state.

For the Estado Novo, established under Antonio Salazar in 1931, any orientation of foreign policy that did not have the alliance as its central pillar, which did not in effect comply with British international interests and priorities, was unthinkable. All three of the principal strategic purposes of the 'Atlanticist' foreign policy defined by Salazar in 1935 had as their common thread the preservation of the Luso-British alliance:[2] (1) the protection of the 'empire' from the appetite of the Great Powers, (2) the defence of Portuguese national independence from the 'Spanish danger', and (3) the preservation of his regime from the opposition 'Reviralhista' at home,[3] and the Communist threat from abroad, particularly in the form of the republican movement in Spain.[4]

[1] On Anglo-Portuguese economic relations in the period see Fernando Rosas, *O Estado Novo nos Anos Trinta* (Lisbon, 1986). Glyn Stone, *The Oldest Ally. Britain and the Portuguese Connection 1936–1941* (Woodbridge, 1994) and 'The Official British Attitude to the Anglo-Portuguese Alliance, 1910–1945', *Journal of Contemporary History*, 10/4 (1975), 729–46.

[2] Official note of 20 September 1935 in Oliveira Salazar, *Discursos e Notas Políticas*, vol. II, 65 ff.

[3] 'Reviralhista' was the name given to the revolutionary republican resistance against the military dictatorship and the *Estado Novo* at the end of the 1920s and during the 1930s, meaning the ones who wanted to 'turn' or return to the situation of the 1st republic.

[4] See Fernando Rosas, 'A Neutralidade Portuguesa Durante a II Guerra Mundial no Quadro da Política Externa do estado Novo (1935–45)', in Hipolito de la Torre (ed.), *Portugal, España y Europa, cien años de desafio* (Merida, 1991).

THE TACIT REVISION OF THE ALLIANCE TERMS IN THE AFTERMATH OF THE SPANISH CIVIL WAR

The new element to influence the terms of the alliance in the second half of the 1930s resulted from changes in the international situation, marked by the heightened sense of tension in Europe, and the emergence of a continental power, Germany, capable of challenging Britain's maritime hegemony. The Portuguese government's exploitation of this situation to broaden its room for manoeuvre – especially regarding the Spanish Civil War and a short but extremely strained period in Luso-British relations, particularly in 1937 – can be regarded as a tacit revision of the terms of the alliance.[5] Portuguese neutrality during the war was to be the main fruit of this process.

However, even in the context of the conflict in Spain, Salazar 'did not cross any Rubicon that would alienate Portugal from the English policy for the Peninsula'.[6] Though it resisted, postponed and evaded the issues – always with the objective of gaining time and further advantages for the Nationalists' cause – during these years Lisbon ultimately ended up complying with Britain's views. It adhered to the Non-intervention Committee, accepted the fiscalisation of the borders with Spain and deliberately delayed granting official recognition to Franco's regime in Burgos.[7] In all these cases, while Portugal negotiated hard on every point, it was always careful to avoid any action which might be construed as a departure from the Anglophile orientation of its foreign policy.

In reality, only in extreme situations, in which the defence of the regime (as in the case of the Spanish Civil War) or the sovereignty of the country ran counter to Britain's immediate interests, did the Salazarist government run the risk of initiating crises in the alliance, by arguing or resisting British demands. In so doing, however, Portugal always kept in mind the fact that Britain's demands or threats were conditioned by the actions of other counter-powers in the international system. And she always acted in such a way as not to risk the existence of the old treaties, even at the height of the harsh political and economic disputes of the Second World War.

The expanded room for relative autonomous action by Lisbon, provided by the changes in the international situation, permitted a

[5] Fernando Rosas, *O Salazarismo e a Aliança Luso-Britânica* (Lisbon, 1988), 33 ff.

[6] José Medeiros Ferreira, 'Características históricas da política externa portuguesa entre 1890 e a entrada na ONU', *Política Internacional*, 1/6 (1993), 139.

[7] See César Oliveira, *Salazar e a Guerra Civil de Espanha* (Lisbon, 1987), 303 ff.

redefinition of Portuguese attitudes towards Great Britain, even although they remained restricted to within the limits of the alliance. As will be seen, some innovative characteristics of the Portuguese declaration of neutrality at the beginning of the war resulted from this redefinition.

## CONDITIONING ELEMENTS AND CHARACTERISTICS OF THE PORTUGUESE DECLARATION OF NEUTRALITY

Whether it was Britain's strategic interests, or Salazar's personal and political experience (formed as a university student and doutrinador in the aftermath of the First World War), or even the particular characteristics of the Second World War, all pressures seemed to propel the regime necessarily towards the option of neutrality. The war of 1939 appeared to be, at its outset, an overwhelmingly ideological struggle between 'democracy' and 'totalitarianism'. For some, the authoritarian, anti-liberal, and anti-democratic Portugal appeared to align itself with those who challenged the interests of Portugal's old ally and the guarantor of Portuguese continental and colonial sovereignty. For others, Portugal seemed to be a cautious ally of Britain, especially when faced with the danger of a Francoist Spain, based on German–Italian support and espousing a 'New Spain' which called into question Portugal's independent position in the peninsula. In certain Spanish circles, the appetite for expansion into Portugal was no secret. Any rash action on Portugal's behalf might jeopardise either the empire, Portuguese independence or, at the very least, the existence of Salazar's regime. Even standing aloof from the conflict was no guarantee that the inevitable shock waves of war would not inflict damage on Portuguese interests.

Therefore, as well as the persistent rejection of the political–ideological character of the conflict, the central concern of Portuguese foreign policy since the end of the Spanish Civil War was to distance Portugal from the imminent world conflict. The policy of neutrality, defined in an official note on 1 September 1939, immediately following the German attack on Poland, emerged as a way of guaranteeing the great strategic objectives of Portuguese foreign policy as we have defined them, that is, in a context of unaltered fidelity to the British alliance.

As has been seen, Lisbon knew how to take advantage of the international circumstances surrounding the Spanish Civil War in order to gain some room for manoeuvre in its relations with Britain. In a sense, Portugal was trying to redefine the terms of the alliance without abandoning those aspects which it considered essential for its own interests.

This experience gave rise to some of the innovative characteristics of Portugal's declaration of neutrality of 1 September:

(a) Portugal's declaration of neutrality was 'unilateral'. The initiative came from Lisbon, and although the British Foreign Office was consulted prior to the declaration it was in no way a response to a British request. This was quite different from the events in August 1914, when Bernardino Machado's ministry was unsure of what action to take and willingly agreed with the policy suggestions proposed by London.
(b) Portugal's declaration was of 'neutrality' and not of 'non-belligerency', as had been the case in 1914. In articulating a policy of neutrality, Lisbon wished to place a greater distance and autonomy between it and London, even though, on both sides, such neutrality was accepted and understood within the framework of the alliance. This was especially the case regarding economic warfare matters where Lisbon hoped for sufficient latitude to enable it to articulate its neutrality in a more balanced or 'collaborative' fashion, depending on the political–military conjuncture of the moment, and with an eye to the fabulous business opportunities which looked set to open up with both belligerent sides.
(c) Lisbon also hoped to pursue a 'politically active' neutrality within the alliance and thereby avoid being marginalised. London attributed a vital role to Portugal's non-alignment in the conflict, especially in ensuring the neutralisation of the Iberian peninsula. Since the end of the Spanish Civil War, Salazar had frequently drawn to London's attention the potential threat posed to British interests in the North Atlantic by the existence of Franco's regime, as an ally of Germany and Italy. The need to guarantee the security of Gibraltar, the western access to the Mediterranean, and the Portuguese coast and its archipelagos (both pivotal to the defence of the Atlantic sea lanes), not only led Britain to improve its relations with Franco from the summer of 1937, but also encouraged it to see Portuguese neutrality as an essential condition if Spain were not to enter the war on the Axis side.

This meant that London accepted and actively supported the good offices provided and developed by a neutral Portugal and its ambassador in Madrid, Pedro Teotónio Pereira, in the hope that through Portugal's intercession with Franco and his regime, Spanish belligerency might be averted. Pereira's private correspondence with Salazar sheds particular light on three important components of this work: (1) the important role of the Portuguese government's action in containing the Germanophile and interventionist faction of Franco's regime, which has been until now underestimated by foreign historians; (2) the close co-ordination, both at a political and economic level, of British and Portuguese diplomacy towards Madrid in an effort to hold Franco back from entering the war; and (3) the role of the Luso-Spanish Friendship and Non-Aggression Pact of 17 March 1939 and of its additional protocol of 29 July 1940. All three aspects were fundamental instruments in British and Portuguese attempts to neutralise the peninsula.[8]

The functions and characteristics of Portuguese neutrality, coupled with the fact that Portugal became a key port of entry and exit from occupied Europe after the fall of France in June 1940, and the exceptional strategic value of the Portuguese Atlantic islands (especially the Azores), gave Lisbon an international role and prominence without precedent in its recent history.

Salazar reaped important domestic political dividends from Portugal's short and golden period as an elevated member of the international community. He was able to negotiate the maintenance of a neutrality which, in its functioning, was favourable to essential Allied interests, in return for their discreet but decisive support in upholding his regime, especially during the agitated period at the end of the war.

## FROM 'GEOMETRIC NEUTRALITY' TO 'COLLABORATIVE NEUTRALITY': THE ACCIDENTS OF PORTUGAL'S POLICY OF NEUTRALITY DURING THE WAR

Portuguese policy of neutrality can be said to have evolved through three distinctive phases during the world conflict:

### *From September 1939 to the summer of 1940*

This was the period of the Phoney War. In relation to Portugal's international standing, this was a phase of little significance. The neutral peninsula was far from the conflict. It was widely believed that the war would be of short duration, and end, after the consolidation of Germany's occupation of Poland, with a new 'Munich' between Hitler and the western 'appeasers', whose governments, after all, had clearly entered

[8] *Correspondência de Pedro Teotónio Pereira com Oliveira Salazar*, vols. I to IV (1939–44), 1989 to 1991.

the war reluctantly, and conducted it with conspicuous circumspection thereafter. From this perspective, neutrality was easily understood and practised as a policy of goodwill towards Britain. It was generally assumed in Lisbon that the new 'Munich' would not bring about any profound change to the relationship between the maritime power of Britain and the continental power of Germany. Portugal's position would therefore remain relatively unchanged.

The peninsula stood outside the conflict and had, at that point, still not attracted the attention of the belligerents. Britain enjoyed good and solid relations with the general political, military, and police circles in Salazar's regime, as well as with the economic and financial community, and was not excessively worried by the burgeoning scale of German propaganda in the country. This was even more so since, despite the official effort to play down the ideological aspect of the conflict, Britain unquestionably benefited from the strong antipathy with which the Church and regime viewed Hitler's ungodly pact with Stalin and his ferocious assault on conservative and Catholic Poland. A 'close cooperation' of the British services with the censorship and the generally anglophile attitude of the press secured a comfortable supremacy for British interests in the country.

## *From June 1940 to November 1942*

This was the most critical phase in Luso-British relations, during which the collaborative attitude which had previously underpinned Portuguese neutrality was replaced by a more balanced or 'geometric' relationship. Portugal conceded significant political and economic favours to Hitler's Germany, but was careful not to put at risk the essential terms of its old alliance with Britain.

Several factors helped bring about this change in Lisbon's foreign policy, in particular factors relating to the evolution of the war and to Portugal's own bilateral relations with the British:

1. The dramatic change in the course of the war favouring Germany after the resounding success of its Western offensive, in June 1940, placed German Panzer divisions in the Pyrenees and prompted German planners to consider the possibility of executing Operation Felix,[9] the seizure of Gibraltar and eventual invasion of Portugal. Surrounded by an aura

[9] 'Operation Felix' was the codename given by the German War Directive No. 18, of 12 November 1940, for an attack on Gibraltar and the subsequent invasion of Portugal. See Rosas, *O Salazarismo e a Aliança Luso-Britânica*, 121–5.

of invincibility, Germany sharpened the tone of its political and even military demands in Portugal.[10]

2. For Portugal, the German menace was inextricably bound up with the threat posed by Franco's Spain. The German victories and the entry of Fascist Italy into the war on 10 June, lent weight to calls from the Falange for Spain's active belligerency in the war, commencing with a joint Spanish–German attack on Gibraltar. This also provoked a resurgence of Spanish Irredentist feeling towards Portugal, a country which the Falange had long considered a suitable target for Spain's 'imperial' expansion. Far from soothing Lisbon's anxieties, Spain's unexpected declaration of 'non-belligerency', on 13 June 1940, merely underscored the difference between the two countries, coinciding as it did with Portugal's simultaneous reaffirmation of its neutrality. Teotónio Pereira's skilful negotiation of an additional protocol to the Pact of Friendship and Non-Aggression of 1939, signed in Lisbon on 29 July, did little to ease tensions between the two countries. Franco, for one, gave little thought to the vague terms of the protocol.

3. The German attack on the Soviet Union, in June 1941, raised throughout Europe the banner of a 'crusade against Bolshevism', and had an immediate effect in Portugal. Politically, it exacerbated the Germanophile, anti-Communist and anti-Allied feelings in the regime circles, with the Portuguese Legion taking a public and official position of support for the Nazi aggression.[11] At the same time, Portugal's cultural and economic links with Berlin were tightened. The announcement of the Anglo-Soviet Alliance of 26 May 1942 obviously strained Lisbon's political relations with Britain. In a speech on 25 June 1942, Salazar indulged in such explicit criticism of the Anglo-Soviet Alliance and democratic systems in general, that the British government felt it necessary to demand an official explanation.[12]

4. Like Hitler, Salazar clearly underestimated the importance of America's entry into the war, after the Japanese attack on Pearl Harbor in December 1941. Nevertheless, for several reasons the regime saw it as a worrying development, particularly in relation to the long-term effect it might have on the outcome of the war. Moreover, it had immediate

[10] The military aspect of this pressure, related to the economic disputes and included the sinking of Portuguese merchant vessels by German U-boats.

[11] The Portuguese Legion's order of 10 July 1941 pledged to Germany 'Portuguese solidarity in her fight against Communism', *Anais da Revolução Nacional*..., vol. V, 219.

[12] Salazar, *Discursos e Notas Políticas*, vol. III, 321 ff.

consequences for the Allied blockade policy, which was much strengthened by American participation. Roosevelt's forthright intention of liquidating the old European empires was also clearly a cause for concern. Finally, America represented the forces of 'mechanic barbarism', which were seen as ideologically and culturally threatening to Portugal's traditional way of life.

5. Secret Anglo-Portuguese conversations for an eventual retreat of the Lisbon government to the Azores, in the event of a German attack on Gibraltar (1940–2), were both inconclusive and prolonged, on account of the divergent opinions over the correct moment and conditions in which such an evacuation should take place, and the level of destruction required to hold up a German advance in Portugal.[13] This issue was seriously complicated by the discovery, in early 1942, of a clandestine British organisation in Portugal, tasked with executing acts of sabotage in the event of the Portuguese government reneging on its commitments or failing to stand up to German demands.[14]

6. The Australian and Dutch landings in Timor, on 17 December 1941, without Portugal's previous knowledge and without its consent – despite Portuguese conversations with London on the subject – almost led to the temporary severance or suspension of diplomatic relations between the two countries.[15]

7. The extremely hard and prolonged dispute over Britain's imposition of an economic blockade on 'adjacent neutrals', the conditions of its application and the effects it had on the general standard of living in Portugal, as well as the functioning of the Portuguese economy, created great strain in bilateral relations.[16]

8. Last, but not least, until mid-1942 Salazar held to his conviction that this would be a war 'with neither winners nor losers'. Salazar certainly did not believe in a German victory but, equally, he did not

[13] For Lisbon's attitude towards the Azores see Antonio Telo, *Os Açores e o controlo do Atlântico 1898–1948* (Oporto, 1993), 289–349.

[14] The organisation was to diffuse pro-British propaganda and organise acts of sabotage and armed resistance to a German invasion. It involved employees of the Shell oil company as well as members of the opposition and even members of the Portuguese Communist Party. See Júlia Leitão de Barros, 'O Caso Schell: a rede espionagem anglo-portuguesa (1940–1942)', *História* (1991), 54–83.

[15] For the Timor incident, see Carlos Teixeira da Motta, *O Caso de Timor na II Guerra Mundial* (Lisbon, 1999), esp. 54–103.

[16] See Fernando Rosas, *Portugal entre a Paz e a Guerra* (Lisbon, 1990). For studies in English on the wolfram issue: Douglas L. Wheeler, 'The Price of Neutrality: Portugal, the Wolfram Question, and World War II', *Luso-Brazilian Review*, 23, 1 (1986), 107–22; 23, 2 (1986), 97–111, and Christian Leitz, *Economic Relations between Nazi Germany and Franco's Spain, 1936–1945* (Oxford, 1996), 170–99.

believe a British triumph was possible. As he admitted to Teotónio Pereira, it looked as if the war would be resolved in a 'compromise peace.'[17] Moreover, Salazar believed that in the search for this settlement and in the discussions over the re-organisation of the post-war world, the 'Latin and Christian block' of conservative regimes (i.e. Spain, Portugal, and Vichy France) might come to play a decisive role: one which would be politically, culturally, and strategically extensive to South America. Behind Salazar's efforts to keep the South American countries out of the war lay a hope of containing the rising influence of the United States.

All these reasons led the Anglophile sections of the Salazar regime to draw back, and Portugal's previous policy of a collaborative neutrality was shifted towards a more equidistant policy of collaboration with both sides. For a brief period, the collaboration would be more inclined towards Germany.

## *From November 1942 to 1945*

The end of the year 1942 saw the upturn in Allied military fortunes: the defeat of Rommel in El Alamein, in Egypt; the first American victories in the Pacific; the dangerous German impasse in Stalingrad; and, on 8 November, the beginning of the Anglo-American landing in Northern Africa (Operation Torch). For Allied strategy in the peninsula and for their relations with Salazar and Franco, the winter of 1942/3 marked a turning-point. The German threat to Gibraltar and the peninsula slowly evaporated, while American troops now stood at Europe's doors, occupying and administrating French Northern Africa.

Generally, it could be said that the Allies, with their eyes set firmly on the great offensive operations in Europe, placed political–strategic questions above the more contentious measures of economic warfare. Although the latter were tightened or relaxed according to the strategic needs of the moment, there was in general a clear toughening of Allied blockade practices after this time, as the Allies endeavoured to capitalise on their new position of strength and galvanise their economic warfare campaign in support of their land and air offensives.

In addition, in relation to Portugal, it was understood that the survival of Salazar and his regime would be called into question if the Portuguese continued to resist demands which the Allies considered politically vital.

[17] *Correspondência de Pedro Teotónio Pereira com Oliveira Salazar*, vol. II, p. 480.

This was certainly the case regarding the two great disputes of the period: Britain's request for military facilities in the Azores Islands in 1943, and the demand for an embargo on the sale of wolfram to Germany the following year.

It is clear that on the British side, especially in the Foreign Office, direct confrontation was eschewed whenever possible and preference given to finding a diplomatic solution to the two countries' economic disputes. In principle, maintaining Salazar in power was the most convenient way for Britain to achieve its interests in the country. It is, however, unquestionable that the relationship between the two countries had changed; when the British addressed demands to the Portuguese, they did so as the future victors. Thus, in May 1944 Salazar came close to being overthrown by a London-backed initiative, when his refusal, to implement an embargo on wolfram exports to Germany exhausted Britain's patience. The Allies were by this date no longer prepared to tolerate delays, refusals, or compromises, when these might have a direct bearing on the conduct of decisive military operations. Salazar was compelled to give in to the essential Allied demands, despite his preference for resistance, which at times verged on the suicidal.

Salazar knew where the winds of victory were blowing from. Already in 1942 he no longer had any doubts about Germany's chances of resistance. He also knew that part of the very serious and disquieting economic and social difficulties which lay ahead would have unforeseeable consequences for Portugal. Salazar believed that the root cause of these difficulties was to be found in the Allied blockade, and that they could be easily aggravated if the Allies chose to adopt reprisals or discriminatory measures against Lisbon. He was aware that the future of his regime was at risk, and that it was time to redefine its foreign positioning and return to a 'collaborative neutrality'. There was no alternative and the issue therefore merely revolved around whether he could sell this neutrality at the highest price, and extract as much profit as possible.

There are three reasons for this attitude. Firstly, Salazar hoped to sever any perceived link between the outcome of the war and his regime's destiny. At the same time, he wished to guarantee his government's sovereignty by making it clear that he would not meekly accept any harmful effects to Portugal's internal order which an Allied victory might bring in its wake. Secondly, Salazar recognised that it was absolutely vital for Portugal to obtain significant concessions in terms of fuel, food, essential raw material supplies, and merchant tonnage, which were necessary to alleviate the social–economic crisis which threatened the country. Finally,

Salazar sought to sell Portuguese 'neutrality' in return for benevolent Allied support for his regime at home and the empire across the globe.

Even though he frequently failed to appreciate the real gravity of the situation and extent of the risks he faced in mid-1944, Salazar nevertheless showed acute intuition, conceding only at that moment when any further intransigence would have meant courting political suicide. This was the case in both great disputes of that period – the Azores and wolfram – and it permitted Salazar to safeguard the objective which he held most dear: the survival of his regime.[18]

At the end of the war, despite tough disputes, bartering, compromises, and domestic troubles, in exchange for the Azores and wolfram, Salazar managed to achieve what was essential in his objectives concerning the Allies. Confronted with a possible political crisis in Portugal at the end of the war, the Allies clearly favoured maintaining Salazar's regime, even actively, and were prepared to safeguard Portugal's colonies.[19] Lisbon managed to ensure that part of its most pressing needs were met, both in its agreement over British access to Azores bases on 18 August 1943 and, especially, after agreeing to embargo all exports of wolfram, by securing a favourable trade agreement on 26 January 1945. Finally, Lisbon succeeded in safeguarding its 'war-businesses', and accumulated substantial quantities of gold and foreign exchange, which were to be used to promote economic growth and social harmony in the post-war period.

## THE CONDITIONS IN WHICH IT WAS POSSIBLE TO MAINTAIN A POLICY OF NEUTRALITY

In the light of the principles of foreign policy defined and practised by the Estado Novo since the mid 1930s, it is possible to advance some general conclusions on the significance of the neutrality adopted by Lisbon during the Second World War, trying also to understand how its maintenance was possible throughout the diverse phases of the world conflict.

First of all, it is necessary to understand the viability of the policy of neutrality in the framework of the Luso-British alliance and, as such, as an expression of Britain's strategic interests with regard to the preparation and conduct of the war; that is, as a central element in achieving Britain's

[18] See António Telo, *Portugal na Segunda Guerra Mundial (1939–1945)*, vol. I (Lisbon, 1991), 137 ff.

[19] In exchange for the military facilities obtained in the Azores, Britain and the USA committed themselves to respect and defend the integrity of Portugal's colonial possessions, specifically Timor, which was still under Japanese occupation. The American commitment played a definite role at the end of the war, by blocking Australian attempts to gain control of Timor after the Japanese surrender.

objective of securing the neutralisation of the peninsula. Portuguese neutrality and its efforts to neutralise Franco's regime, through political and economic means, was of no marginal importance to British efforts to survive the German challenge. This policy could be considered to have been achieved in its essentials by the autumn of 1942.

Against the wishes of Francoist Spain, the political content of such neutrality became more directly and immediately 'collaborative' and pro-Allied, notwithstanding the tough and permanent negotiations to which Salazar always subjected the rendering of requested services: the concession to Britain (18 August 1943), and later America (18 July 1944), of military bases in the Azores, or the embargo on wolfram exports to Germany on 5 June 1944.

The collaborative complexion of the Portuguese neutrality was, however, usually more apparent in its political aspects than it was in the area of economic warfare and war economics. In this field, Salazar was anxious to maximise the economic and commercial advantages to Portugal in the Allied markets whilst at the same time conceding some economic concessions to Germany. To achieve this end, Salazar deliberately interpreted neutrality in a more equidistant fashion. Concessions to Germany were designed not only to placate the pressures of a Great Power whose divisions were stationed in the Pyrenees, but also, from 1943–4 to prevent the total collapse of a country that Salazar regarded as the last defensive bastion against the Slav, Bolshevic menace from the East.

It is necessary to note, however, that dissension between Lisbon and London, whether in the political sphere (the Azores question, or East Timor), or in the economic domain (the functioning of the blockade, the embargo on wolfram), never assumed such proportions as to jeopardise either the existence of the alliance or Portugal's policy of neutrality.

Of course, on each side there were different 'sensitivities' regarding the role and functioning of the neutrality. On the part of the British government, it was a question of making the most out of Portuguese neutrality, especially in decisive moments of defence (1939–42) and counter-attack (1943–5). For Lisbon, on the other hand, it was a question of conducting a pro-British neutrality without running the risk of provoking German–Spanish aggression, and of taking advantage of the tensions between the Great Powers in order to create room for the 'autonomous' development of the Portuguese economy. An analysis of the main disputes between the Allies and Lisbon allows us to conclude, however, that not only were these disputes never allowed to undermine the essential relationship between the two sides, but that they were always, in the end and despite Salazar's penchant for bartering, resolved in the Allies' favour.

The second fundamental characteristic of Portuguese neutrality was that despite being in essence a British policy, it never ceased to be an option which simultaneously satisfied Portugal's national interests, those of its ruling classes, and enjoyed a large measure of public support. On the one hand, neutrality was as far as Portugal could go without jeopardising its alliance with Britain and the Portuguese interests guaranteed by the alliance. On the other hand, neutrality represented the only possible policy in face of a possible German–Spanish attack, which might have resulted in an occupation of Portuguese continental territory and, more than likely, an end to Salazar and his regime.

From a political point of view it must also be said that Salazar managed to safeguard his regime in return for Portuguese neutrality during and after the war, through the support of the Anglo-American allies. During the conflict, London used opposition circles to keep the pressure up on Salazar's regime and to act as a possible nucleus for military resistance in the case of a Nazi invasion. The Allies never used the opposition, however, with the intention of overthrowing the regime, despite Salazar's own delusions on the matter. On the contrary, with the exception of a brief altercation over Portugal's continued export of wolfram in 1944, the Allies, publicly and in private, strenuously denied any intention of putting the Salazarist regime under threat.

It must not be forgotten that, economically, the conflict would come to represent an exceptional opportunity for Portugal's industrial and commercial bourgeoisie in various ways. It allowed the accumulation of public and private capital, via fabulous 'war businesses' connected with domestic supplies and exports to lucrative markets. It provided an impulse to the process of industrialisation and import substitution and intensified the economic occupation of the colonies by the metropolitan capital. The war would be connected in Portugal not only with the most important period of industrialisation the country had ever experienced, but also as a turning-point in the Portuguese colonisation of its 'empire', established with the export of metropolitan capital and in its productive investment in the African colonies.

It may not be unfair to say that the political forces opposed to Salazarism never really offered an alternative to the policy of neutrality. An attentive re-examination of the positions of the diverse forces within the clandestine opposition to the regime (as with the whole of the opposition when it organised itself as a unified front from 1943, the Anti-Fascist

National Unit Movement – MUNAF) allows us to draw some conclusions: from a political position which was markedly partisan towards British interests, the Liberal Democrats, as well as the Portuguese Communist Party (with the exception of the period between the Hitler–Stalin Pact and Germany's attack on the USSR),[20] never formulated a policy that would be more than just a reflection of their anglophile inclinations. For the same reason, the opposition did not represent, in their attitude towards the war, a real alternative to the regime, but functioned instead as merely a radical wing of the anglophiles.

Finally, it should be mentioned that, while it was, in its essentials, a policy which suited both Britain and Portugal, Salazar's neutrality could never have been maintained had it not been, at certain moments and in certain ways, also a policy that suited Hitler as well. This was especially the case during the critical period from 1939 to 1942. Berlin gained undeniable advantages in having a neutral Portugal, capable of buying oil and its derivatives from the USA, phosphates from northern Africa, and several colonial raw materials of equally important strategic interest, all of which, despite the British blockade, were sent on, legally or illegally, to Germany. These lines of commerce and supply would inevitably have been lost to Germany had she occupied the peninsula. Such an occupation would have left the Portuguese colonies at Britain's mercy, and given London a heaven-sent excuse to seize the Portuguese archipelagos in the Atlantic.

To Hitler's strategists the advantages of occupying Portugal in 1940 and 1941 seemed greater than the disadvantages already mentioned. Portuguese neutrality was thus seriously threatened at a time when Britain was capable of offering no tangible assistance. Only contingent circumstances during the first half of 1941 – the need for German divisions to move to the Balkans, and the later attack on Soviet Russia – led to the cancellation of the projected invasion and to the maintenance of Portuguese neutrality in the conflict. Fate would also be an important factor in the maintenance of Portuguese neutrality and therefore of Salazar's enviable ability to survive.

[20] Fernando Rosas, 'O PCP e a II Guerra Mundial', *Estudos sobre o Comunismo* (1983), 2–26.

CHAPTER 12

# *Irish neutrality in the Second World War*

*Eunan O'Halpin*

Irish neutrality in the Second World War cannot be understood without reference to the overwhelming influence of the legacy of the independence struggle on Anglo-Irish relations, on Irish foreign policy considerations, and on the Irish public's perceptions of where the new state's interests lay and who its natural enemies were.

Independent Ireland was the product of the Anglo-Irish treaty of 6 December 1921, under which twenty-six counties of the 32-county island were recognised as a separate dominion within the British empire. The six counties in the north-east of the island had already been separately established as the self-governing province of Northern Ireland, an integral part of the United Kingdom. As Irish separatism had long regarded the national territory as encompassing the entire island of Ireland, and as Northern Ireland contained a large and alienated nationalist minority, many in the new Irish state regarded partition as an unnatural evil, Britain's last malign act before she reluctantly ceded qualified independence to the rest of the country. As head of successive governments from 1932 until 1948, Eamon de Valera constantly characterised partition as the greatest blight on Anglo-Irish relations (although after 1923 he always sought to channel nationalist resentment against it into conventional political channels).[1]

From the first day of its existence, independent Ireland adopted a policy of military neutrality. Although the independence struggle had seen some flickers of ambition for a large-scale military and naval establishment, by the time the state came into being these had evaporated. The rulers of the new Ireland wanted only a small land force capable of subduing internal threats.[2] A determination to stay out of other states' wars spanned the 1922/3 civil war divide within the political elite. However,

[1] John Bowman, *De Valera and the Ulster Question, 1917–1973* (Oxford, 1982), *passim*.

[2] Ibid., 18–42; Sinn Fein publicity leaflet of 1918, quoted in Maire Comerford, *The First Dail January 21st 1919* (Dublin, 1969), 100–1.

after 1922 the most militant anti-treaty republicans pursued opportunistic alliances with what they judged to be Britain's likely enemies, as Irish separatists had done since the late eighteenth century, firstly with the Soviet Union and from 1936 with Hitler's Germany. These links with Germany were to cause acute security and diplomatic difficulties for the state between 1939 and 1945.[3]

Like the new European states which had emerged through the Versailles Peace Conference, Ireland subscribed enthusiastically to the principle of the pacific settlement of international disputes. To Britain's irritation, it quickly joined the League of Nations, despite the implicit dilution of absolute neutrality which membership involved. Ireland displayed considerable commitment to the League for as long as it appeared an effective instrument of international governance: thus the state supported the sanctions imposed on Italy following her invasion of Abyssinia, despite vocal public and clerical support for a fellow Catholic state, and withstood similar confessional pressures to recognise Franco's regime until the Spanish Civil War was effectively over in February 1939.[4] Underpinning this apparently naïve attachment to the ideal of the League were realistic calculations based on the dismal fate of small European states during the First World War: in accepting the League's practical failure in 1937, de Valera observed that the small states of Europe were once more at the mercy of aggressors.[5]

While crucial to the direction of Irish external policy, such principles of international relations were underpinned by an even more fundamental reality: geography. The island of Ireland is the most westerly part of Europe, surrounded on three sides by the Atlantic Ocean, shielded from the continent by the intervening bulk of Great Britain, and sheltered by the British strategic defence umbrella from all likely air and sea attack. Ireland's isolation from mainland Europe was, however, partly offset by another strategic fact of life, her position lying across the trade routes upon which Britain's power in the world depended. The island was, consequently, central to the defence of Great Britain. This had prompted the British government, in reaching an accommodation with Irish separatism in 1921, to insist on elaborate treaty provisions to protect Britain's strategic interests. These covered the retention of naval and

[3] Eunan O'Halpin, *Defending Ireland: The Irish State and its Enemies Since 1922* (Oxford, 1999), 71–3, 126–9.

[4] Michael Kennedy, *Ireland and the League of Nations, 1919–1946: International Relations, Diplomacy and Politics* (Dublin, 1996), 35–6, 211–13, 232–4.

[5] Kennedy, *Ireland and the League of Nations*, 228–35.

communications facilities along the southern and north-western coasts of the new state; the continuation of all 'existing cable rights and wireless concessions'; the right to 'land additional . . . cables' and to set up additional wireless stations; and a right of veto should anyone else seek to set up such facilities. Britain was also accorded 'in time of war or strained relations with a Foreign Power such harbour and other facilities . . . for the purposes of defence' as she might require. The treaty stipulated that 'the defence by sea of Great Britain and Ireland' would be Britain's sole responsibility, although it anticipated that after some time Ireland might undertake 'a share of her own coastal defence'. It also provided a formula restricting the size of any Irish 'military defence force'.[6] While de Valera opposed the treaty on other grounds, the alternative agreement which he canvassed set out to address British defence concerns in much the same manner – as early as February 1920 he had publicly stated in the United States that Britain need never fear that an independent and neutral Ireland would ever pose a threat to her strategic interests.[7] This became a cardinal rule of Irish foreign policy.

Unlike the other British dominions, the new Irish state did not become involved in the ongoing Committee of Imperial Defence (CID) planning processes for concerted imperial defence in a future war. From the Irish point of view, these would have been both domestically embarrassing and strategically pointless: British defence of Ireland from sea or air attack could be taken for granted simply because of geography. For her own reasons, this also suited Britain, where the argument was quietly made during the 1920s and 1930s that for defence purposes Ireland was not a dominion both because of her own defencelessness and because her territory and waters were strategically inseparable from those of the United Kingdom itself.[8]

For a combination of reasons, not least the civil war of 1922/3 and the ongoing problem of republican violence, the new state took little interest in problems of external defence. When that conflict ended in 1923, the army had about 55,000 men. By 1932, when their former *béte noire* de Valera came into office, the defence forces had less than 6,000 men, no reserve worth the name, and virtually no equipment. In 1934 a

6 Articles 6 and 7, and Annex, in 'Articles of Agreement for a Treaty between Great Britain and Ireland', 6 December 1921, in R. Fanning, M. Kennedy, D. Keogh and E. O'Halpin (eds.), *Documents on Irish Foreign Policy*, Volume I: *1919–1922* (Dublin, 1998), 357, 360–1.

7 Bowman, *De Valera and the Ulster Question*, 38–9; 'Proposed Alternative Treaty of Association . . .', 14 December 1921, in *Documents on Irish Foreign Policy*, 363, 366–7.

8 Paul Canning, *British Policy Towards Ireland, 1921–1941* (Oxford, 1985), 176–204. This work deals admirably with Anglo-Irish defence relations.

'Volunteer Force' was established, primarily as a device to bring the bulk of the IRA under government control, but while it served its political purpose of absorbing militarists its defensive value was minimal. As one staff officer put it in unusually forthright terms in 1936, 'external defence . . . has been in the practically unchallenged control of Great Britain for a long period'. Ireland was 'not relatively but absolutely disarmed', yet the public 'do not realise that in the usual European sense' the state had no defence forces at all. This was possible because it 'lies within the sphere of British defence influence and . . . the British forces intervene between it and all other possible external enemies'. Furthermore, such paltry equipment and weapons as the defence forces did have came almost entirely from Britain, thereby compounding Irish dependency on the neighbouring power.[9]

The possibility of maintaining neutrality in a European war involving Britain consequently arose not from the strength of Irish defensive preparations – there were none worth the name – but in a diplomatic triumph achieved in the spring of 1938. Then, in return for the settlement of a financial dispute, the resumption of mutually beneficial trading relations and a reiterated public guarantee that the Irish state would never allow itself to be used to harm Britain's security interests, Britain relinquished her defence rights under the 1921 treaty. This remarkable settlement, on the British side predicated on erroneous assumptions about the likely nature of the coming struggle against Germany and pragmatic calculations about the impossibility of using landlocked facilities without Irish assent, for the first time made Irish neutrality at a time when Britain was at war conceivable. This was because Britain no longer had any bases on Irish territory and no rights to demand them. It is significant that, in addressing this new situation, the government's immediate response was not seriously to build up its largely notional defence forces but, rather, quietly to move to allay British concerns about espionage, security and possible German/IRA activities. This was done through the cautious initiation of contacts between the British security service MI5 and the Irish army's intelligence directorate G2. Apart from very occasional swaps of information on Communist activities, these were the first Anglo-Irish security exchanges since the end of the civil war.[10]

[9] Quoted in O'Halpin, *Defending Ireland*, 136–7.
[10] Canning, *British Policy Towards Ireland*, 140–2; O'Halpin, *Defending Ireland*, 140–2.

For Ireland, the 1938 settlement was decisive in terms of neutrality. The state's willingness to keep to its side of the bargain was soon tested, as G2 and the police began investigating traces of German espionage directed against British, French, and American interests. The state also responded quite firmly to the initiation by the IRA of a bombing campaign in Britain in January 1939 (at the time it was not realised that this campaign had been indirectly encouraged by Germany, as the British had feared). These developments meant that when war came in September 1939 the state had at least limited experience of espionage problems as well as established lines of contact with British security and police organisations.[11]

## DEFENCE AND SECURITY POLICY AND PRACTICE BETWEEN 1939 AND 1945

In September 1939 Ireland had about 6,000 soldiers and airmen scattered in a myriad of ex-British barracks and camps around the state, plus about 13,000 in the largely untrained Volunteer Force and a handful of other reserves. There was no naval arm, no air service worth the name, and no air defence system (in 1940 the state possessed just four searchlights for anti-aircraft defence against a requirement of seventy-two, and one anti-aircraft battery of two 3.7 mm guns plus a few lighter AA weapons). There were acute shortages of all weapons other than rifles and medium machine guns, and apart from a miscellaneous handful of British, Swedish, and improvised Irish armoured cars there were no fighting vehicles. Mortars, artillery, transport, radios, explosives, and ammunition of all types were in short supply. Full mobilisation was ordered on 1 September 1939, but the chief of staff later recalled that 'there were no striking forces available capable of offering prolonged and organised resistance', while the imperative of assigning small groups of troops on internal security duties throughout the state meant 'we were weak everywhere'. Few units had the equipment or transport to operate above company strength, and there was 'almost a complete absence of the most important weapons'. There had been no pre-war manoeuvres of any consequence, and almost every defensive arrangement and security procedure had to be started from scratch. Compounding this

[11] O'Halpin, *Defending Ireland*, 144–9.

parlous situation was the absence of Anglo-Irish dialogue on defence questions.[12]

The defence forces' problems were compounded three months after mobilisation, when the government decided, because nothing much seemed to be happening in Europe, to economise by cutting numbers on full-time service from 19,000 to 13,000 men. Many of those let go simply enlisted in the United Kingdom, a practice that the Irish authorities were unable to prevent. After the fall of France the government issued a renewed call to arms, which within weeks produced 25,000 volunteers for full-time service. The army struggled to cope with this influx while at the same time preparing for a German invasion which for some months was thought to be imminent. They were handicapped in this by three factors: firstly, the acute shortages of weapons and equipment; secondly, the absence of any coherent plan for external defence; and thirdly, the paradox that the only possible source of outside help in the event of a German attack was simultaneously the only other state likely to violate Irish neutrality.

Although secret discussions between Irish and British staff officers in June 1940 laid the foundations of what became quite elaborate plans for joint action in the event of a German invasion (including the destruction of facilities and the establishment of 'stay-behind' groups should the invasion succeed), the Irish defence forces' weapons and equipment problems were never satisfactorily resolved.[13] In addressing Irish requests, the British government had complicated and shifting calculations to make: the desirability of encouraging the Irish to mount some defensive action should Germany intervene had to be set against the danger of providing weapons which conceivably might be turned against Northern Ireland should Germany attack there and invite Irish intervention to regain the lost province. In addition, the more heavily armed the Irish were the better they would be able to resist British moves to seize facilities should these become necessary. Furthermore, Churchill argued that the supply of weapons, like other trade questions, should be treated in terms of the aim of extracting Irish concessions on defence facilities. When the chiefs of staffs recommended the sale of some anti-aircraft artillery in 1941, for example, their recommendation was overruled, much to Irish annoyance: as one officer complained to a visiting American, while Ireland 'would ... fight without the equipment if necessary we would

[12] 'General Report on the Army for the year 1st April 1940 to 31st March 1941', Military Archives, Dublin; Donal O'Carroll, 'The Emergency Army', *The Irish Sword*, 19, 75 and 76 (1993–4), 23–6.

[13] Papers on these discussions released in 1999 are in PRO, HS6/305.

naturally be very sour with our friends if they allowed a situation to arise where we had to fight without equipment while tons ... lay unused within easy reach'.[14] Efforts to secure arms in the United States also fell on deaf ears, primarily because of Roosevelt's hostility to Irish neutrality. In consequence, only dribs and drabs of equipment reached Ireland. In March 1942, an American military observer, while commenting very favourably on the spirit of the army, described its troops as 'very raw', concluded that equipment was so sparse that it would be capable only of a 'spirited but brief resistance to a German invasion', and advised that it would be best to discount it entirely in Allied planning to resist a German attack on Ireland. Even when the army finally completed its planned wartime configuration of two mobile divisions – one guarding the southern and western coastlines against a possible German assault, the other geared to resist a British attack from Northern Ireland – plus supporting units in November 1943, it was, as one historian has written, 'gravely lacking in air support; it had no armour; its artillery ... was well below the desired level; it had little anti-armour defence; and its air defence was seriously inadequate'. However, it is also argued that given the problems which a German amphibious or air expedition would have faced, and the certainty of British participation in resisting any such expedition, the defence forces were by 1943 adequate for their task.[15] It can also fairly be said that, by as early as the spring of 1941, the defence forces were sufficiently well organised to provide sustained resistance to British action. Any British use of force would, in any case, probably have provoked considerable nationalist disruption within Northern Ireland, and might well have threatened discipline amongst the many thousands with Irish backgrounds serving in the British services. It would, furthermore, have brought to an end the very considerable *sub rosa* cooperation which developed after 1939 on a range of matters, from the sharing of meteorological data and coast-watching reports to security, espionage, and counter-intelligence problems. It was this covert cooperation, both on security issues and on operational matters – for example the acceptance of overflights of Irish territory and the provision of navigational aids for aircraft – which sustained Anglo-Irish relations once

[14] Canning, *British Policy towards Ireland*, 291, 302; Col. Mulcahy's report of his talk with Commander Gallery, 31 March 141, NA, DFA A/3; memorandum on his visit to Ireland by R. G. Menzies, prime minister of Australia, undated (between 5 and 10 Apr. 1941), in W. J. Hudson and H. J. W. Stokes (eds.), *Documents on Australian Foreign Policy 1937–49* vol. IV: *July 1940–June 1941* (Canberra, 1980), 552.

[15] Report by Lt-Col. Reynolds, 9 March 1942, quoted in O'Halpin, *Defending Ireland*, 165 and 171; O'Carroll, 'The Emergency Army', 45–6.

the immediate prospect of German invasion had faded by the summer of 1941.

## FOREIGN RELATIONS AND INTERNAL SECURITY BETWEEN 1939 AND 1945

Ireland's adherence to neutrality in September 1939 was domestically highly popular. No significant political figure in any party argued against it, and even de Valera's bitterest enemies saw neutrality both as the litmus test of sovereignty and as the only way of avoiding a civil war. Once the war began, public debate on neutrality and on the course of military affairs abroad was almost completely stifled by the imposition of a remarkably inelastic and thorough press censorship, far stricter than that applied in other neutral states, which made it difficult to publish even the most anodyne remarks in support of one set of belligerents or the other or to question the moral or pragmatic basis of neutrality, which was also used to suppress discussion of domestic economic problems on the grounds that to air such matters would be to imperil national morale, and which even made it impossible for sports reporters to describe the weather conditions at the events they were covering. The only reliable barometers of public opinion during the war were the two general elections of 1943 and 1944, both of them held under conditions unnaturally favourable to the government because of press censorship and both won by de Valera.[16] There is nothing to suggest that many Irish people favoured joining in on Britain's side at any time during the war: in fact the evidence suggests that de Valera was ahead of opinion within his own party in 1939–40, where many who had fought for independence against Britain hoped for her quick defeat and believed that a united Ireland would follow from a German victory. This was also the thinking within the IRA, already under pressure in both Britain and Ireland because of its ill-timed 'S plan' bombing campaign launched in January 1939.[17]

In European terms Irish neutrality was unexceptional, but in the context of the British Commonwealth, neutrality was a bizarre anomaly. Ireland received no sympathy from her fellow dominions, committed as they were to supporting the mother country: their antagonism towards Irish neutrality was qualified only by occasional private criticism of London's perceived highhandedness, something which they too had

[16] On the censorship see especially Donal O'Dreisceóil, *Censorship in Ireland 1939–1945: Neutrality, Politics and Society* (Cork, 1996).

[17] Bowman, *De Valera and the Ulster Question*, 241–2.

to endure and which was anyway outweighed by their fear that de Valera was jeopardising the security of the British Isles.[18] Dublin's vague hopes that, egged on by Irish America, President Roosevelt could be persuaded to endorse neutrality, were soon dispelled: in fact, frustrated by his own difficulties in persuading his country into war, he was outraged at the Irish position, famously ending an acrimonious meeting with the Irish minister for defensive measures in 1941 by pulling the tablecloth from under his lunchtime crockery.[19] Irish American support for Irish neutrality also evaporated after Pearl Harbor, and in reaction to de Valera's futile protests at the stationing of American troops in Northern Ireland.

Ireland rubbed salt into Allied wounds by maintaining diplomatic relations with all the belligerents, as well as with Vichy France from June 1940. This was regarded by Churchill and by Roosevelt almost as a personal affront, and at times their irritation threatened the very close covert relations which developed between Dublin and Allied security agencies.[20] Throughout the war years Ireland played the diplomatic part of a cautious neutral, seeking only to steer clear of trouble and not to offend any of the belligerents. This proved easier with some states than with others. There was little to disturb the tranquillity of Irish–Japanese relations until the spring of 1944, when surveillance of the two-man consulate uncovered some undesirable activities: the consul 'got as pale as a Japanese can, and looked astonished and very guilty'. Although the Irish security authorities were not to know, American codebreakers had broken Japanese cable traffic to and from Dublin and knew that the consulate was not a centre for intelligence gathering.[21] Irish–Italian relations were also cordial, despite the Italian legation's enthusiastic distribution of fascist propaganda. Again, British and American decryption of Italian diplomatic traffic indicated that the mission was not involved in espionage. The perceptive reports of the Irish minister in Rome on Italian politics were, it now transpires, sometimes read with appreciation not only in the Department of External Affairs but in 10 Downing Street, as they featured amongst the selections of intercepts provided daily for Winston Churchill by British codebreakers.[22]

18 David Day, *Reluctant Nation: Australia and the Allied Defeat of Japan 1942–45* (Oxford, 1992), 7–10, 59–60.
19 C. S. Andrews, *Man of No Property: An Autobiography*, vol. II (Dublin, 1982), 124.
20 O'Halpin, *Defending Ireland*, 163–4.
21 Walshe to Taoiseach, 27 May and 1 June 1944, NA, DFA, A8/1; O'Halpin, *Defending Ireland*, 193.
22 Eunan O'Halpin, '"According to the Irish Minister in Rome . . .": British Decrypts and Irish Diplomacy in the Second World War', *Irish Studies in International Affairs*, 6 (1995), 95–105.

Irish/German diplomatic relations also remained reasonably good throughout the war years. There was, however, one exceptional moment in Irish/Axis relations: in May 1940 de Valera publicly denounced Germany's invasion of Ireland's fellow neutrals, Belgium and The Netherlands. While entirely consonant with declared policy this was, arguably, a highly impolitic gesture given the direction in which the war appeared to be going. It caused a protest from the German minister in Dublin, whom Irish officials sought to mollify by every kind private word they could think of as the spectre of German victory loomed larger. As the secretary of the Department of External Affairs testily put it in June, it 'appears to be entirely within the probabilities that we shall soon have to deal with the German government, without any hope that we can look to another government for support'.[23] Good relations were duly maintained, despite repeated German efforts to use Ireland for espionage purposes against Britain, German involvement with the IRA, a handful of probably accidental German bombings of Irish territory in 1940 and 1941 in which about three dozen people were killed, and frequent German attacks on Irish shipping plying the dangerous waters between Ireland, Britain, and the Iberian peninsula. The latter half of 1940 was the period of greatest tension, because of Irish and British fears that a German invasion was likely and because of German overtures both to the Irish government and to the IRA airing the possibility of Irish unity if Germany were to make a landing in force in Northern Ireland – a scenario which 'particularly terrified de Valera' because of its emotional appeal for committed nationalists, not least in his own party.[24] At the height of Anglo-Irish tensions in December 1940, however, the government evidently briefly contemplated an approach to Germany to secure military assistance should Britain invade, a puzzling moment given the close liaison arrangements already in being between the army and British forces in Northern Ireland. Apart from loud protests when the Irish refused to agree to the attachment of meteorologists to his staff – a demand which if granted might well have provoked British military intervention, so grave an intelligence threat did the German presence pose for Britain – the German minister, Hempel, generally softened the tone of instructions received from Berlin and played up Irish difficulties in his reports home. By any rational analysis it was entirely in Germany's interests, once Hitler's preoccupations switched in

[23] Dermot Keogh, *Ireland & Europe 1919–1948* (Dublin, 1988), 120 and 129; Walshe to Roche, 11 June 1940, DFA A23.

[24] Bowman, *De Valera and the Ulster Question*, 211.

the winter of 1940 from an invasion of the British Isles towards the defeat of the Soviet Union, that Ireland should remain neutral and should continue to deny the British any facilities, and as long as this was the position Hempel eschewed a confrontational approach. He was as reasonable as could be expected in respect of his clandestine radio set once the Irish detected it following a tip-off from the British, firstly in promising early in 1942 not to transmit messages and finally concluding a gentleman's agreement in December 1943 under which the set was removed by G2 and placed in a Dublin bank vault, apparently without the prior knowledge of the German Foreign Office.[25] He was, furthermore, wary of involving his mission in active intelligence gathering, although in 1943 the British learned from decrypts that in the autumn of 1942 he had assured Berlin that he would pass on 'any vital operational intelligence' that came to hand.[26] As the war wore on and the likelihood of German victory faded, the Irish took less heed of his complaints about toleration of British activities within the state, but his personal relations with the government remained good, so much so that after Germany's defeat he was afforded assistance to stay on. His good standing may go some way to explain de Valera's bizarre formal visit to the legation in May 1945 to convey his condolences on the death of Hitler, a gesture made against official advice which baffled observers and obscured the reality of his pro-Allied sympathies and of Irish/Allied cooperation since 1939. The successive Irish diplomats accredited to Berlin, similarly, remained on good terms with their hosts until the end, although a certain testiness began to manifest itself in German responses to Irish queries about the fate of groups of European Jews in 1944 and 1945. Decrypted Irish cables from Berlin to Dublin occasionally found their way to Churchill's desk.[27]

The most difficult problems arising from German policy towards Ireland came from her efforts to maintain links with the IRA and to use Ireland as a base for intelligence and sabotage operations against the United Kingdom. The government took the diplomatically convenient view that these operations were mounted independently of the German legation: post-war evidence suggests that this was broadly true. The IRA–German link was dogged by misfortune: in August 1940 the movement's most active leader, Sean Russell, died while on passage

[25] O'Halpin, *Defending Ireland*, 178, 189–90.
[26] F. H. Hinsley and C. A. G. Simkin, *British Intelligence in the Second World War*, vol. 4: *Security and Counter-Intelligence* (London, 1990), 195.
[27] O' Halpin, Defending Ireland, 183–5.

back to Ireland in a U-boat, and with him went the prospect of concerted IRA action in furtherance of German war aims.[28] Between the autumn of 1939 and December 1943, twelve German agents reached Ireland on a variety of missions. Only two, one of them a courier, were under orders to make contact with the IRA. The rest were variously to collect information on the British war effort, to carry out sabotage in the United Kingdom, to radio back weather and shipping reports, and to infiltrate Scottish radical groups. The majority of these agents, three of whom were Irishmen, were ill-prepared, and most were captured within a short time of arrival. One surrendered to the British authorities in Northern Ireland, and for a time MI5 considered using him as a double agent. Amongst those sent in 1940, however, was one experienced agent, Herman Goertz, who regarded himself as as much an emissary as a spy. He saw it as his personal mission to bring about Irish unity, and he attempted to open lines of communication with senior army officers and some politicians to this end. He also established an intelligence-gathering network inside Northern Ireland, some material from which he fed back to his army contacts. Goertz plainly enjoyed a degree of protection – it transpired that at least five men within the police Special Branch were betraying operations – but his work was hampered by two factors.[29] Firstly, he found the IRA, already under intense pressure as a result of ill-judged confrontations with the state, to be inefficient and faction ridden. Secondly, although he had 'a first class cipher ... the best in our experience used by the Germans during the war', he had lost his radio on arrival by parachute and had no efficient means of communicating with his superiors. He was eventually captured in November 1941, but two years later his former courier began using his cipher to send intelligence to the Germans via a ship plying between Ireland and Portugal. By then Allied interest in Ireland centred not on the possibility that Germany might attack but on the danger of the leakage of information about invasion plans. In fact the messages did not get through, as they were intercepted by the British in Lisbon and were eventually broken in a combined British/Irish exercise.[30] Formal protests about the dispatch of agents were registered with the German legation, and formal denials of knowledge and responsibility

[28] Russell's whereabouts remained a mystery to both the Irish and British governments for almost two years. Hinsley and Simkin, *British Intelligence*, 90n; J. P. Duggan, *Neutral Ireland and the Third Reich* (Dublin, 1985), 151–3.

[29] O'Halpin, *Defending Ireland*, 205.

[30] Valedictory report of Richard Hayes, Director of the National Library of Ireland and G2's expert on codes and ciphers, 2 January 1946, quoted in O'Halpin, *Defending Ireland*, 243–4.

were forthcoming from Hempel. Both he and his interlocutors knew perfectly well, that Berlin would continue to do whatever it wished.

As a dominion and as a strategic client of the United Kingdom which nevertheless refused to join in the war, Ireland's relations with the Allies inevitably proved very difficult. The United States minister in Dublin, David Gray, who was on close terms with Roosevelt, was openly hostile throughout to de Valera's government and to neutrality: at the end of 1940 G2 described his mission as 'probably a greater centre of pro-British influence' than the office of the British Representative.[31] An ill-informed alarmist – he forced out the first US intelligence office in Ireland at the end of 1942 because of his positive reports on Irish security – he continually pressed both Washington and London to use every means up to and including force to secure whatever facilities they required and to prevent Axis intelligence gathering. This line of argument was to lead to the 'American note' crisis of February 1944, when Ireland was presented with a demand for the closure of the Axis missions in Dublin as a mortal threat to security in the build up to the invasion of Europe. This demand went directly against the professional advice of the British Joint Intelligence Committee, which had concluded that 'there could be very little, if any, security advantage in the removal of the German Legation whose communications we then controlled'. If it were removed, there was a real danger of renewed German espionage in Ireland which might be far harder to thwart. Both America's Office of Strategic Services and Britain's MI5 were also alarmed by the note, as they feared it might jeopardise their close working relations with the Irish security authorities.[32]

Despite, or perhaps because of, the greater volume of business to be dealt with, the Irish found the strangely styled 'British Representative', Sir John Maffey, sent in haste in September 1939 to provide a link between the governments in the anomalous situation in which Ireland found itself as a neutral British dominion, a far more understanding and perceptive presence than his American colleague.[33] He was soon joined by a naval attaché, with whom the Irish liaised on coastal security questions, and other attachés and an MI6 representative were later posted to Dublin. In addition to liaison with the Irish defence forces on

[31] Ibid., 229, quoting G2 draft annual report for 1940.

[32] Security Service *Official History*, 272–3, PRO, KV4/2.

[33] Nicholas Mansergh, *The Unresolved Question: The Anglo-Irish Settlement and Its Undoing 1912–1972* (London, 1991), 308–9. The title 'British Representative' was agreed between the two governments as a fudge to provide a diplomatic presence without using a diplomatic term such as 'minister' which would imply British recognition of Ireland's independence.

all manner of military and security business, covert 'stay behind' and invasion warning networks were set up along the southern coast, and considerable counter-intelligence operations were mounted against the Axis legations and Axis aliens in Ireland. Some efforts were also made to penetrate the army and the police. So far as can be judged, G2 got well on top of such clandestine activity and was content to let it continue under observation. The rather less extensive undercover work of the Americans from 1942 on was observed with similar sang-froid.[34]

British concerns about Irish neutrality initially revolved around the Admiralty's calls for action to regain the ports, but these were outweighed by arguments about the undesirability of violating Irish neutrality. The calculations changed considerably after the fall of France. The strategic case for getting Irish bases was strengthened by the need to defend the Irish Sea against German action: Ireland was now an obvious target for a German invasion, a possibility undreamt of a few months earlier, and in the IRA Hitler would have a willing fifth column. There were, consequently, strong arguments for putting British forces into the state in anticipation of a German attack. The problem was that this would provoke a conflict with Ireland, and while the military outcome was certain there would be the likelihood of serious guerrilla warfare once the occupation was complete. Such a move might also draw the Germans in, while the forcible occupation of a neutral democracy could have serious repercussions for Britain in the United States. British ministers decided to pursue a middle course, attempting to coax de Valera into participation in the war by holding out the prospect of post-war Irish unity, subject only to the consent of the Unionist majority in Northern Ireland. These overtures provoked accusations of treachery from the prime minister of Northern Ireland, while de Valera reasoned that Britain could not possibly deliver on her offer.[35] In any case, he believed that overt participation would provoke a civil war; he thought that the impact of bombing on Ireland's undefended cities and towns would be catastrophic; and he feared that Britain was about to be defeated anyway. His reaction to the proposal prompted concerns as to 'his real attitude ... we cannot allow Eire to be handed over to the enemy', but in the event the British government kept its nerve, continued to work with the Irish army on a joint strategy to counter a German invasion, and refrained

34 Security Service *Official History*, 267, PRO, KV4/2; O'Halpin, *Defending Ireland*, 237–9; author's conversations with Col. Dan Bryan, deputy director and from 1941 director of G2, December 1983.

35 Bowman, *De Valera and the Ulster Question*, 175; Canning, *British Policy Towards Ireland*, 283–5.

from moving against Ireland.[36] Britain had her air and naval facilities in Northern Ireland, the significance of which for Atlantic defence grew as the war went on, and British troops stationed there also served as an insurance policy should a rapid deployment into the Irish state be required in response to a German attack. The day after Pearl Harbor, Churchill sent de Valera a dramatic telegram which again held out the possibility of post-war unity in return for Irish participation in the war, though without any indication of how Unionist opposition would be overcome or of how Ireland might be protected from the kind of aerial assaults which Britain was already suffering. Once more de Valera declined to rise to the bait.[37] From 1942 onwards, British concerns about Ireland shifted from her vulnerability to a German invasion to problems of maintaining security and preventing leakages of information as preparations began for amphibious landings in Europe. These were matters of procedure and detail which could best be dealt with through discreet collaboration at official level. The success of such collaboration was reflected in some after-dinner remarks by the British Foreign Secretary Ernest Bevin in 1948 during a discussion in Brussels. Recalling the build up to D-Day, he wanted 'our Irish friends to know that ... not a single leakage of information occurred through Ireland ... we had to take the top Irish officials into our confidence .... they gave ... cooperation unstintingly.'[38]

Up to 1941, Irish neutrality was preserved by a combination of nerve, prayer, luck, German indifference, and British restraint, the latter based firmly on fine calculations of where the balance of advantage lay given American opinion, neutral Ireland's importance as a source of manpower and supplies, and the operational difficulties in using Irish facilities if the general population were hostile. The evident determination of the Irish to resist any invader, however briefly, undoubtedly had some influence on British thinking. After 1941, Britain's main concerns about Ireland were security ones arising from German espionage and from the leakage of war information. These were ones which by definition could best be addressed by the Irish government, whose security and police agencies had all the advantages of local knowledge and legitimacy. As the Admiralty director of naval intelligence afterwards wrote, 'having only recently emerged from a ... civil war', these were 'particularly good at detecting underground conspiracies'.[39]

[36] Minutes of Chiefs of Staff sub-committee, 2 July 1940, quoted in O'Halpin, *Defending Ireland*, 176.
[37] Bowman, *De Valera and the Ulster Question*, 246–7.
[38] Quoted in O'Halpin, *Defending Ireland*, 233–4. [39] Ibid., 206.

Irish neutrality was bitterly resented in Britain, where propaganda portrayed the state as a parasite, basking in the shade of the British defence umbrella, relying on the British merchant marine for supplies, expecting Britain to employ its surplus population, and yet allowing Britain's enemies to run amok. We might, however, note some sympathy for Ireland in informed circles: the mercurial Sir Warren Fisher, who as permanent secretary to the Treasury until 1939 had taken a deep interest both in Anglo-Irish relations and in British defence planning, remarked in March 1945 that

> Irish neutrality was easily explained. If Mr de Valera had come in against German tyranny, he would have had a civil war on his hands and we should have had a quarter of a million fewer fighting men . . . Mr de Valera's detestation of Prussianism was as great as anyone's; but there was the 20 per cent minority which would cause trouble.[40]

## UNAVOIDABLE INTERDEPENDENCIES: TRADE, COMMERCE, AND PEOPLE

In 1939 Ireland's external trade, transport and communications were dependent almost totally on foreign – mainly British – providers. She controlled less than 5 per cent of her own shipping requirements, a factor which saw the belated establishment in 1941 of a small shipping company in order to carry supplies from the Iberian peninsula after Britain reneged on shipping agreements.[41] Air travel was in its infancy, with only a handful of flights each week between Dublin and Britain by the state's tiny airline and by a British firm. There was also a significant civilian sea plane facility on the Shannon (near what is now Shannon Airport), which became an important hub in civil air travel between the United States, Britain, and neutral Europe and West Africa. Ireland's telecommunications links also operated under British sufferance. All cable communications to and from Ireland were, by agreement, routed through London on the outbreak of war, ensuring that British code-breakers could study all such traffic at their leisure. Similarly, all mail emanating from or destined for Ireland passed through British controls.

Although the separatist movement had unfailingly blamed Ireland's economic woes on Britain's determination 'to retain Ireland as a barren

[40] Fisher's comments to a Chatham House study group, 12 February 1945, quoted in Eunan O'Halpin, *Head of the Civil Service: A Study of Sir Warren Fisher* (London, 1989), 257.

[41] J. J. Lee, *Ireland 1912–1985: Politics and Society* (Cambridge, 1989), 233; B. Girvin, *Between Two Worlds: Politics and Economy in Independent Ireland* (Dublin, 1988), 134–5.

bulwark for English aggrandisement', the advent of independence in 1922 had had surprisingly little impact on Anglo-Irish economic and commercial relations in the succeeding decades.[42] The Irish pound was linked at par to sterling, and the Central Bank operated more or less as a diligent branch office of the Bank of England. The Dublin stock market was little more than a provincial clearing house for the London Stock Exchange, while the commercial banking sector remained largely oblivious to the new state and continued to operate in essence as a subset of the British banking system.

Economic and commercial interdependence were compounded by Ireland's historic role as a supplier of manpower for British industry and the British armed services. The realities and mutual conveniences of contiguity had been recognised the two states amicably operated a common travel area after 1922, and there were no movement controls or labour or residency laws to prevent Irish people from moving into and working in the United Kingdom. This arrangement allowed Ireland to continue her historic if dismal role as an exporter of manpower to her more prosperous neighbour.[43] From all of this it might appear that Ireland was simply a British satellite, entirely dependent for national survival on London's goodwill. But, even in the spheres of trade and commerce, it is more accurate to characterise the relationship as one of interdependence.

In contrast to the experience of the First World War, when the island had enjoyed a transient boom in both industrial and agricultural production, Ireland's economy contracted severely after 1939. This was because the imports of raw materials and semi-manufactured goods on which many firms depended dried up: industrial employment fell by about 15 per cent between 1938 and 1943, while capital investment fell by four-fifths. Furthermore, even agricultural exports declined in volume and value due to 'shortages of imported feeding-stuffs and fertilisers'.[44] Economic activity was also hit in the winter of 1940/1 by an ill-judged British attempt to use her economic power to force Ireland to concede defence facilities: Churchill's private secretary noted the prime minister's hope that British 'refusal to buy her [Irish] food ... lend her our shipping' and other measures 'seem calculated to bring de Valera to his

[42] 'Message to the Free Nations of the World', 21 January 1919, *Documents on Irish Foreign Policy*, 2.
[43] O'Halpin, *Defending Ireland*, 75–7.
[44] L. M. Cullen, *An Economic History of Ireland since 1660* (London, 1972), 188; K. Kennedy, T. Giblin, and D. McHugh, *The Economic Development of Ireland in the Twentieth Century* (London, 1988), 210–11.

knees in a very short time', although 'the Irish are an explosive race and coercion might mean trouble'.[45] In fact the restrictions fitfully imposed on trade, some in violation of earlier understandings, while they deprived the Irish of some comforts and had a serious impact on the economy, were incapable on their own of producing the results desired: as an agricultural state with an indigenous though despised source of domestic energy – turf – Ireland could subsist on her own produce if needs be, while Britain's appetite for industrial and military manpower meant that she remained an obvious haven for Irish people unable to secure work at home. The fitful efforts to use control of supplies as a lever to secure Irish concessions on strategic questions, while they may have assuaged British public opinion, were intensely resented in Ireland, where people blamed shortages on Churchill rather than on de Valera and took British behaviour as proof of the value of neutrality rather than as an argument for joining in a war which, until 1942, it was thought Britain was going to lose. Furthermore, British officials were uncomfortably aware that the prolonged attenuation of trade with Ireland would hurt some British exporters. It might also harm Britain's finances, if the Irish chose to repatriate their large sterling balances and to increase their trading outside the sterling area.[46] In fact, this danger did not materialise: indeed, a Treasury official later recalled that they generally found their Irish analogues, with whom relations had always been excellent despite diplomatic vicissitudes, 'more papist than the Pope' in their observation of regulations about currency transactions outside the sterling area.[47]

What saved Ireland from the worst consequences of economic hypothermia during the war was the old stand-by of emigration: using the number of travel permits issued between June 1940 and 1945 as an index, a recent study argues that at a conservative estimate perhaps 130,000 Irish people emigrated to Britain.[48] To that figure must be added firstly the numbers who went before permits were introduced, secondly the uncounted thousands who travelled to Britain via Northern Ireland, and thirdly those who, while they remained resident within the state, worked in Northern Ireland during the war (in 1942, for example, a weekly average of 20,000 people crossed the open border at supervised check-points, together with an unknown number who avoided

[45] John Colville, *The Fringes of Power: Downing Street Diaries*, vol. I: *1939–October 1941* (London, 1985), 363, 3 December 1940.
[46] Canning, *British Policy Towards Ireland*, 295–307.
[47] Sir Edward Playfair to the author, 9 August 1980.
[48] Cormac O'Gráda, *A Rocky Road: The Irish Economy since the 1920s* (Manchester, 1997), 18.

official controls intentionally or otherwise).[49] In January 1944 MI5 put the number of Irish 'labourers ... many working in ... operational areas' at 150,000.[50] In addition, in accordance with pre-war tradition many thousands of Irish joined the British forces – in 1938 the War Office had recorded about 10,000 (5.7 per cent of strength) of serving soldiers as 'Irish', and in 1946 the Dominions Office put the number of servicemen and women 'born in Eire' who had joined up during the war at 43,000, probably an underestimate. On the other hand, the figure of 150,000 serving by the end of 1941 which one Irish official suggested appears far too high. Whatever the true figure, the government believed that given freedom of movement within the British Isles it could not prevent its citizens from joining up. After 1940 even the Irish army found it impossible to prevent desertions by men hungry for the more active life, and better pay and conditions, which the British forces offered.[51]

The minor hardships which Ireland endured up to 1945 soon passed into folklore. What consumers failed to realise, in 'an era of brown bread, damp turf, weak tea, and of unpleasant coffee substitutes', was how very lightly they got off: this was reflected in the improbable emergence of Dublin as a gastronomic Mecca for visitors from the United Kingdom.[52] One public servant afterwards pointed out that 'no one died of cold ... or had to eat uncooked food' in neutral Ireland, but gratification at successfully resisting British pressure obscured serious long-term social damage. Not only did economic activity dwindle and emigration rise, but there was an alarming increase in infant mortality amongst the poor. Privation also encouraged the spread of tuberculosis in the population, with consequences which were only adequately dealt with at great public expense in the early 1950s.[53] The economic problems experienced also had a deleterious impact on planning for post-war development:

[49] Memorandum by Herbert, with minutes of 66th meeting of the Security Executive, 29 April 1942, PRO, HO 45/21985.

[50] O'Halpin, *Defending Ireland*, 234.

[51] Keith Jeffery, 'The British Army and Ireland Since 1922,' in Thomas Bartlett and Keith Jeffery (eds.), *A Military History of Ireland* (Cambridge, 1996), 438; MS notes by Walshe, undated, on TS 'Most Secret' memorandum for Taoiseach, 24 May 1941, NA[rand], DFA A/3; Defence Council minutes, 3 July 1940, NA, Department of the Taoiseach, S. 11896; interview with Li-Col. Sean Clancy (who joined the National Army on its formation in January 1922), July 1997.

[52] O'Gráda, *A Rocky Road*, 16; J. A. Gaughan (ed.), *Memoirs of Senator Joseph Connolly (1885–1961), a Founder of Modern Ireland* (Dublin, 1996), 404.

[53] Andrews, *Man of No Property* 170–80; O'Gráda, *A Rocky Road*, 17.

they lent succour to isolationist arguments bordering on autarky about industrial policy, and they reinforced a sense of economic fatalism which was to bring the Irish state almost to the verge of collapse before the final abandonment of protectionist delusions in the late 1950s.[54]

### THE CONSEQUENCES OF NEUTRALITY

Irish neutrality during the Second World War was a policy based firstly on principle, secondly on political pragmatism, and thirdly on the fear of the consequences of war for a virtually defenceless state. The principle of neutrality had been one of the keystones of the independence argument; pragmatism dictated that de Valera keep the country together by uniting all parties under the neutrality banner, since the alternative would undoubtedly have been much greater armed conflict with the republican movement both within the state and in Northern Ireland, and a split within the army; defencelessness, the product both of geography and of the new state's fear of militarism, prompted the fear that Ireland might have to suffer much the same aerial warfare as did the United Kingdom without any comparable air or AA resources.

The policy's success was made possible ultimately by two factors: geography, and Hitler's decision to head eastwards after securing victory in Western Europe. It was sustained by a combination of popular support, adroit diplomacy, de Valera's conscious decoupling of the questions of partition and Irish participation on Britain's side, a great deal of *sub rosa* cooperation on security and military matters which lessened the impact of neutrality on Allied air and sea operations, and the peculiar intimacies of Anglo-Irish economic and social relations.

What were the foreign policy consequences of neutrality? On this opinions differ considerably: some argue that neutrality deepened the divide between the Irish state and Northern Ireland, and contributed to Ireland's wider isolation in the post-war world. Yet there is scant evidence that Irish participation would have persuaded the unionist majority in Northern Ireland to abandon their British identity. What Irish neutrality undoubtedly did, however, was seriously to alienate American élite opinion on partition. It was to be almost another fifty years, and in the vastly changed circumstances of the post-Cold War world, before an American administration was persuaded to take an

[54] Lee, *Ireland*, 271–93, 299–328; John Horgan, *Séan Lemass, The Enigmatic Patriot* (Dublin, 1997), 112–20, 174–8.

independent interest in the Northern Ireland problem. While neutrality was neither forgotten nor forgiven in Westminster, it had no serious impact on Anglo-Irish relations after 1945. The Labour administration which was swept into power in June 1945 had an enormous domestic and foreign policy agenda to tackle, and set out to 'limit their ... involvement in Irish affairs' rather than to exact revenge. Memories of covert cooperation may have had some influence.[55] It is clear that what bedevilled Ireland in the decade after the war was not so much isolation consequent on Allied resentment as self-imposed insulation from the currents of economic and social reconstruction and renewal which swept through western Europe once the Marshall plan provided the means for rebuilding the continent.

Ireland's difficult military experience during the war occasioned no changes in its approach to defence policy after 1945. Limited cooperation continued with the British and later the American governments on counter-espionage and anti-Communist surveillance, but no wider defence relationships were established (although in declining to join NATO in 1949, the Irish government adduced partition as the sole obstacle, and later sought a bilateral defence pact with the United States). Ireland instead pursued a policy of independent defence of its territory, seas, and skies which existed only on paper. However costly this might have been had a further Atlantic war broken out, it has proved remarkably cheap as compared with how other European neutrals set about defending themselves. It has, unfortunately, also fostered enduring illusions about the moral basis for and the nature of Irish neutrality during the Second World War. These continue to bedevil discussion of the state's defence and security obligations as a member of the European Union in the vastly altered world of the new millennium.

[55] Thomas Hennessey, *A History of Northern Ireland 1920–1996* (London, 1997), 86; Bowman, *De Valera and the Ulster Question*, 231–2, 248–51; Mansergh, *The Unresolved Question*, 316–17.

CHAPTER 13

# *Swedish neutrality during the Second World War: tactical success or moral compromise?*

*Paul A. Levine*

> Swedish humanitarian action during and after the war did much to erase the ignominy the country had suffered from gymnastics of its neutrality policy.[1]
>
> Peter Tennant, British Legation, Stockholm, 1940–45.

When the Second World War ended in Europe, the democratic kingdom of Sweden remained as it was when the war commenced – intact and at peace. In May 1945 as in November 1918, Sweden had escaped Europe's fratricidal violence and destruction. What explains Sweden's nearly two-century-long ability to remain outside armed conflict between states? What explains the overwhelming desire of the nation's politicians to remain outside a conflict in which its system of governance, democracy, was so clearly at risk in a Hitler-dominated Europe?[2] More so now than perhaps at any time since the war's conclusion, the current debate about the nation's experience with neutrality, and importantly, its future, is characterised by discussions about its moral content, or lack thereof. Indeed, the importance of neutrality in shaping Sweden's character is difficult to exaggerate, for, as a result of the generations of political and military neutrality, one can virtually speak of a 'mentality of neutrality'. For the Swedish people, 'neutrality' is far more than merely a security policy. As historian Alf W. Johansson has written, 'Neutrality was not only the country's chosen security policy during the war years; it also created a certain mentality, a particular state of mind.'[3] All scholars agree that the

[1] P. Tennant, *Touchlines of War* (Hull, 1992), 37.

[2] Even during the war, the nature and content of Swedish neutrality created interest in the West. See, for example, two articles printed in *Foreign Affairs* in 1945: J. Joesten, 'Phases in Swedish Neutrality', 23/2, 324–9, and B. Hopper (wartime OSS officer in Stockholm), 'Sweden: A Case Study in Neutrality', 23/3, 435–49. See also the early defence of Swedish neutrality by Gunnar Hägglöf (Swedish diplomat intimately involved in Swedish trade negotiations with both belligerent sides), 'A Test of Neutrality; Sweden in the Second World War', *International Affairs*, 36/4, 153–67.

[3] A. W. Johansson, 'Neutrality and Modernity: The Second World War and Sweden's National Identity', in S. Ekman and N. Edling, *War Experience, Self Image and National Identity* (Södertälje, 1997), 170.

tactical goal of remaining outside the conflict was reached, but increasingly the question is being asked (mostly outside of the academy) – at what moral price?[4] It seems obvious to note that Sweden's foreign policy during the Second World War is a complex and often ambiguous period of modern Swedish history, one which will always require new perspectives, questions, and explanations. Perhaps surprisingly, as a new century dawns the controversies surrounding Swedish neutrality during the Second World War are growing rather than receding. Thus, at the same time as a description of Swedish neutrality is offered, a newer perspective from the one dominating existing historiography will be advanced.

Though the various aspects of political, economic, and social life comprising 'neutrality' have been subjected to extensive historical exploration and debate, there is surprisingly little empirical debate concerning Sweden's political and economic response to the Second World War.[5] Historians are in general agreement regarding the *where and when* of Swedish foreign policy (for instance, the quantity and quality of Sweden's trade with the belligerents, primarily Germany, has long been detailed in academic publications). However, the *why* – that is, the political decisions comprising the policy, and its implications – are more controversial today than ever. There are two primary reasons for this. The first is that Sweden has been affected by the general European trend to re-examine its history during the war. The second, and more important, reason, is that two generations after the war, the Swedes hold a rather different understanding of neutrality's moral implications than do most scholars, establishment politicians, and other defenders of what might be called the traditional or standard view of neutrality.

There are two basic and conflicting interpretations of the 'rightness' of the political decisions taken during the war, and these interpretations form the background for the following review. The first has dominated the debate since the war, while the second has long struggled to be heard. The former, here labelled the 'traditional' school, essentially argues that the coalition government led by Social Democratic Prime Minister Hansson *succeeded* in keeping the nation at peace, a political status with

[4] See, for but one recent example, *Dagens Nyheter*, 10 January 1999.

[5] Swedish literature will be cited throughout. Scholarly literature in English on Sweden and the world war is limited, with the most important studies now almost a generation old. The dean of Swedish diplomatic historians, Wilhelm Carlgren, published an abridged English version of his influential *Svensk utrikespolitik 1939–1945* (Stockholm, 1973) as *Swedish Foreign Policy during the Second World War*, trans. A. Spencer (New York, 1977). Useful but dated is H. Nissen (ed.), *Scandinavia during the Second World War*, trans. T. Munch-Petersen (Minnesota, 1983), and T. Munch-Peterson, *The Strategy of Phoney War: Britain, Sweden and the Iron-Ore Question 1939–1940* (Stockholm, 1981).

a higher moral value than freedom. This accomplishment also, importantly, provides moral shelter for the many painful political concessions made to Nazi Germany during the war's early years – concessions which all agree were violations of declared neutrality. According to this school, the concessions were not only necessary, they were (and are) morally defensible. Sweden had limited choices during the war, and made the correct ones. Crucially, this view maintains that trade with Nazi Germany was a matter not only of necessity, but one morally defensible through reference to international law.

The country's deep bow towards Nazi Germany is defended by constant reference to the strategic and tactical situation. Criticism is also deflected by emphasising, for example, the minimal military aid given to the Allies and to the country's Nordic neighbours late in the war, the value of Stockholm and other locations as intelligence-gathering posts against Nazi Germany, humanitarian assistance provided to Greece and Norway, the tens of thousands of refugees taken in, and, recently, help given to some Jews who escaped the Holocaust. This 'school' understands Swedish foreign policy during the war as an unquestioned success, even with its flaws and stains.

Using much the same evidence, the opposing view calls for a substantive revision of the understanding which can be drawn from the experience of neutrality. This interpretation credits the government with far less effort and will to maintain anything approaching genuine neutrality, and finds the moral credibility of many of the policy decisions made questionable. Essentially, this view argues that the political and economic concessions made to Germany were greater than required and continued far longer than was necessary. Perhaps most problematically, Swedish neutrality did nothing to help the cause of the democracies, whilst providing substantial material benefits to the Nazis. This view was articulated during the war both by outsiders, and Swedes. In the summer of 1944 Winston Churchill wrote that, 'In the last War the Swedes were definitely pro-German. In this War they have shown themselves animated only by "safety first". I should like to see them pressed hard privately by us, and warned of the dangers if they come out of this war as non-contributory neutrals to our victory.'[6] More recently and even more acutely, this interpretation questions the necessity and morality of

[6] W. Churchill, cited in L. Leifland, 'They Must Get in Before the End; Churchill och Sverige 1944 och 1945', in Mats Bergquist, Alf W. Johansson, and Krister Wahlbäck (eds.), *Utrikespolitik och Historia; Studier tillägnade Wilhelm M. Carlgren* (Stockholm, 1987), 116.

a foreign trade policy which aided an abhorrent, genocidal regime.[7] For young Swedes, this aspect is the hardest to understand today, and they often react with anguished confusion when confronted with the realisation that government and business leaders, long after any threat to their country existed, continued to facilitate the shipment of massive amounts of militarily vital raw materials and finished products to a regime which was known to be murdering countless Jewish men, women, and children. As historian Stig Ekman recently wrote, 'Ultimately, indignation about Sweden's adaptation to Germany must be seen in the light of the fact of Swedish collaboration with the regime responsible for the Holocaust.'[8]

After being raised on what can usefully be called 'the myth of neutrality', younger Swedes, whether students or housewives (particularly those who support closer engagement with Europe), are demanding a more honest and open discussion of this 'holy relic' of their country's history. We see this gap between academic history and general understanding expressed clearly by one citizen in a recent letter to the government.

> The picture which only recently is beginning to emerge about Sweden's German-friendly policy through the war's end says something different. It would be honest to stop sweeping history under the carpet . . . and speak frankly about how we acted during the war before [the government's book] is translated and distributed into countries where citizens really fought against Nazism.[9]

This opinion, in a nutshell, sets the terms for any contemporary discussion of Swedish neutrality during the Second World War.

In a lengthy memorandum sent to all legations in January 1940, Erik Boheman, the gifted diplomat who served most of the war as permanent secretary of Sweden's foreign office (hereafter Utrikesdepartementet, or UD), wrote that 'Sweden's policy of neutrality is not founded on

[7] Recent scholarship has clearly demonstrated that the Swedish government, and people, knew of the on-going campaign of extermination against Europe's Jews as early as late summer 1942. See, for example, my *From Indifference to Activism, Swedish Diplomacy and the Holocaust, 1938–1945* (Uppsala, 2nd edn. 1998), and "The Swedish Press and the Holocaust, June 1941–October 1943" (MA thesis, The Claremont Graduate School, May, 1987). The full extent of press coverage of Germany's war against Europe's Jews can be seen in I. Svanberg and M. Tydén's *Sverige och Förintelsen; Debatt och dokument om Europas judar 1933–1945* (Stockholm, 1997).

[8] S. Ekman, 'Skilful Realpolitik or Unprincipled Opportunism. The Swedish Coalition Governments, Foreign Policy in Debate and Research', in Ekman and Edling, *War, Experience*,' 205.

[9] Fax from Karin Rebel to Prime Minister Göran Persson, 19 August 1998, *Regeringskansliet Levande historia*. Italics in original. The book referred to is P. A. Levine and S. Bruchfeld's *'Om detta må ni berätta, en bok om Förintelsen i Europa 1933–1945*, which describes the Holocaust and is now in some one million Swedish households. Teachers of the Second World War in Swedish universities are often confronted with exactly the same questions and attitudes. Such articulations are particularly telling in light of the extensive scholarly literature describing Sweden's wartime experience, which Ms. Rebel believes has been 'swept under the carpet.'

any political ideology, but rather on the determined understanding of Sweden's leaders and the Swedish people that this policy is the only or at least the surest way of preserving Sweden's independence or freedom.'[10] Boheman could be sure that such a policy was supported by popular opinion, for the Swedish people had long grown used to non-involvement in the often bloody affairs of continental Europe. By 1940, some 125 years had passed since the Swedish army engaged in active combat, and even though the nation had achieved its 'great power period' in the seventeenth century almost exclusively through military success, this extraordinary period of non-belligerency left a profound mark on the politics and culture of the nation. This experience was the first pillar of Swedish neutrality during the Second World War. The second was international law, which by the first years of this century had codified a nation's right to declare itself neutral, and articulated the concomitant political, economic, and military responsibilities of that status.[11]

Prior to the First World War, Sweden announced its desire to remain neutral by standing apart from the many alliances. This determination was aided immeasurably (then and now) by the luck of geography and the lack of imperial designs by its powerful Baltic Sea neighbours. Relying heavily on the power of the written word, Sweden declared neutrality when the war started and succeeded in staying that way, although as historian Wilhelm Carlgren has written, 'Sweden's policy of neutrality from 1914–18 descended from a rather pretentious and bombastic level to a quieter realism.'[12] The country suffered some economic privation during the war which led to what is called the 'democratic breakthrough', and at no time was its neutrality seriously threatened. Understandably, this success gave rise to a political and popular post-war consensus that Sweden's interests were best served by utilising neutrality.[13]

During the inter-war period neutrality became an almost permanent feature of foreign policy, a trend helped considerably by the rise

[10] *Promemoria* of 25 January 1940, HP 1 Ab, *Riksarkivet*. Erik Boheman occupied this critical diplomatic position for almost the entire war. (Unless otherwise indicated, all translations from Swedish to English are mine.)

[11] For Sweden's understanding and utilisation of the two Hague Conventions which constitute the legal foundation of international neutrality, see B. J. Theutenberg's article, 'Folkrättsakkunniga i UD och folkrätten i Sverige,' in Bergquist, Johannson, and Wahlbäck (eds.), *Utrikespolitik och Historia*. 299–322.

[12] W. M. Carlgren, 'Svensk neutralitet 1914–1918 och 1939–1945', *Historisk tidskrift*, 4 (1979), 386.

[13] American historian Steven Koblik argued, in what remains the best study of neutrality during the First World War, that in spite of some difficulties, Sweden benefited by remaining neutral during that conflict. *Sweden: The Neutral Victor; Sweden and the Western Powers 1917–1918* (Lund, 1972).

to political prominence of the Social Democratic Party (SAP). Throughout the 1920s, most political parties supported the League of Nations and its efforts at disarmament, both as a way of promoting international stability and to reduce defence expenditures. The election of 1932 brought the SAP to its (still dominant) position as the country's most powerful political party.[14] International demilitarisation (and with it the greater possibility for successful neutrality) was of central importance to the SAP as it sought to build Sweden's welfare state, generally called *folkhemmet*. Indeed, insight into the formulation of neutrality during the Second World War can be gained by looking at the response of the Social Democrats to Hitler and Nazism. The rise of Fascism in general and Hitler in particular gave a party which had made its mark by attacking bourgeois society an important chance to portray itself as a defender of the homeland (*fosterlandet*) and state. Importantly, though the dream of unilateral disarmament was reluctantly abandoned in the late 1930s, SAP leaders have never given up the ideological dream of building the *folkhemmet*. The Party was led from its rise by Per Albin Hansson, who is still referred to as a *landsfader*. Most observers agree that Hansson was the overall architect of Swedish foreign policy during the war, even if his leadership style was modest and his interest in foreign affairs often vague. His reaction to being forced to choose guns over butter is clear from the following quote. 'It is a damn shame that everything which I and my comrades wish to create is now going to waste. We have chosen social equality, security for the sick and old and so much else. Now we are going to have to invest everything in military affairs; artillery, cruisers and airplanes. Isn't this a damn shame?'[15]

Though Sweden was consistently pro-German during the First World War, and Germany its dominant trade and cultural partner in the interwar years, the SAP defended itself and the state against Nazi penetration. No politically significant Nazi movement developed in Sweden, either before or during the war.[16] Yet, in a response shaped by Hansson, the government refused to participate in any manifestations, domestic or

[14] Since 1932 through today, the SAP (Svenska Arbetar Partiet) has led Sweden's governments with only three exceptions. The coalition government of the war itself, and two more recent periods; 1976–82 and 1991–4. This one-party dominance in a democratic state is unquestionably why neutrality is associated with Social Democracy.

[15] G. Hägglöf, *Möte med Europa 1926–1940* (Stockholm, 1971), 196.

[16] See H. Lööw, *Hakkorset och Wasakärven: En studie av nationalsocialism i Sverige 1924–1950* (Göteborg, 1990).

international, against fascism or Hitler's Germany.[17] Any understanding of the tenacity with which Sweden and the Social Democrats maintained their neutral stance during the war must begin with an analysis of Hansson.

There were, however, Swedes who not only warned of the dangers of Nazism, but predicted that in the event of a conflict between (social) democracy and Fascism, neutrality would be difficult if not impossible to maintain. Among the most prominent was Torgney Segerstedt, editor of Gothenburg's most important newspaper, and destined to become a thorn in the government's side throughout the war. In daily columns laced with irony and sarcasm, Segerstedt immediately perceived Hitler as a threat not only to neutrality, but to civilisation. Less than a week after the Nazi takeover of power, Segerstedt labelled Hitler 'an insult', and predicted that peace was in the long run impossible with such a violent ideology.[18] Indeed, Segerstedt's incessant criticisms of Hitler and Nazi Germany became an important incentive for the government to impose, upon the urging of the Nazis, a temporary policy of censorship and newspaper confiscation. Particularly in the war's first years there was great fear within the government that an unchecked free press would incite German reprisals.

The Swedish government followed events carefully as storm clouds gathered, particularly in the Baltic Sea region. And though the shock of the Molotov–Ribbentrop pact was considerable, it was not entirely undesirable from a Swedish point of view. Before the war Swedish concerns regarding Soviet designs on Finland were acute. This concern, combined with the traditional distrust (one heightened with the Bolshevik takeover) of the powerful neighbour to the East, turned Swedish eyes as much to the east as to the south. While the Pact upset calculations about the balance of power in the region, it also made it seem less likely that the small nations of the region, especially Sweden and Finland, would be drawn

[17] See A. W. Johansson's 'Den svenska socialdemocratin och fascismen på trettiotalet. Några reflexioner', in M. Bergquist, Johansson, and Wahlbäck (eds.), *Utrikespolitik och historia* (Stockholm, 1987). Interestingly, although the SAP passed a law which forbade Swedish volunteers from joining the Spanish Republicans (although some did), during the Second World War, some 200 Swedes joined the Waffen SS, of whom some forty died. See L. Westberg, 'Svenska krigsfrivilliga i tyska Waffen-SS 1941–1945', *Meddelande Armémuseums årsbok nr. 45–47 (1984–86)*, 222–34.

[18] T. Segerstedt, *I Dag* (Stockholm, 1945). Segerstedt was editor of *Göteborgs Handels- och sjöfarts tidning*. Many of his daily columns, entitled *I Dag* (Today), between 1933 and 1945 are re-printed in this collection.

into a war – with the important exclusion of Poland.[19] Unsurprisingly, when war broke out, few if any Swedes called for involvement. As Alf Johansson wrote, 'The policy of isolation which before the war was discussed and criticised became the natural base around which the government could keep public opinion gathered.'[20]

The view of Sweden's government after 1 September 1939 can be seen in a UD circular written earlier that year by Erik Boheman. 'It must lie in both coalitions' interest that Sweden is not drawn into the war. The Swedish military establishment is of sufficient size to evoke respect, and seen from the outside, Sweden's internal resolution is sufficient to exclude fears of foreign involvement.' Boheman can be accused of exaggerating the capacity of Sweden's military, which was in every way (armour, aircraft, and sea power) badly under-armed and antiquated (but to have admitted otherwise would have been considered defeatist), although it could after mobilisation field close to half a million men. Yet his perspicacity was on display when he also wrote that, 'It is obvious that the neutrality anticipated will be exposed to extremely difficult trials. To a certain extent in the way it will be carried out, neutrality will be a 'negotiated' thing, especially in the area of commercial activities.'[21] Decisions made outside Stockholm would decide the fate of military neutrality, but the nature of its commercial relationship with the belligerents would be created in Sweden.

Even before the war broke out, a clear dichotomy existed in the anticipation of how neutrality would be shaped in the event of a Great Power war between Nazism and the democracies. Simplifying matters, two lines of thinking were clear. The Per Albin Hansson line, which might be paraphrased as 'peace at any price for Sweden.' And the Rickard Sandler (foreign minister before the war) line, which argued that democracy in Scandinavia was dependent on the success, indeed survival, of democracy elsewhere in Europe. Sandler believed that 'absolute neutrality' was both a moral and an ideological impossibility, particularly if there was an ambition to contribute to the struggle for democracy against Fascism.[22]

Hansson had one thing, and virtually one thing only in mind when the war began – to keep his country at peace. In a speech to the Swedish people on 1 September, he said that the primary task for the Swedish

[19] Carlgren, *Svensk utrikespolitik*, 17–19. Carlgren's study is the most authoritative work on the period and has exercised a considerable, even decisive influence on the historiography. It was commissioned by a Social Democratic government while Carlgren served as head of UD's archive.

[20] A.W. Johansson, *Per Albin och kriget* (Stockholm, 1984), 57.

[21] UD Memo of 11 April 1939, HP 22 Ab, *Riksarkivet*.

[22] R. Sandler, cited in Johansson, *Per Albin och kriget*, 41.

people was 'to join together with calm determination around the great task of holding our nation out of war'. One analyst wrote that with this speech, 'Per Albin had laid out *his* foreign policy programme; to keep the nation together around a policy which avoided dissension and foreign policy conflicts. It was a programme to which he would remain indefatigably true for the entire war.'[23] In December 1939, as a result of conflicts over Sweden's response to the Finnish Winter War, the Social Democrat Sandler resigned the post of foreign minister, virtually ensuring Hansson's domination of Swedish foreign policy for the entire war.

The traditional interpretation of neutrality likens it to a pendulum which swung back and forth during the war. By Swedish design it began in the middle, only to be pushed far to one side by German demands. When they lessened, the Swedes sought to regain equilibrium, only to lose it again to pressure put on by the Western Allies. Divided within these movements are four fairly distinct phases.[24] The first begins with the outbreak of the war through the shock of 9 April 1940, when Germany invaded Denmark and Norway, and cut off Sweden from the West. The second begins that month and lasts through late spring/early summer 1943. The standard historiography and popular memory both record and memorialise this period of pro-German concessions and appeasement as the most controversial and indeed difficult period in modern Swedish history. The third phase, when the Allies put increasing pressure on Sweden to cease immediately all trade with Nazi Germany, commences in autumn 1943 and lasts through late 1944. The final phase consists of the war's final months when Swedish leaders sought to understand the country's place in the post-war era, and provided limited aid to their neighbours.

The newer interpretation divides the war into three basic periods. The first two are generally the same as the traditional interpretation, with some differences of emphasis on the importance of certain issues and circumstances. It is, however, in the third phase where substantive differences of interpretation occur. The traditional school emphasises

[23] Johansson, *Per Albin och kriget*, 62.

[24] Scholarly literature about the Second World War in Swedish is comprehensive. Yet the standard historiography is easily discerned in two important 'series' of publications. The first is SUAV (Sweden during the Second World War) series. The product of Stockholm University's Department of History, this research project produced nineteen doctoral dissertations, mostly in the 1970s. The second is the series published in the first half of the 1990s of seven books of essays, one for each year of the war, originating from the Division of Military History, Military College of Stockholm. Although different subjects, theories, points of departure, etc., are evident in both series, the over two dozen books published give clear evidence of the predominance of the standard interpretation of Swedish neutrality.

the fears and possibilities of the coming post-war era. The newer interpretation appraises Swedish actions from the autumn of 1943 far more critically, primarily because for at least a year after the threat of invasion was completely gone, and the ultimate outcome of the war in little doubt, the trade of militarily vital supplies, mostly in the form of iron ore and ball bearings, continued. Not coincidentally, production of German armaments reached their wartime peak during this period. The newer interpretation centres its analysis on the economic, political, and above all moral significance of this third period, arguing that the emphasis on the approaching post-war period is misplaced. This is also the period when, for example, the Swedish railway leased hundreds of freight cars to Germany, easing at least somewhat the strain on the hard-pressed Reichsbahn, when Sweden continued to take shipments of gold in payment for trade even after warnings from the Allies, and when, generally, the Western Allies pressed Sweden to contribute something to the Allied cause, and when Sweden did its political best to resist.

Apart from the overriding goal of remaining at peace and separate from the conflict, Sweden's primary concerns in September 1939 were twofold. The first was to secure sufficient food and fuel supplies in order to avoid the domestic unease and violence created by shortages near the end of the First World War. The second goal, intimately connected with the first, was immediately to avail itself of the rights and responsibilities of legally recognised neutrality; that is, to secure long-term trade agreements with both sides.

Armed with diplomatic assurances from Germany and Great Britain that its neutrality would be respected (which confirmed for Sweden that its neutrality was in the belligerent's interest), the government prepared for what they knew would be difficult negotiations. The Germans' primary goal was to secure and increase the supply of the invaluable iron ore. For the British, who understood the importance of Swedish ore for Germany's armaments industry, the first goal was to limit the amount of ore shipped to Germany to pre-war levels. Convincing the Swedes to reduce shipments was desired, but impossible.[25] Sweden's response was that as long as their neutrality was respected, they sought neither a reduction in trade with either side, nor any substantive restrictions. The government's main task in the complicated negotiations was to secure its

[25] In 1938 Sweden sold approximately 8 million tons of iron ore to Germany, which desperately wanted an increase, something the British strongly opposed. The issue was resolved when London was told that 8 million tons were to be maintained, while the Swedes moved amounts previously sold to Poland and Czechoslovakia into the German allowance. Carlgren, *Svensk utrikespolitik*, 33.

needs; food and fuel supplies from the West, coal, coke, fertilisers, and other chemicals from Germany. With surprisingly little difficulty, broad and detailed agreement were reached first with the British and then the Germans. 'Sweden's trade policy', wrote Carlgren, 'was successfully shifted from peace to war . . . Both belligerent camps had acknowledged Sweden's policy of neutrality and were willing to admit that Sweden had trade needs separate from their own . . . [yet] . . . The danger that Sweden would become pressed hard between the belligerents was apparent.'[26]

The relative political calm of the first months regarding the main belligerents was quickly overshadowed by events in Finland. Throughout the autumn, the Soviet Union had made diplomatic 'inquiries and invitations to negotiations' to Finland, creating great consternation there and in Sweden. Helsinki had been pressing Stockholm to offer a clear declaration of willingness to help, primarily but not only in the Åland Islands, the small island group lying between the two countries. But Sweden's cabinet was divided. Sandler argued that Finland must receive some guarantees. Hansson and other important Social Democrats like Finance Minister Ernst Wigforss argued for a much more cautious line. Aiding Finland would, they argued, be tantamount to abandoning neutrality, obviously an unacceptable option. Portions of public opinion called for an activist, even interventionist policy – something not heard in government circles. When the Winter War began, the unforgettable phrase *Finlands sak är vår* (Finland's fate is ours), became the failed rallying cry of those who sought immediate and substantive help for their Nordic neighbour.

Finland's place in the pre-war Swedish world-view is fundamental. That small country had been an integral part of Sweden for some 500 years, and its recent independence from the Soviet Union (Russia) was of vital importance and urgency for almost all Swedes, particularly conservative nationalists. Finland played a far larger role in the imagination of many Swedish politicians and the public than did many other seemingly more important European states. Traditional feelings of solidarity for Finland and antipathy for Russia were enhanced by the Bolshevik victory. Not surprisingly, this situation has played a role in the historiography of the war, as Swedish historians have paid considerable, even exaggerated attention to events in the East.[27] Also important in understanding

[26] Ibid., 35.

[27] To give but one *ad hoc* but illuminating (historiographic) statistical example, one can look at the space the Finland question takes in Carlgren's influential book. Of approximately 560 pages of texts and footnotes, over 160, that is, well over 30 per cent, are devoted to Finland. Similar concentration is evident in the two major series on the war already cited.

Sweden's 'pro-Finnish' is the factor of the Swedes' traditional cultural, political and economic ties with Germany – that is, Germany before Hitler. The reason why thousands of Swedes volunteered to fight for Finland against the Soviet Union but so few for Norway against Germany is given by historian Göran Andolf. 'In Finland the battle implied a defence against the centuries-old arch-enemy Russia, which stood for despotism and Asiatic barbarism, for atheism and oppression, and to fight against it was an obvious task. To fight the "*kulturstat*" Germany could, on the other hand, as Ribbentrop expressed it, appear "unnatural."[28]

The immediate impact in Sweden of the Soviet attack against Finland was purely internal, with the consequences for Swedish foreign policy for the remainder of the war considerable. The conflicts within the cabinet became intolerable, and with Sandler's resignation, Sweden lost its strongest voice for active participation, in some form, in the struggle of the democracies against Fascism. A government of national unity, still led by Hansson, was formed in the middle of December with all important parties, including the conservative *Högern* (Rightists), participating. The new foreign minister was career diplomat Christian Günther. In this conflict Sweden never announced its neutrality, but rather maintained a position of non-belligerence, refusing to send troops either to the Åland Islands, or to Finland itself.[29]

Ironically, Finland's remarkable defence against the Red Army created a number of problems for the Swedish government. One was the actual stance taken by the Swedish government in the question of directly helping Finland. We have already noted that direct military involvement was out of the question for the new government, yet it did decide 'to give material support within the framework of possibilities under consideration of our own needs'. And though no substantive organisational work was permitted in Sweden, the government did eventually allow some 10,000 volunteers to fight in Finland.[30] Secondly, Sandler's resignation created something of an ideological crisis for the Social Democrats, for he had given their neutralism at least a hint of anti-Nazism and a slight pro-western lean. Thirdly, the war's effect on Swedish–German, German–Soviet and Soviet–Swedish relations was frighteningly

[28] G. Andolf, 'Den svenska frivillinginsatsen i Norge', in B. Hugemark (ed.), *Urladdning; 1940–Blixtkrigens år* (Stockholm, 1990), 319.

[29] Detailed accounts of the government's crises can be found in the studies already cited. See also P. G. Andreen, *De mörka åren; Perspektiv påsvensk neutralitetspolitik våren 1940- nyåret 1942*, (Stockholm, 1971).

[30] Carlgren, *Svensk utrikespolitik*, 81; K. Zetterberg, 'Samlingsregeringen och den 9 april 1940', in Hugemark (ed.), *Urladdning*, 191.

unclear – an ambiguity which would again become evident in June 1941. Finally, Per Albin's refusal to help Finland more openly (for which he was roundly criticised) brought Sweden, according to some, closer to direct military involvement than at any other time during the war. Sweden's refusal to help caused the Finns to look south-west.

The Winter War gave the Western Allies a chance to strike against the regime in Moscow, and of possibly bringing Norway and Sweden into the war on their side. They sought to do this by landing at Narvik in northern Norway, then crossing through Sweden to aid Finland. Not incidentally, leaders in London and Paris saw this as their chance to occupy the iron-ore mines in northern Sweden, and thus cut off supplies to Germany. The importance of Swedish iron ore for Germany's armaments industry was recognised at the highest levels. On 16 December 1939, Winston Churchill wrote that, 'stopping the delivery of Swedish ore to Germany has the same significance as a larger offensive action. Not for many months forward will we have any better opportunity to act.' Two months later, French Prime Minister Daladier added that in planning the action to help Finland, 'We must not lose sight of our most important goal. This is the cutting off of ore deliveries to Germany.'[31] At the same time, Swedish public opinion demanded armed intervention in Finland, precipitating what is known as the 'February crisis'. In the end, however, the relative military success of the Finns was insufficient to win, and they were forced to ask Stockholm to mediate with the Soviets to end the conflict. On 12 March 1940, an armistice was signed which gave the Soviets large areas of Finnish territory, but which maintained Finnish national independence.

The Winter War ended somewhat strangely. Though Moscow dictated the peace conditions, its military had been humiliated by tiny Finland. The Western Powers were seen by the world as still paralysed by indecision, while their mistrust for Sweden had grown as they suspected that Sweden, urged by the Germans, had pushed Finland into the peace. Finland, which lost vast territories in the east, was bitterly disappointed by Sweden's unwillingness to help. In fact, only Sweden had reason to be pleased with the outcome. It had achieved a diplomatic success that the Soviets seemed willing to reward; its limited help to the Finns stimulated the domestic armaments industry; and, most importantly, its hasty mediation fended off the very real threat of armed incursion from the West. Neutrality, it seemed, was saved and the

[31] Both cited in W. Wilhelmus, 'Det tyska anfallet mot Skandinavien', in Hugemark, *Urladdning*, 60–1.

government could breathe a bit more easily. The respite, however, proved shortlived.[32]

It is important to note that, even within the government, not everyone agreed that the preservation of neutrality at all costs was the correct policy for Sweden. One such voice in Utrikesdepartementet was Sven Grafström, a mid-level diplomat who represents an opinion and attitude not often acknowledged in the dominant historiography. On the eve of Germany's invasion of Scandinavia, he wrote that,

> Our government's point of departure has been above all to manoeuvre so that Sweden does not become a battlefield in the 'great' war. More than anything else, this view is the guiding light for the government's actions [Yet] ... it is important to remember that the little Finnish–Russian interlude is only one detail in the large drama, which again shakes poor Europe. With all their sins – appeasement and others – which one can with all justice accuse the Western powers of, one must not forget that in the end this fight is between two world views, and there are rather small chances for us to maintain our sovereignty if we remain only observers in the fight ... We should from the beginning cheer on the right horse.[33]

On 9 April 1940, the severest test neutrality would face began when Germany attacked Denmark and Norway. Not only was the occupation of Sweden's closest and most important political and cultural neighbours a severe shock for all segments of society, most now understood that neutrality actually depended less upon Sweden's own unilateral wishes than it did on a balance of power prevailing in the region. The necessary conditions for maintaining neutrality seemed to have vanished. Interestingly, the Swedes were fairly sure in advance that the invasion would take place, although the Germans attempted to disguise the impending invasion. Yet the Swedes possessed both hard information and geo-political logic pointing towards the sparing of their country from Operation Weserübung.[34] On 8 April the prime minister wrote in his diary that 'England is mining Norwegian waters. The Germans are moving. No measures against Sweden yet, but who knows when? Certain preparatory mobilisation measures decided upon.'[35] For both strategic

[32] The literature on the Winter War is extensive. See T. Munch Petersen (note 5), A. W. Johansson, *Finland's sak, svensk politik och opinion under vinterkriget 1939–1940* (Stockholm, 1973), and Carlgren, *Svensk utrikespolitik*, esp. 81–131.

[33] S. Grafström, *Anteckningar 1938–1944*, entry for 25 March 1940, 219.

[34] See W. Wilhelmus, 'Det tyska anfallet mot Skandinavien', in Hugemark, *Urladdning*, 58–73.

[35] P. A. Hansson's *Dagbok*, cited in K. Wahlbäck, *Regeringen och kriget; Ur statsrådens dagböcker, 1939–1941* (Stockholm, 1972), 70. After the war Günther said that the government was fairly certain that the German attack would be directed only at Norway and Denmark. See W. Wilhelmus, 'Det tyska anfallet mot Skandinavien', in Hugemark, *Urladdning*, 69–70.

and tactical reasons, Germany didn't invade Sweden. The vast size of the country and the fact that the Swedish army was expected to put up a stout, if short lived, defence, meant that Berlin could not assume a swift or painless victory. Yet in the run-up to the invasion of France, the Germans could not undertake the operation. Most importantly, the Germans could not run the risk that the iron ore would become harder, or impossible, to obtain.[36]

Reactions in Sweden to the undeclared invasion of Scandinavia were varied. The press registered shock and outrage, with some calling for immediate Swedish intervention. Others counselled patience and caution, while still others called on the Swedish people to face reality, and adapt to the new situation. For Hansson, there was simply never any question of intervention. Opposing him was, for instance, Crown Prince Gustav Adolf, who argued in a government meeting that 'the most important thing for a people was not to preserve peace but to save its soul'.[37] Segerstedt reminded his readers that, 'It is a great and good thing to be, in this eternal battle, on the side which fights for right and reason. What is a life worth which doesn't participate in this battle? Without this it lacks all content. And if it is sacrificed, so it has given its power to the one holy thing which exists – humanity.' When considering the defeatists within the government and foreign office, diplomat Sven Grafström lamented that 'Swedes have forgotten their humane values.'[38] Actually, the greatest impact of the German invasion on Sweden's government may well have been psychological. Alf Johansson judged the impact in the following way. 'Before the 9th of April there was still an under-appreciation of German willingness to take merciless and reckless military actions. After the 9th of April there would be instead an exaggerated fear of the Germans.'[39]

Surrounded now by the German army, and almost completely cut off from trade with the West, Sweden's prospects for remaining neutral and outside Germany's political and economic hegemony seemed dim indeed. The situation worsened two months later with the catastrophic defeat of France and the isolation of Great Britain. It now appeared that democratic Sweden would have no choice but to live in a Europe

[36] Berlin knew the disposition of Swedish forces around the iron-ore mines, and also knew that they were mined. Military action against them would probably have made the ore unavailable for an extended time period.

[37] Cited in Minister of Justice K. G. Westman's diary, 9 April 1940, in Wahlbäck, *Regeringen och kriget*, 70–71.

[38] T. Segerstedt, 9 April 1940, *I Dag*, p. 130. Grafström, *Anteckningar*, 10 April 1940, 222.

[39] Johansson, *Per Albin och kriget*, 145.

thoroughly dominated by Nazi Germany, and at least until the first defeats of the Wehrmacht in the Soviet Union, the situation seemed likely to become permanent.

This was a critical phase of the war, which Swedes generally consider the most difficult period in their modern history. Contact with the West was subject to German control, and Berlin lost no time exploiting the situation. Berlin demanded and received a series of economic and political concessions which were even then considered painful and controversial. These included the mass transit on Swedish railways back and forth to Norway of over 2 million German soldiers and large amounts of war material, permission for German warships and other shipping to enter Sweden's coastal waters (thus out of reach of Allied forces), an increase in the shipment of iron ore, the already mentioned unconstitutional censorship of not only newspapers, but even theatre plays. The bottom of appeasement was reached when the government, in a very controversial government decision, permitted a fully armed German division to transit from Norway to Finland in the first days of Operation Barbarossa, prompting the so-called 'Midsummer crisis'. For the most part the government never made the concessions willingly and almost always declared them a matter of political (i.e. military) necessity required to forestall invasion. Yet many in the Swedish press and public argued that the government went too far too fast in accommodating and appeasing the Germans, and that, later, Hansson's government was too slow, even obstructionist, in accommodating the Allies with a more rapid diminishment of trade.[40] At the same time the cultural (journalistic, academic, artistic, etc.), political, military, and even sport connections between Sweden and Germany were quite extensive, creating a situation of some normalcy with Nazi Germany.[41] Indeed, had the fortunes of war not shifted in favour of the democracies, it is easy to imagine that many in Sweden, particularly some from the political, economic, and military élites, would have learned to live, and live well, in a Nazi-dominated Europe, one 'freed' from its Jewish and gypsy populations.

Many of the above concessions have been thoroughly investigated and debated by Swedish historians of the traditional school, and judged by them as the severest violations of neutrality during the war. However,

[40] In addition to Segerstedt collection *I Dag*, see those of Johannes Wickman, senior editor of *Dagens Nyheter*, one of Sweden's most important daily newspapers. *Seger: kommentar till de utrikespolitiska dagshändelserna* (Stockholm, 1944) and *Befrielsen: kommentar till de utrikespolitiska dagshändelserna* (Stockholm, 1945) fully reflect the frustrations dissenters from government policies felt.

[41] On these connections, see G. Rickardsson, *Beundran och fruktan; Sverige inför Tyskland 1940–1942* (Stockholm, 1996).

it appears more and more that, with the advantage of time and new perspectives, their importance has been exaggerated. In fact, even during the war the Allies considered this range of concessions (apart from that associated with the 'Midsummer crisis') as 'minor . . . and within the framework of neutrality under international law'.[42] What the Americans (mostly in concert with the British) did not consider minor was the sale of Swedish iron ore and ball bearings to Germany.[43]

Manifestations of psychological pressures can be both individual and national, and the manner in which Swedish neutrality was exercised was as much an expression of the ideas and psychology of individuals as it was an articulation of some larger theory of statecraft. Apart from Hansson, whose attitudes have been spotlighted, most historians agree that three other figures played the key roles in shaping Swedish foreign policy – Foreign Minister Günther, Minister (the earlier title for ambassador in UD) to Berlin, Arvid Richert, and kabinettssekreterare Erik Boheman. The first two, though committed to Sweden's national security, were accused during and after the war of a too-ready willingness to stretch neutrality in Germany's direction. Boheman was considered by all parties to be thoroughly pro-western, without his loyalty to Sweden ever being called into question.

Described as everything from a 'defeatist' to a 'very good foreign minister', Günther's influence on Swedish foreign policy was strongest during the years when appeasement of Germany was greatest. He often persuaded the cabinet that Sweden's long-term interests were best served by agreeing to most if not all concessions demanded by Germany. Gunnar Hägglöf, a gifted diplomat who conducted some of Sweden's most difficult trade negotiations, found Günther uncomfortably sanguine with the prospect of living in a German-dominated Europe. Boheman worked closely with Günther throughout the war, and thought the foreign minister's statecraft altogether too pro-German.[44]

[42] See the long and detailed evaluation of Sweden's political situation given by Herschel Johnson (US minister in Stockholm) to C. Hull (US Secretary of State), no. 1688, 2 July 1942, *Foreign Relations of the United States 1942, Sweden*, 342.

[43] In response to the renewed academic debate about neutrality which took place at a conference in Stockholm in August 1995, eminent German historian Hans Mommsen said: 'The aspect that I miss completely is this: it is not so important whether you [Sweden] sent (*sic*) one or two divisions from Sweden to Finland. The crucial point is that the German war industry was constantly supplied with iron ore from Sweden . . . what . . . impact [did] the Scandinavian countries have on the Axis war economy?' See the 'Summing-up debate', in Ekman and Edling, *War Experience, Self Image and National Identity*, 216.

[44] See G. Hägglöf's post-war account in English, *Diplomat; Memoirs of a Swedish Envoy in London, Paris, Berlin, Moscow and Washington* (London, 1972), 155–6, 164–5. E. Boheman, *På vakt; katinettssekreterare under andra världskriget* (Stockholm, 1964), 38–9.

Richert exerted considerable influential beyond that which such emissaries normally do because he controlled information coming out of Berlin and strongly influenced its interpretation. Even after the years of greatest exposure had ended, Richert argued that appeasing Berlin enhanced Sweden's neutrality and freedom. He helped to craft the much-resented policy of censorship, arguing incessantly that criticism of Hitler, the Nazis, and German policy would sooner or later result in invasion.[45] Ironically, it was permitted to criticise the government and the Allies, but not Germany, a situation which led Herbert Tingsten, one of Sweden's leading intellectuals, to note dryly that 'The only thing which can't be criticised are governments in countries which threaten our government.'[46] Indeed, though both Günther and Richert were undoubtedly loyal Swedes, it is not unreasonable to believe that had Sweden been occupied, these civil servants would have been all too willing to 'translate' German demands into domestic Swedish policy.[47] The list of others responding in that way is long and geographically well distributed.

On the other hand, Boheman consistently argued that Sweden had to do more for the West and less for the Germans. Not surprisingly, he was highly regarded by the Americans and British, particularly the latter.[48] Yet even though Churchill believed the Swedes should contribute militarily in a fashion which did not interest the Americans, the British Foreign Office was throughout the war more willing to accept Swedish arguments than did Washington, leading some UD diplomats to accuse the Americans of unfair treatment.[49] Sir Victor Mallet, British ambassador to Sweden, worked closely with Boheman. His appraisal of the Swede is important, because in the final evaluation, the latter's attitudes and arguments went far in balancing Hansson's domestic parochialism and Günther's appeasement. Mallet wrote in his memoirs that,

> Thanks to the mutual trust and respect which grew up between Erik Boheman and myself, we were able to discuss the most delicate matters with a proper understanding of each other's point of view. Erik is a most wholeheartedly patriotic Swede, but he understood more quickly than most of his compatriots what a disaster for the world a victory for Hitler would be and

[45] On this see L. Drangel, *Den kämpande demokratin; En studie i antinazistisk opinionsrörelse 1935–1945* (Uddevalla, 1976).

[46] Cited in Johansson, *Per Albin och kriget*, 103.

[47] Swedish historians have been reluctant to subject either of these diplomats to in-depth studies.

[48] In the opinion of British diplomat Peter Tennant, Boheman was talented enough 'to measure up to top civil servants anywhere in the world'. See his *Touchlines of War* 92.

[49] See V. R. C. Montgomery's unpublished doctoral dissertation, 'The Dynamics of British Policy towards Sweden, 1942–1945', King's College, London (1985).

he also, even in the worst times, had a firm belief that we would win in the end.[50]

In order to appreciate Sweden's reluctance to meet Allied demands one should note that most Swedes, inside the government and outside, believed that trading with Germany was not only a national right under international law, it was also morally defensible. Moreover, this attitude suffuses Swedish attitudes during the war and in the post-war historiography. Therefore it is not surprising that most concessions to Germany were ended only after severe Allied pressure, pressure put on simultaneously with increasing Allied power and commensurate German weakness. From early 1943 forward, the Americans demanded in increasingly strident tones an immediate end to what one US representative called 'the very substantial aid you are giving Germany every day'.[51] Of interest is the fact that some cabinet members were irked at giving in to the Americans when they had just begun to enjoy more freedom *vis-à-vis* the Germans.

In fact, the dispute between Sweden and the Allies centred overwhelmingly not on a violation of neutrality *per se* but rather on the sale of militarily vital supplies of iron ore and ball bearings to the Germans.[52] By the time shipments were finally halted in November 1944, Sweden had delivered approximately 50 million tons of high-grade iron ore. Not only was the quantity of ore critical for German arms production, its high quality translated directly into important savings for the Nazi's war economy. As economic historian Martin Fritz notes, 'it is transparently obvious that the continuance of imports from Sweden was an exceedingly critical factor in maintaining steel production at a satisfactory level. [Moreover] . . . by using [Swedish ore] . . . the German economy probably made great savings – especially having regard [*sic*] to the shortages of coke, labour, transport and blast-furnace capacity . . . the German economy was able to make huge savings by utilising Swedish ore.'[53]

[50] Victor Mallet Memoirs, Churchill Archives Centre, Churchill College, Cambridge, UK, 94.

[51] Cited in A. W. Johansson, 'Sverige och västmakterna 1939–1945', in S. Ekman (ed.), *Stromaktstryck och småstatspolitik* (Stockholm, 1986), 85.

[52] Literature in English on Swedish trade with Germany is limited, but valuable. See, primarily, the work of Martin Fritz, *German Steel and Swedish Iron Ore, 1939–1945* (Gothenburg, 1974) and his article 'Swedish Iron Ore and German Steel', *Scandinavian Economic History Review*, 21/2 (1973), 133–44. See also 'Swedish Iron Ore and Ball-Bearings in the German War Economy', with several other valuable contributions, in Martin Fritz, Ingemar Nygren, Sven-Olof Olsson, and Ulf Olsson (eds.), *The Adaptable Nation; Essays in Swedish Economy during the Second World War* (Stockholm, 1982). Older but still useful is W. N. Medlicott, *The Economic Blockade*, vols. I-II (London, 1952–9).

[53] M. Fritz, 'Swedish Iron Ore and Ball-Bearings in the German War Economy', in M. Fritz, Nygren, Olsson, and Olsson. *The Adaptable Nation*, 22–3.

All concerned parties understood also the military value of the high-quality ball bearings shipped in massive quantities to Germany. These shipments peaked in 1943, when Swedish ball-bearings constituted 70 per cent of those imported by Germany, which was in turn 10 per cent of the total German usage.[54] The Allies put tremendous pressure on Sweden to cease immediately all shipments of finished ball bearings, but Stockholm consistently and successfully resisted. Indeed, even after shipments of finished products were finally halted, the transfer of difficult-to-produce ball-bearing steel and production machinery continued, without Allied knowledge. Stockholm's position of 1944 was taken during a period when German war production reached its height, producing ten times more tanks that year than in 1939. Such an increase would obviously have been impossible without the vital raw and finished products supplied in 1943 and early 1944 by Sweden.[55] The Allies were so determined to stop this trade that American representatives informally threatened to bomb SKF (*Svensk Kullagar Fabrik*, by far the most important Swedish producer) factories in Gothenburg and threatened to blacklist the company after the war.[56] Sweden deflected the pressure while maintaining production and profit:

> The example of ball-bearings demonstrates with admirable clarity how, then general political developments brought demands for a reduction of trade with Germany from 1943 onwards, Sweden certainly endeavoured formally to comply but at the same time in fact employed a variety of expedients, most of them hidden to view [*sic*] and not susceptible to control on the part of the Allies, in order to maintain its trade with Germany at as high a level as possible.[57]

A look at negotiations concerning shipments of ball-bearings illuminate the attitudes prevailing in Stockholm. On 25 April 1944, Erik Boheman met Herschel Johnson, American minister in Stockholm. Johnson inquired about the feasibility of halting shipments to Germany. Boheman replied that 'it is impossible for SKF to stop entirely all of its exports under existing contracts with Germany . . . but said he realised the importance we attach to immediate cessation of these exports'.[58] Three days later Boheman advised the American that direct negotiations

[54] Ibid., 28–9. [55] R. J. Overy, *Why the Allies Won* (London, 1995), 215.

[56] Efforts to halt German production at the SKF-owned VKF (Vereinigte Kugellagerfabriken AG) factories in Schweinfurt resulted in devastating losses in October 1943 to the American Eighth Air Force. VKF factories accounted for some 55–60 per cent of German bearing production. See Gerard Aalders and Cees Wiebes, *The Art of Cloaking Ownership. The Case of Sweden* (Amsterdam, 1996).

[57] M. Fritz, 'Swedish iron ore,' 32.

[58] H. Johnson to Secretary of State, 25 April 1944, no. 1454, *Foreign Relations of the United States, 1943, Sweden*, 524.

between SKF and the US government were desirable. 'He (Boheman) spoke rather strongly about what he believed is our mistaken attitude as to intrinsic importance of Swedish ball-bearing exports to Germany, and said that as we attach such inordinate importance to it he felt that it had almost a sinister significance . . . I asked him if the matter was out of hands of Foreign Office and was being decided at highest level of policy. He hesitated a moment and said it was true.'[59]

Some ten days later American negotiator Stanton Griffis met Marcus Wallenberg, one of Sweden's most important businessmen and bankers, and a government negotiator. Griffis stressed that the US considered it critical that shipments be halted immediately. Responding to Wallenberg's concerns, he assured the Swede that the American government was prepared to pay for all unfilled orders to Germany, and to protect SKF against any possible legal actions for breach of contract. 'Wallenberg stated that he feared this was impossible and that the company would under no circumstances agree.' Wallenberg, who was conversant with all relevant details about negotiations with both belligerent sides, said that 'commercial negotiations in the matter were inextricable from the relations of the Swedish government with Germany'.[60] An exchange followed which points to the heart of the differences, and which illuminates the attitudes of many Swedes (then and now), about their economic 'neutrality', as well as that of representatives (then and now) of the Allied democracies.

Mr Wallenberg continually referred to the sanctity of contracts and the unwillingness of either the Company or the Swedish government to be charged with violation of the German contract. We endeavoured to point out that far above the morality of contracts was the duty and responsibility of the Company and the Government towards the Swedish nation and that any move which was a defined advance towards the safety and integrity of Sweden was in a category higher than the sanctity of a commercial contract.[61]

This conversation took place less than a month before D-Day, long after men such as Wallenberg knew with some precision of the on-going 'final solution', and with the end of the war increasingly in sight.

One important and illuminating aspect of Swedish neutrality is the manner in which the government and people responded to the genocide of Europe's Jewish population. Curiously, yet for a variety of identifiable

59 Ibid., H. Johnson to Secretary of State, 28 April 1944, no. 1506, 528–9.
60 Ibid., S. Griffis (through Johnson) to Secretary of State, 9 May 1944, no. 1634, 532.
61 Ibid., 533–4.

reasons, this fascinating side of Swedish neutrality has escaped the attention of the Swedish historians of the traditional school.[62] This lack of scholarly interest stands out even more starkly considering that it is a morally positive side of neutrality which balances Sweden's dubious trade policy. Striking as well is the fact that the story of Raoul Wallenberg, perhaps this century's most famous Swede and a hero of the Holocaust, remains unexplored by Swedish political historians.[63]

As in other western democracies, Sweden knew of Nazi Germany's anti-Jewish policies immediately after January 1933. However, apart from regular newspaper reporting on the persecution and its increase throughout the 1930s, there was little that the government of Sweden did, or wanted to do, about Hitler's rapidly expanding anti-Jewish campaign. Hansson's government refused to condemn the outrages, nor was any thought given to liberalising immigration restrictions which might have helped some Jews find refuge, even if only temporarily. By 1941, when the doors of Europe were finally sealed, Sweden had provided shelter for approximately 2,000 Jews, far fewer than most other European nations, even smaller ones.[64]

When the 'refugee crisis' reached its height following the *Anschluß* of March 1938, Sweden responded by tightening border restrictions. At this time, in unknown conjunction with the Swiss government, Stockholm urged the Germans to mark Jews' passports, leading to the infamous large red 'J' stamped into the document. Students at the country's three main universities demonstrated against the 'import of Jews', and generally, in spite of its well developed humanitarian traditions, UD and other government officials responded to the plight of European Jewry with cold indifference – an attitude based largely on anti-Semitic feelings.[65]

In popular and scholarly literature of the Holocaust, Sweden is called a 'bystander', a categorisation which holds true until late October 1942,

[62] On this neglect, see my forthcoming 'Holocaust Historiography in Sweden Today; New Promise after Years of Disinterest?' (Studentlitteratur (in Swedish), Umeå, 1999). See also my doctoral thesis, 2nd edition, 'Swedish Historiography and the Holocaust – A Generation Delayed', 286–301.

[63] The only two scholarly studies of Sweden's reaction to the genocide are S. Koblik, *The Stones Cry Out; Sweden's Response to the Persecution of the Jews, 1933–1945* (New York, 1988), and P. A. Levine, *From Indifference to Activism; Swedish Diplomacy and the Holocaust, 1938–1944*, (Uppsala, 2nd ed, 1998). There is to date no full-scale scholarly study of Raoul Wallenberg, or Count Folke Bernadotte, another important individual connected to Sweden's response to the genocide.

[64] On this see H. Lindberg, *Svensk flyktingpolitik under internationellt tryck 1936–1941* (Stockholm, 1973), 217. Part of the SUAV series, this important study details Sweden's response to the refugee crisis, but concludes when the extermination itself commences.

[65] I have addressed this issue in my article, 'Anti-semitism in Sweden's Foreign Office – How Important was it?,' *Historisk tidskrift*, 1 (1996), 8–27, as well as in ch. 5 in my doctoral dissertation.

when the 'final solution' struck Norway. From then on, Stockholm's response changed from a policy of restrictive indifference to one of committed activism. The change was largely effected by one man, Gösta Engzell, a lifelong civil servant and wartime head of UD's Legal Division. At his direction, Sweden's diplomats came to use their neutral status as fully recognised interlocutors to lobby, sometimes successfully, sometimes not, for the lives of many Jews – the vast majority of whom were not Swedish citizens. As noted, this shift began in Norway, when the government allowed some 800 to 900 Norwegian Jews to cross the border, as well as aiding some by issuing different types of Swedish diplomatic documents which served, sometimes, to protect Norwegian and stateless Jews from deportation. Then, throughout 1943 in such cities as Vichy, Paris, Amsterdam, Berlin, Prague, and elsewhere, protective assistance was given to dozens of Jews. The acceptance of Denmark's Jewish population in October 1943 brought over 7,000 Jews into safety, and then, in Budapest in 1944, between 15,000 to 25,000 Jews received some form of Swedish assistance. This of course is when, after July, Raoul Wallenberg made his historic contribution. The war's last months saw Swedish assistance given in the form of Count Folke Bernadotte's 'White Busses', as well as the reception of several thousand survivors after May 1945.

In fact, after autumn 1942, with specific regard to the implementation of Nazi racial policy (which of course formed the very core of Nazism, and motivated many of Hitler's decisions from 1933 to 1945), Sweden abandoned its neutrality. Saving Jews from the murderous ravages of Nazism was a decidedly unneutral act, one which other neutral nations could have done, but mostly did not. Thus at the same time as Sweden sold militarily vital supplies to Germany, it also was responsible, at least indirectly, for the salvation of tens of thousands of Jews. However, it is not the heroic individual efforts of Raoul Wallenberg which characterises Sweden's rescue of Jews, but rather the normative diplomacy conducted by civil servants connected with UD. The method by which they assisted Jews can usefully be called 'bureaucratic resistance'. Using their recognised status as representatives of a neutral sovereign state, Swedish diplomats placed their 'good offices' between the putative perpetrator and the potential victim. By using normative bureaucratic procedures, Swedish diplomats were able, in individual cases, to block the implementation of Nazi racial policy. This was done generally by forestalling deportation, and always because of specific choices made by individual Swedish diplomats interacting with their German counterparts.

Proceeding from a basic assumption that the Jews in question were of political interest to the Swedish government, a claim was made for their wellbeing, one generally manifested by issuing a document articulating this connection.[66] Swedish diplomats bent rules and practices to help Jews who under normal circumstances would never have had a chance of obtaining Swedish diplomatic protection, and these representations were often made in the face of German protests. It is a striking fact that even during the height of the killing, merely by doing their jobs, Swedish diplomats did something which few others during the war, even other neutral diplomats, ever attempted – they took advantage of a gap in Nazi ideology which they understood was there, and which they worked to exploit. And when German bureaucrats were confronted with an official from a sovereign state authorised to make an appeal on behalf of individual Jews, even Nazi officials could and did give way. Not always, but at least sometimes.

These tactics worked because, for reasons detailed above, Germany had a strong interest in maintaining normal diplomatic and trade relations with Sweden. Because of this, even in matters concerning the lives of Jews, German officials were compelled to respond to Swedish appeals in a serious fashion. A report written by Gösta Engzell during the Danish episode of October 1943 encapsulates much of what the Swedes did:

> During Jewish deportations from Norway the German occupation authorities adopted a viewpoint based on the principle that Swedish government decisions to grant Swedish citizenship to Norwegian or stateless people could not be legally recognised. From a formal point of view the German standpoint is unquestionably well founded ... Nonetheless, in spite of this attitude, in many cases, if the person in question knew that he had been naturalised and this had been confirmed with the German authorities, this led to a forestalling of deportation. Furthermore, this made it possible to conduct negotiations concerning the person's release, which sometimes succeeded. In light of this experience it is urgent that all people who have in the last days been granted Swedish citizenship ... be informed immediately and receive a passport. In Norway it even proved possible to inform some people who were in hiding.[67]

By maintaining some semblance of neutrality, Swedish diplomats could have chosen, as did so many of their counterparts elsewhere, to stand by. They did not, and their choices led to Jewish lives being saved.

[66] Such claims lie at the heart of Wallenberg's famous '*Schutzpass*' of which he distributed many hundreds. More valuable, even in Budapest, were legally recognised provisional passports. See Levine, *From Indifference to Activism, Swedish Diplomacy and the Holocaust*, esp. ch. 12.

[67] Report by G. Engzell, 8 October 1943, HP 21 Ad, *Riksarkivet.*

Any understanding of Swedish foreign policy during the war must be based on an understanding of the primacy of choice. Just as some Swedish officials chose to help Jews, other officials and businessmen chose to trade with Nazi Germany when they could have done otherwise. More than ever it appears that Swedish leaders made some correct choices, as well as some very bad ones. The issue is not that Sweden traded (as international law gave it every right to) with Nazi Germany during the first phase of the war, roughly from 1939 to 1941. No fair-minded observer did, or has, argued that this trade violated either legal or moral neutrality. To that date Sweden's policy – that is, the choices made – was founded upon history, precedent, and a morally tenable interpretation of international conduct. During that initial phase, Hitler's war was still considered by most to be a 'normal' conflict. Nor is the enduring controversy centred in any real way on the so-called 'midsummer crises,' or other relatively minor concessions granted to the Germans when Sweden was most vulnerable. Although not true, defenders of what can be labelled the 'myth of Swedish neutrality' would have us believe that little of interest happened after 1943, and it is not a coincidence that the standard interpretation mostly avoids substantive consideration of the subsequent period. For them, policy decisions made after that date were based on the rapidly approaching post-war world. In this interpretation, continuing trade with Germany remains a matter of legally justified necessity. Yet it is after that date that the Allies put increasing pressure on Sweden to cease immediately all trade with Germany, which finally happened in late autumn 1944. The Germans still fought on for another six months, a fact which gives reason to note that some 600,000 Jews were murdered in the last twelve months of the war, as well as thousands of Allied soldiers and countless civilians.

*In fact, neutrality as such really is not the issue, it is the morality of how it was applied, which is.* Tellingly, there has never been a national debate because the government violated neutrality (in whatever slight fashion) to help the nations led by Winston Churchill and Franklin Roosevelt achieve their *war* aims. The limited assistance given the Allies also violated neutrality, but this has not been, nor will ever be, controversial. The acute moral discomfort felt by the Swedish people for some two generations arises from and remains because, during the war, their nation economically collaborated with and thus aided militarily Germany's Nazi regime *far beyond reasonable necessity*. Relations with Hitler's Germany were controversial then, and will remain so, because the help given Nazi Germany's war-making capacity created, justifiably, deep moral concern in a democratic people such as the Swedes. Continuing normal trade with Nazi Germany during the first half of the war may have been a legitimate form of *Realpolitik* but was scarcely so afterwards. The massive amounts of iron ore, ball bearings and other commercial connections, after mid-1943, provided direct aid to a genocidal government doomed to lose the war.

It is sometimes said that 'people didn't know' the real nature of Hitlerian evil until the war ended. Yet Richard Overy reminds us that, 'Hatred of Hitler and Hitlerism long pre-dated the final evidence of the Holocaust and the catalogue of crimes exposed in 1945. Its roots go back to the 1930s . . . The belief that their cause was on the side of progress in world history gave a genuine moral certainty to the Allies, which the Axis population largely lacked . . . It is this contrast that helps to explain the eventual outcome of the war.'[68] And it is this contrast which underlies the moral discomfort felt by young Swedes when they learn the details, and not only the myths, of their nation's wartime history. This discomfort is particularly understandable considering that Sweden's post-war social welfare state is based on notions of progress, justice, and democratic solidarity.

*Indirectly to be sure*, but undeniable all the same, it is a fact that by trading with Germany as it did, Sweden materially assisted the commission of genocide. This alone ensures that Sweden's relations with Germany, that is, the nation's 'neutrality' during the war, will for generations to come remain a profoundly troubling issue. Yet this problem, while bad enough, is made more complicated because by aiding Germany far longer than reasonably necessary, Sweden's coalition government took very real steps towards ensuring its own ultimate destruction. For Hitler, democracy was, along with the Jews, the ideological enemy to be obliterated from the face of Europe. No one alive during the war, when viewing German occupation policies, could possibly have believed that democratic political systems were safe. Had Germany stabilised its hegemony over Europe, Swedish social democracy would have been crushed.

Holocaust historian Raul Hilberg has written that, 'Neutrality is a zero quantity that helps the stronger party in an unequal struggle.'[69] Democracy in Europe was genuinely at risk when the war began, and this threat did not begin to diminish until the end of 1942 or early 1943. Yet even after the apogee of the threat was reached, Social Democratic Sweden

[68] Overy, *Why the Allies Won*, 286.

[69] R. Hilberg, *The Destruction of the European Jews* (New York, 1983), revised and definitive edition, vol. 1, 309.

did precious little – indeed, almost nothing – to diminish the threat. It could have contributed in some fashion by cutting off trade earlier than it did, but its leaders decided that it was not in the state's interest to do so. This problem is followed by another. For nor did Swedish leaders decide to do anything substantive to aid the approaching Allied victory. This is why Swedes, and particularly the younger generations, struggle to understand the meaning of their nation's 'neutrality' during the Second World War. This moral imbalance formed the basis of Allied complaints against Sweden during the war, and it continues to frame the problem today. Nonetheless, this is not just an opinion made with facts in hand long afterwards. For in early summer 1944, Winston Churchill again had occasion to ponder Sweden's continuing trade with Nazi Germany. In his view, and that of others, reference to international law no longer sufficed. 'Surely it is right', he wrote, 'to put pressure on Sweden to sharpen her attitude to Germany. Neutrals who have played a selfish part throughout ought to be made to suffer in the post-war world.'[70] As a new century begins, we see a clear echo of Churchill's ideas in a recent editorial. It opined, among other negative judgements upon Sweden's wartime neutrality, '[Our] neutrality during the war was based far more on national egoism than principle.'[71] This judgement, equally harsh then and now, does not make for pleasant reading. Yet it is reasonable to conclude that, had Per Albin Hansson made other choices after the first few months of 1943, Sweden's long-term interests would have been better served. His understanding of neutrality could have been different – it should have been different. 'Business as usual' with Nazi Germany has left a nasty legacy in Sweden's *folkhemmet.*

[70] W. Churchill, cited in Leifland, 'They must get in before the end', 121.
[71] *Uppsala Nya tidning*, 8 March 1999, 2.

CHAPTER 14

# *Switzerland: a neutral of distinction?*

*Neville Wylie*

> Of all the neutrals, Switzerland has the greatest right to distinction. She has been the sole international force linking the hideously sundered nations and ourselves. What does it matter whether she has been able to give us the commercial advantages we desire or has given too many to the Germans, to keep herself alive? She has been a democratic State, standing for freedom in self-defence among her mountains, and in thought, despite of race, largely on our side.
>
> Winston Churchill, 3 December 1944.[1]

Churchill's famous pronouncement provides a good starting point for any discussion of Swiss neutrality. In it Churchill highlighted four elements that, to his mind, gave Swiss neutrality its distinctive quality: Swiss democracy, its 'armed neutrality', humanitarian mission, and business activities. At the end of the war, the Swiss government in Berne did its best to construct an image of Switzerland's war that reflected Churchill's glowing testament. Serious debate was discouraged and 'unpalatable' information suppressed. When this was no longer possible, the country's pre-eminent diplomatic historian, Edgar Bonjour, was hired to present a sanitised version of the wartime events as a culmination of 'four hundred years of federal foreign policy'.[2] Although Bonjour's 'report' was by no means uncritical of Swiss policies, nor did it go unchallenged by other Swiss historians, it has been the recent 'revelations' about Swiss refugee and financial policies that has provoked a thorough reassessment of Switzerland's part in the war. This chapter will not chart the evolution of Swiss historiography on the subject, as a comprehensive

[1] Cited in Martin Gilbert, *Winston S Churchill*, vol. VIII (London, 1986), 1028, note 1.

[2] Edgar Bonjour, *Geschichte der schweizerischen Neutralität. Vier Jahrhunderte eidgenössischer Aussenpolitik* 6 vols. (Basle, 1970, French transl. 1970). Vol. IV to VI deal with the war years. For official attitudes towards Switzerland's wartime record, see Luc van Dongen, *La Suisse face à la Seconde Guerre Mondiale, 1945–1948. Emergence et construction d'une mémoire publique* (Geneva, 1998), 84–93.

survey has recently been published in English.[3] Rather, it will draw on the findings of the new scholarship and offer an assessment of the four issues that caught Churchill's attention in late 1944, and which remain to this day central to any judgement of Swiss neutrality during the last war.

## POLITICAL NEUTRALITY

As with the other neutrals, Swiss behaviour during the war was coloured by its historical development and political culture. Neutrality was central to Switzerland's historical identity. In no other country was neutrality so deeply ingrained or so critical to the political fabric and survival of the state. Only by fostering consensual politics at home and adhering to a strict neutrality abroad could the federal government accommodate the diverse national, ethnic, and religious interests of its disparate population. At an international level too, Swiss neutrality enjoyed a unique status. The Great Powers had pledged to respect Swiss political independence in 1815, and despite the temptation they remained true to their word thereafter. Swiss democracy was not universally admired, but by 1939 its neutrality had become such an established and revered feature of European politics that all states, even those of a Fascist hue, would think twice about flagrantly infringing its rights. Switzerland's adherence to a policy of neutrality in 1939 was thus predetermined. The only choice facing Berne was how best to ensure the belligerents would respect all Swiss neutral rights in practice. A voluntary renunciation of neutrality or the adoption of policies that openly flouted Switzerland's neutral obligations was out of the question.

If Switzerland's historical traditions committed Berne to a policy of neutrality, it was the immediate experiences of the 1930s that ultimately shaped Swiss perceptions of what constituted a 'neutral foreign policy' within the context of the 1940s. The key foreign policy debate during the inter-war period concerned Switzerland's adherence to the League of Nations. Berne had been exempted from the League's military obligations when it joined in 1920, and many Swiss had won international acclaim for their work in Geneva, but the federal government had never been comfortable with Switzerland's 'partial' (or 'differential') neutrality as a member of the League. The decision to distance itself from Geneva and return to its former 'absolute neutrality' in March 1938 was

[3] Georg Kreis (ed.), *Switzerland and the Second World War* (London, 2000). This excellent survey should be the starting point for any serious research into the subject.

thus in part a matter of the Swiss learning the error of their ways and appreciating the value of their traditional policies. It was also, however, in large measure a direct response to the deterioration of European political and economic relations over the preceding years. Swiss neutrality may have been guaranteed by *all* the Great Powers in 1815, but in times of crisis it was Switzerland's nearest neighbours – France, Germany, and Italy – whose voices were heard loudest in the federal council. In the circumstances, especially in light of the Berne's unfortunate experience in 1935/6 over the League's imposition of economic sanctions on Italy, neutrality was perceived not simply as an end point in itself, but rather as a tactical device to unshackle Switzerland from the discredited League and reconcile Swiss political interests with those of its Fascist neighbours.

The return to 'absolute' neutrality reflected a broader shift in Swiss diplomacy, in which Berne slowly narrowed its diplomatic horizon and disengaged from the wider international community. This process continued after war began. Swiss officials did not ignore Anglo-French wishes, nor were they under any illusion that an outright German victory would be to Switzerland's advantage. But priority continued to be given to convincing Rome and Berlin of Switzerland's unflinching commitment to neutrality, irrespective of the democratic nature of its political institutions and pro-Allied sentiments of the bulk of the population. During the Phoney War Swiss diplomats spent most of their time assuaging German irritation over the appearance of 'unneutral' articles in the Swiss press, defending Swiss business interests against the Allied blockade, and preventing the Allies from coaxing the League back into life as a tool for western diplomacy. The assumption, then, that were it not for the cataclysmic events over the summer of 1940 Swiss foreign policy would have remained orientated towards the Allied camp, is a faulty one. Though popular sympathies lay with the democracies, Switzerland's foreign political interests diverged markedly from those of the Allied governments.

Berne's attitude towards the war was also influenced by domestic political considerations. Until the turn of the century political allegiances had followed confessional lines, between Protestant radicalism and Catholic conservatism. While religion continued to affect political and social values, the introduction of proportional representation in 1918 transformed Switzerland's political landscape by finally enabling the socialists to translate their electoral support into tangible parliamentary gains. By 1935, the socialists had become the largest single party, were in a position to contest the bourgeois parties' grip on Swiss political life and demand a seat on the country's political executive, the seven-man federal council. Political tensions were not as acute as elsewhere in Europe, but many Swiss viewed the rise of organised labour and socialism as a threat to the country's social fabric and to the system of consensus politics that had been carefully nurtured since the civil war of the 1840s. Switzerland's political and business élite naturally looked at the war not only for its impact on Switzerland's place in Europe, but also for its effect on their own political and social circumstances. And while none of the mainstream parties questioned Switzerland's adherence to neutrality, federal officials inevitably addressed foreign policy issues with an eye to their potential impact on the balance of political forces at home.

Over the past century, the Swiss had become accustomed to distancing themselves from the national and religious convulsions of their neighbours. In the 1930s, faced with the need to isolate the country from the ideological and nationalist paroxysms that gripped the continent, the federal authorities embarked on a programme to heighten Swiss national consciousness. The various measures enacted – from elevating Romansch to an 'official' language to show-casing Swiss achievements in a National Exhibition in 1939 – promoted an awareness of a distinctive Swiss identity that probably helped Switzerland overcome the psychological shocks of the war. In contrast to the First World War, when opinion fragmented along linguistic lines, after 1939 Switzerland's population hung together behind the banner of neutrality. There was, however, a hidden price to pay. In self-consciously insulating their country from corrosive foreign influences, the Swiss inadvertently blinded themselves to the wider moral and political issues at stake in the conflict. During the Phoney War the sense of detachment was manifest most conspicuously in Switzerland's business-as-usual attitude, the general disinterest shown in the rights and wrongs of the war, and an inclination to value Swiss freedoms and neutrality above those of all others. France's fall accentuated the trend, leaving Switzerland as a beleaguered outpost, whose citizens, while intensely interested in the course of the war, felt distanced from it. As one astute observer remarked in early 1945, the Swiss were like the passengers of an air-conditioned liner; they 'could see through the portholes the storm and stress of the weather or the heat of the tropics', but failed to appreciate 'the conditions which the captain and crew were facing and by which they were hardened and influenced'.[4] In short, the federal

[4] Clifford Norton (British minister, Berne) to Foreign Office, 13 February 1945. Public Record Office (PRO), FO371/49714 Z2778.

authorities were more concerned with fine tuning the air-conditioning for their well-heeled passengers, than assisting the sweltering souls suffering out on the deck. Swiss neutrality, especially during the middle war years, was treated in an increasingly restrictive fashion. Instead of providing a mandate for intervention, neutrality was invariably used as a justification for inaction.

The collapse of France dealt a shattering blow to Switzerland's foreign and domestic political position. The balance of power upon which Swiss neutrality had rested since 1815 was gone: so, too, the faith in French republicanism which the Swiss had drawn on selectively since the 1790s. In May 1940, Germany looked set to put an end to Swiss independence by force, and by mid-June, the fall of Paris and Italian entry into the war shattered the political equilibrium considered essential for the maintenance of Swiss neutrality. Berne's political reaction to this crisis has dominated historical debate.[5] Attention has rightly focused on two related issues. The first was Switzerland's diplomatic response to the emergence of German hegemony. What most troubled the federal authorities, especially the foreign minister and federal president in 1940, Marcel Pilet-Golaz, was the fear that Berlin would present demands which were incompatible to Swiss neutrality, such as the transiting of troops or insisting on the severance of diplomatic relations with London. The defence of Swiss political independence was therefore given precedence over all other issues. Conceding minor political points or granting economic and financial favours were all considered appropriate if they helped bring about the desired result.

The second issue related to Switzerland's domestic political situation. On several occasions in the summer and autumn of 1940, most famously in a radio address on 25 June, Pilet appeared ready to go beyond a tactical adjustment of Swiss foreign policy, to instituting wholesale political reform at home. Pilet's dubious utterances can be interpreted as masterful strokes to forestall possible German demands in this direction. This behaviour, however, is more likely to have sprung from deeper beliefs that had been sharpened and clarified by the traumatic events that summer. Though alarmed by the rise of German power, a sizeable proportion of Switzerland's ruling élite was inclined to make a virtue of necessity and seize the moment to create a more unified, centralised government, devoid of 'alien' liberal influences and capable of

[5] See, among others, Jean-Claude Favez, 'La grande peur de l'été 1940 – La Suisse entre résistance et adaptation', *L'année 40 en Europe* (Caen, 1990), 85–99. G.-A. Chevallaz, *Le défi de la neutralité. Diplomatie et défense de la Suisse 1939–1945* (Vevey, 1995), 55–152.

tackling the socialist threat. Talk of political 'renovation' in the summer of 1940 was not a knee-jerk reaction to Switzerland's predicament, but reflected the long-held aspirations of Switzerland's conservative right.[6] Such thoughts were accommodated with greater or lesser ease by the bourgeois parties, while in the federal council, the infirmity or inexperience of most of the federal councillors meant that those most susceptible to the reformist ideas – Pilet and the interior minister Philipp Etter – held the upper hand for several critical months after France's collapse.[7]

In retrospect, the defence of Swiss political independence after the summer of 1940 was remarkably successful. The momentum behind domestic political reform slowly dissipated over the autumn, despite Pilet's meeting with Swiss Nazis in September: caution prevailed, and pressure for reform was held in check. On 10 September, after affirming the need for a 'total revision of the federal constitution', the council agreed to withhold further discussion so long as the economic and political dangers facing Switzerland remained.[8] Although this curtailed neither the aspirations of Swiss conservatives nor the council's efforts to meet German demands, its significance should not be underestimated, for despite the reformers' attachment to neutrality, it is difficult to see how instituting wholesale political changes would not have affected Swiss standing abroad. To British listeners, Pilet's speeches had a sufficiently 'Pétainist ring' to raise doubts over his intentions, and had political reform been pushed through, there is no doubt that Swiss protestations of political neutrality and impartiality would have been given little credence in London or Washington.

At the same time, in judging Swiss success, it must be remembered that Berne was never confronted with demands that openly contradicted its claim to political neutrality. The Swiss were never asked to introduce racial laws or suspend the constitution, far less adhere to the Tripartite pact or join the war on the Axis' side. Berlin's restraint might be explained by the belief that Berne would never willingly abandon its political freedoms and neutrality, or conversely that, given time, the

[6] A referendum on constitutional reform was held in 1935. On the radical Right see among others Aram Mattioli, *Zwischen Demokratie und totalitärer Diktatur. Gonzague de Reynold und die Tradition der autoritären Rechte in der Schweiz* (Zurich, 1994), and Roland Butikofer, *Le refus de la modernité. La Ligue vaudoise: une extrême droite et la Suisse (1919–1945)* (Lausanne, 1996).

[7] Of the seven councillors at the start of 1940, by December two had died and another two retired.

[8] 'Richtlinien für die bundesrätliche Politik', Department of the Interior, 10 September 1940. *Documents Diplomatiques Suisses* (hereafter *DDS*), vol. XIII, 379.

council could be trusted to carry out the necessary reforms on its own. German behaviour is most readily explained, however, by the fact that, on purely political grounds, Berlin had little reason for dispensing with Swiss neutrality in 1940. Riding roughshod over Swiss neutral rights would have damaged German diplomatic interests at the time – particularly its efforts to woo Vichy into the Axis camp. Though irritated by Berne's lackadaisical response to British overflights and the 'unneutral' attitude of the Swiss press, Berlin was content to limit itself to expressing its displeasure through diplomatic channels. By the end of the war Germany had lodged some 169 official protests with the federal government.

Compromises were nonetheless made which affected Swiss neutrality. Apart from tightening press censorship and lifting a six-year-old ban on the sale of the *Völkischer Beobachter* newspaper, Berne took a number of foreign political initiatives that required a creative reading of Swiss neutrality in order to justify them. Over the second half of 1940, Berne introduced a 'blackout' at Berlin's behest and agreed to repatriate 45,000 French troops who had sought sanctuary in Switzerland to avoid capture during the fighting in June. It also released German pilots who landed in Switzerland, claiming that their flights were of a 'non-operational' character. The same courtesy was not extended to Allied airmen. In other areas, however, Berne held the line. The Polish legation remained open and those Polish soldiers who had entered Switzerland with the French were allowed to stay. Berne turned a blind eye to British economic and intelligence activities in the country, and despite strong domestic pressure to cut its ties with the League, it limited itself to simply suspending some of the privileges previously enjoyed by the League staff.[9] Berne thereby maintained a semblance of political neutrality that accorded with the interests of both sides. It 'leaned' towards Germany in some respects, yet sufficiently catered for Allied interests to prevent a complete breakdown of trust and confidence. For the Allies, the existence of 'a democratic State, standing for freedom in self defence' was, as Churchill rightly noted, of considerable significance in itself. The survival of thriving parliamentary institutions in the midst of Fascist Europe demonstrated the vitality of democracy far more effectively than the Allied propagandists could hope to accomplish.

[9] For the importance of intelligence considerations, see. N. Wylie, '"Keeping the Swiss Sweet." Intelligence as a Factor in British Policy towards Switzerland During the Second World War,' *Intelligence & National Security*, 11/3 (July 1996), 442–67.

## ECONOMIC NEUTRALITY

In the absence of decisive German or Italian political demands, the greatest test of Swiss neutrality proved to be an economic one. This was not unexpected. During the First World War the belligerents had so encroached on Swiss economic freedom that the body charged with defending Swiss commercial interests, the 'Société Suisse de Surveillance économique' was quickly dubbed 'Souveraineté Suisse Suspendue.' Admirable attempts were made to stockpile reserves and increase agricultural production before and during the war, but the dearth of indigenous sources of raw materials and solid fuels, coupled with the export orientation of most of Switzerland's leading firms, inevitably limited what Berne could realistically achieve. Economic isolationism was not a luxury the Swiss could afford.

Switzerland's economic success in surviving the war, at least in material terms, is indisputable. Although some sectors fared better than others, the Swiss economy passed through the war relatively unscathed and was in a good position to profit from the upturn in the European economy in the 1950s.[10] Furthermore, on purely statistical terms, it can be argued that the Swiss met their neutral obligations. Over the war as a whole, the value of trade with both camps was remarkably similar, while in the thorny issue of gold receipts, the Swiss National Bank received almost double the amount of gold from the Allies (2,262.5m Swiss Francs) as it did from the Axis (1,356.8m Swiss Francs).[11] In its broad outline, the shape and scale of Switzerland's commercial interaction with both sides has been known for some time. What has been less well appreciated, and where new research has been particularly illuminating, is how federal officials approached the country's economic predicament, how policy was made, and the extent to which economic policy was driven by non-economic considerations.[12]

In their official discussions with the belligerents, Swiss negotiators consistently presented their trade policy as a function of the terms and conditions of Swiss neutrality. At no time were Switzerland's economic contacts with either side completely severed, and Berne could claim that its trade

[10] Only in 1944 did the value of Swiss exports drop below 1937 levels: in 1941 and 1943 they exceeded 1937's figures by 10 per cent and 20 per cent. Imports were worse affected. Pre-war (1937) levels were maintained until late 1943, but then collapsed by 30 per cent in 1944. Jean Hotz, 'Division du commerce et politique commerciale pendant la guerre', in *L'économie de guerre en Suisse, 1939–1949* (Berne, 1951), 62.

[11] Net figures. Independent Commission of Experts, *Switzerland and Gold Transactions in the Second World War. Interim Report* (Berne 1998), 51.

[12] See H.-U. Jost, *Politik und Wirtschaft im Krieg. Die Schweiz 1938–1948* (Zurich, 1998).

policy had been governed by a sense of impartiality. Nonetheless, the fluctuations in the war inevitably impacted on Switzerland's trade with the two camps. Germany's complaint in May 1940, that Switzerland was 'a huge armaments plant . . . working almost exclusively for England and France', was not entirely inaccurate given the scale of Allied war contracts with Swiss firms at this time.[13] By the end of the year, however, exports to Germany had trebled and accounted for nearly a third of all Swiss trade. Generous credit facilities appended to commercial agreements in August 1940 and July 1941 pump-primed Swiss–German trade for a further three years, and allowed Berlin to accumulate a debt of over 1000mSF by early 1944.[14] With exports to Britain slumped to a mere 2 per cent of the total after June 1940, it was only the maintenance of trading links with the United States, and Britain's successful commercial smuggling operations, that saved Switzerland from a complete economic *Anschluß*.[15] Substantial reductions in Swiss–German trade were eventually introduced in late 1943, partly due to Allied pressure and partly to Berlin's failure to meet its quotas of coal and raw material imports for Swiss industries. But from mid-1940 until mid-1943 Berne was essentially obliged to plead *force majeure* in its economic relations with the Allies, in the hope that they would sympathise with Switzerland's predicament. For most of this period, as Churchill's minute shows, Swiss faith in British (if not American) forbearance was not misplaced.[16]

Given the obvious economic dependency on German goodwill, there has been a tendency amongst historians to assume that Berne had no alternative other than to meet German demands. It is clear however that Swiss policy decisions were guided by more than just a calculation of the country's economic needs or a reading of its neutral rights. Over the crisis-filled months in mid-1940, Switzerland's looming economic difficulties were only part of a broader set of problems facing policy-makers in Berne, including the collapse of Swiss security and a deterioration of its political relations with Berlin. The sense of crisis encouraged the federal

[13] Memo by Ritter, 30 May 1940, *Documents in German Foreign Policy*, Series D, vol. IX, (London, 1956), no. 329.

[14] This represented three-quarters of Germany's total debt to continental neutral countries at the time.

[15] Bourgeois makes the valid point that while Switzerland's debt to Germany was substantially larger than any other neutral state, it was much less than the debts accrued by German satellites. Daniel Bourgeois, *La Troisième Reich et la Suisse* (Neuchatel, 1974), 180–1.

[16] One senior official wrote of the Swiss–German trade agreement of July 1941, 'I don't hold it against the English that they are unhappy with it. We are not filled with enthusiasm for it either . . . but it is not Switzerland's fault that France collapsed.' Homberger to Haettenschwiller 6 October 1941. Schweizerisches Bundesarchiv, Berne (hereafter BA.) E7110 134/4. Enclosure V.

council to seize on any means to 'repair' its relations with Berlin, and not to quibble over the scale of Swiss commercial and financial concessions. As Pilet blandly remarked on 21 June while discussing the size of credit to be offered to Berlin, 'il sera inopportun de discuter sur un million de plus ou de moins'.[17]

Berne's 'appeasement' (Pilet's word) of Germany in mid-1940 might have been an entirely understandable, even appropriate, policy, but Berne's continued commitment to the Axis in subsequent years and its apparent deafness to Allied wishes is harder to justify. Two factors appear to have been critical in shaping Swiss attitudes towards its economic predicament during the war. First of all, Berne's exaggerated fear of social and political unrest and its likely detrimental impact on the bourgeois political establishment at home, meant that a premium was placed on securing access to German sources of coal and raw materials so as to guarantee employment for Switzerland's industrial work force. For most of the war, the maintenance of good labour relations was probably more influential in shaping the country's external commercial relations, at least at the level of federal policy-making, than the search for profit or the desire to forge good relations with the Axis. The elevation to the federal council in December 1943 of the socialist politician, Ernst Nobs, did not materially alter the council's political outlook. By this stage, the socialists had discarded their earlier radicalism, and were determined to prove themselves responsible partners in federal government. Moreover, they were as anxious as their bourgeois colleagues to secure full employment at home even if this entailed supping with the devil in Berlin. Memories of the General Strike of 1918 kept the goal of 'industrial peace' at the forefront of Berne's attention right up until the moment the guns fell silent. Allied threats to suspend food and fodder imports and the freezing of Swiss assets in the United States in June 1941 might make Swiss workers hungry, aggravate inflationary pressures on the Swiss franc and alarm Swiss investors, but neither affected the council's main domestic priority of maintaining the country's social stability and political harmony.

Secondly, Berne's economic policy was tailored to meet the interests of the country's powerful business and banking élites. Berne had developed close links with Switzerland's major business and banking associations during the 1930s. These contacts were further consolidated once war began, when Berne drew on the services and expertise of Swiss businessmen

[17] *DDS* XIII, 314/1.

to reinforce the federal bureaucracy, committees, and delegations.[18] Hans Sulzer, owner of the engineering firm, Gebrüder Sulzer, and Peter Vieli, executive board member of Credit Suisse, both led trade missions abroad: the latter's success in dealing with the Italians made him the obvious choice to become Swiss ambassador in Rome in 1942.[19] Switzerland's professional business associations, especially the Chamber of Commerce, which represented Switzerland's largest employers, and the Association of Swiss Bankers, were afforded privileged access to the higher reaches of federal policy-making, and their members were allowed to expound their views freely on political, diplomatic and press matters.[20] It would be wrong to think that Switzerland's business class simply imposed their views on a docile federal bureaucracy. Many of Switzerland's politicians and officials came from commercial backgrounds and shared the same outlook as the country's business community. However, the war brought about a much higher degree of cooperation, even coordination, between the public and private sector than had been the case hitherto. While few of Switzerland's commercial élite were as extreme as Paul Rossy, board member of the Swiss National Bank, who in July 1940 recommended that Switzerland 'consciously seek its place in [the] new world and endeavour to play an active role in it', most were sufficiently fearful of the incipient threat of unemployment at home to press Berne to safeguard their access to Germany's raw-material supplies and export market.[21]

It was primarily this convergence of Switzerland's political and economic interests that accounts for the priority given to commercial interests in Swiss foreign policy once the crisis of 1940 had passed. By early 1941 Swiss foreign political policy had become the handmaiden to the country's commercial interests. Hitler's invasion of the Soviet Union was probably decisive in this respect, not so much in winning the Swiss over to the benefits of National Socialism, but in massively expanding Germany's demand for Swiss manufactures and locking key industrial sectors into Germany's economic production requirements. This process

[18] Swiss commercial interests in northern Italy had a decisive influence on Swiss attitudes during the sanctions crisis in 1935/6.

[19] Oswald Inglin, *Der stille Krieg. Der Wirtschaftskrieg zwischen Grossbritannien und der Schweiz im Zweiten Weltkrieg* (Zurich, 1991), 53.

[20] See, for example, minutes of the chamber's meeting on 15 August, when it expressed its support for 'a deepening of economic relations' to improve relations with Berlin, but also pressed for tighter press censorship and criticised Berne's handling of Swiss foreign policy. Archiv für Zeitgeschichte, ETH Zurich. Nachlass Homberger. Dossier II.

[21] Rossy cited in Independent Commission of Experts, *Switzerland and Gold Transactions*, 77 note 64.

can be measured in statistical terms – in the first half of 1942 Swiss exports to the Axis were valued at 1,166mSF, as compared to 1.7mSF to the Allies – but it is perhaps best seen in the initiatives taken by sections of the Swiss business community to curry favour amongst their German clients. The most celebrated instance of this practice was the dispatch of four medical missions to tend wounded German soldiers – though not their Russian counterparts – on the eastern front. The missions were the brain-child of the Germanophile Swiss minister in Berlin, were sponsored by the Swiss Red Cross and, the early ones at least, were fully funded by contributions drawn from companies involved in Switzerland's export trade with Germany.[22] A few companies even went so far as to provide guarantees for the 'racial purity' of their board members and used forced labour to work in their expanded production facilities in Germany. The massive profits accumulated by firms operating in Germany, which do not feature in the official trade statistics, suggest that Switzerland's economic contribution to the belligerents' war economies was very much greater than has been assumed hitherto.[23] The close relationships forged between Swiss manufacturers and financiers and their German counterparts over many years inclined many Swiss to ignore the implications of their business transactions and overlook the criminal nature of the regime that their urbane business partners ultimately represented. As late as April 1945, the Reichsbank's vice president was struck at 'how strong the cultural ties are that bind our two countries, even when today the political attitudes of the majority are not really in our favour.'[24]

Political considerations – which included the preservation of Swiss neutrality – inevitably encroached on commercial policy, through the negotiation of trade, transit, and credit agreements with foreign governments or the provision of export guarantees for Swiss firms. But control of commercial policy lay in the hands of a 'standing economic delegation' whose frame of reference and composition reflected the interests of the economic department and the business community rather than the political department (foreign ministry). While 'neutrality' was used abroad to defend Switzerland's commercial freedom, and while federal officials

[22] See Daniel Bourgeois, 'Operation "Barbarossa" and Switzerland', in Bernd Wegner (ed.), *From Peace to War. Germany, Soviet Russia and the World, 1939–1941* (Oxford, 1997), 593–610. Daniel Heller, *Eugen Bircher – Arzt, Militär und Politiker* (Zurich, 1988).

[23] Sophie Pavillon, 'Trois enterprises suisses en Allemagne du sud et leur développement durant la période nazie', *Etudes et Sources*, 23 (1997), 209–51, and Daniel Bourgeois, *Business Helvétique et Troisiéme Reich. Milieux d'affaires, politique étrangère, antisémitisme* (Lausanne, 1998).

[24] Emil Puhl to Walther Funk, 6 April 1945, cited in Marc Perrenoud and Sébastein Guex, 'Business as Usual', *Traverse*, 2 (1995), 59–60.

were well aware of the political benefits derived from Switzerland's trade with the Axis, direct political intervention in Swiss commercial activities after 1940 was slight. It was only in the last years of the war that political interests reasserted themselves. In 1943, when the Allies intensified their economic warfare campaign and attacked Hans Sulzer, Berne jettisoned the luckless businessman and agreed to meet Allied demands: protecting political relations with the Allies was considered more important than salvaging Sulzer's dignity. It was not until the last months of the war, however, during negotiations with the Allies in February–March 1945, that political imperatives were allowed to dictate federal economic policy. The need to secure raw materials and mend relations with the victorious Allies forced Berne into all but suspending its financial, transit, and commercial relations with Berlin.

Far from guiding Swiss policy, then, neutrality provided either rough guidelines or *post factum* justifications for the commercial activities of the business community. A good indication of this practice is found in the Swiss National Bank's purchasing of gold from the German Reichsbank. The bank began receiving gold in late 1941 in order to halt the decline of its own gold stock, precipitated by the increased demand for gold on the domestic money market and its inability to repatriate its reserves from America on account of the US freezing legislation. The bank's records reveal that its purchases were in no way connected with Berne's need to deter German aggression or conform to the 'dictates' of Swiss neutrality. Nor did either of these views affect the bank's decision to continue receiving Reichsbank gold in 1942 and 1943, despite the full knowledge that most had been acquired through dubious means. It was only under the pressure of Allied questioning in mid-1943, that the bank constructed a series of arguments to defend its earlier actions. Switzerland's neutrality was central to this defence, both in 1943 and the later years of the war.[25] 'To refuse gold', Allied delegates were informed in February 1945, 'is to operate a discrimination which is incompatible with our policy of neutrality.'[26] As with many aspects of Switzerland's commercial activities during the war, therefore, neutrality was only introduced into the discussion *after* the transactions had already taken place. For all its attempts to centralise control in its hands, Swiss officials had less

[25] See Independent Commission of Experts, *Switzerland and Gold Transactions*, ch. 2. Michel Fior, *Die Schweiz und das Gold der Reichsbank. Was wusste die Schweizerische Nationalbank?* (Zurich, 1997).

[26] Minutes of meeting between Swiss and Allied economic delegations 24 February 1945, BA. E2001 (D) 3/348 Internal discussion of the Swiss negotiating delegation, 9 February 1945. BA. E2800 1967/61 vol. 97.

influence over its business community than they would like to think. Their success in covering Swiss trade during the war with a cloak of neutrality ultimately says more about their ingenuity and the flexibility of the concept of neutrality than it does about the attitudes and intentions of the country's businessmen and financiers.

## ARMED NEUTRALITY

By far the most enduring depiction of Swiss neutrality to emerge from the war is that of the hardy Swiss soldier, rifle in hand, defying aggression and defending his homeland. This image has been cultivated by successive generations of Swiss military historians whose emphasis on Swiss military prowess in 1940 helped justify and reinforce the country's continued commitment to 'armed neutrality' during the Cold War. The reputation of the Swiss army during the war lies not just in its defence of the country's borders, but also in its symbolic value, in galvanising the population and federal leadership into resisting external pressure and defending Swiss independence.

Before examining the so-called Réduit strategy, it ought to be stressed that before France's collapse, Swiss defence arrangements were at odds with their professed policy of neutrality. Had Germany attacked any time before the third week in May, carefully laid joint Franco-Swiss plans would have swung into action, leading to the deployment of French troops on the western flank of Switzerland's fortified line running from Zurich to the Jura mountains west of Basle. These plans, initiated by Francophile elements within the Swiss army, made a mockery of Berne's claim to 'armed neutrality'. Moreover, their discovery by Germany gravely undermined subsequent Swiss protestations of neutrality and the standing of Switzerland's commander in chief, General Henri Guisan.[27]

Switzerland's military accomplishments during the war are certainly impressive. The militia system produced an army of some 800,000 men, including local defence groups and auxiliary army units. In the last years of peace, a serious effort had been made to re-arm and while defences were still weak in several key areas – notably heavy artillery, tanks, and anti-aircraft defences – Switzerland was capable of offering sufficient

[27] Georg Kreis, *Auf den Spuren von La Charité. Die schweizerische Armeeführung im Spannungsfeld des deutsch-französischen Gegensatzes 1936–1941* (Basle, 1976). Willi Gautschi, *General Henri Guisan. Die schweizerische Armeeführung im Zweiten Weltkrieg* (Zurich, 1989, French transl. 1991), 113–40, 355–78.

resistance to warrant serious consideration by any potential aggressor.[28] France's collapse inevitably prompted a rethinking of the country's strategic arrangements. In a speech on 25 July 1940, symbolically delivered on the Rütli meadow where the early cantons had sworn to resist alien rule in 1271, Guisan unveiled what became known as the Réduit strategy: a staged withdrawal of the army from the frontier regions into a defensive Alpine redoubt (Réduit). In theory, the Réduit offered a potent deterrent against an attack. Germany and Italy, Switzerland's most likely assailants, could not hope to knock out the Swiss army in a single blow, nor stop Guisan laying waste to Switzerland's industries or its two Alpine railway lines, upon which the Italian economy relied for its imports of German raw materials and coal.

The apparent success of the Réduit strategy has, however, tended to overshadow many of its complexities and ambiguities. One of its most glaring weaknesses was the fact that it entailed abandoning Switzerland's populous northern cantons at the first sign of trouble. While Guisan talked tough, foreign observers could legitimately question his ability to carry the country with him in a crisis. The Réduit was a high-risk strategy involving enormous sacrifices on behalf of the Swiss population: it is difficult to see how its existence could conceivably comfort Switzerland's political leadership, far less embolden them in their discussions with the Axis. The Réduit might, then, have provided for Switzerland's 'armed neutrality', but it did little to ease the country's economic or political predicament. At no time did the Swiss ever use the threat to destroy the trans-Alpine railways to strengthen their hand in discussions with the Axis. Swiss faith in the Réduit might be gauged from the decision to sell Switzerland's armaments production abroad rather than reserving it for their own army, or equally on the emphasis placed, in both civilian and military circles, on the army's role in guaranteeing social control and political stability at home.[29] Furthermore during the time of greatest danger, Guisan's deterrent strategy rested on shaky foundations. The Réduit only began to take shape in the spring of 1941, and reached completion a year later, when the St Gotthard railway tunnel was made ready for demolition. Had Axis forces invaded in the late summer or autumn of 1940, all major tunnels would have fallen into their hands intact, and the small number of sabotaged viaducts, ramps,

[28] Hans Senn, *Der schweizerische Generalstab Vol. VII. Anfänge einer Dissuasionsstrategie während des Zweiten Weltkrieges* (Basle, 1995), 299–302.

[29] For the social role of the army see Guisan's views in early 1945 cited in Dongen, *La Suisse*, 32–3, 72–3, and Pilet's remarks on 1 July 1940. *DDS*, vol. XIII, 325.

and bridges would not have posed insuperable difficulties for German engineers.[30]

Those who emphasise the importance of the army rest their case on two assumptions: firstly that the German invasion threat was genuine and secondly that Berlin was dissuaded from attacking because of the resolute attitude of the Swiss army. There is no doubting the menace posed by Hitler's Germany. On linguistic and ethnic grounds, Switzerland had a hard time convincing the Nazi leadership that it belonged outside the Reich. At his most charitable Hitler was prepared to 'use the [Swiss], at best, as hotel keepers', offering well-earned winter breaks for his Aryan supermen. Normally, however, he wanted to eradicate the unsightly 'pimple on the face of Europe'.[31] Whether this latent hostility was translated into a clear desire to invade Switzerland is, however, a matter of conjecture. The Swiss themselves felt most threatened during the German invasion of France, when the thought that Germany might outflank the French Maginot defences using Swiss territory triggered a wave of panic across the northern cantons. But although Hitler retained sizeable military formations in the south, there is no evidence that an attack on Switzerland ever occupied a prominent place in German grand strategy at this time.[32] Indeed, the most sophisticated invasion plans belong to the period after France's capitulation. According to Klaus Urner, Germany had both the means and the will to invade Switzerland in June, after the fighting in the north had reached its climax. Hitler himself appears to have taken a more active interest in Switzerland's fate than has previously been appreciated, largely out of his irritation at Switzerland's shooting down of German aircraft.[33] The absence of conclusive evidence as to why the various plans were not put into effect leaves the issue of a German 'threat' very much open.

There are, however, powerful reasons for thinking that Germany's plans were not as serious as some have assumed. If Berlin was earnest about adding Switzerland to its shopping list, it is difficult to explain why the task of drafting the first plans was given to a junior staff officer,

30 Neville Wylie, 'Le rôle des transports ferroviares en Suisse, 1939–1945: les aspects militaire, économique et politique', *Relations internationales*, 95 (1998), 361–80.

31 Hugh Trevor-Roper, *Hitler's Table-Talk. Hitler's conversations recorded by Martin Bormann* (Oxford, 1988), 25, 660.

32 Alfred Ernst argues that Swiss defences discouraged Germany from including Switzerland in its plans against France: 'Die Bereitschaft und Abwehrkraft Norwegens, Dänemarks und der Schweiz in deutscher Sicht', *Neutrale Kleinstaaten im Zweiten Weltkrieg* (Münsingen, 1973), 7–73, esp. 59–60.

33 Klaus Urner, "*Die Schweiz muss noch geschluckt werden!*" *Hitlers Aktionspläne gegen die Schweiz* (Zurich, 1990, French transl. 1996), 64–73.

with no previous experience on working on a project of this size. The military obstacles to a successful occupation were not insurmountable: Switzerland's partial *demobilisation* on 6 June, which left only 150,000 men under arms, would have laid any lingering concerns to rest. What did give cause for concern, however, was the possible shape of future political arrangements. When informal soundings were taken in Rome it was discovered that the Italians were going to cause difficulties, not because of their affection for the Swiss (something the Swiss consistently exaggerated), but because of the disproportionately large slice of land they would demand in any territorial carve-up.[34] Occupying Switzerland would, then, merely provoke awkward and unwelcome tensions between the two Axis partners. The planning and military posturing on Switzerland's frontier might more accurately be seen as part of a general campaign of pressure to bend the Swiss to Germany's will. As Hitler explained to Mussolini on 18 June, Switzerland was to be compelled to adopt a 'more conciliatory position in the question of [railway] transit, and, more generally, in its political attitude and that of the press'.[35] Most of these objectives were obtained over the coming weeks, through German pressure on Vichy France and the signing of the German–Swiss trade and credit agreement on 8 August. Guisan hit the mark on 22 June when he remarked that 'henceforth the Germans would primarily exercise political and economic pressure and [that] military action would scarcely be considered'.[36] The Swiss army's success in actually *deterring* a German attack in the summer of 1940 was minimal.

In fact discussion over the Réduit's deterrent effect overlooks the point that its success had nothing to do with its capacity to flummox German staff officers. German observers were clearly impressed with the Alpine Réduit, and if the voluminous intelligence reports recently discovered in the archive of the Abwehr chief, Admiral Canaris, are anything to go by, Berlin had no shortage of intelligence on all aspects of Swiss defence preparations upon which to base their views. But the secret of the Réduit's success lay not so much in Guisan's determination to defend the mountain chamois or destroy Switzerland's railways, but on his willingness to protect the vital artery linking the two Axis partners

[34] Tamaro (Italian minister, Berne) to Ciano (Rome) 18 July 1940, *I Documenti Diplomatici Italiani 1939–1943*, vol. v (Rome, 1965), no. 53.

[35] Andreas Hillgruber (ed.), *Staatsmänner und Diplomaten bei Hitler. Vertrauliche Aufzeichunungen über Unterredungen mit Vertretern des Auslandes 1939–1941* (Frankfurt, 1967), 140.

[36] *DDS*, vol. XIII, 317.

from Allied sabotage or aerial action.[37] The enormous increase in transit traffic across Switzerland's railways may indeed have enhanced the deterrent effect of Guisan's strategy and helped the Bundesbahnen recover from the effects of the Depression, but it was, at the same time, an integral element in Switzerland's economic relationship with the Reich. As chairman of the Swiss Chamber of Commerce cryptically remarked in mid-August 1940, the economic importance of Switzerland's transit facilities for the Axis was such that 'in the last few months the Gotthard [Massif through which the Alpine railways ran] has been more than just the symbol of our independence!'[38]

The ambiguities of the army's role during the war are further complicated by Guisan's political activities. Most historians agree that Guisan's ostentatious military manoeuvres, carefully choreographed speeches, 'house and army' system (whereby Swiss society was inculcated with military values and discipline), and timely interventions in the federal palace helped stem the tide of defeatism and raise civilian morale over the crisis months in 1940. Guisan became the personification of Swiss resistance and unity at a time when the country desperately needed visible leadership. The difficulty with this depiction of Guisan is that while outwardly calling for resistance, the general twice argued in favour of dispatching a delegation to negotiate a 'political and cultural' arrangement with the Führer.[39] Why Guisan recommended such a pilgrimage, when foreign dignitaries visiting Hitler were known to return home with little more than the shirts on their backs, has intrigued historians.[40] Guisan clearly felt disenchanted with Berne's handling of Swiss foreign policy and thought a more proactive style of diplomacy was required. The knowledge that Germany knew of his secret military contacts with the French no doubt sharpened his sensitivity to the state of Swiss standing in Berlin.[41] Whatever the reason, Guisan clearly appreciated that 'armed

[37] For Swiss defences against Allied sabotage and air attack, see my forthcoming *Britain and Switzerland during the Second World War.*

[38] Minutes of meeting of Vorort 15 August 1940. Archiv für Zeitgeschichte, ETH Zurich. Nachlass Homberger. Dossier II. On economic appeasement and military deterrence see Jakob Tanner, 'Or & Granit. La défense nationale et les liens économiques entre la Suisse et le Troisiéme Reich durant la Seconde Guerre mondiale', *Les annuelles*, 1 (1990), 31–48, Ph. Marguerat, *La Suisse face au IIIe Reich* (Lausanne, 1991), and Markus Heiniger, *Dreizehn Gründe. Warum die Schweiz im Zweiten Weltkrieg nicht erobert wurde* (Zurich, 1989).

[39] Guisan to Minger, 14 August and Pilet-Golaz, 9 November 1940. *DDS*, vol. XIII, 367 and 410.

[40] Oscar Gauye, 'Le général Guisan et la diplomatie suisse, 1940–1941', *Etudes et Sources*, 4 (1978), 4–63.

[41] A similar attitude can be discerned in his decision to the Abwehr official Walter Schellenberg in early 1943 regardless of the dangers to Swiss relations with the Allies. See Pierre-Th.

neutrality' was not sufficient on its own to provide for Switzerland's security. The problematic nature of Guisan's behaviour is further complicated by an assessment of his political ambitions within Switzerland. Guisan's political outlook was markedly conservative and authoritarian. He hated Communism, abhorred social and political disorder, and was quite prepared to use the army as a bulwark for traditional bourgeois values, a function he had performed with notable enthusiasm in suppressing the strike movement in 1918. As the war progressed, Guisan took an increasing interest in Switzerland's home front, and, much to the irritation of the federal council, made no secret of his contempt for civilian leadership. For Guisan then, Switzerland's mobilisation under the banner of 'armed neutrality' had two components: it provided for the defence of Switzerland's frontiers but also created the opportunity to forge a national consensus behind traditional military values, some of which unquestionably ran counter to Switzerland's cherished political pluralism and culture.[42]

## ACTIVE NEUTRALITY

The final component of Swiss neutrality to attract Churchill's attention in late 1944 was its humanitarian work. For Churchill, Switzerland's work in 'linking the hideously sundered nations' with the free world, was entirely in keeping with the country's traditions. Switzerland had been a favourite sanctuary for Europe's radicals, republicans, and revolutionaries in the nineteenth century, and had been closely associated with humanitarian initiatives, especially after the founding of the International Committee of the Red Cross (ICRC) by Genevan worthies in 1863. More recently, Switzerland had developed a reputation for its skill as a 'protecting power', most notably during the First World War, when Berne held a total of thirty-six mandates and in some form or other acted on behalf of all the major belligerent parties.

In discussing Switzerland's 'active neutrality' during the war, we must distinguish between two separate activities. The first was Switzerland's work on behalf of the belligerents. The importance of this activity was widely recognised before the war, and was the basis of talks between federal officials and representatives of the Swiss Red Cross and the ICRC in

Braunschweig, *Geheimer Draht nach Berlin. Die Nachrichtenlinie Masson-Schellenberg und der schweizerische Nachrichtendienst im Zweiten Weltkrieg* (Zurich, 1991).

[42] Oscar Gauye, '"Au Rütli, 25 juillet 1940." Le discours du général Guisan: nouveaux aspects', *Etudes et Sources*, 10 (1984), 5–52. Gautschi, *Guisan*, 51–66.

1938/9 with an eye to drawing up a list of humanitarian services which Switzerland could offer in any future protracted conflict in Europe. In contrast to the First World War, when Switzerland was conveniently situated to provide a range of medical and convalescent facilities for the battle scarred and war weary of both sides, for most of the Second World War, Switzerland's geographical isolation prevented it from developing its 'active neutrality' as originally envisaged. One of the few projects Berne brought to fruition was a child-relief programme, whereby over 60,000 children, mostly from France and Belgium, spent periods of several months in Switzerland safe from the deprivations and dangers of war.

The most prominent area in which Berne fulfilled its mandate as an 'active neutral' was in its work as protecting power. By May 1945 Switzerland had represented the interests of some forty-three different countries across the globe, providing them with a means of transmitting confidential communications to their adversaries, guaranteeing the security of their diplomatic premises abroad, and ensuring that their citizens in enemy hands were not mistreated. Surveying their accomplishments after the war, Swiss officials had little doubt as to the importance to their work of Switzerland's pedigree as a neutral. Without this, it would have been hard to retain that semblance of impartiality necessary for the success of their delicate negotiations and discussions.[43] The breadth and expertise of Switzerland's diplomatic net, and the dearth of alternative candidates by early 1942, clearly worked in Berne's favour. But perhaps the main reason for Berne's success in this field was its determination to make protecting-power work a central pillar of Swiss wartime diplomacy. This was unquestionably the case in September 1939 when Berne eagerly accepted Germany's mandate in Britain and France in the hope that it might make Berlin more amenable to Swiss wishes. A similar approach was taken in late 1942 when a series of incidents, culminating in Germany's shackling of British prisoners in October, encouraged Pilet to use Switzerland's good offices as a way of facilitating an improvement in Anglo-Swiss political relations. From early 1944 Berne's protecting-power work assumed such importance in Allied eyes that it largely eclipsed the sense of bitterness created by Swiss commercial collaboration with their enemies in the preceding years. As the war drew to a close, and the fate of Allied prisoners in German (and Japanese) hands increasingly hung in the balance, Berne devoted enormous time

[43] J. de Saussure to D. Secrétan (both FPD), 22 January 1946. *DDS* vol. XVI, 56.

and resources to its protecting-power activities and building up a reserve of good will which would ease the country's passage into the post-war world. The success of this policy can be no better seen than in Churchill's glowing remarks in December 1944.

The second aspect of Switzerland's 'active neutrality' concerned its treatment of refugees. Even during the nineteenth century, when Switzerland's reputation as a haven for Europe's unwanted was forged, Berne had been careful to balance lenient asylum laws with a range of restrictions designed to limit the number of people able to enter and reside in Switzerland. Distinctions had been made between desirable and undesirable refugees, and the refugees assessed on their financial circumstances. The twentieth century saw a continuation of this outlook. Berne had supported the various international initiatives in favour of Russian and Armenian refugees at the end of the First World War, but by the late 1930s it had given up on the search for an international solution, and instead increasingly focused on 'defending' itself from the increasing number of people forced to leave Nazi Germany. As with the League's collective security measures, Berne justified distancing itself from the various international humanitarian projects by referring to its 'special position' as a permanent neutral. In reality, however, appeals to Swiss neutrality merely obscured Berne's increasingly insular attitude towards the refugee problem. The reasons for this outlook ranged from an exaggerated fear of the economic danger posed by refugees – as a burden on the national economy and competition for Swiss workers – to anxieties over the risk they posed to Switzerland's social and political security. In September 1943, the veteran socialist Robert Grimm spoke out against letting in too many Italians on account of the detrimental impact this would have on the Swiss workforce. The army repeatedly counselled against relaxing the country's border controls, and was largely responsible for the negligent attitude shown towards the refugees' psychological and social needs in the internment camps. More influential in colouring attitudes towards the plight of refugees during the war was the anti-Semitism and xenophobia prevalent in official federal circles, and the concern to defend 'pure' Swiss society from contamination from alien biological, cultural or commercial influences. The fear of Swiss society being 'corrupted' by alien influences, or 'inundated' with Jews gave an added impetus to the discriminatory attitudes which had always existed along side Switzerland's avowedly liberal asylum policies, despite the fact that the percentage of foreigners living in Switzerland actually declined as the century progressed.[44] By the late 1930s, while paying lip-service to Swiss humanitarian traditions, officials set out to reduce Switzerland's own refugee population rather than helping those in need of assistance. The most notorious instance of this attitude was Berne's insistence on the introduction of a 'J' stamp on German passports for Jews in 1938, in order to facilitate Swiss discrimination between 'desirable' and 'undesirable' emigrants. The remark of police chief Heinrich Rothmund – 'we have not spent twenty years fighting excessive foreign influence and especially "Jewishification" in Switzerland with everything . . . at our disposal, just to have emigrants forced upon us today' – encapsulated the kind of attitude found in official circles before the war and which continued, with disastrous consequences, after war began.[45]

The small numbers of people who sought sanctuary in Switzerland during the early war years ensured that Switzerland's rigid border restrictions could in practice be relaxed. Swiss relief work in France in 1940 and Greece in 1941 – whether organised from Geneva or Berne – and the official child-relief programme was warmly appreciated on both sides. Matters changed however in 1942, as the onset of Hitler's extermination programme convinced thousands of people across Europe to seek neutral sanctuary. Despite possessing extensive information on the gruesome fate awaiting Jews and other refugees, in August 1942 Berne decided that, with 9,600 refugees already in the country, 'the boat was full.' Frontier guards were instructed to eject refugees found crossing the border, 'even if [this] could have serious consequences for the foreigners in question (danger of life and limb)'; repeat 'offenders' were to be handed over to the Vichy or German police authorities. The federal council also used its influence in the ICRC to prevent the organisation from making a public statement on the Holocaust. Blame for Switzerland's actions has traditionally been laid on the shoulders of the chief of police, Rothmund, but a recent report on the subject concludes that the measures were generally 'approved by the majority of the members of Parliament, as well as by a whole influential sphere of political and social circles'.[46] Minor, momentary relaxation of the border controls

[44] Jacques Picard, *Die Schweiz und die Juden* (Zurich, 1994). The percentage of foreigners to the total population declined from 14.7% in 1910 to 10.4% in 1920, 8.7% in 1930 and 5.2% in 1941.

[45] Rothmund to Arthur de Pury (Swiss minister, the Hague), 27 January 1939. *DDS* vol. XIII, 9.

[46] Independent Commission of Experts, *Switzerland and Refugees in the Nazi Era* (Berne, 1999), 96. André Lasserre, *Frontières et camps. Le refuge en Suisse de 1933 à 1945* (Lausanne, 1995). But see Jean-Christian Lambelet, who disputes Bergier's figures; 'Die Macht der Mythen. Politik und Praxis der Schweiz gegenüber Flüchtlingen im Zweiten Weltkrieg', *Neue Zürcher Zeitung*, 19 August 2000.

were introduced to satiate public complaints over the winter of 1942, but the border essentially remained closed until the autumn 1943, when Switzerland opened its doors to Italians fleeing German occupation forces.

Several aspects of the policy demand particular attention. Firstly, the Allied response to Swiss actions was largely mute: partly because of the inadequacy of their own programmes, and partly out of a concern not to embarrass the Swiss government which was doing so much to protect their prisoners in German hands. The absence of any overt Allied criticism of Swiss refugee policies during the war helps account for why the issue has taken so long to seep into Swiss public consciousness.[47] Secondly, while economic constraints were used to justify Swiss actions, these had little direct bearing on the actual decisions. Berne deliberately discouraged the Allies from increasing food shipments to Switzerland for the refugees so as to retain maximum freedom of action in its relations with the refugees both during and after the war.[48] Thirdly, although individual Swiss officials, soldiers, and citizens went out of their way to help Jewish refugees, it was only in 1944, with the creation of the US government's War Refugee Board, that Berne decided to emulate the Swedes and actively search for ways to alleviate the suffering of Europe's refugees. Swiss initiatives, such as trying to save Hungarian Jews and provide sanctuary to concentration camp victims, hardly compensated for Berne's neglect in the preceding years, when there were over 24,500 documented cases of refugees being refused entry.[49] Nor was there any fundamental shift in basic attitudes towards the 'refugee problem' as it affected Switzerland's social and political fabric. In July 1944 Rothmund was ready to offer sanctuary to 'industrialists who produced goods for Germany in order to keep their plants running and prevent their workers from

[47] Even though refugee policy was made the subject of an official report in 1957, and attracted considerable media attention: see Carl Ludwig, *La politique pratiquée par la Suisse à l'égard des réfugiés au cours des années 1933 à 1955* (Berne, 1957) and the popular work of Alfred A. Häsler, *The Lifeboat is Full. Switzerland and the Refugees 1933–1945* (New York, 1969, from German, 1967).

[48] See minutes of federal meeting 7 May 1943. BA J17 1990/98, vol. 35. 'He who pays, directs', was Rothmund's view. 'The Anglo-Saxon powers are perhaps today only too pleased to give us Navicerts for this purpose, so they can recall them after the war, in order to prevent Switzerland from rejecting those refugees which have already been accepted.'

[49] See Andre Lasserre, 'Les réfugiés de Bergen-Belsen et Theresienstadt ou les déboires d'une politique d'asile en 1944–1945', *Schweizerischen Zeitschrift für Geschichte*, 40 (1990), 307–17. Theo Tschuy, *Dangerous Diplomacy. The Story of Carl Lutz, Rescuer of 62,000 Hungarian Jews* (Grand Rapids, 2000, from German, 1995). For an analysis of the statistics: Guido Koller, 'Entscheidungen über Leben und Tod. Die behördliche Praxis in der schweizerischen Flüchtlingspolitik während des Zweiten Weltkrieges', *Etudes et Sources*, 22 (1996), 17–136. Some 51,000 refugees were given temporary asylum during the war.

being transferred to Germany', but 'planned to deal more strictly with accepting (refugees)'. Since the latter 'now have better possibilities . . . of avoiding being caught by the Germans' they should 'no longer simply be let in'.[50]

During the one hundred and fifty years before the outbreak of the Second World War, Swiss neutrality had acquired such a revered status that its existence and preservation had become a 'settled norm' of European international relations. Even if Hitler and Mussolini dismissed Switzerland as a relic of some bygone age, both appreciated that they could not treat Swiss neutrality with quite the same disdain as was meted out to the other small neutrals. Likewise, while the collapse of France might have transformed the political landscape, neither belligerent considered it appropriate to ride roughshod over Swiss rights with impunity. Even in the midst of total war, Swiss neutrality had a cachet which could not be ignored, and which was at least of equal importance in the eyes of the belligerents as the tangible benefits they obtained from Swiss services. Yet however much the belligerents might hold Switzerland's venerable neutrality in awe, the Swiss themselves clearly felt less inhibited by their country's historical traditions. True, neutrality established the guidelines for Swiss diplomacy and accorded to the wishes of the overwhelming majority of the population, but in practice Berne's outlook was anchored in its immediate experiences in the 1930s, its political culture and the psychological outlook of its leadership. As a result, during the war Swiss neutrality served Switzerland's national interest, not the interest of the international community. Swiss neutrality may well have been distinctive, but its record was by no means as distinguished as Churchill assumed.

[50] Cited in Independent Commission of Experts, *Switzerland and Refugees*, 99.

# *Appendix*

The sheer size of Europe's neutral club prevents us from offering a fully comprehensive survey within the confines of a single volume. Regrettably certain countries that could qualify as neutrals or non-belligerents have been omitted. In terms of its impact on the war, the 'neutrality' of the Soviet Union and United States before 22 June and 7 December 1941 respectively was of course of enormous significance. Historians have studied the attitudes of both exhaustively and there is little benefit in rehearsing their findings in the present survey. Despite America's fervent attachment to its neutrality acts, the actions of both countries were ultimately guided less by concepts of neutrality than by considerations of their Great Power status and resources. Neither went out of their way to assist Europe's neutrals, even although most states tried to court American support during the Phoney War.

As its foreign relations were handled by Denmark, Iceland was covered by Copenhagen's declaration of neutrality on 3 September 1939. Reykjavik promptly declared its temporary independence from Denmark after the German occupation on 9 April 1940, since it was clear that Denmark's continued claim to 'neutrality' would find few takers in London, in whose hands Iceland's fate ultimately lay. The ploy did not succeed and the following month British troops landed at Reykjavik in order to compensate Britain for the loss of Norway and pre-empt any possible German action against the country.[1] Finland's neutrality lasted barely two months, brought to an end by Russia's attack on 30 November 1939. It was resurrected, if in a distorted form, after the conclusion of hostilities in late March 1940 and lasted until its occupation by Germany in June 1941. During this period, although Helsinki permitted Soviet troops to pass across its territory, it maintained a tenuous trading link with the outside world via the northern port of Petsamo. Any hopes that

[1] See Donald F. Bittner, *The Lion and the White Falcon: Britain and Iceland in the World War II Era* (Hamden, 1983).

the Baltic States (Latvia, Lithuania, and Estonia) might have entertained of remaining neutral in the coming war were dashed with the signature of the Hitler–Stalin Pact on 23 August 1939 and Germany's agreement that they would form part of Moscow's sphere of influence. Until this time, Germany had actively promoted Estonian and Latvian neutrality, even going so far as to conclude non-aggression pacts with them in June, in the hope of isolating Poland from potential Soviet aid. Nevertheless the collapse of Franco-British talks in Moscow over the summer reduced the value of Baltic neutrality even before the Hitler's pact with Stalin effectively sealed their fate.[2] The luckless republics were first occupied and then, in August 1940, annexed outright into the Soviet Union.

Few people suffered more than the Greeks from the collapse of their neutrality. The war brought partition, alien rule and, within a year, a famine that claimed the lives of over 250,000 people before it ran its course. The avoidance of war made sense for a country whose territory was coveted by three of its neighbours, Bulgaria, Italy, and Yugoslavia, and whose relations with a fourth, Turkey, were only beginning to return to normal after a disastrous war which ended in 1922. Traditionally close to Britain, Athens willingly accepted an Anglo-French guarantee in April 1939, despite the increasingly Right-wing character of the Metaxas regime. So long as Britain and France dominated the Mediterranean, Athens had no reason to doubt the wisdom of its choice. The collapse of France, Italy's entry into the war and the demise of British power in the Mediterranean inevitably upset these calculations, and Italy's attack on 28 October 1940 brought home their worst fears. Significantly, however, Italian aggression did not signal a complete rejection of neutrality. Athens remained wary of relying wholeheartedly on London lest it antagonise its relations with Italy's Axis partner in Berlin. The high-wire act ultimately ended in disaster. Germany was not willing to see its ally humiliated, nor countenance any British presence in the region at a time when it was planning the invasion of Soviet Russia.[3] When diplomatic efforts to enrol the support of its various neighbours collapsed during the spring of 1941, Greece was left with no option other than to turn to Britain and place its faith in the contest of war. Regrettably, neither its own forces,

[2] See Rolf Ahmann, 'Nazi German Policy towards the Baltic States on the Eve of the Second World War', in John Hiden and Thomas Lane (eds.), *The Baltic and the Outbreak of the Second World War* (Cambridge, 1992), 50–73.

[3] See, among others, P. Papastratis, *British policy towards Greece during the Second World War* (Cambridge, 1984); J. S. Koliopoulos, *Greece and the British connection, 1935–1941* (Oxford, 1977); G. Schreiber, Bernd Stegemann, and Detlef Vogel (eds.), *Germany and the Second World War*, vol. III (Oxford, 1995), 308–448, 451–551.

nor those of its ally were any match for the Wehrmacht when Germany struck on 9 April 1941.

Pétain's government in Vichy France might be said to have pursued a policy of non-belligerency from its installation in June 1940 until its occupation by German forces in November 1942. Though rarely free from direct German pressure, Vichy was able to carve out a certain amount of freedom in its foreign relations through its possession of the French fleet and the loyalty of the majority of France's overseas empire. It was the existence of these two strategic assets that probably convinced Hitler to leave Vichy intact after his meetings with Pétain and Laval at Montoire on 22 and 24 October 1940, and at the same time rebuff suggestions that Spain be offered the pick of France's North African colonies. Vichy's relations with Britain were restricted to intermittent, secret discussions. Its success in having its non-belligerency respected by London can be partly explained by the support it received from Washington, with whom it retained diplomatic relations until November 1942, and partly through London's interest in seeing the French fleet and empire remain beyond Hitler's immediate grasp. In being able to defy British wishes, to the point of having no diplomatic relations, while at the same time forging such intimate relations with Berlin, Vichy operated at the limits of what might be considered non-belligerency.[4]

Turkey's foreign minister for most of the war, Sükrü Saraçoğlu, frequently described his country's external policy as 'alliance with Britain and friendship with Germany'. The subtle distinction between Turkey's relations with the two belligerents arose from its different treaty obligations. Ankara concluded a security pact with Britain on 19 October 1939, with the intention of insuring itself against aggressive Italian designs in the Eastern Mediterranean. The collapse of the Anglo-French position seven months later, coupled with the arrival of German troops on its borders in April 1941, necessitated a deft piece of political acrobatics on Turkey's behalf. Its treaty of friendship with Germany signed on 18 June 1941 reflected Ankara's appreciation of the new strategic situation; one which included the possibility of mounting German demands, but also, more worryingly, the prospect of pressure from Turkey's historic foes in Russia. Relations with Moscow had cooled after the signing of the Hitler–Stalin Pact and continued to deteriorate thereafter. Allied efforts to bring Turkey into the war, which reached a crescendo in 1943 and

[4] See, among others, Martin Thomas, *The French Empire at War, 1940–1945* (Manchester, 1998); R. T. Thomas, *Britain and Vichy. The Dilemma of Anglo-French Relations, 1940–1942* (London, 1979); Philippe Burin, *France under the Germans. Collaboration and Compromise* (New York, 1993), esp. 98–159.

early 1944, confronted Ankara with the difficult choice of either joining the war and risking German reprisal or delaying entry and losing any hope of future western help against the Soviets. Turkey's foot-dragging infuriated Churchill, who saw Turkish belligerency as the key to unlocking southern Europe for the Allies, but there is little doubt that it was effective. As one British official grudgingly noted, although there was 'something Ghandi-esque and positively immoral' in Ankara's effort to be all things to all men, 'its astuteness and cleverness cannot be denied'.[5] Turkey suspended its important chrome exports to Germany in April 1944, withdrew its ambassador from Berlin in August and entered the war in February 1945, in time to secure a seat at the United Nations conference at San Francisco.

[5] Cited in Selim Deringil, *Turkish Foreign Policy During the Second World War* (Cambridge, 1989), 136. See also J. Robertson, *Turkey and Allied Strategy, 1941–1945* (New York, 1986); K. Schonherr, 'Neutrality, "Non-Belligerence", or War: Turkey and the European Powers' Conflict of Interests, 1939–1941,' in Bernd Wegner (ed.), *From Peace to War* (Oxford, 1997), 481–97; B. Millman, 'Turkish Foreign and Strategic Policy, 1934–1942', *Middle Eastern Studies*, 31/3 (1995), 483–508. Scholarship has suffered on account of the unavailability of official Turkish sources. Researchers may, however, now profit from an examination of the Allied decrypts of Turkish diplomatic traffic: see Robin Denniston, *Churchill's Secret War. Diplomatic Decrypts, the Foreign Office and Turkey* (London, 1997).

# Index